The Rise
of
Hispanic
Political Power

The Rise
of
Hispanic
Political Power

José de la Isla

Archer Books
Los Angeles

Published in the United States by:
Archer Books
P. O. Box 1254
Santa Maria, CA 93456

Printed in the United States

First edition

Cover photo © 2003 by Photodisc, Inc.
Cover Design: John Taylor-Convery, JTC Imagineering

ISBN 1-931122-04-0

Library of Congress Cataloging-in-Publication Data

De la Isla, Jose, 1944-
    The rise of Hispanic political power /José de la Isla.-- 1st ed.
    p. cm.
    Includes bibliographical references and index.
    ISBN 1-931122-04-0
    1. Hispanic Americans--Politics and government--20th century.
2. United States--Politics and government--1945-1989. 3. United
States--Politics and government--1989- 4. United States--Ethnic
relations--Political aspects. 5. Political campaigns--United States--
History--20th century. I. Title.

E184.S75 D376 2003
320.973'089'68--dc21

                                                        2002026081

E-mail: info@archer-books.com
Web site: http://www.archer-books.com

In memory of

José de la Isla Jr.
My father

"I'll give you a phone number right by my bedside. You won't [ever] have difficulty reaching me."
—Candidate Jimmy Carter, speaking to Hispanic political leaders, (1976)

"People are recognizing that the Latino agenda is synonymous with the American agenda. There is nothing radical about our goals of improving schools, expanding health care, making our communities safe through gun control and law enforcement, and expanding economic opportunity. . . ."
—Richard Polanco, Chairman, California Democratic Latino Legislative Caucus

"And I have to tell you, this presidential election year, it is somewhat frightening to see two white, middle-aged men campaigning around the country speaking better Spanish than your own niece and nephews."
—Arturo Vargas, Executive Director, National Association of Latino Elected Officials (September 29, 1999)

George Magazine: "How do you feel about being Hispanic?"
Bill Richardson: "I'm very proud, but try not to wear it on my sleeve, don't overemphasize it. I am not a professional Hispanic. To get ahead, you must deal with mainstream issues, not just Hispanic ones."
—Interview (August 2000)

"I believe in the Constitution—and groceries too."
—Congressman Henry B. González

Acknowledgements

I owe much to many. Among them are Charles Ericksen, Gerald García, Blanca Hernández Blanco, Kathryn Lawlis, Patricia Fuentes, and Francisco García, Jerry Rankin and Alfonso Vásquez. Joy Estela Hansen suffered through the early drafts and was consistent with her research assistance. Carol Lumpkin helped prepare the final manuscript. And Fanny Riva Palacio gave me moral support to the finish. My publishers, Rosemary Tribulato and John Taylor-Convery, made the completion of this work easier than a task like this ought to be.

Also, I want to thank the University of California-Berkeley Ethnic Studies Department for a lectureship that provided me time to collect my thoughts and organize my ideas. Some of the material in this book first appeared as articles in *Society*, *Aztlán*, *Houston Post*, *Houston Chronicle*, *Hispanic Link Weekly Report* and in newspapers that are part of the *Los Angeles Times* Syndicate.

Contents

The Rise
of
Hispanic
Political Power

Prologue

Writer Mike Davis has provocatively stated, "To be Latino in the United States is rather to participate in a unique process of 'cultural syncretism' that may become a transformative template for the whole society." Latinization, is the fusion of histories, traditions, and social understanding. It is a practice, rather than a representation. It would be a mistake for us to search for an essence of the Hispanic identity, "the Rubik's Cube of ethnicity" in Davis' words. Hispanic/Latino is an artificial "box," he says, that was invented to contain individuals of "disparate national origins who may subsequently develop some loosely shared identity as a reaction-formation to this labeling." Davis, of recent commentators, comes closest toward grasping the identity-force (movement, purpose and action) and dispels the identity-label (provoking a victim-of-circumstances characterization and a stereotype).[1]

There is still a tendency to portray the several major Hispanic groups as a single mindset. However there are just too many national origin, regional, linguistic, cultural, class, and educational matters that differentiate the groups and the individuals. By the same token, it is a simplification to imagine that the differences lead to antagonisms between the Hispanic groups. There may be competitions, of course, but estrangement is another matter altogether. What brings Hispanic groups together is the shared notion of a common experience, recognition that each one lives in the same national context, and that something has to be done to extend opportunity to those that prosperity does not reach. These are not arguable points but shared values and the stuff of strategy. The direction mostly taken has been to avoid offshoot ideologies and head, instead, toward mainstream politics.

---

1. Mike Davis, *Magical Urbanism: Latinos Reinvent the US City* (London: Verso, 2000) pp. 14-15.

Altogether, Hispanics number 32 million, or 11 percent of the U.S. population. It increases by about a hundred thousand persons per month. By 2050, Hispanics will make up 24 percent of the United States population. While Hispanic historical roots go back to the nation's founding, current developments began soon after the Second World War. Hispanic soldiers, returning home from liberating countries, witnessed how our government made reconstruction investments abroad at a scale unmatched or rarely seen at home. Some of them returned to communities that loved their heroism but disdained or discriminated against them as members of an ethnic group. That part of the story is not generally well known, nor are the predating landmark civil right challenges in the 1940s, leading to the desegregation of Hispanic children in Texas schools.

While many people became better off in the post-World War II period, that prosperity was not evenly spread. Government reluctance to intervene and extend equity more uniformly at the local level was part of the problem. The lack of government representation, especially in the southwestern region where most Hispanic people—mainly Mexican Americans—lived was patently obvious and became the issue.

There was even a general belief that the progress and welfare of the people was not the stuff of government. That seems to be the ideology mainly among those whose neighbors, friends and relatives were unaffected by underdevelopment. Yet, despite it all, there was some progress when the economy was strong enough to continue incorporating people, albeit ever so slowly. But the political introspection of the 1950s helped the next generation's leaders, who looked at education and neighborhood conditions as the benchmarks for government-sponsored help that they wanted.

The belief that the arriving immigrant generation must sacrifice so that the next generation can climb up the middle-class rungs wasn't working. Many Hispanics coming of age during this period were now a generation or two removed from the immigrant experience. In fact, some people were now centuries removed from it. The political beliefs and ideologies that resonated with Middle America just didn't strike a cord with many Hispanic Americans. Notions about equality and democracy looked more like folklore then as an achievable reality. A dissatisfaction—and in some places disaffection—festered throughout the 1950s. All that began changing during John F. Kennedy's presidential campaign when the Hispanic vote was actively sought for the first time and Kennedy won by a razor thin margin over Richard Nixon in 1960.

Mexican-Americans, the largest of the Hispanic groups, had by then adapted to a hyphenated ethnic identity, similar to the Irish-Americans and the Italian-Americans and other immigrant populations. While the term "Hispanic" was not applied prior to this time, none of the three major "Latin American" groups was significantly large to command a national identity. Mainly Mexican or Puerto Rican and a smattering of other groups were a hybrid that did not quite fit into the conveniently simplistic racial categories white, black, red or yellow. They were distinguished by—of all things—culture, Spanish-language and historically Latin American roots. This "Latin American" proto-identity distanced Mexican Americans, Puerto Ricans and the others from racial identification and segregation in the 1950s. But they were mis-typified, except to themselves.

By the time of the Civil Rights and racial and ethnic assertion movements of the 1960s, "Chicano" became the term for the so-called "brown movement." The older regional distinctions (Californios, Tejanos, Hispanos, Manitos, Spanish-surnamed, and Spanish-speaking) gave way to Chicano, and captured the imaginations of political activists and young people (mainly students). The new term implied—beyond ethnicity—an identity with a cause. So much so that in the early days, some Chicanos recruited Puerto Ricans, before many of them joined their own *Boricua* movement. Some of the fervor still remains. "Today," says Richie Pérez, a political participant in the tumultuous 1960s, "the majority of [Puerto Rican] activists from this period, myself included, recognize electoral participation as an important weapon in our political struggle."

The need to change the terms to designate Hispanics arose from the need to include more people and get greater congruence for a larger place in the national picture. They were not included if they lacked a name.

"Hispanic" was adopted in the early 1970s, during the Nixon administration. "Spanish-speaking" (not everyone was) and "Spanish-surnamed Americans" (nor was everybody), although used, just didn't fill the bill. While some people to this day object to "Hispanic" as the encapsulating category, the others were worse. "Hispanic" was originally as much a demographic as it was a political device. "Hispanic," as a political term, was one included in the Nixon "heritage groups," used to distinguish among potential constituencies. The choice of "Hispanic" grates on some people because of its association with the Nixon administration's policies and political intentions, but it did facilitate the first significant U.S. Census enumeration under this category.

Both "Hispanic" and "Latino" are generally accepted today. Author Earl Shorris conducted one interview in which his respondent refused any term other than national origin: "No other word was acceptable," said Shorris, "not because there were no other nouns or adjectives available, but because any less specific, more encompassing word was damaging: To conflate cultures is to destroy them; to take away the name of a group, as of an individual, is to make pale the existence of the group."[2] It is like having your name as the address and "Latino" or "Hispanic" is the name of the city.

Our intention is certainly not to do violence to anyone's identity. Either "Hispanic" or "Latino" will just have to serve as neither satisfactorily expresses national, regional, ethnic and class identity. "Hispanic," because it gained acceptance first, and it is the choice of most Hispanics, is mainly used in this book.[3] In either case, both represent a drifting away from mixing racial and ethnic and political identities under one term, as was so popular in 1960s and '70s.

Hispanic" is the meta-category first applied in forging the early political collaborations, alliances and coalitions between groups. "Hispanic" was the meta-term applied to adhere the various nationality, rural-urban, ethnic-class, public-private interests. The term had currency then and it is one still in general use now. It is not used exclusively in this book because "Latino" shares billing among many people. [4]

Mexican Americans, Puerto Ricans and Cubans are the largest Hispanic groups. Since the 1970s and 1980s, Central and South Americans are the fastest growing segments and Dominicans (among the Caribbeans) have significantly increased in number. The Hispanic bond extends to the newcomers as the affinity goes to those with a historical origin in Latin America. Yet for some—such as the Hispanos of New Mexico and some colonial and land grant Mexican-American families—"Latin America" might have to include parts of the present United States when those regions were culturally part of Latin America. Yet, our purpose is not to resolve all the seeming contradictions and describe the nuances but to avoid posing a fiction. The

2. Earl Shorris, *Latinos: A Biography of the People* (New York: W.W. Norton & Company, 1992), p. xvi.

3. John A. García found in the National Latino Political Survey a preference for the term "Hispanic" much more than "Latino." *Latino National Survey, 1989-1990: Explorations into the Political World of Mexican, Puerto Rican, and Cuban Communities*, ICPSR Bulletin, September 1997). A Hispanic Trends, Inc. survey found that 65 percent of Latino registered voters preferred the term "Hispanic" and 30 percent chose to identify themselves as "Latino." "Hispanic vs Latino," *Hispanic* (December 2000).

4. Writer Mike Davis warns: "The debate is unlikely to be resolved. Indeed, there is a broad critical awareness that both labels fail to acknowledge the decisive quotient of indigenous genetic and cultural heritage in the populations described," *Magical Urbanism,* ibid., p. 12.

task here is to show how the Hispanic distinction came about in politics and how it is increasingly less foreign and is more a part of the American experience.

Mexican Americans form the largest Hispanic group. Their tie to the United States is as old as the Republic itself and as recent as the last bus to arrive at the terminal. Historically, this population has been mainly concentrated in the Southwest. Immigration and mobility have made it a national population with significant clusters in every state, and virtually every urban and suburban population center. In the formative years, the farm workers movement crystallized a political consciousness, especially among youth, liberals, idealists, and progressives. They established a connection between social justice, representation, and legislation. The lessons learned from those early struggles (that still continue) were taken to other efforts for economic opportunity and civil rights. While traditionally Democratic, we will see how and why Republicans made inroads.

In the late 1960s, Puerto Ricans—concentrated in the northeast, mainly New York—received Democratic party attention, however with many notable progressive Republican exceptions. The Puerto Rican population has been fed historically by migrations from the island. Underlying Puerto Rican concerns is the sovereignty status of Puerto Rico, which became a territory in 1898 and a free associated state in 1952. Puerto Ricans became U.S. citizens in 1917, under provisions in the Jones Act, but island residents are still not allowed to vote in presidential elections nor do they pay federal taxes. Free associated state status won a plebiscite in 1967 and in 1993 by a bare plurality (48.4 percent) over statehood (46.2 percent). The *Independistas* only garnered 4.4 percent of the vote that year. Puerto Ricans, like Mexican Americans, have focused on ethnic assertion but have directed much of their attention on urban revitalization, migration from the island to the city, and island sovereignty.

The Cuban influence on South Florida and Tampa predated the 1959 revolution in Cuba led by Fidel Castro. In the early twentieth century, up to a hundred thousand Cuban visitors traveled annually between Havana, Key West and Tampa for business and pleasure. After 1959, about 215,000 Cubans—including wealthy businessmen, government officials, and professionals—went into U.S. exile. Miami's Hispanic population increased tenfold from the 1960s to the 1980s. Although Cubans settled in other parts of the United States, the largest concentration was in South Florida.

In 1966, Congress passed Public Law 89-732, providing federal assistance through the Cuban Adjustment Act. Medicaid, food stamps, free

English courses, scholarships, business credit and loans, low-interest college loans, ability to secure visas, and less than the normal five-year waiting period to gain citizenship. The law became a sore spot with Mexican Americans and Puerto Ricans whose displacements never received that kind of concentrated aid as provided the Cuban refugees. Cubans were routinely elected to school board, city, county and judicial positions in South Florida only a decade later after their mass arrival and contrasted sharply with the other Hispanic groups.

Central and South Americans comprise a large 14 percent of the rest of the U.S. Hispanic population. Their numbers are not to be minimized, however. For instance, Dominicans, Colombians, Mexicans and Ecuadorians have a significant presence in New York. So do Nicaraguans and Puerto Ricans in Miami. As do Salvadorans and Guatemalans in Los Angeles. While traditionally one tries to telescope in and zoom out, the truth is that we need a kaleidoscope to embrace the true social setting on the ground. Furthermore, these populations may be the link to the United States' international future. U.S. Latinos, considered as a whole, would make up the fifth largest Latin American nation—after Brazil, Mexico, Colombia, and Argentina. By 2050, U.S. Latinos will be the equivalent of the third largest Latin American nation.

Of the three major Hispanic groups, Mexican Americans occupy much of our attention.[5] As the oldest and largest group, Mexican Americans have a longer representational history than the others, making them more prominent in forming alliances across local, regional, rural and urban, education and class distinctions. These are political alliances and coalitions, not blood brotherhoods. Detractors sometimes confuse the difference.

This book, purposely, does not compare and contrast between Hispanic groups. That provincial approach, prevalent until the end of the 1990s, is frivolous. Instead, looking at what brought distinct Hispanic groups from different parts of the country together and how they gained political capital is a more fruitful discussion. In the end, we see that this is part of the continuing story about how the United States brand of democracy is acquired. It is also the story about how power is gained—it is not given freely—and

5. Current convention refers to "Puerto Ricans" and "Cubans" by place of cultural origin, although "Cuban American" (without a hyphen) is occurring more often in writing. "Mexican American" was written with a hyphen in the past but it has been largely discontinued. The hyphen suggests a verisimilitude "hyphenated" American, so the thinking goes, that gives equal footing to both places. Without the hyphen, "Mexican American" makes "Mexican" the modifier, an adjective, with no ambiguity about national identity.

the controversies involved in acquiring it, and the progress that can be made from its pursuit.

Abelardo L. Valdéz, former White House chief of protocol, once said, "History is to a nation what memory is to a person." This story of the emergence of Hispanic political power recollects what happened and why, and who played a part in support or reaction to what. Not long ago, this would have been an interesting story about politics, local color, assimilation and accommodation. The unfolding globalization allows this story to become, instead, an adventure tale about how our nation is transforming, adapting to a new time and to different circumstances. The grand sweep of events foretells how the next chapter in the nation's story will unfold and gives us a glimpse into the emerging history of the future. But before we lunge into that future, we are wise to draw from our national memory—that is to say, from our history.

1
The Brown Mafia

New Mexico Senator Joseph Montoya was outraged (somewhat disingenuously) when he learned the Nixon administration had blatantly tried to buy the Hispanic vote. Investigators from the U. S. Senate's Watergate Committee had uncovered an elaborate scheme to influence how Hispanics voted in the 1972 presidential election. The whole thing was an "incredible insult," said Montoya, after hearing testimony on the White House plan.

Senator Lowell Weicker (R-Conn.), who heard the same testimony, saw it differently. The White House was merely "maximizing on the incumbency," as he put it. "Why in heaven's name do you think the Democratic Party became the majority party? It was just these types of efforts made on behalf of other minority groups over a period of decades."[1]

In fact, many Hispanic leaders had been led to believe before the election that unless they supported Nixon, the federal government might stop giving financial support to their communities. They had fought hard to get assistance for education, employment, and self-help projects and feared this would come to a halt if they supported George McGovern, the Democratic candidate. Put bluntly, Hispanics were vulnerable because they needed help and had few elected officials who looked out for their interests. Why not play it safe and support Nixon?

Why would the Republican White House undertake a strategy to focus on Hispanics in the first place? The reason was one that Democrats had long understood and Republicans were only now catching on to.

Hispanics formed a potential voting bloc that could mean the difference between winning and losing a close presidential race. Robert Kennedy

---

1. "'Brown Mafia' Sought Chicano Votes," *Washington Star-News* (November 7, 1973).

had recognized this years before. As his brother's campaign manager in 1960, he supported the formation of the Viva Kennedy organizations in the southwestern states and requested Henry B. González, an unsuccessfully candidate in the Texas gubernatorial primaries, and U.S. Senator Dennis Chávez of New Mexico, as national co-chairmen to help organize the Viva Kennedy Clubs. John Kennedy got 85 percent of the Mexican American vote in his razor thin victory over Richard Nixon.

Mexican Americans made a difference in the Texas election that year when Democrats failed to win a majority of the Anglo precincts. Republican local gains were offset when 91 percent of Mexican Americans voted for the John Kennedy-Lyndon Johnson ticket, which won the state with 50,000 votes to spare. In New York, Puerto Ricans (especially in Spanish Harlem and the South Bronx) turned out for Kennedy three to one. They gave him a 125,000-vote plurality—approximately one-third of the New York victory margin. That unprecedented political organization by the Kennedys swept Los Angeles City Councilman Edward Roybal into the U.S. House of Representatives. The next year, Henry B. Gonzalez (D-Texas) was elected in a special election to fill a House vacancy.

In 1964, during the next presidential campaign, Lyndon Johnson won 90 percent of the Mexican American, and 86 percent of the Puerto Rican, vote. He carried all the southwestern states, except Arizona. In the following presidential election of 1968, 87 percent of Hispanic voters favored Hubert Humphrey. Richard Nixon received only 10 percent of the Mexican American and 15 percent of the Puerto Rican vote.

The 1960, 1964 and 1968 presidential elections clearly demonstrated that the Hispanic vote was allied with Democratic candidates and was potentially (if voter turnout could be kept at a high level) far more important than previously recognized. The pattern was so evident that the League of United Latin American Citizens and the Mexican American Bar Association issued a white paper arguing that a small shift in the Mexican American voting pattern in the southwestern states plus Illinois could tilt the balance in future presidential elections.[2]

Local and state candidates were also well aware of what the Hispanic voting potential meant. Democrat John Connally failed to carry a majority of Anglo precincts, but won the 1962 Texas gubernatorial race with a 150,000 vote victory margin coming from Mexican American precincts that voted

2. "The Electoral College and the Mexican-American: An Analysis of the Mexican-American Impact on the 1972 Presidential Election." Privately circulated. N.D.

for him by 93 percent. Similarly, Democrat Joseph Montoya won New Mexico's U.S. Senate election by 16,000 in 1970 over Republican Anderson Carter. Hispanics made up the victory margin in a record turnout for an off-year election.

As Richard Nixon's reelection campaign in 1972 approached, the respective campaign histories suggested that success required voter-switching to the Republican Party and/or a low Hispanic turnout in key states. Other events also played into the White House's 1972 election design. The La Raza Unida party, founded by José Angel Gutiérrez, turned into an important pawn. Unlike other third parties, Raza Unida had the ability to divert a crucial number of Hispanic protest votes to its own candidates and away from the major parties.

La Raza Unida was part of a new generation of organizations that arose around San Antonio in the late 1960s. In 1967, the Ford Foundation granted $630,000 to the Southwest Council of La Raza to help accelerate the rise of Mexican American leadership. About the same time, the aforementioned José Angel Gutiérrez, who was born and raised in Crystal City, Texas, headed a group called the Mexican American Youth Organization (MAYO). The Ford Foundation, said Gutiérrez—in the arrogant, demanding, even menacing tone characteristic of the time—"didn't have much choice in the matter. It was one of those situations that either you come across with the money and [are] able to plug us into the system or we just tear the hell out of everything out there."[3]

In 1968 Gutiérrez supported Congressman Henry B. González' Republican opponent and encouraged several members to enter a city council race. The next year, after Gutiérrez made some public comments not dissimilar to those of the so-called radical youth of his time but considered inflammatory rhetoric by some, González countered from the floor of the House of Representatives, attacking the Ford Foundation for supporting the "Brown Bilbos" and the "new racism." Subsequently, MAYO was told by the Ford Foundation it would no longer grant them support. Period.

---

3. Neil R. Pierce, *The Megastates of America: People, Politics and Power in the Ten Great States* (New York: W.W. Norton & Co., Inc., 1972), p. 560. José Angel Gutiérrez was to become one of the leading Chicano activists and political leaders of the 1960s and '70s. Besides co-founding La Raza Unida Party, which helped to raise consciousness about Chicano civil rights issues. In 1966, Gutiérrez had received a B.A. from Texas A&I University in Kingsville, Texas and an M.A. from St. Mary's University in San Antonio. Later he was to receive a Ph.D. in Political Science from the University of Texas at Austin in 1976.

Gutiérrez returned to his hometown and, in 1970, formed La Raza Unida party. The idea of a third party alternative to the predominantly conservative Texas Democrats had a certain appeal to Gutiérrez and his followers. The love affair between Mexican Americans and the state Democrats had turned acrimonious. Dissatisfactions ran deep. "When President Kennedy and Bob Kennedy died, the Democratic party died for the Mexican Americans in Texas," said one labor official.

By the spring of 1970, Raza Unida party candidates had won control of Crystal City's school board and positions in Carrizo Springs and Cotulla. This success, however, was short-lived. In the fall elections that year, Mexican American voters deserted Raza Unida candidates and voted Democratic, electing, among others, Democrat Lloyd Bentsen to the U. S. Senate.

In response, Gutiérrez set out to extend Raza Unida beyond south Texas, and found success in that year's special election to fill the State Assembly seat in Los Angeles. Chicano Democratic nominee Richard Alatorre was the clear favorite in the race against eleven other candidates, including Raza Unida candidate Raúl Ruíz and Republican Bill Brophy. When Alatorre, Ruíz and Brophy were forced into a runoff, Ruíz doubled his primary total by cutting into the traditional Democratic vote. As a result, Alatorre was defeated and the Republican won. Raza Unida had proved it could upset a close election by drawing votes away from Democrats, act as a spoiler and even help Republicans come out ahead.

Alex Armendáriz, a staffer at Richard Nixon's reelection campaign committee (Committee to Reelect the President), had been studying Raza Unida and proposed a strategy to weaken Democratic strength and help Raza Unida win votes, namely that his party provide covert assistance to Raza Unida. "Republicans," he wrote, "are in a good position to help attract to La Raza [Unida] . . . [the Hispanic voters] who already approve of that party." He assured that "any help given them would not be identifiable as Republican. . . ."

In formulating the strategy he estimated that Republican core support would come from the 19.4 percent of the group who "may be the most conservative members." However, the main target was the 33 percent of Hispanics who had no strong political opinion. The goal was quite simple: [It] "will be our job to try to crystallize" [that segment] "toward La Raza [Unida], toward the Republican party, or staying at home."[4]

4. Committee for the Reelection of the President memorandum for Henry Ramírez from

To accomplish this, the federal bureaucracy would have to be enlisted to provide incentives for Hispanic leaders to either turn Republican or to allow the Republican incumbent to win by going passive. The mechanism for doing that had been established earlier.

President Johnson's Inter-Agency Committee on Mexican American Affairs was formed in response to the Viva Johnson support of 1964. Headed by Vincente Ximénez, a former U.S. Equal Employment Opportunity Commissioner, the agency held hearings in El Paso (attended by the President and Vice President Hubert Humphrey) and heard testimony from virtually every major Mexican American leader about the need for a greater federal commitment. Witnesses demonstrated how the population was much more diverse than the prevailing wisdom, which typified Hispanics as a predominantly rural, regional, unorganized group, forming an insignificant population in political terms. They were, instead, a heterogeneous group whose problems and issues were, in fact, national in scope. However, federal programs continued to elude them, even when economic conditions demanded attention. Hispanics were getting left out of the national scheme of things. Government agencies, they argued, needed to become more involved to ensure that federal assistance reached individual communities. Cabinet members and the Office of Economic Opportunity's (OEO) director, Sargent Shriver, were briefed on the uniqueness of the problems.

A year after the hearings, Senator Joseph Montoya introduced a bill to keep the momentum going. He proposed a new agency to continue the Inter-Agency Committee's work. The Senate Government Operations subcommittee held hearings, and Congressman Frank Thompson (D-N.J.) introduced companion legislation in the House of Representatives. Then the bill dropped out of sight.

Several years later, Representative Edward Roybal "found" the bill in the Foreign Affairs Committee. "Mexican American" had been presumed to mean relations between Mexico and the United States.

Roybal's intervention got House Government Operations Committee chairman Chet Holifield (D-Calif.) to refer the bill out of Foreign Affairs and into his own committee. With only two weeks remaining before a recess, the

Alex Armendáriz. Subject: Spanish-speaking study, June 19, 1972. In "Activities of the Cabinet Committee on Opportunities for Spanish-Speaking People," Hearings Before a Subcommittee of the Committee on Government Operations, House of Representatives, Ninety-Third Congress, First Session (Washington, D.C.: US Government Printing Office, July 23 and September 12, 1973), pp. 27-33.

House passed the legislation. In December 1969, with a new administration now in place, Congress finally established the Cabinet Committee on Opportunities for Spanish-speaking People.

Martín Castillo, a deputy director at the Civil Rights Commission, became the Cabinet Committee's chairman. He was experienced in Washington's ins and outs and moved quickly to persuade the Bureau of the Census, as a matter of policy, to identify Hispanics as such (referred to as the "Spanish-speaking"). The data was vitally needed to form advocacy offices inside federal departments.

Numerous bureau chiefs had already noticed that the Hispanic population was growing fast. Still, progress was slow. Hispanics had not received the amount of attention they deserved for a population their size. "We're not doing so well," Castillo admitted to Vice President Spiro Agnew, who presided over the Cabinet Committee. The bureaucracy itself was the main problem. It didn't have enough Hispanic Americans among its ranks to count on, causing a lack of insightful understanding about how to apply existing policy. Agnew agreed. Too few policymakers came from Hispanic backgrounds, leading to the recommendation and President Nixon's approval of a sixteen-point program to significantly increase federal employment opportunities for Hispanics.

Then one month after the 1970 mid-term congressional elections, Castillo and Small Business Administration director Hilary Sandoval suddenly resigned. Their inability to move any noticeable Mexican American votes into the Republican column had upset the White House. The first and second highest ranking Hispanic presidential appointees were out. The election had ushered in no new Hispanic Republican strength. Instead, Herman Badillo, a liberal Puerto Rican Democrat, had been elected to the House of Representatives from New York's South Bronx, ousting a Republican, and becoming the first Congressman born in Puerto Rico to represent a district in the continental United States.

Overall, Hispanic congressional representation increased to six (one senator and five representatives; five Democrats and one Republican). With this, the two highest-ranking Hispanic presidential appointees, failing to produce any noticeable Republican gains, were turned out.

The White House didn't replace Martín Castillo for eight months. When it did, President Nixon said in his speech nominating Henry Ramírez that he was concerned about how slowly the federal government responded to Hispanics. The Senate confirmed Ramírez in November, a year before the presidential election, and a lot of federal activity followed, but little had much bearing on the Cabinet Committee's statutory responsibilities.

Tony Rodríguez, the Cabinet Committee's acting executive director, then became a White House aide. Ramírez, with little experience in bureaucratic hardball, didn't see the important contradiction signaled by his appointment. While the Nixon administration had encouraged Hispanics to seek assistance from federal programs, the broader New Federalism policy it pursued (including revenue sharing) was designed to discontinue the programs that targeted Hispanic communities. If the administration continued along this path, even fewer federal programs would be available to Hispanics. Local groups would be forced to seek local support to obtain grants and contracts.

Community advocates and leaders were activated to petition Washington for help in addressing their self-help proposals to the federal government. Inside President Nixon's Executive Offices, a small group concerned with this confronted the basic problem: How could the government avoid giving direct support and still gain Hispanic loyalty? They had learned from the failed Castillo and Sandoval experience that well-meaning bureaucrats could not orchestrate this delicate political maneuver. Instead, a task force was created to carry out what was named the "Responsiveness Program."

In January, 1971, Jeb Stuart Magruder, a White House staff member, began planning a general campaign strategy[5] and, in June of that year, William Horton, a White House aide, recommended that the president should have control over selected grants. The White House could then determine which ones were politically important enough to warrant a positive response. With this, the Responsiveness Program, designed by Fred Malek, was hatched.

At thirty-six, Malek was one of the most ambitious persons on the President's staff. When he joined the Nixon administration in 1969, he was assigned to assist Health, Education & Welfare Secretary Robert Finch. Malek unsnarled HEW's confused, overlapping programs and successfully applied management-by-objectives and cost-effectiveness measures.

In early 1971, H.R. Haldeman, the President's chief of staff, took Malek into the White House to recruit personnel. As part of this job, he evaluated the Office of Communications, headed by Herbert Klein. After a White House staff fight over lines of responsibility, Malek recommended that Chuck Colson get authority over project managers and the speakers bureau.[6]

5. *The Senate Watergate Report: The Final Report of the Senate Select Committee on Presidential Campaign Activities* (the Ervin Committee), Volume One. (A Dell Book, 1974), pp. 322-324.
6. Jeb Stuart Magruder, *An American Life: One Man's Road to Watergate* (New York: Atheneum, 1974), pp. 143-144.

The reorganization made Colson supervisor of the Spanish-speaking Constituency Group Task Force, headed by William Marumoto. Marumoto's career paralleled Malek's. He had entered government service in 1969 as an assistant to Health, Education and Welfare Secretary Robert Finch. He joined Malek's recruitment staff in 1970. Marumoto reported to Charles Colson on programs concerning Hispanics.

The Committee to Reelect the President (CRP) was in disarray toward the end of 1971. Malek—with Magruder, Attorney General John Mitchell, and H.R. Haldeman agreeing—took on the additional duty of supervising the CRP's voter response program. That section included the Spanish-speaking Division, now headed by Alex Armendáriz. When Attorney General Mitchell resigned from the CRP, Haldeman put Malek in charge of field operations and the Responsiveness Program.

The Responsiveness Program was intended to remain a covert operation but it was exposed by the Senate Watergate Committee investigating President Nixon's campaign activities following the 1972 election. Secret memoranda moved into reporters' hands in such abundance that Washington insiders described the flow of documents not as a leak but as a "hemorrhage." One report in particular, titled "Administration Efforts in Support of the Reelection" provided the most revealing look into how the Responsiveness Program worked.[7]

Each Cabinet officer was told which states, counties, and voting blocs the White House considered important. Each was asked to "sensitize" "loyal" appointees to White House political priorities. The departments were asked to plan what they intended to do to advance the campaign's target groups.

In early 1972, key persons were identified for honorary appointments to gain "stroking value." One report humorously pointed out that a leader of the Sons of Italy in New York had been placed on a traffic safety board. "He was ecstatic," said the report. In a similar move, Alfred Hernández, a Houston municipal court judge, was "stroked" and told he was being "considered" for a possible federal judgeship. Hernández, at the time, headed the League of United Latin American Citizens, the largest Hispanic organization in the nation.

But the bureaucracy was Malek's main concern. He reported to Haldeman in a "confidential" March, 1972 memorandum that the departments

---

7. "Administration Efforts in Support of the Re-election." The report was unaddressed and undated. A summary of the Responsiveness Program takes up Chapter 3 of *The Final Report of the Select Committee on Presidential Campaign Activities*, United States Senate, June 1974. U.S. Government Printing Office, pp. 361-444.

needed to respond quickly to the White House's political priorities if the Administration was to take full advantage of the discretionary funds available during that fiscal year. The Responsiveness Program was only channeling a fraction of what it could. The departments took too little initiative, and the White House had to virtually direct the whole program, he said. If only 5 percent of the money in five of the Commerce Department agencies alone were re-channeled, Malek believed, the campaign could effectively reach its "target groups and geographic areas."

It was also deemed necessary that the White House set the campaign's political priorities and stop micromanaging the details. Department officials needed to take their own "positive" and "negative" actions to help cultivate support from organization leaders who were awarded grants.

"There would be no written communications from the White House to the Departments," Malek instructed. Knowledge about the operation would never become public, and "all information about the program would be transmitted verbally." As if to wipe the fingerprints from the evidence, "The only written material submitted by the Departments to the White House would be their plans," said the secret report. Only two copies were permitted—one for the White House and one for the Departmental contact.

By June 1972, Malek and his staff had already intervened in twelve responsiveness issues. "All of them," wrote Malek, "originated in the field and were channeled to us" by CRP, the Committee to Reelect the President. Three of the five examples he highlighted concerned Mexican American projects in Los Angeles that were losing their funding (one program concerned possible conflicts with the Watts black leadership). The Department of Housing and Urban Development agreed to fund the three projects.

In another situation, the Department of Labor agreed to reverse an earlier commitment to fund a so-called "anti-administration" consortium made up of community action agencies that wanted to train migrant farm workers. The responsiveness group intervened and Labor was instead asked to make the $2.2 million award to the "pro-administration" Lower Rio Grande Valley Development Council. Malek reasoned that, by pulling the rug out from under the Office of Economic Opportunity, a possible antagonistic group was silenced. The administration would also gain Senator John Tower's (R-Texas) goodwill.

In the other intervention, Senator Tower had informed them that Edward Peña, a compliance director, had recommended to Equal Employment Opportunity Chairman William Brown that the agency sue the University of Texas over employment discrimination. Brown agreed, even if the action would be detrimental in a key state. (Brown later denied to responsiveness group inquisitors that the suit was even considered.) The matter "should be followed carefully," said Malek.

Malek's deceptively simple Responsiveness Program politicized every important department and strong-armed the government into conformity with the election campaign's priorities. Previous administrations might have had similar plans, but never before had campaign goals been as pervasive, nor carried out to the same extent.[8]

Congressman Edward Roybal, who represented a predominantly Mexican American district, was disturbed about the Responsiveness Program. At a House Appropriations subcommittee hearing, he confronted Malek. Roybal was from the Kennedy generation that had looked at public service and government as the source of public assistance and social direction. Now he was seeing it used for deliberate manipulation "It seems to me," he said, "that this whole set up was to reward your friends and punish your enemies, and that this matter of contracts was actually used as a stick over someone's head to get them to fall in line with regard to the campaign. Doesn't that indicate to you that the main objective was to reward your friends and punish your enemies?"

"Absolutely not," said Malek.[9]

Later, Malek even suggested to the subcommittee—and afterwards to Les Whiten, columnist Jack Anderson's associate—that the Responsiveness Program was never fully put into effect. "That wasn't done," he said. Instead, the memoranda had just been "talking points which never came up in meetings with Mitchell and Haldeman." Columnist Anderson reported that, despite Malek's denials, "we have obtained evidence that among blacks and Spanish-Americans, at least, the program was in full swing."

---

8. The Watergate Committee accounted for seventy-one exhibits (mainly memoranda, other communications, and affidavits) related to the incident. Fifteen of them were "Not for publication." *Presidential Campaign Activities of 1972, Senate Resolution 60.* Hearings Before the Select Committee on Presidential Campaign Activities of the United States Senate, Ninety-third Congress, First Session. "Watergate and Related Activities. Phase III: Campaign Financing." (Washington, D.C.: U.S. Government Printing Office, November 7, 8, 13, 14 and 15, 1973, Book 13), pp. 5532-5766. See also, "Everybody's Done it?" *The Washington Post* (January 21, 1974).

9. Hearings of the Subcommittee of the Committee on Appropriations, House of Representatives (Ninety-third Congress), *Treasury, Postal Service, and General Government Appropriations for Fiscal Year 1975, Part 3, Executive Office of the President* (Washington, D.C: U.S. Government Printing Office, 1974), p. 745.

Alex Armendáriz, also, denied he had any significant involvement in the Responsiveness Program. "I never engaged in specific discussions on any particular grant or contract of any sort," he said.[10] But the evidence didn't support that claim. In fact, he even contended that the memorandum outlining the strategy to neutralize the Hispanic vote was merely a point of view put on paper resulting from a public opinion survey. His plan wasn't much more than that, he said.[11]

But it was. It was much more than that.

To make the Responsiveness Program possible, White House aides Charles Colson and William Marumoto helped form the "Brown Mafia." The group went by that designation until it was changed to "Spanish-speaking Constituent Group Task Force" in May, 1972.

"Please drop mafia title," Malek wrote to Marumoto, "it would look bad if it ever got out."

Indeed word did get out and it was Marumoto—who had joined Fred Malek's staff in 1970—who did it. On programs affecting Hispanics, Marumoto reported to Charles Colson. Under Colson, Marumoto focused his attention on grants, personnel appointments and programs to "fill any gaps in the President's record," as he described it. He also kept an eye on federal subsidies that could serve as havens for the "opposition." The Brown Mafia was originally comprised of Marumoto, A.F. (Tony) Rodríguez, Carlos Conde, Henry Ramírez, and Alex Armendáriz. Rodríguez and Conde had both worked at the Cabinet Committee before taking staff jobs at the White House. Ramírez was, of course, the Cabinet Committee's current chairman.

Armendáriz (of the campaign staff and not a government official) coached the President's Domestic Council staff on what minority grants to approve and eventually he was involved in "signing off on" (meaning, giving approval to) an Office of Economic Opportunity grant application. Marumoto admitted as much to the Watergate Committee. But the Brown Mafia's concern, he said, was "more than grants."

"What we tried to do," he said, "was [to] select any department or agency . . . and we asked that [the agencies] cooperate in trying to involve our particular constituency." In matters dealing with the Office of Minority

10. The *Senate Watergate Report*, ibid., pp. 332, 338.
11. Hearings of the Subcommittee on Minority Small Business Enterprise and Franchising of the Permanent Select Committee on Small Business, House of Representatives, Ninety-third Congress, First Session, *Government Minority Enterprise Programs—Fiscal Year 1974*, Volume I (Washington, D.C.: Government Printing Office, October 3 and 4, 1973), pp. 81-83.

Business Enterprise, John Evans of the White House Domestic Council was assigned to coordinate those requests and took coaching from Armendáriz and Rodríguez on who would receive grants.

"Would it be fair to say," asked Samuel Dash, the Committee's Chief Counsel during the investigation, that "included in that group of new recipients of government grants and contracts were also those [people] sympathetic to the administration, [and whom you would call] the right people?"

Marumoto said they were looking for supporters.

"But [would that] also [include] those who are sympathetic to the administration or supportive [of it]?" Dash wanted to know.

"Yes," said Marumoto, "and I think here I would like to clear the air in terms of any . . . of the fact we weren't just looking for Republican contractors because in the Spanish-speaking communities there are very few [Republicans]. So we were really looking for those [potential recipients of grants and contracts] who were supportive and qualified."[12]

During the eight months they were in operation, the Brown Mafia did not, of course, supervise all government grants and contracts that went out to Hispanic recipients. They, however, attempted to do so.

The government's grant-making process, intended to be equitable and free from partisan shenanigans, was made partisan and biased. Approvals and rejections, with Brown Mafia influence, were based on the applicant's political qualifications. In some instances, people were "stroked" if they were undecided or if their loyalty was in doubt about supporting the president's reelection campaign.

Richard Nixon's Hispanic reelection strategy was also helped by Lyndon Johnson's Great Society. Nixon got credit for programs beginning to show promise after Johnson had left office and Nixon was president. To his credit, Nixon had measures of his own to show off. He had proposed bilingual education. Also, during his term, greater numbers of Mexican American and Puerto Rican youth—helped by projects to recruit and provide financial assistance—enrolled in colleges and universities. The federal government even attempted to establish Mexican American and other Hispanic higher education institutions. While the Johnson administration had expanded training programs to reach Hispanic applicants, new organizations during Nixon's first term were forming an infrastructure to improve housing, advance economic development, and provide project management.

12. Hearings of the Select Committee on Presidential Campaign Activities, op cit, p. 5285.

However, the broader policy to decentralize the federal government threatened Hispanic organizations that were becoming dependent on centralized federal funds. These organizations didn't think they could compete successfully at the local level for revenue-sharing funds if Nixon's reform measures were adopted during the second term.

Richard Nixon, as president, had proposed to decentralize most "social" programs—and most of Johnson's "Great Society" legacy. Under a new policy, Nixon wanted to channel federal money to state, county and municipal governments through "revenue sharing." Local governments would become responsible for funding local groups. This "New Federalism," as the policy was called, would force Hispanic leaders back into negotiations with the same city, county and state officials who had driven them to search for federal assistance in the first place. Few Hispanic leaders had any confidence in the kind of future that Nixon proposed. They had little, negligible, or no representation in the nation's city halls, county court houses and state legislatures to assure fairness, even when they formed a large part of the population.

The Nixon White House had to smooth over the discrepancy between what it had done (continue some programs) with what it wanted to do (replace them with decentralization).

Starting in early 1972, the Brown Mafia met every Monday afternoon to develop strategy. William Marumoto was the Brown Mafia's group leader. His boss in this matter, Charles Colson, had originally persuaded Nixon that "special interest" groups were a key to winning the election by cutting into traditional Democratic ties. Marumoto was particularly concerned that some groups opposing the administration could find jobs and political havens within organizations funded by the government. Just before the election, he wrote to Colson that he wanted suspect projects supervised closely "so they are devoting all their energies toward solving the problems of [the] Spanish speaking poor (particularly in September and October)," preceding the November election.

Brown Mafia members most feared negative publicity, as had occurred when the National Economic Development Association (NEDA), a Mexican-American organization, opposed the appointment of Cipriano Guerra to become deputy director at the Commerce Department's Minority Business Enterprise section. Marumoto wanted a Commerce Department undersecretary to threaten withholding a $2 million grant to NEDA. Later, when they seemed to have the group under control, Marumoto wanted one of the organization's vice-presidents to stage a demonstration protest over a *Los Angeles Times* editorial as a loyalty test.

Marumoto and Armendáriz made the rounds of federal agencies to encourage officials to make grants, let out contracts, and appoint "safe" Hispanics supportive of the administration. In some cases—documented for the Office of Economic Opportunity, at least—Armendáriz approved new grants.

"He [Armendáriz] was involved in terms of signing off on any grants," Marumoto testified to the Watergate Committee.

"When you say "signing off," did that mean he would have to agree?" Chief Counsel Samuel Dash asked.

"Approve, yes," said Marumoto.

"He would have to approve?"

"Yes," Marumoto affirmed again.

"And he was not actually a staff member of OEO, was he?"

"No, he wasn't," said Marumoto.

"In fact," Dash continued, ". . . a political signing off was necessary for the making of a grant to a Spanish speaking grantee. Is that your testimony?"

"Yes, sir," Marumoto answered.[13]

Meanwhile, Henry Ramírez's job was to make sure that highly visible awards went out. The Cabinet Committee, which he headed, was responsible for "spinning off" large sums of federal money through a special initiative called "Project Alfa." It yielded $47 million to first-time Hispanic grantees. Small Business Administration loans increased by 23 percent in 1972, a boost from $57 million to $74 million. The SBA also awarded $18 million to Hispanic firms through 248 contracts.

The reelection campaign correctly claimed to the public that the Nixon administration had made a greater effort to help Hispanic Americans than any previous administration. The message was that this group was finally getting out from under Democratic social-welfare handouts that only looked like progress, or so it seemed.

The Republican outlook was especially appealing to entrepreneurs and businesspeople. Bureaucrats who expected local organizations to come hat-in-hand, and who solicited proposals for projects while dictating the terms, offended them. The middle-income sector didn't want to become dependent on social development programs. Republicanism was a quantum jump into self-reliance and respectability, the likes of which welfare-oriented Democrats

13. Select Committee on Presidential Activities, Vol. 49, Hearings held Wednesday, November 7, 1973, p. 9556-9557. From an early transcription of the hearings.

didn't understand. The new approach promoted improved living standards, increased government employment, and expanded business opportunities.

Alex Armendáriz, meanwhile, came to some curious conclusions from an opinion survey conducted in New York, Chicago, Los Angeles, and San Antonio. He detected that East Coast Puerto Ricans, Florida Cubans, and southwestern Mexican Americans were uneasy within the generic "Spanish-speaking" alliance. Instead of devising one campaign to appeal to all, a divide and conquer strategy was considered more effective. "Puerto Ricans are unpromising voters for anyone," Armendáriz wrote in June 1972. "They are undermotivated, easily divided, and rely extraordinarily on luck for [the] betterment of their lives." When asked what the best thing that might happen to their families might be, they put the perception of money gifts first. When probed, they answered that the form that this might take would be the winning of *la loteria.*"[14]

His memorandum, after it was leaked to the *New York Times*, began to rekindle some old antipathies between Mexican Americans and Puerto Ricans, based on their earlier competition to get government attention. These differences had been resolved earlier when the "Spanish-speaking" alliance was formed. One of the agreements reached was to collaborate in forming the Cabinet Committee on Opportunities for Spanish-Speaking People, but Armendáriz' approach threatened to destabilize that relationship.

Armendáriz believed Republicans could capture about a third of the Hispanic vote. He reasoned that some voters were already predisposed to the Raza Unida party, and that they should be encouraged to waste their votes in that direction because those ballots wouldn't go to the Democrats. Then, Republicans would chalk up numbers by appealing to the Hispanic middle class, using the influence of Henry Ramírez, Treasurer of the United States Romana Bañuelos, and other campaign surrogates.

The campaign encouraged undecided voters to not vote at all by satisfying them with information about Republican accomplishments and creating an ambivalent attitude. The thought was their divided loyalties would make them stay home.

A "negative campaign" against McGovern (making drugs, crime, and

14. Committee for the Reelection of the President Memorandum to Henry Ramírez from Alex Armendáriz, June 19, 1972. The Subcommittee on Government Operations published this and the memorandum from Armendáriz to Frederic Malek of June 16, 1972 (that included the analysis of the survey) in "Activity of the Cabinet Committee on Opportunities for Spanish-speaking People," Ninety-third Congress, First Session, July 23 and September 12, 1973 (Washington, D.C.: U.S. Government Printing Office), pp. 27-33.

abortion the central campaign issues) would work best, he thought. To get President Nixon to advocate bilingual and other educational efforts was "our strongest and most effective issue."

The Brown Mafia now had a broad plan: the Responsiveness Program on the right and Armendáriz' strategy on the left. Marumoto was proceeding along these lines when he met with Southwest Council of La Raza (SW-CLR) members (the organization later became the National Council of La Raza) in an attempt to neutralize them. "There was some discussion about SWCLR supporting the President," said Marumoto. "They, in turn, said they would, provided they could get some federal contracts. . . . I think . . . the Committee to Reelect, the Spanish speaking division, recommended a strategy for working with them. . . . That they be funded for $30,000 for a national conference they wanted to hold. . . . I believe they were looking for either two or three grants. . . ."

Five weeks before the election, Marumoto reported that Brown Mafia members agreed any proposal submitted by SWCLR should be held up for the next few months. "We would like to have final sign off in the event any funds are given to them."[15] The Brown Mafia also worried about the Mexican American Unity Council, an SWCLR affiliate, and wanted their grant monitored closely.

Just a month before the election, George McGovern made a thinly veiled reference to José Angel Gutiérrez and a health project in Crystal City, Texas. He asserted that the Republicans had offered money to discourage the militants from voting in the presidential election. Gutiérrez quickly denied the charge, calling McGovern a "damn liar."

Yet ten months prior to McGovern's allegation, an "action memorandum" sent to John Mitchell (despite claims to the contrary) ordered a plan that called for "consideration of undercover funding of La Raza Unida, a splinter party, in exchange for an agreement that La Raza Unida runs Presidential candidates in California and Texas."[16]

Colson had communicated to H.R. Haldeman a year earlier that Raza Unida was "a very fertile political opportunity" and to give "some sub rosa financial and/or organizational support." The idea was to encourage the

15. The Southwest Council later denied reciprocating with the Brown Mafia. It rejected allegations that anyone from their group "was ever authorized to discuss or initiate on behalf of the organization any support for the reelection of the president as a condition for receiving federal grants or contracts."
16. Select Committee on Presidential Activities, Vol. 49, op. cit., p. 9662.

splinter party to run candidates and draw votes away from Democrats. "Money spent this way," said Colson, "can be as effective, if not more so, than money spent for our own advertising and promotion."[17]

Raza Unida entered the Texas gubernatorial race. An upset Democratic Governor Preston Smith had refused to approve OEO funds for a health project. "So we saw the Republicans and they overrode it," said Gutiérrez. But a September 14, 1972 memorandum indicated it wasn't as simple as that. Instead, Gutiérrez had actively sought Republican money, and Armendáriz responded by pressuring for more federal grants to Zavala county (Crystal City) up to a week before the election.

Armendáriz went so far as to recommend an $8,000 contribution to Ramsey Muniz, Raza Unida's Texas gubernatorial candidate. When he got the news, Malek became suspicious. It "seems too cheap. Raza Unida principles should be [worth] more than that," he said.

The Chicano party's election role was approaching a critical point. Soon, Raza Unida would register enough votes to hold its own primary elections. It could already divert as many as 200,000 "liberal-left" protest votes that cut into Democratic strength. The disaffections could make the difference in a Democrat winning or losing a close statewide race.[18] Evidently, La Raza Unida party, sanguine about its position to leverage a bloc of votes, was reported to have tried to shake down the McGovern organization for $200,000, as well.

Besides a preoccupation with organizations, the Brown Mafia was also concerned with certain careers in and out of government. Edward Peña, contract compliance director with the Equal Employment Opportunity Commission was a long-standing League of United Latin American Citizens (LULAC) member. He had been an aide to Indiana Democratic Senator Birch Bayh before taking the civil service job and had participated in forming an alliance with the G.I. Forum (a Mexican American civil rights group comprised of veterans). Together, they organized the largest Hispanic worker-training program in the nation, called Service, Employment and Redevelopment (Project SER). Peña remained active with LULAC while holding down his government job. The Brown Mafia tried to have him fired.

17. Memorandum to H.R. Haldeman from Charles Colson, December 20, 1971 in Bruce Oudes (ed.), *From: The President—Richard Nixon's Secret Files* (New York: Harper & Row, Publishers, 1989), p. 351.
18. Select Committee on Presidential Activities, Vol. 49, op. cit., pp. 9661-9662.

The Brown Mafia was also concerned about Armando Rodríguez, a distinguished educator from California who went to Washington in 1967 to head Mexican American advocacy in the Office of Education. In 1971, Nixon appointed him, a Democrat, assistant commissioner of Education. Rodríguez screened Hispanics for important jobs, which made some Brown Mafia members nervous. Tony Rodríguez—no relation—was assigned to keep an eye on him so that he could be "kept in line."

The Brown Mafia was not concerned with Democrats per se, only unfriendly ones. In a quid pro quo, Marumoto promised former LULAC president Judge Alfred J. Hernández that "the President will adequately recognize you" for conducting a news conference declaring his support. Hernández later headed Spanish-speaking American Democrats for the President. Marumoto communicated to John Clarke, a White House aide in charge of recruitment that "If any vacancies come up for the Federal bench in Texas . . . our operation would like to see Judge Hernández appointed." But the likelihood was very remote since the Republican senior senator from Texas, John Tower, would not clear a federal judgeship for a Democrat, and junior senator Lloyd Bentsen, a Democrat, would not favor Hernández after he endorsed Nixon.

Marumoto wanted nothing to mar the upbeat campaign. He even recommended that the Census Bureau suppress a report that showed Hispanics were falling seriously behind the rest of the population in certain economic categories. The report had been earlier slated for release before the election.

Sometimes, campaign exuberance motivated the Brown Mafia. Other times, they seemed like skilled plotters. But they were only part of the picture. The campaign surrogates were the other part of the strategy.

★ ★ ★ ★ ★

2

The Price of Influence

A lex Armendáriz had U.S. Treasurer Romana Bañuelos in mind when he recommended that Republican campaign surrogates should appeal to the Hispanic middle class. She had been a successful businesswoman, had name recognition, many people identified with her struggle, and others aspired to be like her.[1]

Nixon had nominated Banuelos despite a series of embarrassing raids by the Immigration and Naturalization Service on her food processing plant. The raids were staged for the media to draw attention to a developing illegal immigrant problem and to discourage union efforts at her operation. The incident's coverage in the *Los Angeles Times,* that Nixon interpreted as reflecting badly on the administration's ability to enforce the law, enraged him. He told Attorney General John Mitchell that he wanted retaliatory Immigration and Naturalization Service action taken against the newspaper owner, to have the INS area director replaced, and to have tax records of Otis Chandler, the paper's publisher, examined. "I want to go after this goddamn *Los Angeles Times*," said Nixon to his assistant . "I want the whole goddamn bunch gone after."[2]

---

1. Romana Acosta Banuelos was the first Mexican American woman to be nominated to a such a high federal position. Born in Miami, Arizona in 1925, she was raised and educated in a Chihuahua, Mexico, mining village before returning to the United States. In 1949, with young children at home, Romana Banuelos bought a $400 part-interest in a small Los Angeles tortilla factory. By the 1960s Ramona's Mexican Food Products had expanded into a major company, preparing 25 different products and hiring 300 employees. At the time of her nomination to become U.S. Treasurer, she was 46, and Ramona's Mexican Food Products had completed new construction on a 23,000 square foot plant addition. Banuelos was a founding member and chair of the East Los Angeles Pan American National Bank. She had also established a scholarship foundation for East Los Angeles high schools graduates. In 1971, at an Oval Office ceremony, President Nixon nominated Banuelos for U.S. Treasurer.
2. Ken Hughes, "Absolutely No Sense of Humor," *American Journalism Review* (March 26-31, 1997); and Jack Nelson, "Nixon Targeted The Times," *Los Angeles Times* (March 22, 1997).

Despite it all, those who knew about Nixon's nominee Romana Banuelos understood she was an American success story, a clear example of perseverance and ultimate triumph by a small businesswoman. She represented the type of individual who succeeded through hard work and persistence, in spite of criticism and adversity. Not surprisingly, United Farm Workers leader César Chavez had opposed the nomination.

Armendáriz believed that the careful use of Henry Ramírez, Philip V. Sánchez, and Romana Bañuelos in particular, would influence the middle class to support Nixon.[3] "There's a helluva push on," said one administration aide, to name Latinos to high-level positions and to publicize those appointments. "We were told by the White House to do it," said another official.

After March, 1972, Romana Bañuelos's schedule was arranged by the White House and the Committee to Re-Elect the President. Eighteen appearances were arranged that month. A television taping at the Spanish International Network—for broadcast to New York, Miami, San Antonio and Los Angeles—was arranged by Carlos Conde and also featured Phillip Sánchez and Henry Ramírez.

On March 17, 1972, Mrs. Bañuelos spoke at the San Antonio Chamber of Commerce. More than 200 persons picketed the hotel entrance, protesting what they described as the Republican administration's bias against the United Farm Workers Union. In her speech, Bañuelos said that the nation was moving toward greater equality for all citizens. "Discrimination is still a painful fact for Mexican Americans." We already "know about our problems," she said. "We need action and I think the action has begun," she told the 400 dignitaries in attendance.

The following month, a Denver celebration to honor Bañuelos—organized by *La Luz*, the first national Hispanic magazine—was canceled after the United Farm Workers Organizing Committee (UFWOC) threatened to picket the event. In Houston, Bañuelos spoke to a banquet organized by the local Hispanic Committee for the Reelection of the President. "These doors," she said to the five hundred attending the event, "will open still wider if we continue our active interest in public affairs and our traditional independence of spirit." A "poor people's dinner" was held outside the hotel

3. Committee for the Reelection of the President Memorandum from Alex Armandáriz to Henry Ramírez on June 19, 1972, Subject: Spanish Speaking Study in Subcommittee on Government Operations, "Activities of the Cabinet Committee on Opportunities for Spanish-Speaking People," Ninety-Third Congress. First Session, July 23 and September 12, 1973 (Washington, D.C.: U.S. Government Printing Office).

while she spoke. '$50 IS A MONTH'S RENT,' read some of the protest signs. Referring to the pickets, banquet organizer Benjamin Fernández said "there would be other occasions" when all Hispanic people could participate, "including $5 dinners and $100 dinners." Another sign across the street from the Shamrock Hilton read, 'BAÑUELOS, GO BACK TO YOUR TACO FACTORY.'

"The main objection" to the Republican showcasing, according to protest organizer Ben T. Reyes, was that Nixon's "few token appointments" didn't reflect community sentiment. "The people inside," said Reyes, "will be bank chairmen, funeral directors, furniture merchants, and other middle-class Mexican Americans who fancy themselves as part of the elite. The real majority of Mexican Americans will be represented outside."

Treasurer Bañuelos, in response, said, "I don't know why they say I am a token Spanish-speaking appointee. If we can go back and compare President Nixon's appointments of Spanish-speaking people to those of previous administrations, they don't even compare."

"The announced 'poor people's dinner' outside the hotel . . . fizzled," *Houston Chronicle* political editor Gayle McNutt observed. "The only food served the demonstrators was a pair of tamales and a few soft drinks. The protest dissolved in about an hour after demonstrators shouted insults in Spanish at many of those entering the hotel to attend the dinner."

As election day neared, Philip Sánchez, Carlos Villarreal, and Mrs. Bañuelos swept through key cities. The Mexican American Committee to Re-Elect the President sponsored the three administrators in Tucson and an *Arriba Con Nixon* rally in Phoenix. Sánchez, obviously optimistic, said that federal revenue sharing would definitely strengthen the poverty program. He said that municipal tax bases had become so saturated that cities could not do more for the poor, even though they wanted to. Revenue sharing would allow cities to address poverty from the local level.

Only forty persons attended the Phoenix event where Sánchez declared: "We've been telling the people to look at the record of this president in regards to Spanish-speaking people." He pointed out that three of the Department of Health, Education & Welfare regional directors were Hispanics, and "for the first time in history," the chief of the migrant division of HEW was a Mexican American. The Nixon administration has "given the orders to open the door of opportunity" for Mexican Americans, he said. "I dig that."

Sánchez, Bañuelos, and Villarreal flew to Denver for a rally sponsored by the Hispanic CRP. Two hundred persons in attendance heard Sánchez assert bluntly that members of the administration had a responsibility to recruit more Hispanics for federal appointment. "We have to be judged in terms of bringing in more [Latinos to government], and if we don't, the President will kick us out." Outside, United Farm Workers union supporters distributed a leaflet urging the boycott of non-union lettuce.

Going into the election, Mexican American and Hispanic appointees were ubiquitous. They were later credited with helping the president make inroads into the solid Democratic bloc. The campaign surrogates, as part of the Brown Mafia's reelection strategy, created the illusion that Nixon's policies and Hispanic interests pointed in the same direction. At last, Hispanic Americans were considered part of the nation's consensus-building and were taken into account. Or so it seemed.

Going by a cumbersome name, the National Hispanic Finance Committee (NHFC) for the Reelection of the President was organized to raise money, work with the Brown Mafia, and serve as a forum for campaign surrogates. The group also sent out an important message: affluent and middle-class Hispanics controlled their communities and supported the president. The imagery offended many neighborhood-level poverty workers, who had begun acquiring some measure of community control themselves.

Benjamin Fernández dreamed up NHFC as a fund-raising organization in early February, 1972. He wanted Hispanic communities contributing funds to Nixon's campaign. Maurice Stans, former Commerce secretary and chairman of the Finance Committee for the Reelection of the President (Nixon's main fundraising unit), liked the idea and authorized it. The first event was a testimonial dinner honoring Stans.

Upon finding out about these activities, San Antonio Congressman Henry B. González (D-TX) took to the floor of the House of Representative on May 4, 1972 to recount how Fernández, with a $605,360 SBA grant, formed the National Economic Development Association (NEDA) by opening offices in Los Angeles. Between 1970 and mid-1972, the organization received additional grants totaling more than $1.3 million. In two years, NEDA opened eighteen area offices. By May of 1971 NEDA clients had received loans totaling $1.5 million dollars. Applications for about $14.7 million were pending. The 744 loans approved, pending approval, or in progress came to more than $40.5 million, making NEDA a significant factor in stimulating new Hispanic business development.

It was, however, interesting to note that the NEDA San Antonio office ranked first among those cities stimulating activity. González claimed he had received complaints about Fernández's personal profiteering in late 1970. Within six months of NEDA's opening, said González, San Antonio groups paid $23,000 to Fernández's research company in applying for savings and loan association and bank charters.[4] Cipriano Guerra and Dr. Richard Delgado (the San Antonio office director and a NEDA board member), in an apparent conflict of interest, were among the six organizers. The group hired Fernández to conduct the required economic survey for about $13,500.

After organizing NEDA, Fernández separated himself from Research Inc.'s management, then divested himself of company stock. In August of 1971, Fernández resigned from NEDA after failing to get a vote of confidence from his board, following a dispute over the company's books.

Weary over insinuations about wrong-doing, Fernández, declared, "It is the toughest thing I have ever done in my life to try working the Spanish-speaking people into a cohesive unit. We have a tradition of not working together. Indeed, among ourselves we joke that the Mexican American does not talk to the Puerto Rican, the Puerto Rican does not talk to the Cubano, the Cubano talks to no one, and it is tough getting these three diverse groups to talk together."

William Marumoto looked into the affair to see if the administration would get damaged in any way. "We are convinced after some checking," Marumoto wrote to Charles Colson, "that there is no truth to the charges."[5]

From the run-in with González, Fernández drew a curious moral: It "brings to mind a cliché that I learned from my father, a Mexican immigrant from Michoacán, Mexico. He told me as a boy, 'Son, if you ever, as an adult, work with the Mexicans, I want you to remember something, that more Mexicans have died from envy and jealousy than from cancer.'"

In February 1972, under charter from Maurice Stans, Fernández organized the National Hispanic Finance Committee. State committees, each with its own chairman, were installed in California, Colorado, Arizona, Texas, Illinois and New York, with Florida a priority state. The large Cuban-American

4. González' remarks concerning this matter are contained in the *Congressional Record* of May 4, 1972.

5. Memorandum May 12, 1972 (Exhibit No. 262-16) and Memorandum May 19, 1972 (Exhibit No. 262-17), Hearings before the Select Committee on Presidential Campaign Activities, U.S. Senate, Ninety-third Congress, First Session, *Watergate and Related Activities, Phase III: Campaign Financing*, November 7, 8, 13, 14, and 15, 1973, Book 13 (Washington, D.C.: U.S. Government Printing Office, 1973), pp. 5576 and 5579.

population in Florida had more money to contribute than other Hispanic groups due, in no small part, to Cuban entrepreneurial success. Plus, they were staunch Republicans.

Testimonial banquets in cities with large Hispanic populations were staged to honor Nixon's high-ranking Hispanic appointees. The events provided the forums for unprecedented public relations gains.

By August of 1972, the HFC had raised $244,900. One dinner alone in New York City produced $50,000. The black-tie affair brought out businessmen, bankers, and officials who, according to *The New York Times*, "tend to be overlooked amid poverty problems that plague so many other members of the Hispanic community."[6] The talk at the event was about how delighted the president would be with a 20 percent show of support from the Hispanic community since nine-tenths of New York Hispanics were registered Democrats. But New York Republican Senator Jacob Javits pointed out that he had received 25 percent of the Puerto Rican vote. Governor Nelson Rockefeller had drawn a slightly higher percentage in 1970. The President could equal that number, Fernández thought, even though New York's Puerto-Rican voting strength had actually declined while the population increased. High estimates suggested up to 500,000 registered Puerto-Rican voters; others indicated there were as few as 120,000. Either way, it was enough to make a difference in a tight race.

San Juan's mayor, following Stans at the podium, pointed out that President Nixon had increased federal programs to Puerto Rico from $197 million in 1968 to $420 million in 1972. The mayor said that a "permanent union" was established between the island and the mainland, encouraging statehood and benefiting the U.S. with better Latin American relations.

By drawing out the affluent and the influential, the Finance Committee forged an identification between middle class Hispanics and the Nixon administration. The testimonials created the impression that a grateful and admiring community approved of the administration's direction. All the while, Ben Fernández and the Brown Mafia were in constant communication over how to get the most public relations juice from each event.

"The testimonial dinner in Los Angeles on March 19th for our Spanish-speaking Presidential appointees," William Marumoto wrote in a memo to Charles Colson, "is coming along very nicely. The organizing committee has already reportedly sold 2,000 tickets and are projecting an audience of

6. "Hispanic Leaders Raise $50,000 for President at a Dinner Here," *The New York Times* (August 31, 1972).

4,000 people composed of 90 percent Chicanos."

In April, Marumoto reported to Colson that "Rodríguez is working with Ben Fernández on a master list of his fundraising activities so we can plug in our speakers." All worked well. The entire project, in fact, went off as planned and was a screaming success.[7] Yet, later revelations suggested the something else was going on.

John J. Priestes testified before the Sentate Watergate Committee on November 7, 1973, that he was suspended as a contractor by the Federal Housing Administration (FHA) for violating regulations. Benjamin Fernández, representing the Hispanic Finance Committee, allegedly called him to say that several builders and real estate people had mentioned Priestes's troubles to him and that he thought he might be able to help.[8]

Fernández claimed he had assisted people in trouble with FHA before. The suspension could be cleared up in exchange for a $100,000 contribution. A $25,000 check, made out to the "Committee to Reelect the President," would serve as the first installment. After receiving it, Fernández would arrange for Priestes to meet Maurice Stans in Washington. Priestes was to make another $25,000 payment after meeting Stans and pay the remaining $50,000 when the suspension was withdrawn.

In Washington, Priestes was worried after newspapers disclosed that International Telephone and Telegraph had made an illegal $200,000 political contribution to the Nixon campaign. And he thought it was unfair to ask him for $100,000 dollars. This led to a change in the payment schedule. Priestes was to pay the first $25,000 at the meeting with Stans, and a remaining $25,000 when the FHA problem was cleared up.

At the meeting, Priestes explained the FHA controversy and handed Stans some newsclippings. Stans said he would make a call and would return the check if he could not do him any good. Stans jotted something on the check indicating that it had been made out to the wrong committee. Furthermore, according to Priestes, "He [Stans] told me that the final payment would have to be made before April 7" to circumvent certain new reporting requirements.

---

7. The relationship between the Spanish-speaking Task Force and the National Hispanic Finance Committee was documented in Marumoto's weekly reports to Colson and Malek on the following dates: April 3, 32, 28, May 5, 19, 26, June 9, 16, August 18, September 1, October 6, 1972.

8. "Testimony of John J. Priestes . . ." *Watergate and Related Hearings, Phase III, op. cit.,* (November 7, 1973), pp. 5327-5357

Priestes returned to Miami and later found that Fernández was not positive, saying they were working on it and would get back in contact with him. About two weeks passed before a man appeared at Priestes's door. "The man said 'it could be handled but it would require $25,000 in cash, and the check . . . he didn't want the check,'" said Priestes.

Priestes couldn't recall the man's identity. Upset, he called Fernández, who offered to find out what could be done.

"Well," said Priestes, "his conversation [with me] was that he said: 'Well, we can't do anything for you. You can, if you would like to, make a contribution for $5,000 but it would have to be reported. . . .' I said: "Wait a minute, I don't understand this at all. You're talking about $5,000.' He said: 'We never promised you anything,' and I guess I got a little indignant and I said: 'What was I doing in Washington with [the] $25,000 check, and I am not even a Republican?'"

On questioning him, Senator Lowell Weiker asked, "What did you think you were doing?"

"What did I think I was doing?"

"Right."

"I though," Priestes answered, "I was paying $25,000 down, with a promise to pay an additional $25,000 for a political favor."

"A political favor or government favor?" Weiker asked.

"Well, I don't know how, exactly how to describe it. I don't know what type of favor you would describe it as. The end result was that I was going to be an eligible building contractor again. It would have been a favor."

"Did you think of this in your mind as a bribe to government officials?" Weiker wanted to know.

"I didn't give it a lot of thought as a bribe. No, I didn't really give it that thought," said Priestes. "I just thought it was the way things are done."

A statement from Maurice Stans, introduced to the record, acknowledged he met Priestes briefly on March 13. Hugh W. Sloan, treasurer of the Finance Committee to Reelect the President, had arranged the meeting.[9] Priestes offered a $25,000 campaign contribution in the form of a check payable to an organization other than the Committee for the Reelection of the President. After discussing the check, Stans reviewed Priestes's newspaper file and promised to read the clippings more thoroughly later. "I also told him that I could not evaluate the situation without knowing FHA's attitude toward him and his transactions; that I would have to check with

9. Ibid., pp. 5346-5347

HUD. I returned the check either to Fernández or Priestes to hold until I had been able to do so."

Later the same day, Stans had HUD deputy assistant secretary Richard Dunnells look into Priestes's record. He also met with William Gifford of the White House staff to have him check out Priestes. Within days, Dunnells and Gifford advised that any contact with Priestes was inappropriate. On March 18, he told Fernández to terminate any contracts with Priestes, and Fernández said he would do so at once.

When Ben Fernández' testified, he said that "To my knowledge, in no single instance was there ever a promise of political favoritism, coercion, or other similar tactic employed in the solicitation, collection, or expending of these campaign contributions."[10]

"Yesterday, I sat in this hearing room while a man named John Priestes did everything in his power to stain my good name and that of the National Hispanic Finance Committee," he said. "I am appalled, shocked, and disgusted with the tenor of his testimony." Fernandez took the stance that this was a low blow after he had taken ten months from his own business to work as an uncompensated, full-time volunteer.

As it turned out, John Priestes was just one—albeit extreme—type of contributor. There were others. And there was a connection between contributions and political considerations.

John Evans, a White House staff member, admitted receiving "input" from Marumoto and Armendáriz, among others. He acknowledged that political considerations played a role in awarding grants. He admitted that the Brown Mafia recommended "qualified groups" who supported the administration over those who did not. Although Armendáriz, Marumoto, and Ramírez had approached him, asking him to fund political contributors, Evans said he was not involved in specific grants where that had occurred.

In a Watergate Committee interview, Alex Armendáriz denied any wrongdoing or that he had been involved in letting out government grants. He disclaimed having had power to sign-off on federal awards. "I never engaged in specific discussions on any particular grant or contractor of any sort," he said.[11] But that was, of course, untrue.

---

10. "Testimony of Benjamin Fernández . . ." *Watergate and Related Hearings, Phase III, op. cit.,* (November 8, 1973), pp. 5360-5402.

11. *The Senate Watergate Report: The Final Report of the Senate Select Committee on Presidential Campaign Activities (the Erwin Committee)*, Volume One (a Dell Book, 1974), p. 348.

The Senate Watergate Committee documented how the Brown Mafia rewarded Republican friends and punished uncooperative individuals. Joe A. Reyes, president of J.A. Reyes and Associates, and chairman of the District of Columbia, Virginia, and Maryland HFC, had received numerous federal grants. Most of his business came from Section 8(a) of the Small Business Administration, a program designed for the expansion and development of small businesses owned and controlled by eligible disadvantaged persons. Reyes grossed between $400,000 and $500,000 during 1971, and his gross grew to $1 million in 1972. All of the money came from the 8(a) program through seven contracts and one grant, including a $200,000 "sole-source" (non-competitive) contract awarded to evaluate and assist the Office of Economic Opportunity's Emergency Food and Medical Services Program.

Arnold Baker, former head of OEO's field operations in the Labor Division, argued that sufficient data already existed on the program, and an evaluation was unnecessary. Nevertheless, the contract was awarded over the objection. When the political reasons for the award became obvious, OEO decided to withdraw the contract. Then the contract was awarded. Then it was canceled because of substandard work. Then it was reinstated. A contract specialist with the Migrant Division concurred with Baker that the Emergency Food Program contract was not warranted and that J.A. Reyes Associates was unqualified to conduct the evaluation. The contract specialist characterized the award as a "political payoff." The Migrant Division director, denying the allegations, insisted on the award, claiming the contract did not result from political influence.[12]

In another situation, Marumoto and the Brown Mafia supported a $300,000 Office of Minority Business Enterprise grant to Ultra-Systems. Fernando Oaxaca, HFC's national treasurer, was Ultra-Systems' vice president. "This organization," said Marumoto about the grant applicant, "strongly supports the Administration." The company was again the subject in an August 1972 White House memorandum concerning an Office of Minority Business Enterprise application. Steps were taken to expedite the request, even though the firm had not completed the qualifying requirements. Oaxaca denied that the grant, awarded in October, was a quid pro quo. He explained that he failed to get a response after the application was made, so he contacted A.F. Rodríguez, who made an inquiry on Oaxaca's behalf.

12. The subject of numerous "Weekly Activity Reports" from Marumoto to Colson and Malek. *Watergate . . . Hearings, Phase III*, Exhibit 262-15, p. 5572.

In yet another case, Armendariz recommended the Spanish-speaking Business Alliance of Los Angeles (with which Oaxaca was also affiliated). They "are highly recommended by this office," he said.[13] Yet, in his interview with Watergate Committee staff, Armendáriz admitted knowing Oaxaca, but denied knowing that he was national treasurer of the Hispanic Finance Committee.

Influencing favorable decisions was one thing; influencing negative actions was quite another. For example, Marumoto asked for a contribution from Leveo Sánchez, head of Development Associates, a contractor with Democratic ties. Sánchez refused. Consequently, the Small Business Administration announced that Development Associates was "graduated" from participation in the 8(a) program. This meant that the company would lose all government grants awarded on the basis of participation as a minority contractor. Dan Trevino, a company vice president who had served on the Texas Committee to Reelect the President, tried to intervene. He discussed the problem with Henry Ramírez, A.F. Rodríguez, and William Marumoto, but to no avail. Ramírez and Rodríguez admitted that the actions were directed at Sánchez for not cooperating, and not at Treviño. Similarly, other negative actions were considered against the Mexican American Unity Council in San Antonio, but Marumoto wrote to Colson saying, "there are some legal hang-ups to try to cut them off."[14]

In the end, the campaign investments helped yield 31 percent of Hispanic ballots for Richard Nixon, while the Democrats retained 69 percent. The Brown Mafia strategy came close to its goal of obtaining a third of the Hispanic vote.

According to a CBS analysis, 49 percent of Hispanic voters in Texas and Florida voted for President Nixon, as did 24 percent of New York Puerto Ricans, and 11 percent of California's Mexican Americans. Sampling by the Committee to Reelect the President showed that the chances that San Antonio Mexican Americans would vote Republican increased with income: 20 for Nixon in low-income precincts, 49 percent in middle-income precincts, and 58 percent in high income precincts.

The president's coattails had no effect in the Texas election. The gubernatorial election was a seesaw race. In the end Democrat Dolph Briscoe won over Republican Henry Grover with just over 99,500 votes. Raza Unida's

13. Ibid., p. 5633.
14. *The Senate Watergate Report*, op. cit. pp. 353-362.

candidate Ramsey Muñiz drew over 200,000 votes. Earlier, Muñiz had drawn enough votes away from liberal Frances "Sissy" Farenthold to cost her the nomination during the primary. When Muñiz drew just over 6 percent of the vote in the general election, he deprived Briscoe of a majority. Raza Unida, as a third party, had earned a place in future elections. "If we only increase our strength to ten per cent of the vote," said Muñiz, "we'll decide every governor's race from here on out."

Following the election campaign, numerous administrative changes were made. In many cases, high-level Mexican American officials were replaced. Nixon's policy now emphasized revenue sharing as part of the New Federalism plan. The days were numbered for categorical programs focused on human services.

In the same month of Nixon's reelection, the National Labor Relations Board ruled on a complaint brought by the Teamsters against Ramona's Mexican Food Products. The ruling said that the union, on strike since March, had been treated unfairly. The company was ordered to stop refusing to negotiate and discouraging union membership. Eighteen days later, federal immigration agents raided Ramona's Mexican Food Products again. Fifty-three illegal immigrants were arrested.

Romana Bañuelos resigned fifteen months after the President's reelection. She said personal reasons had led to her decision to leave the administration. Speculation pointed to a Treasury Department controversy in which she was embroiled as the cause.

President Nixon appointed Benjamin Fernández as special envoy to Paraguay President Alfredo Stroesner's inauguration in August, 1973. Rumors circulated that Fernández would soon announce his candidacy for lieutenant governor in California. But the plans never materialized in the wake of the Watergate investigation.

A year later, Senator Edward J. Gurney (R-Fl.), who served on the Senate Watergate Committee, was indicted on charges that included conspiracy, bribery, receiving unlawful compensation, and four counts of making false declarations to a grand jury. John Priestes was one of three key government witnesses whose testimony led to the eleven-count indictment. Priestes claimed he would have "exposed" Gurney before the Watergate Committee if minority counsel had not stopped him.

In the middle of all this confusion, Samuel Dash attempted to clarify why the Senate Watergate Committee was concerned with Hispanic policy and politics. The main concern, he said, "was not whether or not the administration sought to give grants to a minority group, but whether or not certain members of that minority group were made enemies . . . that if you were not in favor of the administration, you were cut off." Some contractors were classified as unfriendly and "graduated" out of competition.

Dash said, "perfectly competent" Hispanics were "dropped from grants because they would not support the administration " The question," he said, "is whether or not that is proper politics." Clearly, it wasn't.

The Brown Mafia, Committee chairman Senator Sam Ervin stated, had made federal agencies into "the political plaything of the Nixon administration." They set out to channel federal contracts, grants, and loans to places, groups, or individuals "so as to promote the reelection of the President rather than to further the welfare of the people."

As the Brown Mafia activities began coming to light, Henry Ramírez was called to account for the Cabinet Committee's role before the House Operations Committee. He had succeeded where his predecessor, Martin Castillo, had not, but Ramírez was going to pay a price for it.

Congress had given the Cabinet Committee a five-year mandate to do its work. The charter, Public Law 91-181, due to expire in December, 1974, required most of the president's cabinet and agency heads to meet quarterly to determine a Hispanic policy approach. But the Cabinet Committee only met three times in three years.

The Cabinet Committee's 1972 annual report, required by legislation, was only nineteen pages long and arrived eleven months late. The document suggested that the Cabinet Committee had virtually stopped working as it was supposed to. For instance, the 1971 and 1972, efforts to implement the Sixteen Point Program to increase the federal work force with high-level appointments were dubious, at best.

"You have been in existence four years," Michael McGinn, the Government Operations Subcommittee's analyst said in open hearings. "Are you aware that as of the last period for which figures are available, that fourteen out of twenty agencies in the Executive Office of the President had no Spanish-speaking representation, and that only among groundskeepers do the Spanish-surnamed exceed their portion as a whole?"

McGinn was miffed because he couldn't verify the Cabinet Committee's employment claims. "Fifty people," the report showed, were "employed as a result of your data bank, which you cite as one of your major accomplishments, and last week you cited to the Appropriations Committee there were forty people from all sources. The list sent to me included a major general in the Air Force. Presumably he wasn't in the job bank."

The Sixteen Point Program simply didn't work, but it was postured for election purposes as a great success. Hispanic people, 6 percent of the U.S. population, represented only 3.1 percent of the federal work force.

Under Henry Ramírez' chairmanship, the Cabinet Committee had been deflected from its mission. He could have guided both the president's Cabinet and the U.S. Congress through this Hispanic "domestic council," reporting to both the executive and legislative branches of government. But Ramírez, as a campaign surrogate, let partisan politics overtake the policy's purpose and created only the illusion of progress. After the election, unable to effectively carry out the mandate, he was pulled into an unenviable round of questioning.

"On behalf of the nation's Spanish-speaking," Ramírez pleaded before committee chairman Chet Holifield, " we hope and pray that your deliberations are fair, that your decisions [are] just."

President Nixon revived the "new federalism" idea originally conceived by Walter Heller, Chairman of the Council of Economic Advisors during the Eisenhower administration. Local governments were to become responsible for planning, allocating resources, and making program decisions. They would get revenue grants to spend on the public sector. The money from the federal government would come from anticipated surplus revenues from full employment if the economy remained strong. But the government did not have a revenue surplus by the time revenue sharing was enacted into law in 1972. The United States operated a deficit budget. Critics called it "deficit sharing."

The new approach was presumed necessary because the old grants and contracts, according to its critics, were over-bureaucratized. Categorical programs alone had increased four-fold between 1945 and 1972. The approval process was cumbersome and virtually unworkable. Federal bureaucrats in Washington determined what local problems needed attention.

Richard Nixon first advanced the New Federalism idea in his "welfare-workfare" speeches of 1969. He wanted to give grants to states and cities to plan their own worker training, set welfare payments to benefit the working poor, and give cash incentives to unemployed welfare recipients to get job training. In 1971, the administration also proposed special revenue sharing for law enforcement, transportation, education, manpower training, community development, and rural development. According to Nixon, the first four proposals—resubmitted in 1973—consolidated, decategorized, and decentralized government programs on the assumption the measures would eliminate waste and duplication of services.

State and municipal governments would use revenue-sharing funds to initiate their own new programs. But that level of government had seldom, if ever, seen fit to safeguard—much less promote—Hispanic interests. It was doubtful they would recognize, much less embrace, Hispanic problems that needed solutions. The New Federalism undermined the developing Mexican American influence by displacing sympathetic bureaucrats who were learning how to use available federal programs to their benefit. The prospects were not bright that state and local governments would share the same level of concern as the federal government.

Neither cities nor states had an acceptable record of service to Hispanic groups, who were often overlooked or taken as a nuisance, and who lacked local representation (often due to gerrymandering and at-large elections).

The administration's first major rejection of Hispanic community interests occurred when President Nixon moved to abolish OEO and its Community Action Program. The administration tried to wipe them out with a flourish and, with it, the Great Society's approach to alleviating poverty. Many of the social objectives outlined in the 1960's were rejected. "Phil Sánchez (OEO director) was appointed to preside over the funeral of OEO," said Hector Morales, Tucson's community action agency director, "and that's what really hurts." President Nixon later replaced Philip Sanchez at OEO with Howard Phillips, who colorfully junked existing antipoverty operations in order to substitute the New Federalism.

In a March 1973, in a speech before the National Spanish Speaking Business Development Conference, Henry Ramírez admitted, "We lost Phil Sanchez and then Carlos Villarreal at Transportation." Four months after Nixon's reelection, five other Hispanics were fired from high-level positions. Some observers complained that the loss of policy leaders was part of a Nixon plan to hoodwink Hispanics. "Our people," said Ramírez, "began thinking we had been used, that all the administration had been doing was giving us jobs and money so that it could get our votes." He rationalized, instead, that the losses were the result of simple reorganization and attrition. "I can tell you," he said, "that other high-level Spanish-speaking appointments will follow. I can assure you that there are going to be more brown faces in top government jobs than ever before."

Ramírez, however, failed to address the central issue: The administration didn't want the nation's budget written with particular people's problems in mind. Many community-based service programs faced oblivion under revenue sharing if local leaders couldn't negotiate funding with the established state and local authorities.

The issue was representation. Hispanics did not have enough representation at the local level. And not enough at the federal level, either.

The Nixon government had believed all along that they had no business promoting economic equity through programs providing assistance. The shift was evident in the reelection campaign. A selfish reaction was engendered within the electorate. Nixon's campaign exploited the understandable crassness among citizens who were harassed by high taxes, frustrated by rising prices, worried about bussing to achieve school desegregation, annoyed by political violence and afraid of crime in their neighborhoods. Federal assistance was portrayed as totally profligate and administered by a lot of devious characters concerned only with bureaucratic empire-building, embarrassing the president and dissipating taxpayers' hard-earned money on social programs run by inept administrators to meet questionable aims. The administration promised a "New American Revolution" that would return power to average Americans who had become members of an exploited class, helpless against an omnipotent government, and fed up with social parasites.

During the retreat from social responsibility, the president, without committing himself to anything more than avoiding a tax increase, carried forty-nine states. The new policies, when they were implemented during the second term, reopened old cleavages. The New Federalism was no revolution at all. It was just an administrative adjustment.

While the nation was traumatized by the Watergate Committee's revelations of the president's campaign activities, the economy deteriorated rapidly. This had begun during the 1970-71 recession and continued during the preparation for the 1972 election. The administration imposed the largest peacetime budget deficits and a tremendously sharp increase in the money supply to hold down interest rates.

Nixon had traumatized the nation in 1971 with a ninety-day wage and price freeze, followed by mandatory controls limiting pay increases to 5.5 percent and prices to 2.5 percent. The program seemed to work at first. Inflation receded from 4.4 percent to 3.8 percent. Then in 1973, Nixon abandoned mandatory controls in favor of a voluntary program. Inflation surged ahead again. Wage and price controls produced shortages. Tremendous distortions in the market economy drove prices even higher. When Nixon finally dropped the program for good in 1974, inflation was at 12.2 percent, two-and-a-half times higher than the rate he had inherited.

The deteriorating national economic situation hit Hispanic families very hard. The Census Bureau released a report in August 1974, showing that

Hispanic average income declined while it increased for the rest of the population. Nixon's economic and social policies were largely responsible. To have a better social and economic chance in the future, the only reasonable answer was to replace the stand-ins and surrogates representing Hispanic interests with their own elected officials.

Burdened by the articles of impeachment voted by the House Judiciary Committee, President Nixon resigned on August 9, 1974. Vice President Gerald Ford assumed the presidency, taking office with just two years to establish himself and his program before the Republican Convention.

3

The Transitional Presidency

A month after taking office, President Ford invited Hispanic congressmen and administration officials to the White House. The agenda mainly concerned the economy, bilingual education funding, and worker training programs.

As the first order of business, Congressman Eligio (Kika) de la Garza (D-Texas) insisted that distinctions and differences between Hispanic groups had to be taken into account. Regions such as rural south Texas needed one kind of attention that was distinct from what was needed in urban areas like East Los Angeles or New York City. The differences required better definition and attention. Still, the meeting, said de la Garza, was encouraging. He found Ford "genuinely interested."

"His intention is very serious," said Senator Joseph Montoya. New Mexico Republican congressman Manuel Lujan, Jr. added, in Lincolnesque prose, "Doors of opportunity must be open to all citizens, regardless of ethnic background, with fairness for all and favor to none."

Earlier in the month Henry Ramírez had resigned from the Cabinet Committee and was replaced by Reynaldo T. Maduro, who had been Ramírez' principal adviser during the 1972 campaign. Ford had said he wanted more information about how the agency worked before taking a position on its continuation. Community leaders had mixed feelings about Maduro's appointment. De la Garza favored, instead, a Hispanic advocate in the White House. Coincidentally, Ford was considering Fernando E.C. de Baca to become a White House special assistant.

Soon after the meeting, Ford appointed de Baca as presidential counselor. De Baca had earlier headed Nixon's Sixteen Point Program in the Civil Service Commission. He was at least partly responsible for Nixon's fifty-one Hispanic super-grade appointments. The record compared with six similar appointments by the Johnson administration. Nixon then appointed de Baca to head the Department of Health, Education and Welfare's western region. Now, as a counselor to the President, he was Ford's highest-ranking Mexican American appointee.

De Baca believed Ford needed to understand that language policy was an important concern. "Over half of our people, half of 10.8 million people speak only one language, and it is not English." A 1969 Census survey had found that 87 percent of Cubans, 72 percent of Puerto Ricans and 47 percent of Mexican Americans spoke Spanish at home. Many non-English-speaking Hispanics had a lower earning potential through missed employment opportunities and stood to become more socially isolated.

However, news, information, and entertainment was getting through to many as a Spanish-language communications industry was in place and rapidly expanding. The United States had ten Spanish-language television stations in 1975, and four others broadcasting to the U.S. from just across the border in Mexico. A 1973 survey sponsored by the Spanish International Network, owner of seven stations, found that 64 percent of Spanish-language households in New York City turned their dials to a Spanish-language station at least once during prime time. New York, Miami, and Los Angeles each had Spanish daily newspapers, although their combined circulation reached only 150,000 readers.

The implications were staggering. Most people believed that the Hispanic population, though growing, had no major economic significance. On the other hand, major marketers were feverishly going after their purchasing dollars. Something didn't make sense.

To uncover what that something was, de Baca proposed an accurate census count of Hispanics for starters. "That count plays a major role in the allocation of federal resources," he said, referring to the formula (based on population and need) used to distribute revenue-sharing dollars. A working Hispanic population estimate was 9.2 million. However, the 1970 census undercounted them by at least a million. The actual total may have been even closer to 12 million, not counting undocumented immigrants.

With the nominating convention only two years away, primaries in eighteen months, and the 1976 presidential campaign set to begin within four months, political considerations went into Ford's appointment of Ignacio E. Lozano, a Los Angeles businessman and publisher of *La Opinion*, as ambassador of El Salvador. Ford made sixty-one Hispanic super-grade appointments, accounting for more than any previous president. The most important one came six months prior to the 1976 presidential election when Edward Aguirre was named Commissioner of Education.

Even though White House press releases announced various appointments as the "highest-ranking" Hispanic in the administration—making a virtual mockery of the designation—Aguirre actually had the highest domestic rank of any other Ford appointee. He held the equivalent of what would have been a cabinet post had the Department of Education been established earlier. No Hispanic for twelve years would hold a higher position.

Like his predecessor, President Ford moved on OEO (a symbol of controversial programs testing the limits of political tolerance). The agency's name was changed to the Community Services Administration. Bert Gallegos was named to head the agency, but his nomination didn't go smoothly. Gallegos came under sharp criticism in a House Manpower and Housing Subcommittee report alleging abuse of personnel policies in Denver. The allegations were a rehash, said Gallegos, of the criticisms from two years earlier. His nomination was confirmed.

Samuel R. Martínez later succeeded Gallegos as CSA director. He became the poverty agency's third Hispanic administrator in five years, succeeding Gallegos and Phillip Sánchez. The strategy, as before, was to appease the constituents while ending some programs. In 1976, CSA consisted of 865 community action agencies with a $520 million budget. Ford proposed cutting into CSA by ending recreation and food programs for the poor and reducing the agency's budget to $334 million.

Martínez himself came under suspicion after a report alleging fiscal mismanagement at the agency was turned over to a local U.S. attorney.[1] The allegations against current and previous CSA administrations did not constitute guilt, but the pattern of suspicion seemed to visit Hispanic elected and appointed officials largely because of the networking in which they had engaged.

For example, columnist Jack Anderson reported in November 1975, "The Watergate scandal isn't over." Alex Armendáriz was appointed to head the Office of Minority Business Enterprise (OMBE) in 1973 "as a reward for faithful service to Nixon," said Anderson. Characterized as "a political operative," Armendáriz "apparently learned his lesson well" on how to win federal grants and contracts in exchange for political support. He "continued to reward friends with federal funds and to punish enemies by denying them money." Among the examples, Anderson said Armendáriz helped Tony Rodríguez, a fellow Brown Mafia member, to obtain an OMBE contract. Armendáriz said there was nothing wrong because Rodríguez

1. Marianne Means, Struggling War on Poverty," *San Francisco Chronicle* (June 20, 1976).

was qualified. Armendáriz was also reported to have made grants to benefit a congressman, had funded projects of dubious value and relevance to a minority business enterprise, accepted valuables, and provided junkets for employees. Anderson reported that the Commerce Department—the Office of Minority Business Enterprise's parent agency—was taking "a serious look at Armendáriz' activities."[2]

Watergate-related revelations had cast a shadow of suspicion over most high-ranking Latino government officials. The caper tainted everyone. Presumption of guilt abounded. Nearly all Hispanic officials paid a price for that defamation. Consequently, some of them failed to receive the acknowledgment and gratitude for great efforts and accomplishments. Many anonymous administrators, in addition to their job requirements, did double-duty articulating inside government the demands of America's 10 to 12 million Hispanics.

In October 1974, President Ford met with representatives of eighteen Hispanic organizations for an hour and a half. They told Ford they wanted a decision-making role in addressing emerging problems. Among them was the illegal immigration issue, which was becoming painfully challenging. Some undocumented people, in the United States for decades, were technically illegal entrants. Many family hardships and job disruptions would occur if the threatened deportations took place. Expelling people would not solve the problem, they said. Furthermore, they noted, as many as 16 million people needed bilingual education to become job-ready. But who would serve as their advocate on the issues? The leaders didn't have strong feelings as to whether or not the administration should keep the Cabinet Committee in that role.

About that time, the Senate was approaching a decision on the matter. Senators Charles Percy (R-Ill.) and Jacob Javitz (R-N.Y.) planned to support a bill, coming up for a vote, that would give the Cabinet Committee a six-month extension. The two Republicans had been Cabinet Committee critics but were persuaded to support the extension instead of its outright abolition. Reynaldo Maduro said he thought he could turn negative sentiment around by holding meetings with Congressional members and grassroots organizations. Henry Ramírez' departure had helped win over some major Latino groups, he said. Fernando de Baca joined in the lobbying for the extension. But the bill never came to a vote. The Cabinet Committee's

2. Jack Anderson, "Watergate Scandal Isn't Over," *San Antonio Express* (November 12, 1975).

authority ended on December 30, 1974 after a five-year existence. De Baca said its demise was understandable. The Cabinet Committee had become no more than a complaint desk in its last year. He, subsequently, became the administration's spokesman and the Hispanic communities' chief surrogate representative.

President Ford, after only three months in office, met with Mexican President Luis Echeverría in Arizona. The presidents agreed, respectively, to buy and sell Mexican oil at the going world rate. The meeting was part of a campaign swing by Ford in support of Republican Russ Williams in the Arizona gubernatorial race against Democrat Raúl Castro. The candidates were running neck-and-neck. Castro, not to be outdone, interrupted his campaign schedule to meet with Echeverría. They talked about Arizona-Mexico relations. "He told me," said Castro after the meeting that "I could be of service to better relations if I am elected governor."

Ford and Echeverría also agreed to form a joint commission to study how the United States might admit more Mexican guest workers to farms and ranches facing acute labor shortages. The U.S. had used a *bracero* program, responsible for 200,000 Mexican guest farm workers, before organized labor pressured its termination in 1964. Consequently, farmers mechanized further (and displaced more farm workers) or switched to crops that needed less physical labor. But increased production had made farm workers necessary again.

The two presidents met about the time a new program was inaugurated to control the number of undocumented entries into the U.S. from Mexico. Attorney General William Saxbe estimated that one million illegal aliens, mostly Mexicans, would be deported during the year after 552 officers were reassigned along the Mexican border and other U.S. gateways. The 25 percent Border Patrol increase was intended to show that Ford placed a high priority on the issue.

Undocumented workers were presumed to take "millions" of jobs from American citizens, drain social services, and "mock our system of legal immigration," said the attorney general. Saxbe estimated that one million illegal entrants held 364,000 industrial jobs, nearly as many in agriculture, and about 300,000 service jobs.

He called attention to one Los Angeles police district that reported illegal immigrants accounted for 36 percent of felony arrests. "This matter deserves much closer study nationally," said Saxbe, ". . . if illegal immigrants are a substantial factor in our growing crime rates, this gives even more impetus to the need for prompt action."

But Saxbe had gone too far, said Rosario Muñoz, a Los Angeles activist. Saxbe's policy of threatened deportations was inflammatory and tantamount to "declaring open season on all Mexicans."

"Saxbe's trying to find a scapegoat and he's picking on the most helpless group of people in this country," she said, adding that the attorney general was motivated by worsening economic conditions and the Ford administration's inability to deal with inflation and unemployment. Javier Rodríguez, head of CASA, an organization set up to help aliens, compared the Saxbe remarks to the anti-immigrant hysteria of the 1920s and 1930s. "Mexican people will have to walk around their own communities carrying identification cards."

Saxbe's perspective invited rancor toward immigrants, and encouraged panic and monstrous prejudice. Artfully contrived arguments were rampant about how much the public would save from welfare payments, if they could only get rid of the undocumented immigrants. The administration, many believed, was going too far. Memories about wholesale deportations during the Great Depression were still alive.

Saxbe sought to give the Immigration and Naturalization Service $50 million, but the bill was stalled in Congress. Drafted by Representative Peter Rodino (D-N.J.), the legislation intended to get undocumented Mexican laborers off farms through round-ups and deportations. The bill would also penalize employers (with fines and jail sentences) for hiring undocumented workers.

Rodino's bill had passed the House of Representatives twice. Its Senate companion, sponsored by Senator Edward Kennedy, proposed stiff penalties for hiring undocumented workers but offered amnesty to those who had lived in the U.S. for more than three years. The bill was killed in the Senate Judiciary Committee. A second bill, with stiff penalties minimized, languished in committee until chairman James O. Eastland (D-Miss.) drafted his own version of the legislation that softened penalties against employers.

President Ford supported the Rodino bill. He specifically cited it in a message, saying he wanted legislation enacted before adjournment. Ford estimated "that there are some four million to seven million illegal aliens in the United States." The bill was needed, he said, to make more jobs available.

Eighty delegates to the Mexican American Issues Conference, fed up with the administration's direction, wanted Saxbe reprimanded and unanimously asked President Ford to seek the attorney general's resignation. In addition, a resolution asked for federal legislation allowing illegal immigrants living in the U.S. longer than two years to legalize their residency. Another resolution would give legal residents the right to vote, which was the only right they did not have under present immigration laws.

Fernando de Baca stepped in to speak for the administration. He regretted the "recent unfortunate statements" made, he said. The attorney general's remarks "do not reflect the position of the President of the United States." Saxbe had only reinforced the conventional belief that illegal immigrants depressed wages, drained social programs, and took jobs from Americans. "These questions have to be addressed and answered not on the streets of East L.A. in a confrontation between immigration officers and a brown-skinned person, but at the conference table."[3]

The public was bombarded with facts, exaggerations, and fictions aimed at influencing their opinion to blow off steam with respect to the economic situation. The *San Antonio Express,* for instance, reported that the INS estimated (wrongly) that roughly eight million people, out of a total 210 million population, were illegally in the country. "Can a nation that is sliding inexorably into a recession, is battling inflation and rising unemployment, and is faced with shortages of energy, clean water and air and possibly even food," asked reporter Michael Stachell, "afford to take in millions of extra residents, especially when in this country, zero population growth is close?"

The AFL-CIO meanwhile supported measures to curb illegal immigrants and estimated a cost of $10 billion in wages lost to aliens, who also undermined union strength by working below union scale. INS investigators also expressed frustration, reasoning that the odds of getting picked up by the Border Patrol were the same as getting struck by lightning. Illegal immigration had increased, but their budget had not.

The "crisis" reached comic proportions when a group of leading western ranchers met with INS Commissioner General Leonard Chapman about the west having run out of cowboys. The ranchers wanted permission to import Mexican *vaqueros* to make up the difference. But with six million unemployed Americans, and an estimated two to three million illegal immigrants holding jobs, the Labor Department, scrutinized by the AFL-CIO, would not easily authorize imported labor.

INS reported that its 8,000 member staff had arrested 800,000 illegal immigrants but 25 to 30 percent of those arrested had trickled back into

---

3. "Chicano New Conf. Scores Saxbe on Alien Deportation Plan," *Los Angeles Times* (November 8, 1974).

the U.S. General Chapman argued for staff increases and pressed for the Rodino bill. The legislation would authorize over 2,000 more INS agents to help recover a million jobs for unemployed Americans. The measures were urgently needed, Chapman added, because the U.S. was running out of fuel, food, land, clean water and other vital resources. "They're costing the United States hundreds of millions in unpaid taxes, in the various government, state, or local services they use, and in remittances sent to their homelands."

Conservative commentator William F. Buckley noted that while some Americans blamed Mexican workers in the U.S. for sending money out of the country, they overlooked the fact that 10 percent of investment capital from the U.S. was destined for Mexico. It seemed that money from workers to families was not beneficial to the U.S., but dollars from bankers, investors, and investment houses was.[4]

Fernando de Baca again addressed the illegal immigrant issue, this time at a meeting of the National Association on Counties. President Ford was tackling the problem "head on," he said. The Domestic Commission on Illegal Aliens was gathering data, determining how many there were, what jobs they held, how many attended school, what municipal services they used, and how much money was sent back to the mother country. "We've got to pull together to stop the flow of illegal aliens into this country. It is a fantastic influx," he said, "and it is growing." But de Baca doubted General Chapman's reports that illegal immigrants held ten dollar-per-hour jobs. Those getting high pay were the exception and not the rule.

The issue heated up further when Manuel Fierro of the Raza Association of Spanish Speaking Affairs told the National Congress of Hispanic American Citizens that he favored cracking down on employers. Fierro blamed unscrupulous farmers, industrialists, and businessmen who benefited from illegal immigrant labor. The Rodino bill's penalty provisions were not stringent enough, he said. Cracking down on employers was preferable to cracking down on immigrants. Too many Hispanic Americans would be adversely affected when they were mistaken for foreign nationals.

Monsignor George G. Higgins, secretary of research for the U.S. Catholic Conference, favored blanket amnesty for all illegal immigrants. Deportations would cause massive hardships on legal and illegal immigrants alike. Meanwhile, the Mexican American Political Association's (MAPA) Los Angeles director advocated relief for immigrants similar to the assistance provided Vietnam refugees. People fleeing communism, he said, were no

4. William Buckley, Jr. "Getting Along With Mexico," *Arizona Republic* (September 2, 1975).

more worthy than refugees from hunger. MAPA attorneys drew up guide-lines modeled after Ford's amnesty for Vietnam-era draft evaders. An immigration board was proposed that would allow petitioners to apply without fear of retribution.

If the policy issues were not sufficiently difficult, an incendiary situation arose when G.I. Forum national Chairman Antonio Morales called General Chapman "definitely a racist." Chapman bragged, said Morales, "he had just bagged forty-one 'Polacks' washing windows in Washington." The whole immigrant thing was a charade. "Last year," said Morales, "the country generated 225 million dollars for special programs for the Spanish-speaking. Yet, in a moment of crisis, our President was able to generate 400 million dollars for 100,000 Vietnam refugees." The federal government welcomed one group of immigrants and gave them assistance and tried to throw out another. "While we welcome the refugees," said Morales, "we look at the ironic aspects" that the policy represents for the Spanish-speaking people in the United States. If the U.S. had surplus people, the refugee policy made no sense.

Neither Chapman nor Saxbe anticipated that America's Hispanics would mount enough political muscle to force a reconsideration of the administration's simplistic analyses and solutions. In a conciliatory tone, Chapman said that he had considerable sympathy for illegal immigrants. They often worked hard just to make a go of it. But he believed that sympathy should not blind Americans to the fact that illegal immigrants were knowingly violating the law and exacerbating a serious economic situation by sending $5 billion a year out of the country. Income taxes were evaded, he claimed, and Americans were forced onto the welfare rolls when interloping immigrants took their jobs.

In January 1975, President Ford established a Domestic Council committee on illegal immigration to come up with policy recommendations after assessing how much the federal government spent on programs used by illegal immigrants. The estimates, added together, would determine the impact on government and society. But the first problem to arise was defining "illegal alien," and then estimating their number. The President asked the committee to report to him by September 30 to coincide with a deadline set by a similar committee set up by the Mexican government.

President Luis Echeverría was well aware that solutions also depended on Mexican efforts. They faced losing farm workers going north when jobs south of the border became scarce. For political leverage, he insisted that the migrants should receive fair treatment, referring to problems dating back to the Franklin Roosevelt administration.

Finally, a policy approach was taking shape from the cornucopia of opinions. Fernando de Baca floated a trial balloon. Government should bring millions of illegal immigrants under the protection of the law by legalizing the people already in the country to avoid "turning the U.S. into a police state." "It is imperative," he said, "to regularize the status of such persons so that they will not be exploited and they can better integrate themselves in our society as a whole." The nation needed to understand that some people wanted to enter the country so badly they were willing to break the law to get in.

De Baca's statements, coming right before Ford met with thirty-five Republican National Hispanic Assembly leaders, was taken to mean that, after heating up, the issue was getting cooled off for the election season.

Two Mexican American governors were elected in the 1974 mid-term elections. Forty-year old Jerry Apodaca became New Mexico's first Spanish-surnamed governor since 1918. He won with 51 percent of the vote. Fifty-eight year old Raúl Castro won a narrow gubernatorial victory over Republican Russell Williams in Arizona. Both new Hispanic governors were Democrats.

Raúl Castro had lost to Williams by 7,000 votes four years earlier. But in his comeback, he gained greater name recognition. By the time of the second encounter, Castro was better staffed, better organized and better financed than before. He also had access to a twin-engine airplane to get around. Castro lost Maricopa County (Phoenix) but made up for it by winning the Tucson area, his hometown. However, the winning margin came from Native Americans, where Castro won three Navajo counties by a 9,000-vote margin after a successful voter registration drive by the Tribal Council. About 20,000 of 140,000 Navajos registered to vote, more than triple the previous years' registration. About 60 percent of those who registered actually voted, compared to past elections when only 10 percent turned out.

Apodaca's New Mexico election was not manifest destiny for Mexican American and Hispano representation. Apodaca won by only 2,800 votes. Political experts said the margin would have been larger except for a segment of the Anglo population that still worried about a "Mexican American take over." New Mexico Democratic Chairman Ben Alexander conceded that old prejudices were an election factor. He pointed out that changes were taking place: "Jerry got some Anglos who've never voted for a Mexican American before," he said. In that sense, "I don't guess we done too bad."

The accomplishment showed, instead, that the scales tipped when the right political combination was put in place. Joe Skeen, Apodaca's opponent, had weaknesses. But, more importantly, Apodaca did not repeat the mistakes of the 1968 election between Democrat Fabian Chávez and Republican David Cargo.

Cargo won in 1968 with 50.2 percent of the statewide vote; Chávez got 49.3 percent. Only 2,910 votes separated the two candidates. Joe Skeen almost duplicated Cargo's earlier victory. He carried Bernalillo county (the Albuquerque area) better than had Cargo and did better than Cargo in the Little Texas counties (so-called because of demographic and geographic characteristics similar to West Texas, with strong anti-ethnic preferences). Apodaca was strongest in the northern Hispano counties. Though not from the north himself, he adopted bilingual speech, and mingled with crowds easily. Hispanics took to the energetic, former college football athlete's articulate hand-to-hand electioneering. He consolidated his campaign with the state party after getting support from Democratic bosses and leaders in the northern counties.

The northern Hispano counties voted in record numbers and gave Apodaca the winning margin (67.3 percent to 31.7 percent), enough to offset Skeen's gains in Little Texas and Albuquerque. Even so, Apodaca was one-tenth of one percent short of a majority. Skeen was short by 1.2 percent. Gene Gonzáles of the American Independent Party diverted 4,062 votes to his campaign, or 1.2 percent of the statewide total. Without Gonzáles, the difference between Skeen and Apodaca would have been narrower and a toss-up. But a conservative third party in the race, taking votes away from Republican Skeen, helped Apodaca win.

"For the first time," Fernando de Baca observed, "we have two elected Latino governors, and we've tasted success all the way down to the school board and city council levels." De Baca failed to point out that the victories were mainly Democratic successes. The broader principle was not lost on him, though. Latinos will "have fuller representation than we have had."

The election ball had begun rolling, even though Arizona and New Mexico's political gains were not duplicated to any great extent in other parts of the southwest. G.G. Gutiérrez and Cesar Sereseres, two California commentators, were disappointed in their state, calling the outcome "ethnic politics as usual," or "*nada por nada*," thanks for nothing.[5] They reasoned that Republicans ignored hard issues because Chicanos did not vote

5. G.G. Gutiérrez and Caesar Seréseres, "*Nada por Nada*: The Chicano Political Trap," *Los Angeles Times* (November 7, 1974).

Republican, and Democrats knew that Chicanos made up 18 percent of the state's population but cast just over 7 percent of the general election votes. Why should candidates try to reach this population? They didn't make up enough voters to form a majority virtually anywhere. Neither California gubernatorial candidate had even so much as delivered a major speech concerning Mexican American problems during the campaign.

Chicanos faced a Catch-22. They didn't vote because politicians didn't pay attention, and politicians didn't pay attention because Chicanos didn't vote. On the other hand, Gutiérrez and Seréseres failed to note that California's Hispanic population was very young, much of it below voting age. Its political potential was increasing incrementally, on a year-to-year, or election-by-election, basis. Expectations were running ahead of reality.

Discontent prevailed among many Hispanics. Democrats had gained forty-one congressional seats throughout the nation (giving them a 289 to 147 majority) and three Senate seats (a 65 to 35 majority). Congressman Manuel Luján, a Republican, defeated New Mexico Lt. Governor Roberto Mondragón in a congressional contest despite many Republican losses during the mid-term election.

The Republican Party had tried to consolidate strength when 250 Hispanic Republicans, with GOP party chairman George Bush's help, formed the Republican National Hispanic Assembly. Co-founder Benjamin Fernandez reasoned that Democrats had only paid lip service to Hispanic voters until Texas Senator John Tower and Ambassador George Bush (also of Texas) began attracting Hispanic support in the 1960s. "Republicans," he said, "have made impressive gains among Hispanos in recent years, and must redouble their effort during this period of growing voter independence."

The Republican Party was in search of a new strategy, one that would add strength, especially after crushing defeats in Texas. The Hispanic Assembly was designed as the grassroots organization to encourage participation in GOP activities, said RNC official Raúl Espinose.

Rómulo Munguía, one of the thirty Texas party officials meeting with Espinose in San Antonio, was still smarting over the mid-term election. He especially didn't want the new approach to become a paper tiger, relegated to the outskirts of Senator John Tower's campaign against the "John Connally-Ben Barnes-Waggoner Carr machine," as he called the group that had dominated Texas Democratic politics. The Texas U.S. senate election would test whether the Republican Party could work with the Assembly.

4
Politics and Relevance

The Texas poll tax, before it was declared unconstitutional, stopped many potential voters who could not afford to pay it. Another popular practice was to avoid enrolling registrars who would concentrate on selling the tax in Hispanic areas. Not surprisingly, Mexican American registrations increased dramatically as soon as the U.S. Supreme Court struck down the poll tax in 1967. Only 53 percent of eligible Mexican American voters were registered before the tax was lifted. In 1968, registrations increased to 65 percent, and by 1970 they were up to 70 percent.

But other restraints to voting persisted. Mexican Americans had complained for decades about intimidations, insults, and humiliations when they attempted to vote. Jobs, welfare benefits, and food stamps were taken away from people in some counties. José Angel Gutiérrez, for one, reported those retaliations against Raza Unida Party voters.

In Arizona, the legislature, dominated by Republicans, cleared the voter registration rolls and called for re-registrations prior to the 1970 elections. Mexican Americans could not respond as quickly as other citizens to the requirements. Language barriers delayed word getting out. Sometimes people didn't understand what was asked of them. Democratic Party activists and political analysts pointed out that re-registration was intended to keep Mexican American voters from sweeping Raúl Castro into office. They were right. Castro lost the election, but only by a few thousand votes (he would win the governorship in 1974).

District gerrymandering was also a widespread practice. East Los Angeles, with more than 600,000 Mexican Americans, was divided into nine state assembly districts, seven state senate districts, and six congressional districts. None of them had more than a 40 percent Mexican American population, and none of the districts had more than 35 percent registered

Mexican American voters. Los Angeles County, with the largest Mexican American concentration in the nation in 1970, had a negligible number of Hispanic elected officials until 1977.

Elsewhere in California, no elected official had a Latino constituency greater than 30 percent; no representative was dependent on Hispanic support. Gerrymandered Mexican Americans were clearly being denied representation.

Hispanic constituencies were rarely large enough to consider their group relevant to most elections. A 1971 U.S. Civil Rights Commission report stated that Mexican Americans had no real chance of gaining representation to the state legislatures or the U.S. Congress in proportions approaching their percentage of the population. The lack of representation created another layer of unfairness because the New Federalism strategy virtually required even local-level representation to assure fair distribution of funds sent by Washington.

In 1972, five Hispanics served in the House of Representatives (four Mexican Americans, one Puerto Rican) and one was in the U.S. Senate. There were no governors and California had no state senators and only five assemblymen, none of whom represented districts with more than 28 percent Mexican American constituencies. In short, less than 2 percent of all elected and appointed officials were Hispanics. And, few elected officials meant few appointed officials as well. Finally, less than one-third of 1 percent of federal officials listed in the Congressional Directory of the U.S. Government were Mexican Americans. Under prevailing conditions, the prospects were not good that major changes would occur.

Of course the history of Hispanic elected representation was dismal. For example, the first California legislature (technically an advisory council to the military governor), organized in 1847, consisted of four Mexican-descended residents and three Anglos. Mexican Americans had some representation in the state senate from 1849 until 1864, with at least one Mexican-descended person in each legislative session. In the next forty-seven years, from 1865 until 1912, three Mexican Americans served in the state senate. After 1913, and for the next sixty years, no Mexican American served in the state senate until Rubén Ayala was elected in 1974.

All this considering that, by the early 1970s, California's Mexican American population was greater than the total populations in twenty-six states. Yet, out of 160 state and federal officials elected by Californians in 1972, only three were Mexican Americans.

Of course, unrepresentative elections were of such long standing that the injustice was barely acknowledged. The non-democracy created by gerrymandered districts was an accepted norm. In the southwest, Mexican American interests were not considered particularly important, nor did anyone come to the rescue. In fact, representatives were so distant that they were unaware that there was even a Mexican American interest to represent. Jess Unruh, former California Assembly Speaker, was blunt: "Quite obviously the Mexican American community has been reapportioned more with regard to how it would maximize Democratic [party] representation, than how it would maximize Mexican American representation."[1]

Failure to establish ongoing equitable representation posed a real problem in California and elsewhere. The New Federalism's decentralized programs came under state and local authority. Solutions to social problems increasingly became a state and local government responsibility. That meant that Hispanics were middled. They couldn't get a fair hearing at the national level, and they couldn't get one at the local level. In many cases, local government was the level furthest from the people. Then, in 1974, four months into the Ford Administration, an opportunity arose that changed all that.

As a civil rights issue, support for inclusion of Hispanic concerns was not entirely well received. Mexican American leaders wanted the coverage of the Civil Rights Act of 1965 expanded. Civil rights leaders wanted the act re-authorized by Congress without changes (oriented toward African-American groups).

To complicate matters, a memorandum by eighteen Civil Rights Commission staff members to their director John A. Buggs argued that they had been ordered to "limit" a study into voting problems faced by Mexican Americans and other minority groups. Their position was that if the problem was not studied, how would they understand it? Or do anything about it?

The Voting Rights Act, passed in 1965 and renewed in 1970, concentrated on South Carolina, Georgia, Alabama, Mississippi, Louisiana, Virginia, thirty-nine North Carolina counties, and counties in five other states, including nine in Arizona. The law suspended literacy tests and similar voter qualifications, and authorized supervision of voter registration in federal elections. As a result, seven southern states had increased representation

1. Quoted in Fernando V. Padilla and Carlos B. Ramirez, "Patterns of Chicano Representation In California, Colorado and Nuevo Mexico," *Aztlan* (Spring and Fall, 1974), p. 201.

from fewer than one hundred African American elected officials to 964 by 1974

Civil rights leaders, who didn't want the legislation changed, remembered the trouble they had in 1970. The Leadership Conference on Civil Rights (made up of blacks, labor, Mexican Americans, and other minority groups) finally defeated the Nixon administration's effort to kill the expansion of the law's coverage. Gerald Ford was then House minority leader and among those working with Nixon. As president, Ford offered to support the law's renewal in its present form if it contained no changes.

Clarence Mitchell, the National Association for the Advancement of Colored People's (NAACP) chief lobbyist, contended that some of the problems cited by Mexican American leaders were already covered in the existing federal legislation.

J. Stanley Pottinger, Assistant Attorney General for Civil Rights, on the other hand, wanted to get out of the way of the coming confrontation. "I would hate to see fratricide among any particular groups," he said. He saw African Americans as "sealing off the act because they've got the vote in their pocket."

When John Buggs informed the Leadership Conference leaders of having ordered the Civil Rights Commission staff to cut back on their study, Manuel Fierro of the Raza Association of Spanish-Speaking Americans was especially unhappy. He and Al I. Pérez of the Mexican American Legal Defense and Education Fund, cited intimidation and harassment of Mexican American voters in Texas and other southwestern states as the basis for extending the Act's coverage. The collaboration grew tense. The *Arizona Republic*, without naming its source, stated, "a strong feeling exists among blacks that Spanish-speaking persons in California and Colorado are trying to displace them in jobs, political activities and in other areas. A similar problem exists in Florida with Cuban-Americans."

Congressmen Edward Roybal and Herman Badillo (D-N.Y.) introduced a bill to extend civil rights coverage to Spanish-origin persons. Representative Barbara Jordan (D-Tex.) proposed another bill to extend the law's protection to persons whose mother tongue was other than English. The NAACP and other black groups proposed adding a separate title to the Civil Rights Act to protect language minorities. Clarence Mitchell said he feared the law's renewal was endangered or could result in lengthy court tests (disrupting its enforcement) if it were drastically changed.

By late March, support had increased in the House of Representatives to include Mexican Americans in some southwestern states under the Voting

Rights Act. "We're going to enact it, I'm sure," said Representative Don Edwards (D-Calif.), House Judiciary Subcommittee chairman. At the hearing on the measure, Congressman Edward Roybal testified that more than three million Mexican Americans experienced serious impediments to registering and voting. Discriminatory school-board election practices made electing Spanish-speaking people virtually impossible, as did redistricting, registration and voting irregularities, changes in polling places without notifying the public, and the lack of bilingual registrars and election officials.

Consequently, Mexican Americans, who comprised 16 percent of California's population and 12 percent of its voting age population, held only 0.7 percent of the elected positions in the state and Los Angeles, with a Spanish-speaking population larger than some states, did not have a single city councilman of Hispanic descent. Roybal argued for a more liberal bill, one with enforcement power over political subdivisions whose voting-age Hispanic population was 5 percent or more and where the voter turnout was less than the 1972 national average.

The proposed changes were not popular everywhere. For instance, the *San Antonio Express* opposed extending the Voting Rights Act to include Texas. An editorial demanded proof that abuses had occurred. Rosie Castro answered the challenge.[2]

Arguing like a lawyer, Castro said that the Texas government had been taken before every judicial level throughout its history to defend discriminatory election laws. The state had enacted the Terrell Election Law (allowing a white primary) and defended *Nixon v. Herndon* and *Nixon v. Condon*, the white primary challenges before the U.S. Supreme Court. Upon losing the cases, the state legislature approved measures allowing the Democratic Party to declare itself a "private club," permitting it to exclude "undesirables." The *Smith v. Allwright* decision of 1944 overturned that practice. After the Supreme Court's one-man-one-vote decision, Texas challenged the decision in court "just to be certain that the one-man-one-vote theory was democratic."

Castro pointed out that intimidations had occurred in Pearsall, Cotulla, and Corpus Christi. Chicanos had been harassed and subpoenaed to appear before judges and juries after voting for the Raza Unida party. South Texas police and Texas Rangers guarded polling places, but from whom? Voters?

The clearest example of intimidation came out in the *Bernal v. Lombardino* case. Chicanos who had voted for the Raza Unida party in the

2. Rosie Castro, "Texas Voting Rights," *San Antonio Express* (May 26, 1975).

primary, and crossed over in the runoff election, were interrogated at their homes by members of the District Attorney's staff. They were told they would be taken to court if they refused to sign a statement but were not provided a copy of the statement. They were asked, in some cases, who they voted for, in violation of secret ballot rules. For these voters, said Castro, "it doesn't pay to vote for La Raza Unida, it doesn't pay to vote for Bernal, it doesn't pay to vote. Duty, right, or privilege, it does more harm than good."

In 1975, while the Voting Rights Act moved through the House of Representatives, the U.S. Senate worked up a version to meet an August deadline. House minority leader John J. Rhodes (R-Ariz.) said he was unsure whether the President would sign the legislation if it passed but speculated "he would find it very difficult" not to.

The new measure would cover California, Texas and other western states under its provisions. In California, for example, this meant that fourteen counties—including Los Angeles, Orange, San Diego, and Ventura—would have to print election ballots in Spanish and English. San Francisco ballots would also appear in Chinese. New provisions allowed the federal government to supervise local voting procedures if the Justice Department found voting irregularities and discrimination.

Ten days before the law was due to expire, the House voted 346 to 56 to accept the Senate's version. The bill that passed and went to President Ford called for a seven-year extension of the law instead of the House's ten-year continuation.

Fernando de Baca gloried after Ford signed it. "Spanish-speaking Americans have long been denied equal education opportunities by state and local institutions resulting in severe learning disabilities and continuing illiteracy in the English language," he said. The new Voting Rights Act was the solution. Policy issues and voting rights were interwoven. People could take possession of their own problems and come up with their own solutions. Voting discrimination was part of the past now. The revised Voting Rights Act, he said, was "the most significant landmark piece of legislation" Spanish-speaking Americans had ever had.

However, Ford's passive approach to the Voting Rights Act didn't square with de Baca's enthusiasm. Had Ford come out early and championed it, he would have gotten credit and suffered no losses. A White House statement admitted that "voting discrimination against Spanish-speaking citizens had been pervasive and far-reaching." The statement said the new law would assure "far greater representation of Americans of Spanish heritage in the elected offices of this country." It was one of the strongest and most forceful statements to come from the White House about ending an awful chapter of American history. But it came from Fernando de Baca. The President did not even so much as dignify the measure with a presidential press release.

As the New Federalism took hold at the local level, President Ford muddled through. Meanwhile, Hispanic leaders began raising their voices in protest. They intended to establish a political agenda distinct from Ford's. Federal policy was openly challenged. Spokespersons for numerous Hispanic organizations challenged politics as usual. Greater sophistication was evident, with a better insight into the issues.

Hispanic leaders were impatient and ready for results. The Voting Rights Act provided the leverage they needed. They now had a shield from intimidation and unfair political practices, as well as a tool to wrest power from political opponents. But they needed candidates who would follow through.

"I think that 1976 will show that those public officials who show responsiveness to problems of Spanish-speaking Americans will get their support," said Fernando de Baca. "I'm sure, that at least in eighty-five congressional districts in this country we have 10 or more percent of the population. That may not be many, but 10 percent sometimes can be a very effective swing vote, and that vote's going to swing with a great impact."[3]

Of course, the new legislation met with some resistance, perhaps because of its enormous potential to affect school board, municipal, legislative, and federal elections. Antonio Morales, for instance, announced at the mid-year GI Forum convention in El Paso that Texas Congressman Dale Milford and Illinois Congressman Robert McCory had co-sponsored a bill to remove the bilingual ballot from the Voting Rights Act. "We're still having to fight for citizen's rights," said Morales. "Next thing we can expect is they'll try to bring back the poll tax."

But progress had been made. Attorney General Edward Levi required 513 counties in thirty states to hold elections in more than one language. He proposed new compliance guidelines and ruled that 314 jurisdictions were required to obtain advance approval of new laws under the act, or other political changes that might affect the voting rights of any language minority.

3. "Latin Minority Predicted to be Largest," *El Paso Times* (October 21, 1975).

The states of Alaska, Arizona, and Texas, specifically, were required to get federal "pre-clearances" to change their laws. Portions of twenty-seven other states were required to hold bilingual elections, acquire federal clearance, or both. States with large Hispanic populations—including California, Colorado, Connecticut, Florida, Idaho, Kansas, Michigan, Minnesota, New Mexico, Oregon, Utah, Washington, and Wisconsin—were put on a Justice Department watch. Thirty-eight California counties—almost the entire state—were required to hold elections in English and Spanish.

Some local leaders, unaccustomed to accounting for the politics of the past, grew alienated. One likely mayoral candidate complained about the three identified populations: Black, Mexican American, and Anglo. "According to Webster (and me)," he wrote, going to the best authority he could find on American ethnicity, "an 'Anglo' is an Englishman. Since I am an American of Irish extraction, I wish to protest this blatant racism. . . ."

New Mexico, on the other hand, welcomed the spirit of the new legislation. Three counties were exempt from the federal voting-rights requirements because they had no history during the preceding ten years of denying or abridging voting rights. In fact, the state welcomed the legislation and established a voter assistance and education program. "The cooperation with the Justice Department has been so great," said U.S. Attorney Toney Anaya, "I am sure we will have no problem working out some solution."

The election reforms came in the nick of time. Evidence showed that Hispanics were, in fact, far worse off under the New Federalism reforms than under previous policies. A Ford Foundation study showed Hispanics received substantially less funding under the reformed manpower training programs than they had before the decentralization. Local officials, by channeling the funds to local service organizations, controlled the Concentrated Employment Training Act program (or CETA, as the new employment training programs was called). G.I. Forum chairman Antonio G. Morales estimated that the Spanish-speaking lost $109 million under CETA. Manpower services were cut by 42 percent and one out of 2.4 eligible persons was denied service. He said that before the Nixon reforms, "the Spanish-speaking received 15.2 percent of the services available. Unfortunately, under CETA, the percentage has dropped to 8.8 percent." This occurred when Mexican American joblessness was double the national average.

Education issues faced a similar concern. Vilma Martínez, Mexican American Legal Defense and Education Fund's executive director, said, "In Texas, for example, where the dropout rate is seventy to eighty percent, it's not just a matter of desegregating schools, but of adding bilingual-bicultural components in education." Favorable court decisions had not dramatically improved bilingual opportunities.

Shenanigans replaced overt regional discrimination. From the White House, President Ford sent out memoranda asking the federal government to hire women and minorities. But HEW's Office of Civil Rights told women and Spanish-speaking minorities that the office could not handle their discrimination complaints because the office was not under court order to give them priority.

Peter Holmes, speaking for the Office of Civil Rights, explained that Judge John Pratt had ordered HEW to "commence prompt enforcement activity upon all complaints . . . of racial discrimination." To the OCR staff this meant "racial," and not sexual, religious, or national-origin discrimination. The argument appeared persuasive on the surface, but not to Al I. Pérez, MALDEF's associate counsel. He noted that OCR staff had grown from less than 100 members in 1966, to 400 by 1970, and about 850 in 1975. "OCR requested of Congress no additional positions for the Elementary and Secondary Division, which would have handled most of the Mexican American complaints, and only six new positions for the Higher Education Division for the enforcement of sex discrimination cases. If OCR was hamstrung by staff shortages, why didn't it ask Congress for some staffing relief? Pérez further pointed out that "OCR . . . even had some dead money last fiscal year that it turned back to the Treasury." He concluded that the agency was "playing a very dangerous game of consciously pitting Chicanos against blacks."

Elsewhere, the administration's message was equally confusing. Benjamin F. Holman, director of the Justice Department's Community Relations Service, described the migration of Hispanics as a "brown tide." So what was the problem? He suggested the *existence* of Hispanics as *the problem*. And to him, the Voting Rights Act was just one more disturbing accommodation. "We should stop doing any more demographic studies of our cities that project the needs of blacks and poor whites only," said Holman.

Holman's word picture reflected a fractured national leadership: Republicans in disarray and Democrats disoriented. A new vocabulary was needed (beyond "integration") to mean national inclusion. For a public at-large already feeling overburdened, these Hispanic assertions were the last straw. What they heard provided no redeeming insight into the Hispanic population's role in the nation but suggested, instead, a new burden. As taxpayers underwriting government expenditures, they already felt unappreciated, over-taxed, and under-rewarded. This seemed like yet another obligation for a questionable purpose.

Finally, President Ford began speaking out. Unfortunately, he only made matters worse. Ford urged Congress for a law defining which rights aliens could exercise in the United States. He said he had concluded, "It is in the national interest" to prohibit civil service employment to aliens, "except where the efficiency of the service or the national interest dictate otherwise." The letter, later converted into an executive order, seemed to contradict a Supreme Court decision from three weeks before striking down a regulation barring resident aliens from civil service jobs. The case, filed by five Chinese San Francisco residents, left open the possibility that the president or Congress could establish hiring limitations. Robert Gnaizda, attorney for three major Mexican American organizations, asserted that Ford's action repudiated the spirit of the Supreme Court's decision and was motivated by election politics.

"This greatly affects Asians and Chicanos," said Henry Derr, executive director of Chinese for Affirmative Action. "Because we're in an economic recession, many people find it convenient to pinpoint our economic woes to aliens." Permanent residents, he observed, had to wait five years before obtaining citizenship. Under this order, you have to pay taxes, but you can't work for the man who takes your taxes."

Ed Steinman, lawyer for the five plaintiffs, argued that Ford lacked the constitutional and statutory authority to issue the order. Ford's national interest claim, he said, was an election year ploy to assuage voters' worries about jobs, but it violated the basic tenet of a civil service system designed to secure the "most effective employees" for the government and "not [just] to provide jobs." U.S. Attorney Steve Shefler, in answering the complaint, said that the President exercised his constitutional power correctly, but was unprepared to argue whether the ban violated immigrants' rights to due process and equal protection.

Elsewhere, Ford prepared to limit the number of legal entrants to the United States from the Western Hemisphere. He cut by half the annual number of Mexicans admitted. A new bill, drafted by Representative Joshua Eilberg (D-Penn.), required U.S. citizens to be twenty-one years or older to petition for entry of close relatives. It addressed a legal quirk in legislation that allowed children born in the U.S. of alien parents from the Western Hemisphere to grant their parents immediate priority for entry. Forty thousand Mexicans had entered the U.S. during the previous eight years on that basis. Eilberg steered the bill through the Democratic-controlled

House under a unanimous-consent agreement obtained at a time when Congressman Edward Roybal was absent from the floor. The measure also went through the Senate the same way on the last day of the 1976 session.

Congressman Roybal charged that Ford showed "more concern for the vested interests of agribusiness and industries which exploit illegal aliens than with preserving our humanitarian policy for reuniting families." Manuel D. Fierro, president of the National Congress of Hispanic American Citizens, called the new bill "racist and discriminatory." Fierro tried to talk Ford into vetoing it, but later admitted, "He led us to believe that he would pocket-veto the bill," but he didn't.

The White House, by going along with the popular idea that immigrants were taking jobs away from citizens, reinforced the perception that aliens were the problem. The administration's politics divided public opinion, and the ploy partly succeeded.

The White House seemed unaware that its pronouncements had strained relations with Hispanic leaders. At a town hall meeting in Austin, Texas, Vice President Nelson Rockefeller, out to get advice about issues for President Ford to include in his state of the union message, heard El Paso Mayor Don Henderson say that he wanted action on transportation, commerce, water usage, drug enforcement, and other similar matters relating to both sides of the U.S.-Mexico border. Henderson contended that border cities needed greater involvement with their sister cities on the Mexican side of the frontier. Washington's inattention and provincial outlook compounded problems. Rockefeller was surprised to learn that the El Paso area was home to more than a million people.

The administration was stumbling when action was called for. Meetings by a joint United States-Mexico commission were delayed following the Ford-Echeverría border talks and didn't begin for months. Mayors of Mexican border towns formed their own organization to communicate with their U.S. counterparts. Finally, federal inertia prompted the governors of Texas (Dolph Briscoe), Arizona (Raúl Castro), and New Mexico (Jerry Apodaca) to independently lobby for federal funds to address border issues. California Governor Jerry Brown did not immediately agree, but also eventually went along with the plan.

While border governors built policy bridges to Mexico, U.S. Ambassador to Mexico Joseph Jova, in casual remarks at a Washington symposium, strained relations when he called Mexico's political system "monarchical." President Echeverría ordered his Foreign Ministry to "take appropriate actions." Mexican political officials were indignant, and opposition groups demanded that the government declare the ambassador persona non grata.[4] José López Portillo, presidential candidate of the ruling party, the *Partido Revolucionario Institucional* (PRI), denounced Jova for attempting to "destabilize" Mexico.

The Washington friction could have, but didn't derail the movement toward a new relationship. The U.S. was on a clumsy learning curve, while Mexico sought intermediaries to articulate her desire for new trade. López Portillo met with a delegation of Mexican American businesspeople and community leaders and sent word he was interested in working directly with border governors and mayors. The message signaled cooperation. Four days later, Secretary of State Henry Kissinger, on a visit to Mexico City, announced that López Portillo—who was still two weeks from election—would meet with President Ford at the White House before taking office. He assured the Mexican national television audience that "no change" was expected in the White House—Ford would win in November.

In his eight-month campaign, ending on July 4, López Portillo had pledged in his speeches to continue the same self-determination and non-intervention policies of the Echeverría and previous administrations. He was critical of the Cuban intervention in Angola and deplored the United States' involvement in Vietnam. He proposed to continue Mexico's strong identification with Third World countries, a point of view that made Washington nervous.

"I am of middle class origin, the son of a modest soldier, public employee and intellectual," he had said. "I was educated in the schools of the revolution. I knew shortages and the need to maintain appearances. My mother miraculously stretched the salary from my father's two jobs. I belong to a generation . . . [growing up after the expropriation and nationalization] of the oil industry. Thus one understands my revolutionary calling."

The statement triggered seventy-six congressional members, a month after López Portillo's election, to write an open letter to President Ford asking for assurances that a communist "Cactus Curtain" was not developing along the border. Representative Bob Kreuger (D-Tex.) thought his colleagues might have damaged relations with the regrettable insinuation about Mexico.

Then, during a four-hour farewell address to the nation, President Echeverría made a surprise announcement. He had decided to float the

4. "U.S. Envoy Remark Enrages Mexico," *Denver Post* (March 23, 1976),

peso, causing the money's value to drop sharply against other currencies. Throughout the previous twenty-two years, the peso had been pegged at 12.50, or eight cents, to the U.S. dollar. As a consequence of the devaluation, Mexican exports would cost less, but Mexicans would pay more for foreign goods; vacations south of the border became cheaper for Americans, but thousands of other Americans with high interest-yielding deposits in Mexican banks lost as much as 30 percent. The old exchange rate, Echeverría explained, was not adequate for Mexico's balance of payments, which ran up a $1.2 billion deficit during the first six months of 1976. Mexico's inflation was twice that of the U.S. Exports were increasingly expensive to foreign buyers. Robert A. Balanger, a Bank of America vice president, said that it was "a very smart move. Mexico is joining the international system of floating rates." But bankers and shoppers were having difficulties on the border, as the exchange rate soared to twenty and twenty-five pesos to the dollar.

President-elect López Portillo faced a financial crisis. Border trade almost collapsed altogether. Buyers and sellers were reluctant to trade in pesos. Creditors were nervous that Mexico would devalue the peso again. López Portillo was still three months away from inauguration but was having to assume presidential authority. President Echeverría, meanwhile, prepared for a goodwill mission to San Antonio.

Luís Echeverría set out at the end of his presidency, on one of his most important excursions in trying to build a new policy platform. In his only visit to the U.S. during his presidency (aside from stepping on Arizona soil to meet Ford earlier), Echeverría set out at HemisFair in San Antonio to cultivate relations with Mexican Americans, who might provide the much-needed support base that Mexico longed for.

The United States was Mexico's leading trade partner. Mexicans were increasingly dependent on U.S. goods and capital. But Echeverría's foreign policy had aligned Mexico with the Third World. He exploited domestic resentments over longstanding issues (including the mistreatment of Mexican immigrants in the United States, and Americans serving prison terms in Mexico). Relations between the two countries had hit rock bottom during his term in office.

Echeverría had his hands full counteracting financial speculation against the devalued peso, a Jewish American tourist boycott because of Mexico's pro-Palestinian positions, and U.S. Congressional criticism. If that was not enough, Mario Cantú, a local militant, threatened to sabotage relations with Mexican Americans.

The San Antonio activist claimed that Phillip Agee's book, *Inside the*

CIA, correctly listed Echeverría as an agent with the code name Litempo 2.[5] He claimed to have concrete evidence of political imprisonments, tortures, assassinations and other human rights violations by Echeverría. When the president's entourage headed for a meeting with Chicano leaders at Hemis-Fair and moved past protesters by the hotel entrance, Echeverría spotted Cantú's poster, which read, "FREE POLITICAL PRISONERS." Mexican secret service agents pushed Cantú aside, but he continued waving his sign vigorously in front of Echeverría who grabbed it, tore it in half, and threw the pieces at Cantú, calling him a "little fascist." The incident had no particular importance, said Echeverría. "This young man is trying to interfere with our efforts to establish better relations with the United States." Outraged, Cantú called the San Antonio police "gorillas who won't protect me."

Inside the hall, New Mexico protest activist Reies Tijerina apologized for the Cantú incident and introduced Echeverría to the one thousand Mexican American leaders at the event with a warm *abrazo*.

In his speech, Echeverría admitted that Mexico had ignored news about violations of Mexican Americans' rights in the past. His country had been slow in understanding the implications of that posture. Mexico, in fact, had not shared the responsibility that it should have because they didn't really know enough about the Mexican American population in the United States—who their parents were, why they came to the United States, and what they wanted from the United States and Mexico. But now "In Mexico, there is an understanding of your struggle," he said. He urged the leaders to persevere: "Failure is due to the individual's limitations or putting out a minimum effort. Failure is not due to one's origins." Echeverría understood—he said—the underlying human feats and dramas in the struggle to gain a better living, to acquire better representation, to obtain improved schooling. The issue was not really about the legal status of some residents, but the legitimacy of having a distinct relationship with two countries. He urged Mexican Americans to remember their forefathers and to combine the best of Spanish- and English-speaking cultures.

He said, "There's a third generation of Mexican Americans who speak neither good English nor good Spanish. They must learn to speak them both well." Language, he asserted, would serve as the measure of a successful transcendence beyond mere acculturation to achieving cultural balance and integration, making an important contribution to American culture.

Zavala county Judge, and Raza Unida leader, José Angel Gutiérrez leaped

5. David McLemore, "Echeverría To Be Picketed," *San Antonio Express* (September 5, 1976).

to his feet. "Echeverría has more interest and foresight into the Chicano problem than any other Mexican president and any U.S. president, including Ford and Nixon," he said.

Two days later, a federal grand jury indicted Mario Cantú of conspiring and attempting to shield illegal aliens. Other charges pending alleged he had delivered firearms to groups advocating armed rebellion in Mexico. Cantú claimed the charges were part of a campaign to make him stop criticizing Mexican government policies.[6]

Two weeks after Echeverría's San Antonio visit, President-elect José López Portillo and a small group of advisors met with President Ford in Washington. They provided figures showing that Mexico bought more from the U.S. than the U.S. bought from Mexico by $2.08 billion, making it one of the United States' biggest customers. The Mexican president-elect reassured Ford that Mexico was a democratic friend and dismissed allegations that Mexico was drifting toward communism or that freedom was stifled in his country. He would encourage press criticism during his administration, he said.

President Ford met with López Portillo less than a month before the U.S. election. Although Ford desperately needed Mexican American and Hispanic support, the meeting did nothing, one way or another, for him. He took no measures to establish the appearance of closeness. Nixon's campaign had arranged a 1972 tour of Chicago, Texas, and Los Angeles for President Gustavo Díaz-Ordaz—Echeverría's predecessor—to impress on Hispanic voters Nixon's goodwill toward Mexico. Instead, Ford leaned heavily on his impressive list of appointments to consolidate election support. He had exceeded, with sixty-one high-level appointments in eighteen months, what Nixon took six years to do.

On the heels of the election campaign, the announcement of one departure from the White House came from New Mexico and not from Washington. Governor Jerry Apodaca announced he had named Fernando de Baca to head the state's Health and Social Services Department. De Baca denied he was under any pressure to resign but recommended that whoever took his job should coordinate better with other special presidential assistants. President Ford named Phoenix attorney Thomas Aranda, Jr. to replace de Baca at a Republican National Hispanic Assembly meeting.

6. Bill Mintz, "Cantu Convicted--Now Wanted in Mexico," *San Antonio Express* (September 10, 1976).

5

Symbolism Just Wasn't Enough

Tensions were building a full year before the 1976 presidential election. The Democratic Party's "McGovern reforms," establishing greater population representation in the party, were in place, but not everyone was happy with the procedures. "They expected nothing from us," Alicia Chacón, El Paso County Clerk and national committeewoman, complained, "except to ratify their decisions."

A pressured Democratic National Committee sponsored a meeting to determine how Latino elected officials would work with the party. Over a hundred Hispanic Democrat elected officials from fourteen states and Puerto Rico met to determine ways they could increase their political clout. Governors Jerry Apodaca (N.M.), Raúl Castro (Ariz.), and Rafaél Hernández Colón (P.R.) co-chaired the conference.

Republicans were vulnerable for failing to make more out of current policy initiatives, said Senator Joseph Montoya. The Sixteen Point Program, he said, "so far . . . hasn't raised percentages even one point," adding that, "we hear a lot about bilingual education, but so far it is only reaching about five percent of our children."

When Hispanic elected leaders spoke out on these issues, they were often perceived as single-focus, special interest representatives—no more than elected lobbyists—while their responsibilities called for more than that. For Hispanics to gain broader representation in the eighty-five congressional districts with a Latino swing vote, this perception would have to change. The Voting Rights Act increased the possibility that Hispanic candidates could rise to the national scene from local politics if they marshaled together the right combinations of issues and responsiveness. Ethnic-centered appeals had a place but not if the politicians wanted to get, keep and expand their constituencies. "We know how to serve all Americans, once in office," promised Montoya.

Elected officials and candidates also needed a solid base of support. Hispanic voter registration had slipped severely. Only 44 percent of Spanish-surnamed potential voters were registered in 1972, compared to 72 percent of all eligible Americans. This left a lot of room for improvement. However, even these numbers were in dispute. Joseph Aragón, director of the DNC's Spanish-speaking Affairs Division, used census data to argue that only a third of potential Hispanic voters were registered. He recommended a national voter registration campaign.

Congressman Edward R. Roybal, a ranking Democratic Party official, argued for increased Latino representation within the party. The Latino community, he said, "has come a long way from the confrontation politics of the '60s" and needed to occupy a new role of "active participation within the system." Others voiced concerns with the nuts and bolts of a larger strategy. Rubén Valdéz, Colorado's Speaker of the House wanted a more accurate census. People at the national level, he said, "would begin to understand "what our needs are and start dealing with us" once they realized the true numbers Hispanics represented. The numbers would not only speak for themselves but were needed as leverage for planks in the Democratic Party's 1976 platform.

While the delegates generally agreed on most concerns, the meeting divided over Cuba. A small majority favored slow negotiations. Roybal and New York Congressman Herman Badillo favored normalizing relations. Governor Castro wanted serious negotiations before any reciprocal relations got going. Montoya said that the United States should not commit to doing business with Fidel Castro's regime. The Ford administration was "flirting with it too hotly," he said. And Puerto Rico Governor Hernández Colón thought the United States should not consider relations with the Cuban government until Castro stopped supporting Puerto Rico's independence movement.

In the end, the officials agreed to form a national caucus, affiliated with, but independent from, the Democratic Party. They set a new nationwide voter registration drive as their main focus, intending to get a million new Hispanic voters enrolled by 1976. "It looks like there has been new life breathed into the Democratic Party," said Alameda County, California supervisor Charlie Santana.

Nothing like it had occurred since 1950. A similar conference back then had ended with the delegates failing to even agree on a name for the organization. In 1971, another conference had ended when delegates could not agree on Puerto Rican statehood. This time, statehood wasn't brought up.

Instead, major divisive issues were sidestepped and a steering committee was formed to begin setting the agenda. The first presidential primary was only three months off and the election only a year away.[1]

The steering committee met in Phoenix a month after the conference. They began laying plans for a voter registration drive and fundraising goals to support Hispanic candidates. Congressman Roybal, a DNC executive committee member, reminded those present that the effort was needed because the Democratic Party had not implemented programs to obtain equal representation for Spanish-speaking Americans. He suggested that Hispanic delegates hold a session during the 1976 national convention to draw attention to their needs. The party, he thought, should even consider nominating a Latino for vice president. Roybal was unanimously elected chairman. The new organization was called the National Association of Latino Democratic Officeholders.

The leaders believed they would get reinforcements just as soon as the changing demographics kicked in. Hispanic birth rates were about twice the national average. One White House official had even predicted that Latinos would replace blacks as the largest minority group by the year 2000. A Democratic official had suggested that the population would expand such as to make the next presidential election dependent on Mexican Americans.[2]

Most Hispanic officials felt they could carve a path around the fractious course that previous ethnic and racial politics had followed. But the existence of many Latino interests in different sections of the nation—each with distinct geographical, national-origin, ethnic and racial affinities—posed a challenge as to whether a unified Hispanic agenda was possible.

After voter participation had virtually hit rock bottom, Latino voting was expected to increase dramatically. Only 23 percent of eligible Hispanic Americans had voted in the 1974 congressional elections. The Voting Rights Act would partly repair the problem when hundreds of Hispanic registrars were commissioned in California, Texas and in the other southwestern states. "I would hope," said Joseph Aragón, that "we can register at least 200,000 more Mexican Americans in California alone." He recalled that fifteen years earlier, "John Kennedy lost California in 1960 by only 36,000 votes, and eight years later Hubert Humphrey lost the state by only

1. "Cuba Policy Splits Hispanos," *Albuquerque Journal* (November 3, 1975).
2. Democratic Latinos to Form National Group," *Arizona Republic* (November 3, 1975); Tom Kuhn, "Latino Democrats Form National Group at Meeting Here," *Arizona Republic* (December 14, 1975).

228,000. Next time," he said, "new Spanish American voters in California could decide the whole election."

Governor Jerry Brown, as he had promised in his 1974 campaign, negotiated legislation allowing farm workers to decide by secret ballot on union representation. After more than a decade of labor disputes, the thorny issue needed to be resolved in order to bring stability to California's agricultural fields. In the final moments before he signed the legislation in May of 1975, Brown made a dramatic telephone call to César Chávez, the United Farmworkers' leader, to get his support on the compromise. Farm growers in the state had insisted that Chávez give his personal assurance that the farm workers would not return to the legislature the following year demanding changes in the statute.

The UFW's strikes and boycotts from 1965 to 1970 had been supported by millions of people. Growers, in response, had wanted legislation to curb the organizing rights of farm workers and had even sought to restrict boycotts through a ballot initiative. In 1972, California voters rejected it by 60 percent. Growers then tried to defeat the union by signing sweetheart contracts with the Teamsters union to displace the UFW as the farm workers' representative and bargaining agent. In response, the UFW organized the largest strikes in U.S. agriculture history. Non-UFW grapes, head lettuce, and Gallo wines were boycotted. By October, 1975, 17 million Americans were observing the grape boycott. Brown's support of the farm workers' union solidified his position with labor.

Presidential politics were also in Brown's mind. He planned to enter the Democratic presidential primaries and needed union backing. Former congressman Allard K. Lowenstein, who Brown hired as an assistant, said Brown needed an issue to give him national prominence. The farm worker-grower compromise was just the ticket to bring warring parties together. The only remaining question was whether Brown could produce a compromise before he was distracted by primary campaigns outside the state. After much effort, the payoff came when Brown connected his telephone to the speaker box for everyone to hear Chávez' voice. "I agree. It is a negotiated agreement." The phone confirmation was the final word on the compromise.

With the deal behind them, the farm workers' union recruited hundreds of volunteers and staged a thousand-mile walk across the state to take the news to workers in the fields and in rural areas. Later, the Agricultural Labor Relations Board (ALRB), created under the new legislation, organized a large number of union elections to decide on representation. By April of 1976, the UFW had won 204 of 327 elections to represent the workers. An equally large number of unfair-labor-practices complaints were filed. Consequently, the ALRB ran out of funds. A two-thirds vote in the legislature was needed to approve new funding, but anti-UFW forces succeeded in denying it.

In exasperation, Chávez and his union decided to bypass the legislature and take the issue directly to the voters of California. The Farm Worker Initiative was put on the statewide ballot as a referendum initiative after petitions collected 350,000 signatures. The measure, said Chávez, "will make only a few changes in the existing law." The campaign, he said, "will be difficult and expensive—expensive for the growers, who will spend millions to defeat it; difficult for the farm workers, who will sacrifice themselves and their time." Proposition 14 was scheduled for the November ballot, coinciding with the presidential election.

Jerry Brown received UFW support for siding with the farm workers union after the legislature caused the ALRB slow down. Chávez' volunteers, working with Brown's presidential campaign, were dedicated, disciplined, and organized. They swarmed into Maryland, Rhode Island and New Jersey. Brown came out in those states ahead of former Georgia governor Jimmy Carter each time. Five hundred organizers were sent into Oregon. *Washington Star* correspondent Mary McGrory largely attributed Brown's campaign success there to the United Farm Workers. They were "a new and special force in the politics of the West," she said.[3]

In April of 1976, two months before the California primary, Brown appointed Cruz Reynoso to the state Court of Appeals to become the highest ranking Mexican American judge in recent California history. Reynoso, as head of California Rural Legal Assistance, had been one of former California governor Ronald Reagan's most persistent and successful antagonists. In 1971, the Reagan state administration had tried to get the federal government to end the public-interest law firm's budget after CRLA won a series of court challenges to Reagan's farm labor policies. A three-judge commission ruled in CRLA's favor. After Brown won the California presidential primary that summer, preparations were made for Chávez to deliver a speech seconding Brown's nomination for the presidency.

Republicans, like the Democrats, were busy laying a foundation for future

3. Mary McGrory, "Carter on Brown's Turf," *San Francisco Chronicle* (October 2, 1976).

elections. Benjamin Fernández, with the Watergate investigation laid to rest concerning the National Hispanic Finance Committee to Reelect the President, co-founded the National Republican Hispanic Assembly. A different approach was needed to prevent a recurrence of what had happened during the Nixon campaign in 1972.

Hispanic Republicans had been betrayed, said Fernández. They were entitled to some of the top government jobs but had been cheated out of them. Instead, "We were dropped like hot potatoes." He didn't think that President Gerald Ford's accomplishments went far enough, either. This time, "We're saying '*basta!*' We're tired of Anglo politicians wearing big hats and *serapes.*"

The newly organized Hispanic National Assembly was in the vanguard. It already had, he claimed, a hundred chapters in Florida, Texas, and California, and had the potential to become a powerhouse in the GOP. Fernández envisioned hundreds of chapters in twenty-four states and he wanted the Ford Election Committee to provide $300,000 to make that possible. Hispanic Republicans would not raise funds as they had in 1972 but would organize voter-registration drives for the party, instead. He found, however, that conservatives in the party were still reticent to support these measures vital to Hispanic Republicans. Fernández pleaded with them to "demonstrate by bold direct moves that you care, that you really want to expand the political base of the party."

Ronald Reagan's camp, in its drive for the presidential nomination, had all but excluded Hispanics. The Texas delegation had no Hispanics, even though the state had 2.5 million Mexican Americans. The California delegation had two Mexican Americans and two Cuban Americans. The facts spoke for themselves. Ben Fernández was furious and used mixed metaphors to express it: "They're suffering delusions," he said. The party was "not keeping in step with the times—and that step has a Spanish accent. We're coming in whether the conservatives like it or not. They can protest all they like, but we're coming in, with dynamism. We're hoping to be invited, but we're not waiting to be. We're moving in."

For reasons entirely different from those voiced by Ben Fernández, New Mexico's four-term Republican Congressman, Manuel Luján, had trouble finding common cause with the status quo. He wanted a more conservative party, not a more moderate one. While he'd supported Gerald Ford, Ronald Reagan's presidential bid was more appealing to him, and a third-party bid didn't sound bad either.

Democratic Senator Joseph Montoya, in the same state, had difficulties dissociating from the 'liberal' label hung on him. People often resented federal funding of state and county economic development, social services, and other assistance, even when they—directly or indirectly—benefited from those programs. The public wanted candidates to articulate that ambivalent trend. Lujan could and did, with the result that a full year before his re-election bid, Montoya was at odds with many voters.

Then Bob Woodward, *The Washington Post* reporter known for his coverage with Carl Bernstein of the Watergate case, disclosed that Internal Revenue Commissioner Donald C. Alexander and senior IRS officials had blocked audits and tax investigations into Montoya's affairs. The Senator was in charge of a subcommittee that oversaw the IRS. Woodward wrote that "four highly reliable sources" told him that an IRS official had recommended audits of Montoya's tax returns. Woodward quoted an anonymous source saying Alexander "was inordinately sensitive to Montoya and was horrified at the thought of auditing or investigating him."[4]

"I have never stopped a case for political reasons. Never," said the IRS chief. "All taxpayers are treated alike, whether they are president, vice president, senator, or congressman."

Montoya, a self-made millionaire, had been delinquent twice in paying taxes and late in filing his 1945 and 1946 returns. However, no evidence pointed to tax evasion or his seeking special IRS treatment. "If there's one senator whose skirts are clean," said Montoya, "it's me." A year after Woodward's disclosures, Treasury Secretary William Simon reported that Alexander had in fact blocked an audit, but without Montoya's knowledge. A new audit was ordered, and Montoya was cleared, but his troubles were not over.

Montoya emphasized, during the toughest campaign of his forty-year public career, that he was soon to become the Senate's Public Works Committee chairman. In that role, he said, "You are going to see more highways and byways built in New Mexico than ever before." Three months before the election, the embattled Joseph Montoya was fighting for his political life.

He was also fighting, besides the Republican Party, Albuquerque's two major newspapers. The newspapers charged that Montoya ran a shopping center from his taxpayer-supported state office, and that the shopping center had a post office branch as a tenant, violating a law prohibiting a lease

4. Bob Woodward, "Montoya Audits Blocked," *Denver Post* (October 19, 1975).

between the government and a member of Congress. Montoya responded that the government lease was already in place when he and his partners purchased the property, an assertion the Justice Department was unable to disprove.

Outraged and hounded, Montoya told party workers "if there's one thing I'm going to defend, it's my integrity and honesty." Ironically, Montoya was losing to the politics of morality that he had helped usher in as a result of his participation in the Senate Watergate Committee. Even the appearance of impropriety, in the post-Watergate political environment, was intolerable.[5]

To win, he needed southern New Mexico and conservative support in the Albuquerque "Heights" district. Hispanic support was solid and remained strong, illustrated when two young girls drew Montoya's attention to the threatened termination of their bilingual education program. "Over my dead body are they going to cancel this project," he shouted. Activists planned massive voter-registration drives in Hispanic precincts. In Carlsbad, Montoya personally led backers, advising workers to set up registration tables in front of Catholic churches to enroll people leaving mass. He urged them to work the bingo games and to set up in front of supermarkets. His campaign workers had registered 17,000 voters in 1970, more than his victory margin over Anderson Carter. His orders now were clear: get them registered and on the voter rolls, and turn them out in November.

Early in June of 1976, Bexar County (San Antonio) Commissioner Albert Bustamante met with candidate Jimmy Carter in Los Angeles to shore up influence. Bustamante pointed out to Carter that Mexican Americans were under-represented among U.S. attorneys, federal judgeships, magistrates and marshals. Carter said he had appointed blacks to major positions when he was Georgia's governor, as a way of demonstrating he understood minority concerns and assured Bustamante that he intended to do something. Back in San Antonio, Bustamante tried to consolidate his position with the candidate by criticizing National Democratic Committeeman Joe Bernal and Mexican American Democrats (MAD) for trying to upstage public officials when it came to contact with Carter.

MAD, formed a year earlier to push for better delegate representation of Mexican Americans in the state, was fighting to get a fair share of the Texas delegates to the 1976 national convention. Only four Mexican Americans

5. Paul R. Wieck, "Montoya Gets Ready for Toughest Campaign," *Albuquerque Journal* (August 22, 1976).

had been on the 1968 delegation; the number increased to fourteen in 1972. But the new rules, changed in 1975, called for 75 percent of the delegates to come from the thirty-one state senatorial districts and the remainder from the state convention. According to El Paso County Clerk Alicia Chacón, the new presidential primary law, drawn up by U.S. Senator Lloyd Bentsen's supporters (who expected him to make a presidential bid), was "the greatest anti-people legislation ever passed." MAD members insisted that two of the seven elected Democratic National Committee seats go to Mexican Americans. Coincidentally, MAD Caucus chairman Joe Bernal and Vice-Chair Alicia Chacón both held those positions and were up for re-election.

Bernal, a former state senator, had support from Lloyd Bentsen, Jerry Brown, and Jimmy Carter for the minority proportional-representation plan. But Democratic Texas governor Dolph Briscoe was the stumbling block, and he was intransigent. The governor wanted to overrule Bernal's nomination, giving himself a chance to serve as the gateway between the presidential candidates and the Mexican American constituency.

In California, Abe Tapia, an East Los Angeles businessman and former Mexican American Political Association (MAPA) president, informed a group of seventy-five leaders about the problems in building bridges to the Carter campaign. Tapia, himself a Carter delegate from the 30th Congressional district, claimed staff had taken steps to exclude Mexican Americans from the California campaign. He, and other Latino supporters, wanted a meeting with the candidate and threatened to break with the campaign unless it happened. Assemblyman Joseph B. Montoya (not related to New Mexico's senator), the only member of the California legislature's Chicano Caucus to endorse Carter, introduced the candidate when the meeting finally came about.

Carter said he had little experience dealing with Mexican Americans or other Latino groups. He was from Georgia, he said, a state with few Hispanics. While disarmingly honest and open, Carter was not running for president of Georgia. The presidency of the United States and responsiveness to the Hispanic community's needs were at stake.

The California-based Viva Carter group delivered a list of Hispanic-oriented issues to the candidate. Carter accepted the seven-page position paper and promised to reply within a few days. However, several persons were already critical of Carter for failing to place Hispanics in key campaign staff positions.

Fredrick Mullen, the state campaign coordinator, said that Carter's campaign had not overlooked or excluded California's 800,000 Hispanic voters.

Instead, friction between Chicanos and the campaign staff stemmed, he claimed, from infighting between various Latino factions. Some groups attempted to attach themselves to the campaign while others attempted to barter between the campaign and the Hispanic community as power brokers, he said.[6]

Henry L. Lacayo, head of the National Association of Latin-American Officials and United Auto Workers president Leonard Woodcock's administrative assistant, stepped into the fray before any more splintering occurred. Lacayo arranged a meeting in Houston between candidate Carter and thirty-five Puerto Rican, Cuban, and Mexican American leaders (specifically excluding persons who allegedly "screamed" at Carter at the acrimonious Mexican American gathering in Los Angeles). The leaders originally wanted to meet with Carter in private. But Carter reversed that decision and opened the event to the press.

Carter consolidated many of the Los Angeles concerns into one focal issue. With Arizona governor Raúl Castro at his side, and after having consulted Jerry Apodaca, Carter said he favored extending "legitimate status" to millions of illegal immigrants who had entered and remained in the country for a long enough period. He didn't know what the legal status cut-off date should be—three, five, seven or more years—but some form of legitimacy, removing the illicit aspect that hung over undocumented residents, was preferable to trying to deport masses of people.

In addition, Carter favored strict measures barring future illegal immigration by imposing "heavy penalties" on employers. He did not mean that illegal immigrants should become American citizens, however. He thought only in terms of allowing them to get work permits, knowing that a president could not deliberately fail to enforce the law against illegal residents. Nor was it good politics to allow undocumented workers to cause unemployment, as he believed they did.

I want "a permanent partnership between me and you," said Carter "to ensure that the long-standing discrimination against Spanish-speaking people is eliminated." He also said he supported bilingual education. "Most Americans, like myself in the past, have never been familiar with the special problems of people who don't speak English . . . I will be totally committed as president to providing bilingual education for those who need and want it." He asked the Houston group to form an advisory council to work with him during the campaign, and afterwards, on Hispanic concerns. He said

---

6. Frank del Olmo, "Chicanos Give List of Issues to Carter, " *Los Angeles Times* (June 4, 1976).

he wanted an aggressive group that would be "highly critical if I overlook some effort to get Spanish-speaking persons involved."

Carter drew applause when he said he would base his diplomatic appointments on merit. He would not make diplomatic appointments to pay off political debts, as had been the case under former president Nixon, he said. That practice had led to ambassadors in Latin America who did not even speak Spanish. Few Hispanics were appointed to those posts. That won't happen "when I become President," he added.

Only one question concerning Hispanic American issues came from the press when the meeting was opened to their questions. That was typical of the "Eastern press," said G.I. Forum national chairman Antonio G. Morales. Carmela G. Lacayo, the executive director of the Asociación Nacional Pro Personas Mayores, characterized the gathering as "put together carefully," "hand picked," and attended by "professionals." Another critic, who didn't like the make-up of those attending, criticized the mainly "establishment people . . . so-called 'double-knit Chicanos who wear suits, ties, have a fairly high income." The gathering included few "grass-roots" people, he said.

On the other side, Arizona Governor Castro said, "I was pleased with his candor. I think he won friends. I think it was a very positive meeting." Similarly, Marc Campos of Austin, a lobbyist for the Tejano Political Action Committee and former Sargent Shriver supporter said, "Many of us were skeptical when we came into this meeting about what he would do for us. But now I'm ready to go out and work for him."

"I think he really comes closer than anyone I've seen or heard to understanding the problems of Mexican Americans," said Manuel López, Mexican American Political Association president, whose group had supported Jerry Brown in the California primary.

Abe Tapia, acknowledged that Carter's response to the seven-page position paper at the Houston meeting was "one of the best replies I ever saw." Joe Bernal, in attendance at Houston, praised Carter: "He has a deep understanding of the problem." Even Joe Staley, head of the San Antonio office of the Immigration and Naturalization Service, said Carter was responsive: "I think Carter's plan is exactly what our service wants."

The first Viva Carter headquarters opened in Texas soon after the meeting. Albert Bustamante outlined a state-election strategy at the campaign kick-off. Congressman Henry González and Irma Rangel—state representative from Kingsville—were to head the Viva Carter for President campaign. Throughout the state, a half dozen other headquarters openings soon followed. Texas Democratic Party chairman Calvin Guest pledged $100,000 for a voter registration and a get-out-the-vote campaign. Albert Bustamante took the strategy a step further: "We do not want to exclude anyone who wants to help Carter," and added, "including Raza Unida people and Republicans." Competition and a campaign: this was the antidote to the earlier Republican strategy encouraging voters to stay at home, vote Republican, or vote Raza Unida.

Jimmy Carter met with the two hundred Latino delegates and alternates at the Democratic National Convention in New York. He said, in his opening remarks in Spanish, that, if elected, he would name Hispanics to the White House staff and consider their recommendations to fill jobs at all government levels and judgeships. Carter restated his position on illegal immigrants and about the need for bilingual education. "I came here today not because of any pressure that was brought on me. I came here because I care about you. I need your help as deeply as you need mine . . . I would like to form a partnership with you."

The delegates leaped to their feet. Latino Caucus members finally felt accepted in the family, rather than like unwelcome stepchildren. It was a heady moment and just in time, too.

Earlier, the convention had been frustrating, disappointing, and marred by internal dissension.[7] One segment divided over the word "Latino" to designate all Hispanic-origin Americans. Mexican Americans, Cubans, Puerto Ricans, and other groups were unable to settle other differences. Some Chicanos wanted to take an independent course. "The Latino Caucus has neglected us and has not stressed Mexican American problems enough," said Roberto Reyes of El Paso. Paul Moreno, also of El Paso, wanted to form a "Chicano Caucus." They were among twenty-five Chicanos—representing Texas, Arizona, Colorado, California, Washington, and Michigan—who thought the Caucus focused too much on Puerto Rican and Cuban concerns.

Chairman Robert Revelas disagreed. "The Latino Caucus fairly represented Hispanic concerns. Nothing could present a mirror-like image."

Colorado state senator Polly Baca Barragán blamed the rifts on frustration with the Democratic Party's Latino Division in Washington, D.C., headed by Joseph W. Aragón. The Democratic National Committee had routinely set up meetings between Carter and other groups, but Latinos

7. Charles Overby, "Chicanos Push Complaints," *El Paso Times* (July 14, 1976

had been overlooked and had to go outside the party structure to gain access to the candidate, even though a Latino office had been set up. "We've had no input into the platform. No sustained effort was made to help us to be effective politically. . . ." Latinos had made no new progress and accounted for 4 percent of all delegates, the same level of representation as in 1972. In fact, the Colorado delegation had dropped from eleven in 1972 to four in 1976.

Some disputes continued to dog the campaign after the convention. Carter's handlers chose Arizona Senate Majority Leader Alfredo Gutiérrez to head that state's campaign, but angered Governor Castro who was not consulted. Gutiérrez was positioned to advance as a campaign leader and threatened Castro as state party chief. The Carter campaign hobbled along that way.

Three months before election day, Congressman Henry González' office revealed that a grant to Zavala county (Crystal City), Texas was similar to the funding given to the Raza Unida party in 1972 by the Nixon administration. José Angel Gutiérrez, Raza Unida party founder and leader, called the newspaper accounts ridiculous. No member of the Raza Unida party had contact with the White House, he said, or even with the GOP—for that matter—in connection with votes for Republicans. The million-dollar grant in question was intended to support a cooperative farming project and two related businesses. "This is our first chance" to make an economic dream come true, he said. There was no political trade-off. "We're not for sale."

Governor Briscoe thought otherwise. He asked President Ford to delay the grant until there was further study. In response, Gutiérrez, pointed out that the Governor was himself among Zavala county's absentee landlords, and implied he had a personal staked interest in stopping the project.

Briscoe, González and U.S. Representative Abraham Kazan complained they had not been consulted, as was usual before a grant was approved. Governor Briscoe, believing that the Community Services Administration had violated federal procedures and the Intergovernmental Cooperation Act of 1968 when it bypassed local and state officials, asked Texas Attorney General John Hill to take whatever legal measures were necessary to block the funding.

Attorney General Hill conducted an investigation into Crystal City's Housing Authority. Some board members had complained of possible conflicts of interest. Shrugging off the investigation, the directors of the Zavala County Development Corporation moved ahead on the purchase of a thousand-acre farm.

Hill's investigation led to indictments against Amancio Cantú, a former Crystal City School District Superintendent, who was charged with removing a portable video camera and a tape recorder from school premises. The equipment, bought for about two thousand dollars with federal program funds, accompanied a group on a trip to Cuba a year earlier. "No, no, no," he insisted, when it was suggested the equipment was a gift to Premier Fidel Castro's brother Raúl.

In a letter to President Ford, Governor Briscoe cited three Office of Management and Budget regulations that required state review before the grant was made in August, 1976. The case incited Representative Floyd V. Hicks (D-Wash.), chairman of the House Manpower and Housing Subcommittee, to ask Office of Management and Budget director James Lynn why the grant was expedited, especially when a planning grant was not due to expire until October.

There had been "considerable confusion at CSA," Lynn wrote to Governor Briscoe. The grant application was made in May and was processed during an interim period when regulations were not fully in place. CSA, nonetheless, was considering the Governor's "comments," but would not stop the grant funds. CSA staff members informed Attorney General Hill that an OMB official had written a letter waiving state review but was unable to identify the official, and they were unable to locate the letter in the files. Hill said it would make a difference whether he would proceed with a suit or not if the letter appeared.

Then Governor Briscoe electrified the opening session of the state Democratic convention. He charged, in one of the strongest speeches of his career, that the Zavala county grant was "for the purpose of establishing a little Cuba in Texas, for establishing a communal type form of operation in Texas." He said, "this grant is illegal, but beyond that, without a doubt, it is un-Texan and un-American. It is to be used for the specific purpose of promoting socialism in Texas. This is the way the Ford administration is using the taxpayers' money."

The governor took such rhetorical license that even the conservative *San Antonio Express* editorialized that, contrary to the governor's opinion, "Properly managed, the cooperative might give some help to farmers there who are unable to finance their own efforts." The paper wasn't buffaloed; it could tell the difference between socialism and partisanship: "There is no question that Ford has made a partisan issue of the August 16 grant . . . the President had cleared the way for the grant as an inducement to win voter support from Gutiérrez' political following . . . the grant has the earmarks of an improper political gift of public money."[8]

The controversy began tearing the Raza Unida apart. A pall hung over the public administrators affiliated with the party. All of them came under a cloud of suspicion for possible misconduct and misappropriation. Then the other shoe fell.

Four indictments were returned. A grand jury investigating possible misdeeds charged that the Department of Housing and Urban Development and HEW were negligent in overseeing funds spent by the county. Three of the indicted were from Crystal City, adding to the eleven indictments brought against three others, including two former school district superintendents. All were accused of theft and conspiracy to commit theft. District Judge Jack Woodley set bonds at $25,000 each. The Attorney General's spokesman said he expected a new grand jury to continue the investigations. Not surprisingly, the state Attorney General filed suit to stop the economic development grant.

Influenced by the events in Zavala County, state Democratic party chairman Calvin Guest challenged his Republican counterpart, Ray Hutchinson, to explain his party's role in the "little Cuba incident." Taking momentary—perhaps permanent—leave of his senses, Guest said people wanted to know why "Republican funds [were] channeled to South Texas to support avowed Socialists who want to create a little Cuba in Zavala County."

While the good ol' boys were having some fun witch-huntin' on the socialism bugaboo, U.S. District Court Judge Jack Roberts ruled that the State of Texas had the right to review the disputed federal grant. He enjoined the Zavala Economic Development Corporation from spending any funds during the sixty days of the injunction. Lacking any other means of support to pay staff and costs, the Economic Development Corporation was put out of business. Gutiérrez said he expected to prevail in court and in the Fifth Circuit Court of Appeals, if necessary. "Briscoe has gotten what he wants," he said. "The judge gave him a veto power he didn't even have under the law."

However, there was method to the Texas madness. Briscoe, the South Texas millionaire and large Zavala county landowner, had won election in 1972 after defeating Republican Hank Grover by only 2.8 percent of the state vote—47.8 to 45.0 percent. Raza Unida candidate Ramsey Muñíz polled 6.28 percent, and held the balance of power after siphoning the Mexican

8. "President Pushes a Major Boner in Grant for Farm Cooperative, *San Antonio Express* (September 20, 1976).

American protest vote. Briscoe did poorly in urban areas, except San Antonio and El Paso, where Mexican Americans pulled him through. In 1974, Briscoe won a four-year term, and the Raza Unida party sank into disarray.

Aware that the Raza Unida party could not survive without patronage (made possible through jobs to party workers through federally-funded projects), Briscoe was looking ahead to his reelection campaign in 1978. He was making sure Raza Unida was not going to help decide the outcome if a split occurred between Democrats and Republicans. By now, the state was not unambiguously in any party's column. It had voted for Eisenhower and Nixon, as well as for John Kennedy and Lyndon Johnson. Briscoe wanted to make sure that the Raza Unida party did not exist in 1978, or at least was rendered incapable of fielding a candidate against him.

The way to neutralize it was by destroying its patronage-dispensing capabilities. Plus, a message was going out to Ford and Carter. Briscoe was not going to allow Ford to establish a Republican power base by funding groups working against the established Democratic party, certainly not with any more underhanded project funding as had occurred during the Nixon administration. The message to Carter was that if he won the election, the Texas governor would bolt from party discipline if the Democratic administration did not clear grants through the state.

Later the same year, (a month after the presidential election), Ramsey Muñíz, who as Raza Unida's candidate against Briscoe in 1974 had won enough votes to worry the state Democratic party—to the shock and dismay of many—was indicted by a San Antonio grand jury in connection with a marijuana seizure. A Corpus Christi judge released Muñíz on bond, but he failed to appear for a hearing and was hunted as a fugitive from justice. On Christmas Day, 1976, Mexican police handed over Muñíz in handcuffs to a U.S. deputy marshal at the international border in Laredo.[9]

For all practical purposes, the Raza Unida party was down and out. Only one of the candidates fielded in Zavala County won. Democratic regulars replaced Raza Unida candidates and incumbents.

9. Muñíz fled after a second charge was filed against him of conspiring to smuggle 6,500 pounds of manijuana into the U.S. from Mexico in 1976. He pleaded guilty and served five years in prison. In 1981, Muñíz was released on probation, but he was arrested the following year on a state cocaine charge that was dropped when the drug search was found to have been faulty. In 1994, while the Drug Enforcement Agency (DEA) was in pursuit of Donacio Medina on drug charges (who had been in contact with Muñíz, working as a Legal Assistant as the time), Muñíz was arrested in Lewisville, Texas by the DEA. Muñíz was found behind the wheel of Medina's car that contained forty kilograms (approximately ninety pounds) of cocaine in the trunk. Muñíz is serving a life term at the federal facility at Levenworth, Kansas.

In his own defense, Raza Unida party leader José Angel Gutiérrez believed that Briscoe's landholdings and $40 million personal wealth explained the Governor's motivations. "Fat Dolph," said Gutiérrez, was strictly a political bovine. And Attorney General John Hill was laying the groundwork for his own gubernatorial bid. Hill's investigation had been only one of six others by state and federal agencies. Questionable indictments were returned from Hill's eleven-month probe, and Gutiérrez doubted that the charges would stand up in court.

The resistance to Raza Unida projects from Zavala county landowners, he said, stemmed from their worry that the $2.50 per hour pay rate at the cooperative farm would establish a new benchmark price of labor that would engender discontent among laborers who worked for less. This was "the good old capitalistic system," said Gutiérrez, "but this time [it's] the have-nots [who] would get some of the action." As for Cuba, he said, no one complained when San Antonio's mayor went to China. Why was there such concern about public officials from Zavala county going to Cuba? Over there, said Gutiérrez, he had seen some good things and some things that were not so good, as he put it. He didn't like the regimentation, but he said he didn't see beggars in the streets, either. Everyone could read, he said, and housing and health were good.

Gutiérrez's defenses seemed weak, shallow even, in the face of the political recriminations and banter. The xenophobic witch-hunting had portrayed the Raza Unida party's purpose as fundamentally disloyal—democratic, but against the region's normative interest. Yet, embedded in José Angel Gutiérrez's comments was the heartfelt belief that the local people had a right to work the land, earn a living wage, and improve their life conditions. Contrary to the alleged disloyalty, José Angel Gutiérrez seemed profoundly offended that the reform movement could be evaluated, under any circumstances, as disloyal to the nation's institutions. "We have a stake in this country," said José Angel Gutiérrez after summarizing the countless aspersions and allegations, and before giving up.

6

Turning Politics Into Government

On his first full campaign day following the nominating convention, Jimmy Carter announced from Los Angeles that he supported a Democratic voter-registration drive that might add four million Hispanic Americans to the voter rolls.

In Hollywood the following month, Senator Robert J. Dole of Kansas, the Republican vice presidential candidate, met for a half-hour with seventy Mexican American businessmen and professional people at Lucy's El Adobe Mexican restaurant. He said after the meeting that he would urge President Ford to veto the Rodino bill, the immigration reform bill before Congress that would impose sanctions on employers hiring undocumented workers. In fact, he thought the administration already opposed it in its present form because of its anti-business character. Dole said he favored amnesty for illegal immigrants who had lived in the U.S. for a number of years. Any illegal immigrant law should "protect those who are already here, whether you call it amnesty or whatever." Illegal immigration caused problems, he said, but "I don't see it as harming our society." He opposed Proposition 14 on the California general ballot, however, because it allowed labor organizers onto private property. "I don't quarrel with the right to unionize . . . I just . . . can't go for that second step and say you ought to just have the right to override property rights. . . . I think it's a state issue that should be determined by the states." A reporter quipped he had a tape recording of his earlier statement saying he was neutral on the proposition. "Good. Keep it," Dole snapped. Had Dole made inroads at the restaurant? "I think so," said Lucy's owner Frank Casado—a Democratic activist and Governor Jerry Brown's friend.

The United Farmworkers convention unanimously endorsed Jimmy Carter, who told the delegates by telephone hook-up that he would support Proposition 14. The controversial measure had first gone to the state

Agricultural Labor Relations Board that ruled union organizers had three hours of access time on California farms. State courts upheld the rule, but farming interests appealed to the U.S. Supreme Court, which refused to determine how much access to farms, if any, union organizers should have. When the state legislature failed to alter the access rule, or six other suggested changes to the 1975 state farm labor law, the issue went to the voters as a proposition. It was on the ballot with the presidential election.

Carter was having trouble making friends anywhere in California. At the Mexican Independence Day parade in Santa Ana, Jerry Brown and Jimmy Carter marched together. In East Los Angeles, César Chávez whipped up a crowd and Carter's remarks in Spanish were politely received. But the campaign staff failed to produce much of a turnout at many stops, and the crowds were small.[1]

Carter was losing ground and he knew it. Poor attendance at southern California rallies marred hopes for a big voter turnout. Dismal planning and logistics for Hispanic communities by the national campaign staff allowed Republicans to gain on the Democrats. Latino advisor Alex Aguiar was blamed. The United Press reported California's Hispanic leaders were prepared to sit out the campaign, and Ford and Dole were running ahead of Carter."[2]

Aguiar was fired. Rick Hernández and Franklin Delano López were put in charge of the nine-state western region, Hank Lacayo, head of the Hispanic Advisory Committee announced. "If we carry California, we'll win," said Senator Walter Mondale, Carter's vice presidential running mate. "And if Jimmy Carter loses in California, many will put the blame on Proposition 14."

The analysis was correct. Latinos could elect Carter if they showed up at the polls and carried the winning margin. On the other hand, the unpopular proposition on the ballot could siphon votes away from the Democratic ticket and its defender—Jimmy Carter.

Columnist Abe Mellinkoff believed that the issue in California was not farm workers or farmers. "The issue is César Chávez, as charismatic as they come and as tough as necessary." Mellinkoff was chafed that Chávez had helped elect Jerry Brown governor and then later had seconded Carter's nomination at the Democratic convention. He was piqued at Chávez' ability

1. Mary McGrory, "Carter on Brown's Turf," *San Francisco Chronicle* (October 2, 1976); "Carter Hits the Trail West," *San Francisco Chronicle* (Ocober 3, 1976).
2. "Gov. Carter Fires His Latino Adviser," *San Francisco Chronicle* (September 28, 1976); "Carter Aide Fired," *Denver Post* (September 28, 1976).

to produce large numbers of campaign workers. Chávez was estimated to have added "more than 300,000 to the Democratic majority in California" through registration drives. The issue, said Mellinkoff was whether people would vote for or against Chávez: for Prop 14 and Carter, or against them.[3]

Following Carter's California campaign swing, President Ford met with about thirty prominent Mexican Americans in an attempt to gain new followers. Then he met privately with a handful of Latinos after the public meeting: Julian Nava, Tony Gallegos and David Ochoa. Leon Parma (co-chairman of the state campaign committee), Gilda Bojórquez Gjurich (head of the California Republican Hispanic Assembly), and Al Zapanta (assistant secretary of Interior) also attended.

Nava was a two-term Los Angeles Board of Education member (at a time when no other Latino served in a city- or county-wide elected position); Ochoa had led the short-lived Viva Carter committee during the California primary and had helped produce Spanish-language commercials. Only Gallegos, former GI Forum chairman, indicated he might lean toward Ford.

Carter's weak California campaign generated little excitement. Nor was it helped by the shake-ups in the national organization. Ford's campaigners capitalized on the situation and continued to target civic and political leaders, and well-to-do Hispanics. Nava admitted he was impressed with Ford "as I have not been before." He found the President knowledgeable about the rapid growth of the Mexican American community. The discussion cut across party lines and centered on relations with Latin America and the need for bilingual education, jobs and illegal immigration—issues that "transcend internal Mexican American matters," said Nava.

The Hispanic Committee for President Ford, mostly composed of long-time Republicans and several independent Democrats, did not include the three that Ford had specifically courted. Frank Viega, a businessman and spokesman for the Ford support committee, said he was "still optimistic that some strong Democratic leaders will come out for the President. Republicans are a minority party, especially among Mexican Americans," he said. "If we win 40 percent of the Hispanic vote it's a landslide. I think we can win at least that."

The Republicans were trying to offset the effect that a campaign visit to Los Angeles by Governor Jerry Apodaca was expected to have. The

3. Frank del Olmo, "Ford Intensifies Bid for Latin Votes," *Los Angeles Times* (October 12, 1976).

Democratic Party sent Apodaca to urge Hispanic leaders to work harder for Carter. In the San Fernando Valley, Apodaca told his audience he was campaigning for Carter in two states. "If Carter carries California and Texas, the election is as good as over." But party activists complained that Carter's staff was slow to excite large numbers of barrio residents. "The issue is not to criticize the things the Carter campaign has done or not done," he said to a San Francisco Bay area audience. "The issue is the difference between what a Ford Administration would do and what a Carter Administration would do."

Later, appearing confident and happy after a televised debate with Robert Dole, Walter Mondale met in Hollywood with a group of seventy prominent Mexican Americans, including César Chávez, elected officials, and local activists. Mondale hit hard at the Ford administration for doing little to remedy unemployment and to curb inflation. Conservatism, he said, offered little to independent voters and moderate Republicans. "The other evening, Bob Dole hurt my feelings when he said I was too liberal," said Mondale. "I always thought I was moderate. But then he defined what he meant by liberal. . . . He meant those left-wing, subversive, radical groups like the League of Women Voters." Mondale blamed Ford for the highest unemployment since the 1930s; high interest rates, and monopolistic business practices that lowered middle-class spendable income to 1965 levels. Mondale said that a Mexican American should be placed in the Supreme Court and on the Federal Communications Commission and warned that—Ford's claims notwithstanding—many of the Ford appointments were symbolic and had no real impact on the Hispanic community's problems.

Carter was also buoyed by his own debate performance. Speaking on the West Coast before the Service Employees International Union the day after the debate, and wearing a YES ON 14 button, he said the Ford administration's policies were producing eight-percent unemployment, a higher rate than existed in any other industrial nation. The unemployed are "just statistics to Ford. To me they are 7.5 or eight million Americans who want to work and can't."

The campaign was down to the wire. The outcome could rest on how many new voters were enrolled. César Chávez hoped to add as many as 350,000. He thought he might be able to account for more than a quarter of the 1.2 million Californians registered since the June primary. The voter registration drive was like a mass movement. By the first week of October, over 200,000 new voters were enrolled. In the final days of the drive, Chávez and his people claimed 20,000 new names daily. With characteristic humility in the face of anticipated victory, Chávez said he wanted none of the credit in the event Carter won. "It's a risk trying to act as a broker," said Chávez. "I've seen cases where people make those assurances when they can't even deliver their wives' vote."

In the final month before the November balloting, Proposition 14 was in trouble. Public awareness only increased opposition to it: fifty-three percent of Californians opposed the measure, only thirty-one percent favored it. In the Hispanic community, fifty percent—as polled by the Mervin Field Research Corporation—favored the measure, while thirty-four percent were opposed, and sixteen percent were undecided. Dark clouds loomed over the proposition and consequently around the candidacies of Jimmy Carter, Senator John Tunney, and other Proposition 14 supporters.

In the last week before Election Day, Carter campaigned in South Texas. He called for more jobs. "Viva Carter" and "We want Carter" greeted the candidate in McAllen at a rally attended by ten thousand. Opening his remarks in Spanish, the candidate paused. "I can also speak English," he said. Later in the day, Carter spoke to a crowd of nearly 25,000 at Alamo Plaza in San Antonio: "It is time for a change," he said. "People want a nation of workers, not of welfare." Carter campaigned with his wife Roselyn largely among Mexican American audiences at rallies in Houston the following day and in the final three days of the campaign.

On arriving at an election night rally, César Chávez sat briefly in front of a television set to hear the election returns. News came that Carter carried Louisiana. Chávez beamed: "I predict Carter all the way!" Then he consoled his followers. Proposition 14 had lost by a wide margin—62 percent against, 38 percent in favor. "Our experience in this movement," said Chávez, "is that we never lose. There may be temporary setbacks, but we never lose. . . . The work on Proposition 14 was an investment. . . . Don't be bitter."

No one was bitter in Plains, Georgia where Jimmy Carter waited for the election results. Before the evening ended, Governor Carter and Senator Walter Mondale, narrowly defeated the Republican ticket and won the presidency by a two percent margin of the popular vote and by only a majority plus fifty-six votes of the Electoral College's 538 votes. The 1976 presidential election was one of the narrowest victories since 1916.

Speculation immediately arose about how the opportunity had slipped away from the Republicans, not about how able the Democrats had been. Much of the criticism centered on a rift that prevented a Gerald Ford-Ronald Reagan ticket that many believed would have won the presidency.

The Carter-Mondale campaign had been disorganized from the start. Even Congressman Henry González called the organization an "abomination." Columnist Kemper Diehl speculated that operatives could have lost the Mexican American vote had not state and local party leaders come to the rescue in Texas. The last-minute swing through South Texas and San Antonio, in the company of familiar party leaders, paid off. County Commissioner Albert Bustamante and organized labor brought out a 21,000-voter winning margin for Carter in Bexar County. Carter won there with 53.6 percent to Ford's 44.6 percent and ran better than Nixon in 1968. Ford, with Reagan on the ticket, might have carried Texas and Ohio, two states that went to Carter. The two states comprised 51 of 56 electoral votes that went to the Democrats.

Carter won Texas with only 129,019 votes. Mexican Americans gave him 205,800 more votes than those cast for Ford. In Ohio, Latinos gave Carter an 18,000-vote plurality; and Carter carried the state with only 11,116 votes. All signs pointed to Carter owing the election victory to the Hispanic vote.

Texas' Mexican American voter turnouts were eight percent less than among other voters in the state, yet Ford still would not have won had Hispanics turned out in greater numbers. Larger numbers would have only provided Carter a greater winning margin in Texas. If California Hispanics had voted in the same proportions as their Texas counterparts (81 percent Carter, 19 percent Ford), they would have given Carter enough votes to carry the state.

New York Latinos voted for Carter as a bloc—89 to 11 percent. They provided 84.3 percent of Carter's plurality that was only 15.7 percent short of an absolute majority.

When all states were considered, if Ford had won New York, Ohio, and Texas—even by the smallest of margins—he would have remained President. In the final analysis, Hispanics provided Carter the winning margin.

"It's a statistical fact," said Joe Bernal. "The Mexican American electorate turned out 65 percent of its registered voters . . ." which was significantly greater than any previous major election. The turnout translated into 405,000 voters, or about 22 percent of Carter's total in Texas. "In other words," said Bernal, "we made sure Governor Carter carried Texas and its twenty-six electoral votes." Overall, Texas' Mexican Americans gained one state senate seat and three house seats, for an overall representation of seventeen legislators. The gains came in the face of a court-ordered legislative session in 1975 that carved nine populous counties into single-member districts.

Hispanics had earned an important role in the Carter government, said Hank Lacayo, Carter's Hispanic Advisory Committee chairman. He cited the pivotal turnouts in New York, Ohio, Pennsylvania, and especially Texas.[4] Polly Baca Barragan, also on the advisory committee, stressed, "All we are asking is that he [Carter] . . . open some doors—for both women and Hispanos."[5] As the talent search began, Baltasar Luna, IMAGE's national secretary (an organization formed in 1972 to improve federal job opportunities for Hispanics) noted that Hispanic Americans comprised 7 percent of the population but filled only 3.2 percent of civil service jobs. "The only obligation," he said, "is that 82 percent of the Hispanic vote went to Carter."[6]

Following the election, after the new administration began making appointments, members of Mexican Americans For, a Los Angeles-based civic group, leaked a memorandum to the Carter transition team authored by Herman Gallegos, Monsignor Geno Baroni and David Ushio. The memo denounced the "insensitive" attitude prevalent among transition staff members and the negative screening given Graciela Olivárez of New Mexico, a highly regarded leader.

The flap over the "scrutiny" given Hispanic prospects subsided after the inauguration. "If I had to write another one today I would change it," said Gallegos. Indeed he would, since the publicity served notice on the administration to make good on promises to choose from Hispanic loyalists. Right after the memo, in fact, six Hispanics were appointed to government posts. One of them was Graciela Olivárez, who was appointed Director of the Community Services Administration. After a month in office, President Carter repeated his pledge to appoint Hispanics to high-level government posts.

By June 1979, after two and a half years in office, President Carter had made 1,805 appointments. Eighty-eight of them were Hispanic appointments (including two pending and one interim), amounting to 4.8 percent of the total. The figure was low in relation to the nation's Hispanic population (approximately 7.5 percent at that time). Slightly less than half were sufficiently high ranking to require Senate confirmation. In fact, 59 percent of the Hispanic appointees served on boards and commissions—typically advisory, and not administrative—and on a part-time basis, with relatively little influence on program and public policy decisions.

4. Hispanics Stress Role in Election," *Denver Post* (November 19, 1976).
5. Jane Earle, "Carter Expected to Produce on Promises," *Denver Post* (November 7, 1976).
6. "Minority Job Shortage Cited," *San Antonio Express* (November 20, 1976).

The remaining appointees were scattered throughout the executive and judicial branches of government. None of the thirty-six Hispanic appointees worked in the White House: Three were on the White House staff and worked in the Executive Offices (an important distinction because to work in the White House suggested working directly under the president; serving on the staff meant a full rank removed both from the president and presidential decisions). A special assistant to the president, as well as a deputy assistant to the president and an associate deputy counsel served on the White House staff but were not part of the inner circle.

Twenty-four Hispanic appointees went into twelve cabinet agencies, but none was appointed to the Cabinet itself. The highest positions were held by four assistant secretaries in the departments of Agriculture; Health, Education and Welfare; Housing and Urban Development; and Defense. President Carter later appointed Edward Hidalgo Secretary of the Navy, and Abelardo Valdéz as the State Department's Protocol Chief, with the rank of ambassador.

One Hispanic appointment was made to each of the departments of Commerce, Treasury, and Labor. The Justice Department, on the other hand, received ten Hispanic presidential appointments, including three U.S. Attorneys, five U.S. Marshals and the head of the Community Relations Service. Leonel Castillo was appointed Commissioner of the Immigration and Naturalization Service.

In the State Department, ambassadorships went to Raúl Castro (Argentina), Diego Ascencio (Colombia), Mari-Luci Jaramillo (Honduras), and Frank Ortiz, Jr. (Guatemala). In addition, Frank Pérez was appointed U.S. Representative to the Strategic Arms Limitations Talks (SALT), and Abelardo Valdéz became Assistant Administrator for Latin America. No appointments were made to three other departments, but five were made to independent agencies, while none were made to the remaining seventy-four.

President Carter named Alvin Rubén to the U.S. Circuit Court (one out of 132). James DeAnda, Santiago Campos, José Gonázales, and Cristóbal Duanas were each appointed District Court judges out of 516 similar appointments.

President Carter's eighty-eight appointments represented the highest number of Hispanics appointed by any president up to that time. Not unlike past administrations, the Carter White House published a list in June of 1979 showing 186 appointees. Over half were actually Schedule "C" political appointments made by high level staff and not the president. Yet, even without padding, President Carter's record was sufficiently impressive compared to that of his predecessors.

However, Carter's Hispanic appointees were not strictly or exclusively concerned with Hispanic constituents and issues. Their primary concern was their new posts, followed by Administration concerns, and then Hispanic issues (if, in fact, there was a difference or any decipherable "Hispanic" perspective). Serving the administration could be difficult when contradictory interests arose. But that was the stressful difference between playing on the field and just observing from the stands. Carter's appointees were now unambiguously running plays and not merely spectators calling fouls.

While Leonel Castillo was still Houston's elected controller, he made a dramatic bid for state Democratic leadership and served as the party's state treasurer. He advised the Carter campaign on how to attract and keep a Mexican American constituency. Rumors circulated that Castillo would run for mayor of Houston. He had succeeded in city politics with broad-based support from blacks, Mexican Americans, low- and middle-income groups, when others had failed to form such coalitions. He was unscarred and free of scandal, recognized for high ethical standards in office and a record of success by sticking to policy and the issues. He was a powerhouse in the state, even without a legislative office. So it came as no surprise when Castillo was singled out to serve in the Carter administration, especially since the state had been so crucial to winning.

Soon after President Carter took office, Castillo was offered the job of commissioner of the Immigration and Naturalization Service, one of the toughest in the new administration because labor sought immediate, tough action against illegal immigrants and their employers. To begin with, even determining the extent of the "illegal aliens problem" was itself an issue. In February of 1975, General Leonard Chapman, the INS Commissioner, had testified before a congressional committee that between 4 and 12 million illegal aliens resided in the United States. He gave no basis for his estimates. Unable to get support from the INS's own statistical section, he turned to a Washington D.C. consulting firm for help.

Lasko Associates concluded there were between 4.2 million and 11 million illegal immigrants in the U.S., or about an 8.2 million average. Of these, 5.2 million were Mexicans. The Congressional Research Service evaluated the study, and concluded differently: the estimates were based on weak and indefensible assumptions.

A scary figure was important to the "public education campaign" that the INS had launched, and it proved moderately successful in helping increase its budget. The agency averaged a 16.4 percent annual increase between 1974 (when the campaign began) and 1977 (when Castillo replaced Chapman).

Castillo, upon taking the INS post, embarked on a program to untangle a bureaucratic mess. He soon had the agency's planning and evaluation unit validating the "illegal alien" estimates that INS used. When he found that the figures had no empirical basis, he instructed employees to stop guessing and to confine statements to official figures. As part of the changes, he assigned sociologist Dr. Guillermina Jasso from Johns Hopkins University as an assistant to impose discipline on the research. Some INS observers suspected that Castillo didn't understand the budgetary process, i.e., the more inflated the numbers, the greater the request made of Congress.

His appointment was pure folly, according to some observers. Castillo's own grandfather was, technically, an illegal immigrant. Others criticized Castillo for adopting the term "undocumented worker" over the more pejorative "illegal alien." Others insisted that Hispanic Castillo could not be objective. That was suggested as what was behind the head of the Los Angeles office requesting a transfer to Hong Kong. Anonymous sources told the *Los Angeles Times* that the agent was on Commissioner Castillo's "hit list." The replacement would be required to speak Spanish because "Castillo wants to get a Latino activist like himself here. . . . Then we can forget completely about law enforcement and concentrate on serving the illegals. . . ."[7] The reporter failed to mention that Spanish fluency had long been a requirement of Border Patrol agents in the southwest.

The Administration acted on Carter's promise to get "resident alien" status for long-term undocumented immigrants, but organized labor's contention that undocumented workers were driving down wages and taking jobs away from Americans made progress difficult.

Mexico and the U.S. had operated an open border until 1925. Afterward, the border was relatively more open or more closed as a function of the two national economies, with the United States attracting greater numbers of Mexican workers during boom times. The wage differential was, obviously, a major enticement. In 1978, the minimum wage was $2.65 per hour in

7. Ronald J. Ostrow, "Ban on Hiring Illegal Aliens Questioned," *Los Angeles Times* (February 27, 1980); Millie Budd, "Leonel Castillo: Time Never Stands Still for Man of Many Titles," *Houston Business Journal* (June 2, 1980).

the U.S., while it was $.71 in Monterrey and $.75 in Mexico City. Border towns, where wages were a fraction higher, exploded with newcomers.

The across-the-border population problem became so serious that some experts claimed that Mexico would have 85 million people by 1985. The Mexican economy was unable to absorb a rapidly expanding population, especially rural people lacking the skills needed for a changing workforce. As the tenth most populous country and the fourteenth in GNP, Mexico—beginning in 1978—tried to diversify its markets by making bilateral agreements with its trading partners. Manufacturing output increased, but despite progress, it imported more products than it exported. U.S. cargo to Mexico consisted mostly of production, rather than consumer, goods.

The balance of payments increased from $866 million to $3.04 billion between 1970 and 1976. In 1973, double-digit inflation forced the devaluation of the peso, which had been stable for two decades. U.S. export goods went through price increases. Retail sales on the border dropped; businesses laid off workers. The devaluation aggravated the push by Mexicans to search for any living wage wherever jobs were available, which meant the United States.

After 1978, the Mexican economy improved. Trade balances became more favorable. Inflation was brought slightly under control and dropped from 27.2 percent in 1976 to 20.7 percent in 1977. The oil industry alleviated the economic situation and helped the recovery. However, oil—not a labor-intensive industry—also had a slightly opposite effect. It imported skilled labor and technology while exporting the product abroad. Meanwhile, the U.S. public became increasingly inflamed due to thoughtless histrionics by commentators who should have known better.

Undocumented workers, and those who entered the U.S. with faulty documents or abused their official visas and permits by overstaying, most often took domestic or farmworker or other low-paying jobs in occupations with bad working conditions that no one else wanted. Data obtained in 1978 from McAllen and El Paso, Texas, showed that many were apprehended as often as five times each month—often within seventy-two hours after entry.

However, new data suggested that undocumented immigrants did not bring as many negative consequences as generally assumed. Lasting solutions resided in economics, not in attitudes. "The unemployment experience" wrote Professor Gilbert Cárdenas, "seems to support the notion that their impact is often exaggerated. Still, some see the undocumented alien issue as a 'silent invasion.' Others see the United States-Mexico border as an 'escape valve' for Mexico's unemployed."

In 1977, the Carter administration—based on faulty, inadequate, or unsubstantiated data—proposed to curb the flow of undocumented workers. The administration assumed that undocumented immigrants displaced American workers and had a far greater negative impact on the national labor market than they actually did.

Proposed legislation would grant amnesty to aliens who had entered the United States illegally before 1970 and who had lived continuously in the U.S. since. The plan created a temporary resident-alien category, allowing them to work and remain in the country for five years. Afterwards, a new determination would be made. The proposal took into consideration the concern expressed by Hispanic organizations that many illegal immigrants, after having settled in the U.S., purchased property, paid taxes, and given birth to American citizens, still remained subject to deportation.

The proposed legislation had many problems. Some undocumented immigrants, for instance, could not prove their status and entry dates. Community organizations opposed the measure, believing that temporary status would not assure permanent legal status later. Fearing deportation during or after the five-year period, some people would refuse to register. Concerns also arose that the proposal would actually encourage some people into illegal immigration in order to qualify for amnesty (although 1978 figures later failed to substantiate the concern).

The Carter administration also proposed stricter border enforcement and added two thousand new officers to the Border Patrol. "Employer sanctions" required penalties of up to a thousand dollars per undocumented immigrant employed. A similar measure under the previous administration—passed in the House but defeated in the Senate—was revived. The administration argued that the measure was inevitable. Mexican American organizations and other groups objected, saying that the proposal encouraged widespread discrimination by employers and deportations by the Border Patrol. Congressman Edward Roybal tried unsuccessfully to counter the administration's proposals with legislation granting amnesty to considerably larger numbers of undocumented immigrants and reforming INS enforcement practices. White House staff members tried to persuade Hispanic leaders that the administration's proposals were preferable to the stronger sanctions favored in the House of Representatives.

Finally, Attorney General Benjamin R. Civiletti withdrew the administration's proposal, saying that its wisdom was questionable. A ban "would be outrageously difficult and not very productive." The laws on the books against sweatshops employing undocumented aliens made sense, he said.

Those laws penalized employers who paid less than the minimum wage, failed to pay overtime, or violated the Occupational Safety and Health Administration regulations. The administration denied it had changed its policy and agreed with Congress to create the Select Commission on Immigration and Refugee Policy to study the issues. With this, the administration bought time and a cooling-off period. Those who demanded new statutes and large budget increases for the Border Patrol would have to cool their heels.

While policy gladiators waited, others started a less lofty campaign. Roger Conner—of the Federation for American Immigration Reform (FAIR)—blamed Mexican Americans for the lack of a coherent policy, saying they "feel that preventing the employment of illegal immigrants from Mexico would lead to discrimination against them." He claimed that "if we phased illegal immigrants out of the economy, the life of the average American would hardly change for the worse, and the opportunities for black and Hispanic teenagers and unskilled workers would be greatly enhanced."

Although it wasn't, the infusion of young Mexican labor could have been viewed as an asset. With zero population growth achieved, who would take the jobs and generate the income needed when many more Americans retired? Peter A. Morrison, a Rand Corporation researcher, projected that by 2030 only three active workers would support each retiree, compared to six to one in 1978. Pension expert Merton C. Bernstein was much less worried. "We can solve the problem whenever we want in whatever numbers we want," he said to the President's Select Commission. "Mexican immigration, almost single-handedly, could do the job."

The issues at stake needed serious, sober evaluation. But public opinion had already formed without the benefit of good evidence. Congress wasn't well served either, after authorizing $1 million in 1978 for an INS study of illegal immigrants. The survey was carefully designed and respondents were assured of confidentiality, interviewers came from the same neighborhoods as the persons polled, and residents were given reasonable assurances that law enforcement would not get the interview information. But money for the study ran out before it was completed. Problems in the field and the work's quality were brought into question. The "Residential Survey," as it was known, was canceled, leading to congressional charges that a cover up was taking place "to avoid alarming the country over the extent of its immigration problems." Both the consulting firm doing the work and the INS denied the charge. The data produced was never the issue, rather how the data was obtained and whether confidentiality could be assured was. There simply was no information, one way or another, to release.

In another instance, the Central Intelligence Agency conducted its own study. Leonel Castillo tried unsuccessfully to get the CIA report released, saying that it "would be of value to the public discussion." The report contained no information that others had not already seen. The *New York Times* magazine released leaked portions, which it referred to as a National Security Council report. In it, the U.S. proposed to pressure Mexico to promote small-scale industrialization in rural areas to stem the flow of immigrants. Commissioner Castillo was right. There was nothing new in the report. But former CIA director William Colby picked up the alarmist call. As if he were the first to notice the growing Mexican population's effect on the United States, Colby told the *Los Angeles Times* that Mexican population growth "is a greater threat to the United States than the Soviet Union."[8]

Irresponsible and adversarial officials exploited the issue, inflamed the public, made scapegoats of the helpless, propagated ignorance and misdirected rightful concern. The public worked up anger while most opinion leaders and the press had provided little insight. No balanced appraisal on the immigration phenomenon's impact was in sight. Few people considered that all consumers benefited from cheaper goods and services produced by undocumented workers, that they drove down wages for people in marginal jobs but also made restaurant food, houses, and home improvements more affordable to millions. Many Americans gained access to affordable goods and services due to undocumented labor.

The public policy issue was reduced to how much undocumented workers and immigrants took away, despite the tax revenues they generated and the benefits gained from filling jobs that had previously gone begging. The un-confronted issue was how to reconcile the differences between a poor, native U.S. population and the poor immigrants. The native population was often lost in a vast menu of specialized social welfare agencies and bureaucratic non-profit agencies. They remained unemployed after jobs opened up. The interloping new immigrants, without the benefit of language, conveniences (telephones, cars, lunch money) and most normal services (health care insurance, good housing) willingly took hard, menial jobs. Yes, there was much to concern organized labor, but they missed the real point. Many Americans wanted to find a scapegoat rather than take a serious self-appraisal. The rhetoric of the day took control.

Studies by the Labor Department and the *Colegio de México* showed that illegal immigrants had income taxes withheld, paid Social Security and, like

8. Paul R. Ehrlich, et. al, *The Golden Door* (New York: Ballantine Books, 1979), pp. 189-190.

everyone else, paid sales and similar taxes. Only one-half of one percent of the people interviewed collected any form of "welfare," one-half of one percent received food stamps, four percent had unemployment compensation and four-and-one-half percent took advantage of public health and medical programs.

All the while, the press carried scare stories portraying the large influx of illegal immigrants as a national menace and the INS as an agency under siege. The imagery portrayed Border Patrolmen as working hard, but making little progress in stemming the human tide. Hordes were wading and pole-vaulting across border river crossings, dashing undeterred across the desert and dodging cactus instead of border agents. While bureaucrats in Washington played games and talked about gathering more data, the public wanted action. Congress was getting damned mad. This was no time for wimp paper-shuffling.

The administration, in response, acted prudently by not playing to the crowd, but was politically naive by stopping both legislation and further budget increases for the INS. It was unable to master the alchemy of progress and politics. While the promised amnesty was never enacted, some minor reforms took place as a result of improved information gathering (a task rarely credited to Castillo), and a more reasonable mood took hold for a discussion about this inflammatory issue. Indeed, the administration even made some modest improvements in dealing with the undocumented entrants themselves.

For instance, members of the congressional Hispanic Caucus told Attorney General Griffin Bell that police zeal and lack of knowledge about U.S. immigration law and procedures led to the harassment of Hispanic citizens and legal residents. Police officers around the country reacted to the growing public concern by seeking out and detaining suspects for deportation by the INS. Bell was warned that an explosive situation was developing in some cities between the local police and Mexican Americans, Puerto Ricans, and other Hispanic citizens. The INS, part of the Justice Department, had a longstanding—but unobserved—policy prohibiting local police from enforcing immigration laws. The Mexican American Legal Defense and Education Fund and its Puerto Rican counterpart, had received many complaints that Hispanics were harassed during police searches for illegal aliens. The California state attorney general even issued an opinion in 1977, after a Santa Ana incident, saying that local police could not arrest a person solely on suspicion of immigration law violations. The Los Angeles police force had similar regulations, even though an individual arrested in connection

with a criminal offense could be held for the INS. Attorney General Bell issued a statement following the meeting with the legislators, reminding local
police agencies that they were not authorized to enforce immigration law.

On another front, the Carter administration lost supporters by beginning
construction of a fence the length of the U.S.-Mexico border. Critics called
it the "Tortilla Curtain." The move was widely interpreted to mean that the
government viewed the policy matter as a simple law-enforcement concern.

The new immigrant waves "are changing the face of America," said the *U.S.
News & World Report*. Ten million newcomers, the magazine estimated,
had arrived in the previous ten years after Congress removed quotas that
had previously discriminated against Third World countries. In 1951, 89
percent of the immigrants came from Europe and parts of the world other
than Latin America, Asia, and Africa. By 1976, twenty-five years later, Latin
America, Asia, and Africa accounted for 79 percent of the legal immigration. Mexico alone accounted for 14.5 percent, followed by the Philippines
(9.4 percent), Korea (7.7 percent), Cuba (7.3 percent), and China—including Taiwan—(4.7 percent). The Americas accounted for 27.2 percent
of all legal immigration in 1976, compared to 13.2 percent in 1951 (when
Canada alone accounted for 10.1 percent of the immigrants).

The newcomers' impact—especially the effect of those from Asia, Latin
America and the Caribbean—would be felt even more strongly as U.S.
birthrates diminished. And due to racial and ethnic antagonisms, reasoned
USN&WR: "Darker skins and exotic non-European languages make it difficult for some to melt into the predominantly white, English-speaking
population."[9]

Commissioner Castillo became one of those people coming across the
border by impersonating an immigrant to see how people were treated at
the U.S. entrance gate. "I've made visits to our offices, unannounced and
totally unrecognized, to see how they'd treat me if they thought [I] was just
another immigrant. Sometimes I dressed poorly and spoke Spanish. It's
been very instructive." For instance, in "some places [people are treated]
very well, and [in] some places they tell me to 'get to the end of the line'—
to 'shut up and wait.' In one office I asked to see the district director. I was
told to take a number and wait. After half an hour, I learned he wasn't due
in that day."

9. "New Faces, How They're Changing U.S.," *U.S. News & World Report* (February 20,
1978).

Under Castillo, the INS grew to 9,600 employees with a $250 million budget. He planned increases leading to 11,000 employees and $300 million. The enforcement focus shifted from individual apprehensions to prosecuting organized smugglers of illegal immigrants.

Castillo and the administration sought to legalize undocumented aliens with community roots, and of good moral character, who had been in the U.S. before 1970. Congress had grandfathered legislation like that several times before. The administration wanted persons arriving between 1970 and 1977 to have the opportunity to work for five years, but not draw social service benefits, or bring their families, collect welfare or Medicaid. They could return to their homes and then come back to work, receive the protections and rights of other workers in this country (such as union membership), but could not vote in elections.

Groups divided between those who thought the measures would create an underclass allowed to work (but without benefits) and those who said that the only thing to do with undocumented workers was to throw them out.

Castillo estimated from sketchy figures that undocumented workers displaced some Americans in industrial areas and competed for minimum-wage jobs. The Border Patrol, therefore, concentrated enforcement on the better-paying industrial and manufacturing jobs, where citizens could get hurt the most. But "As best [as] we can tell," he said, "there is no great rush of unemployed persons on the East Coast to go pick onions in 100 degree heat for three weeks." Nor did undocumented immigrants particularly extend their stay. A Massachusetts Institute of Technology researcher found that undocumented Mexicans worked in the United States six to eight months before returning home. In August of 1978, Castillo said he believed that immigration brought on by population pressures was a temporary problem because Mexican fertility rates would soon drop. This was an over-optimistic view. Reforming a government agency was different from changing the flow of human migration.

★ ★ ★ ★ ★

7
Things Could Be Better, Yes

Mexico wanted oil revenues to become its best source of capital for national development. "If we have the wisdom to manage the oil reserves properly," declared President Lopez Portillo, "the possibility exists that there will be work for every Mexican by the beginning of the century." But Jorge Díaz Serrano, director of the state-operated petroleum company PEMEX, countered this newfound optimism. He argued that it would be "an absolute error for Mexicans to pin all their hopes for progress on the oil industry."

Hopes, however, whether well placed in oil or not, had to respond to the exploding population growth. And population expansion was not necessarily all bad. It had come to mean business growth in places that responded to increasing consumer demand. That was especially evident along the border and in southwestern U.S. cities, anywhere there was a crossover population. On any given day hundreds of people could be seen streaming to and from shopping centers, malls, and grocery stores with armloads of packages and grocery bags. New and used car sales skyrocketed. Rental-housing vacancy rates dropped. The new immigrants brought back to economic life hundreds of small Mexican American neighborhoods and communities. Established Mexican American families of previous immigration waves ventured into middle-class neighborhoods.

One-fourth of the people who legally immigrated to the United States became California residents. The pattern led many Californians to wonder whether their state had the capacity to absorb the new populations. The other three-fourths scattered among the remaining forty-nine states, mainly to the major gateway cities and states near oceans and borders.

The average U.S. citizen had virtual amnesia when it came to Mexico—its people, cultures, the whys and wherefores of its situation in the world. Both countries had observed an open border until 1925. Relations had grown tense in 1936 after Mexico expropriated American and European oil interests. Less than a decade later in World War II, a Mexican air corps unit flew missions in the Philippines, Japan and Formosa under U.S. command. To help in the war effort, Mexico provided the U.S. with some farm labor through a guest-worker program. Relations between the two countries alternately improved and deteriorated during the following decades. The discovery of new oil reserves during José López Portillo's presidency created an opportunity for improved relations.

"Mr. President," asked Tom Brokaw of NBC's *The Today Show* of the Mexican president in 1978, "do you sometimes think that the United States takes your country for granted, that it does not give Mexico its due importance?"

"Yes, I think that the United States does not give Mexico its due importance. Yes, I do," said President López Portillo. "We believe that there is a lack of information [about the U.S.] and that the information we do have is sometimes distorted. We believe that we do not as yet have a listing of matters that would make it easier to solve the problems. But this is a problem of the United States, and our problem is the United States."[1]

López Portillo's statement came just as the United States began taking Mexico a little less for granted and began showing a little more deference. At first, the U.S. had viewed the Luis Echeverrría government's drift toward solidarity with Third World countries as foreign-policy poison. Then the U.S. viewed it as less a threat than a necessary tonic forced down its throat. The U.S.'s newfound empathy with Mexico rose as we became sensitive to Mexico's problems—too many people, too much oil.

Oil captured the American imagination, especially after the shortages of 1972 and 1974. High world prices and dependence on Middle-East supplies heightened our interest in Mexico's reserves as a way to help solve the U.S. deficit. At least that was a popular perception that translated into new respect. Mexico, on the other hand, struggled with its own challenges. Soaring food imports threatened to thwart much of its new oil wealth.

Until the early 1960s Mexico had produced enough food for its people and exported large quantities of wheat and corn. The annual corn and bean output (the main staples of the Mexican diet) doubled between 1950 and 1970. Then the government fixed low price supports from 1965 to 1971 to mitigate consumer unrest, which discouraged planting. As a result, the country ran a deficit in corn and dairy products in 1970. By 1977, it had to purchase more than $600 million in foodstuffs.

1. *The Today Show*, September 18, 1978.

As the mortality rate plummeted in response to improved public health and nutrition, the population surged to a 3.6 percent annual growth rate in the mid-1970s. With more mouths to feed, Mexico paid by taking pesos from the federal budget that otherwise would have gone to agriculture. Economic efficiency gains did not come soon enough. When farmers failed, or couldn't afford, to take advantage of available technology, unemployment rose to nearly 40 percent and a portion of the Mexican workforce was lost to the U.S.

Was Mexico embarrassed by having to export people who then became illegal immigrants? "Of course," said President López Portillo, "Very frequently we have said when this point comes up, that we want to organize in such a fashion that we will export goods and not people. The basic problem is that we have not had the capacity to create enough jobs within the Mexican republic, and therefore keep the people here that dare to go abroad, who are usually our best men."

Mexico's revenues were increasingly coming from the sale of oil and gas, its oil reserves were speculated to be perhaps as large as those of Saudi Arabia. Meanwhile, U.S. policy leaders feared Mexico might become a member of the Organization of Petroleum Exporting Countries (OPEC) cartel. "The United States is our . . . logical customer," said López Portillo about the difficulty his country was having. "However," he added, "in the case of oil, there were no tensions, but a misunderstanding."[2] That stemmed from the U.S.'s insatiable demand for oil and gas and Mexico's unwillingness to divert larger portions going to developing countries.

Energy and immigration were the dominant themes at each of the meetings between presidents Carter and López Portillo. Their first meeting in 1977 was largely ceremonial. The Mexican president chastised the U.S. for taking a paternalistic attitude toward his country during a toast at the second meeting in Mexico City in February, 1979. President Carter angered Mexicans and Americans alike during that meeting with a remark about having suffered from the tourist ailment (diarrhea) known as "Montezuma's revenge."

Carter had been under increasing pressure just prior to the trip. Governor Jerry Brown said he intended to make U.S. relations with Mexico an issue in his escalating party nomination campaign against Carter. "When we have a country just a few miles from where we're sitting that has petroleum reserves the equal of most of the other countries of the world," he said, "it makes very little sense that we are dragging our feet in coming to some reasonable understanding on a combination of differences. Sooner, rather than later, this

2. "Mexico Must Help," *The Dallas Morning News* (June 15, 1980).

country is going to have to move into a position that will best be character-ized as a common market between Mexico, Canada and America."

The third meeting came in late September, 1979, after López Portillo had presented an energy plan to the United Nations. At a state dinner with President Carter, López Portillo insisted that the United States exercise its "political will" to avoid world energy depletion and to discipline its oil use. The Mexican vision continued taking the less fortunate Third-World na-tions into account by championing their cause and did not prioritize en-ergy-rich North America ahead of them—at least not yet.

Carter called López Portillo's speech "one of the most profound, the most beautiful speeches I have ever read," whose philosophy "can lay the groundwork for discussions among all nations." This represented a com-plete change of heart from the one that had generated the negotiations that had begun the year before.

Energy secretary James Schlessinger had brusquely rejected Mexico's natural gas selling price in 1978. When the U.S. balked, negotiations broke down. Meanwhile, Mexico reduced the amount of natural gas it was willing to sell the U.S. The delay caused Mexico to find other uses for its product. The U.S. had counted on Mexican natural gas to make up for a projected shortfall, using 19.9 trillion cubic feet of gas per day but finding only 14.4 trillion cubic feet.

In the end, Mexico agreed to limit its oil exports to 1.5 million forty-two-gallon barrels per day for the next fifteen years and said it would not export more than 50 percent of the total to any single country. Exports to the U.S. were to be held to 740,000 barrels a day under the plan, compared to the current 657,000 barrel level, representing 65 percent of Mexico's oil exports.

"He made the right decision," said Robert Krueger, coordinator of Mexi-can Affairs at the State Department, in defense of Secretary Schlesinger, "but he handled it the wrong way." Krueger eventually negotiated to buy 300 million cubic feet a day of Mexican natural gas for a better price than Schlesinger had offered. Krueger noted, just prior to a trip to Mexico City with Secretary of State Edmund Muskie, "We are working increasingly well as two nations but there will always be certain differences of a scale that will pose problems for us." After the oil and gas issue was brought in check, he said, the persistence of the illegal immigrant issue was the next "largest overall problem between our two countries" that needed attention.

The states, meanwhile, were becoming impatient with Washington. Texas Republican Governor William P. Clements proposed a plan to grant Mexican nationals a nine-month temporary work visa. Under it, they could go wherever they wanted. While he opposed a general amnesty for undocumented aliens, the Texas governor proposed a "fast-track" to citizenship for illegal immigrants in good standing. The plan was put before the first joint meeting of Mexican and U.S. border governors. Immigration and Naturalization Service, INS, Commissioner Leonel Castillo and Ambassador Robert Krueger attended the meeting as observers. They were concerned that the governors would venture into immigration and energy policy without consulting Mexico City and Washington, D.C. They were right. Krueger, a former Texas congressman, mainly directed his criticism at Republican governor Clements for meddling in State Department affairs.

"I don't think Bob Krueger knows much about state government," Clements responded. Arizona governor Bruce Babbitt, said, "People for the first time are getting together and understanding that we've got an enormous backlog of problems that we can't leave to Mexico City and Washington. They're too far away." The meeting drew widespread attention because it was the first time the border governors had met to discuss mutual problems. Together they represented forty-million people along the 2,000 mile frontier that INS Commissioner Castillo had termed "the most active border in the world."

Jerry Brown, who championed a North-American economic-union idea was absent from the meeting. He was both an administration critic and an advocate for improved border relations. His idea was not altogether new, as former Texas governor and later Treasury Secretary John Connally had earlier advocated a similar notion of a North American common market.

Under such a plan, imbalances in trade and tariffs tilted toward the United States' advantage, at least in the short run. Realizing that, *Fortune* magazine recommended an incremental approach to trade with Mexico.[3] A small step in the right direction would occur when the U.S. stopped dealing at the State Department with Canada through the Bureau of European Affairs and with Mexico through the Latin American bureau. The time for a North American bureau had come.

Later, Carter nominated Julian Nava as ambassador to Mexico, replacing

3. Herbert E. Meyer, "Why a North American Common Market Won't Work—Yet," *Fortune* (September 10, 1979).

former Wisconsin governor Patrick J. Lacey. The Mexican press suspected Nava's appointment was a move by Carter to shore up Mexican American support and votes in the president's reelection campaign. One Mexico City newspaper asked Carter to rethink the nomination and another said the nomination was an insult. On the other hand, the government-owned newspaper, *El Nacional,* was positive. Nava himself reported that more than a dozen Mexican government officials and scholars, favorable to his appointment, had traveled to Los Angeles to meet with him.

The central issue remained out of focus and was widely reported, although much of it trivial and inane. "I think most of the criticism is simply prejudice," said one high-placed American official. "Upper class Mexicans look on Mexican Americans as sort of undocumented workers once removed." Other concerns tugged and pulled at the administration. What was the U.S. energy policy with respect to Mexico? Was there one? What was the U.S. approach to illegal immigrants? Was Nava to deliver a constituency in a shift from national to hemispheric concerns? Was the administration going to confuse everyone by shifting its focus to Mexican nationals, de-emphasizing Mexican Americans and other Hispanics?

Still, Mexican Americans praised the nomination. "I think his appointment is certain to improve and strengthen U.S.-Mexico relations. . . ." said Rubén Bonilla, League of United Latin American Citizens president. Raúl Yzaguirre, president of the National Council of La Raza said the nomination "signals a new era." Vilma Martínez, MALDEF president, said that Nava had earned respect for his scholarly work and achievements.

The Foreign Relations Committee unanimously approved the nomination, and the full Senate confirmed the new ambassador in one of its last acts before adjourning for the spring recess. Nava was surprised and pleased with the Senate's quick action. "López Portillo wants to have better communications with the Mexican people in the United States and when they found out about my involvement in Chicano activities they were satisfied," said Nava.

Given the staggering increases in border trade and Mexico's importance to the world oil and gas market, the country could hardly remain isolated from its North American neighbors. Trade across the border with the U.S. had increased 47 percent from 1978 to 1979. U.S. investments in Mexico were at heady levels and tourism was flowing in both directions. Just for starters, the new ambassador said his top priority was to make sure that staff at the American Embassy in Mexico City was completely bilingual in English and Spanish.

The need to have professional U.S. representatives able to speak Spanish fluently in a Spanish-speaking country was obvious. But in the U.S., at the local level, matters concerning Spanish-speaking children in an English-speaking country were controversial and heated.

The issues basically stemmed back to the Bilingual Education Act of 1968, which recognized that children with limited English-speaking ability had special education needs. The legislation gave the federal government an opportunity to provide new and imaginative programs. By 1980, the law supported 575 projects at a cost of $108 million and helped 315,000 students. Yet, about 3.5 million children needed bilingual instruction. However, the federal program's intention was to spur on new local initiatives and not necessarily to become a mainstay. Nevertheless, the mix of illegal immigrant children and tight government budgets made for an incendiary situation.

Increasing numbers of children needing language instruction were like a fuse that once sparked went straight to an explosive core. It ignited defensive American values that daisy-chain fashion alienated many Hispanics who saw policy-makers as bent on impeding educational progress. Some politicians now called on plain people to decide pedagogical issues. But getting a handle on the issue was hard enough because it was further confused by the way the federal government approached bilingual education. Far too many teams were on the court for regulation play.

Actually, the Carter administration's support of the Bilingual Education Act, due for renewal in 1978, was a foregone conclusion. Disagreements, however, among the legislation's supporters arose over whether school districts should receive federal funds for more than five years of instruction. Hispanic advocates, in turn, insisted on getting assurances from the administration that projects would not only continue but that the administration would not attempt to divert bilingual education money to assist school districts facing court-ordered desegregation. The administration pressed to use funds for that purpose after Health, Education and Welfare secretary Joseph Califano promised them to Chicago, where desegregation at local expense was resisted. The central disagreement, however, was over how much to increase bilingual education spending. Only the amount was at issue, not whether to provide funding.

But a philosophical debate threatened the policy. A difference arose over "maintenance goals" (maintaining the child's native language) and "transition goals" (transitioning from Spanish to English). The President, secretary Califano and policy advisors within the Department of Health, Education & Welfare believed that the best way to educate language minority children deficient in English was through temporary programs. "Maintenance," favored by Hispanic advocacy groups, was considered by many in the administration as a luxury and, from a social policy point of view, unrealistic. The "Americanization" of Spanish-speaking children was considered preferable and necessary. Administration officials did not understand the complicated prevailing Hispanic point of view and dismissed it readily in order to emphasize transitioning.

In general, Hispanic advocates wanted the Act to help children acquire English-language proficiency by using the native language to compensate for the disadvantages children faced in keeping up with English-language classmates. Eventually, they wanted the act to encourage proficiency in two languages, as well as to promote pride—meaning improved self-worth—among bilingual children. Dual language and pride seemed to cause some problem, as a matter of policy.

The Administration tried to gain a winning edge by quietly lobbying congressional staffs, instead of encouraging public testimony. It pursued an "anti-maintenance" objective. A consulting firm had prepared an evaluation that concluded that the transition goals of the bilingual education program had not been achieved. Someone at the Department of Health, Education, and Welfare made the report public, even though its conclusions were subsequently proven indefensible in light of the study's methodological flaws. Meanwhile, the administration's support of a budget increase was used as proof that the President was keeping his campaign promise. When secretary Califano failed to support part of the administration's position, Vice President Mondale was made the administration's point man. In the end, the administration opposed Latino advocates on several technical issues, while both sides lobbied Congress for the Bilingual Education Act's extension, but from different positions. It was hard to tell that Hispanics and the administration were on the same side.

In some important respects, the administration understood the emotional issues far better than the language-learning proponents. The $170 million bilingual program was popularly perceived as a "melting pot," or an "Americanization" program for children. Columnist Stephen S. Rosenfeld felt, as did many people, that this bilingual stuff was more divisive than unifying in its approach. "Let us concede that bilingualism will do everything its supporters claim. . . ." he wrote. "Will it not also distract his attention from learning English and the social skills that accompany the learning of English,

4. "Bilingualism and the Melting Pot," *Washington Post* (September 27, 1979).

or give him an excuse for not buckling down hard on English?"[4]

There was, evidently, something intimidating about children feeling okay about their origins, which seemed to imply they could not be faithful to the United States if they wasted their time on another language. Why couldn't they be more like—well— typical Americans? Why did they have to be so different?

In practice, it was not the use of Spanish so much as the lack of a clear policy that caused confusion about what this country was trying to accomplish. Bilingualism supported by government was touching a raw nerve, and the debate over the legislation was serving as a receptacle for many confused and sometimes nativistic values. It exposed latent fears of being overrun by a language minority. Philip W. Quigg, writing in *Newsweek*, thought that people should be helped to learn English as a transition to a "different" culture. But he warned that "to do more than this is to invite destructive tensions and endangerment of national unity." He said, "nothing spawns political disunity more effectively than differences in language." And "Since the Latinos in the American Southwest already believe (perhaps rightly) that the territory was stolen from Mexico, what could be more logical than that they should demand complete autonomy or independence or dual citizenship as soon as they constitute a majority in some appreciable area." In a word, language was like a menace.

Opponents made the fight over "maintenance" or "transition" language goals an important rallying point. Any language other than English was a first step "in a degeneration process that will prove uncontrollable," said Quigg. "If ballots and voting instructions must be printed in Spanish, why not the *Congressional Record*?"[5] Conveniently, the debate overlooked the obvious: The legislation encouraged English proficiency among five and seven year old children. Properly instructed, they wouldn't need *La Gaceta del Congreso*.

The chairman of G.I Forum, a civil rights veterans' organization, said plainly, "We want education for our youth. These things . . . [have] been denied for more than 150 years" and he noted that the Treaty of Guadalupe Hidalgo, ending the U.S.-Mexico War had promised Spanish-speaking descendants use of the Spanish language in educational institutions. "And here we are more than 150 years later, still fighting for bilingual education."

A short, but significant, activist period occurred as court rulings and government regulations were promulgated. The Carter Justice Department in

5. Phillip W. Quigg, "Speaking the Same Language," *Newsweek* (October 16, 1978).

one case brought suit against the state of Texas to force mandatory bilingual education in elementary through high-school grades.

A government witness criticized the Texas programs for reaching "the tip of the iceberg" rather that helping to solve the problem. "We lack adequately trained teachers," said Robert L. Tipton, a bilingual consultant and the state's only witness. It's not that nobody wants to do it; it's that we can't, he seemed to reason. "There are 155,000 teachers in the state of Texas and only 7,860 are certified bilingual teachers." Of sixty-three higher education institutions providing teacher education in the state, only thirty-seven offered bilingual programs.

In California, the Brown administration worked behind the scenes to reform the state's bilingual education program while attempting to prevent Senator Newton Russell from scraping the program. It was not the public school's business to maintain a minority student in his or her language and culture, he argued. The sole purpose of bilingual education was to enable a student to master English as fast as possible. Assemblyman Peter Chacón (D-San Diego) led the fight to prevent a program revision. In the face of stiff opposition, he proposed major amendments extending the time for teachers to obtain bilingual certification and allowed local school districts a greater degree of program flexibility. The existing program required elementary schools to provide bilingual teachers. Children were to receive instruction in their native cultures whenever ten or more limited or non-English speaking children were in a school.

Bilingual advocates were in hand-to-hand battle to hold on to the advances they had already made. The language issue had a knack for sparking intense resistance, especially among monolingual, English-speakers. Opponents expressed a sentiment that something was basically wrong—even un-American—when citizens wanted to retain fluency in a language other than English. The very thought pulled at society's fabric. References were made to the federalist quarrel between French- and English-speaking Canadians. The United States could become like Quebec. It could become as diverse as Europe. Language differences were causing problems previously unknown to the U.S., many people reasoned. Instead of becoming one nation, we were becoming many, divided into race, ethnic, religious, and now language groups. What next?

Next, the right of children to attend public schools was challenged. The Houston Independent School District imposed tuition on non-citizen children. De Zavala Elementary School became the main target of the poacher-children issue. The school itself was a reminder how this country was formed historically by diverse people. The school was one of the few monuments to Lorenzo de Zavala—the historian, statesman, and politician—who served as the first Vice President of the Texas Republic. The neighborhood school, not far from the place the city was founded, was a waystation for Mexican immigrant families and others whom economic opportunity had not reached. Nearly all families sent their children to de Zavala School until the Houston Independent School District imposed tuition on non-citizen children.

The fight was led by Alfredo Saenz, the children's lawyer, who appealed the levy to the State Board of Education. He argued that the Houston district had gone beyond its constitutional power and was using federal immigration laws to determine who could go to school free. "The children will not disappear by being turned away from the schools," Saenz argued. "They will remain and they will remain uneducated." He could have saved his breath arguing on "humanitarian and moral right," as was widely reported. The issue was money.

According to Kelly Frels, the school district's lawyer, a 1975 Texas law specified that only Texas residents and legally admitted immigrants were entitled to a free public education. The board of education insisted that the law would have to be declared unconstitutional for illegal immigrant children—mainly between 10 and 11 years of age—to get schooling. Numbering between four and five thousand, they were applying mainly to the first grade because they could not speak or write English. The students cost the district about $7 million, or $1,485 each. "I'm not being callous by talking about how much it costs," said Frels, "but there is only so much money to go around. If that money is used to educate illegal aliens, it deprives our citizens of money for them."

Numerous suits were consolidated into one that went before U.S. District Court Judge Woodrow Seals whose landmark ruling struck down the Texas law. He ordered the school district to enroll the children beginning in the fall of 1980. However, a federal appeals court in New Orleans indefinitely stayed the Seals ruling. Attorneys for the state of Texas argued that ten thousand children would flood the schools and put a damaging financial burden on the state.

How would they know, then, whether the child was illegal or not? Houston schools superintendent Billy Reagan said only that the determination would be made "based on the educational expertise of our principals." A distressed Rubén Bonilla, LULAC president, was more to the point: "The higher court is creating chaos and disorder. It's legally and morally unconscionable. I never thought a federal court would advocate functional illiteracy."

Meanwhile, a 1974 Supreme Court decision would help draw a new defining line between what the public at-large wanted as distinct from what many Hispanics wanted. In *Lau v. Nichols* the court affirmed that limited or non-English speaking children had the right to equal education. But the Court did not prescribe a specific remedy about what a school ought to do. It simply affirmed the right of equal treatment when services were available. To uphold the civil rights of limited and non-English children, the resulting rules were referred to as the "Lau Regulations," based mainly on existing Department of Education practices setting minimum requirements to protect children on the basis of national origin.

Yet, some government officials, in charge of enforcing the regulations, were incensed, and an internal memorandum went out from the Health, Education and Welfare department to "clarify" a "misunderstanding" by some of these education-rights enforcers. The 333 school districts they oversaw (affecting 1.1 million students) were not mandated to provide bilingual education for children whose primary language was not English. How could children's civil rights be protected, as supported by the Supreme Court, and still not require enforcement?

The Civil Rights Act of 1964, Title VI, had established a broad prohibition against denying access to federally-funded education programs because of a student's limited English proficiency. The "May 25, 1970 Memorandum," as the regulatory document was known, provided the guidelines. And the U.S. Supreme Court unanimously upheld the guidelines for schools to eliminate language barriers in local education programs.

Then, HEW developed a set of informal policy directives, outlining the school districts' responsibilities to language minority students; these were known as the "Lau Remedies." They were used by the federal government in nearly five hundred school districts as the basis for compliance. But in order to settle *Northwest Arctic v. Califano* in 1979, the Department of Health, Education and Welfare agreed to publish the Lau Remedies or similar guidelines in the *Federal Register* for public review and comments, and ultimately to issue them as new Title VI regulations.

Instead, the Lau Remedies soon became a presidential election issue. In May 1980, the Carter administration disbanded HEW and created the new Department of Health and Human Services and the Department of Education. Shirley Hufstedler became the first Secretary of Education. She was convinced by the White House in June, 1980, to issue Title VI regulations requiring bilingual education to gain Hispanic support in Texas and California for the Democratic ticket.

In August, 1980, Hufstedler issued a "Notice of Proposed Rule Making" concerning minority-language children. The regulations required virtually every school system that enrolled English-language learners to establish bilingual education and teach subjects in a language the language minority could understand until such time as they learned English. The notice, instead, incited a flurry of legislative proposals in reaction.

Two weeks after Hufstedler issued the proposed rules, James McClure (R-Idaho) introduced in the Senate S.3049, the Local Schools Option Protection Act, directing the Secretary of Education to withdraw the proposed rules. No action was taken on the bill.

Representative Robert Michel (R-Ill), based on a House Appropriations Committee report, proposed changes to bill HR 7998 (concerning funds for the departments of Labor, Human Services, and Education) that local school districts should be left to decide for themselves how they would provide equal educational opportunities to non-English-speaking children. Federal regulations would be restricted from requiring basic courses in languages other than English and from prescribing staff requirements, teacher qualifications, teacher training, specific methods and procedures for identification, assessment, class size or composition.

Three weeks after secretary Hufstedler issued the proposed rules, Representative John Ashbrook (R-Ill) introduced an amendment to HR 7998 restricting the use of federal funds from being used to enforce regulations that required state or local education agencies from teaching students of limited English-speaking ability other than a program of intensive English instruction. The amendment was passed, 213 to 194, within an hour of its introduction.

Five weeks after the proposed rules were issued, Senator McClure offered a similar amendment to a Senate Appropriations Bill for the departments of Labor, Health and Human Services, and Education. Hispanic and civil rights groups looked on actions like those by McClure and Ashbrook as political attempts to obstruct basic rights.

Senator Lawton Chiles (D-Florida) offered a substitute stating that the Secretary of Education could not use funds to promulgate any regulations that replaced the current "Lau Remedies." In September, 1980, the Senate passed a joint resolution that included the Chiles substitute amendment.

In November of that year, Ronald Reagan was elected president. That changed everything. After Terrel H. Bell was named Secretary of Education, he withdrew the proposed Lau Regulations, calling the policies "harsh, inflexible, burdensome, unworkable and incredibly costly . . . fiercely opposed by many, supported by few."

8

A Formidable Giant

Many Americans had been transfixed by the gripping allusion in the 1968 Kerner Commission report on civil disorders which characterized the U.S. as moving toward "two societies, one black, one white—separate and unequal". Overcoming race-based inequality posed a divisive national challenge. Virtually every domestic issue before and since that time has had a racial tone to it. "Race" and "minority" were often used as euphemisms to suggest inequality, inequity and a panoply of unresolved social issues. Increasingly, the image of an emerging Hispanic population was superimposed on the metaphor of the two societies. "Hispanics" (by the late 1970s increasingly known as "Latinos") were coming into their own but in a context of a nation conflicted by unresolved race-based issues. Hispanics, nonetheless, increasingly pressed "ethnicity" as part of the way people thought about society, and that caused dissonance. Some people who thought a lot about these matters were having to stretch their way of thinking beyond their comfort zone.

In the closing days of 1979, Census Director Vincent Barraba, as if to allay fears, sent a letter to the National Black Caucus of Local Elected Officials to say that Hispanics would not outnumber African Americans in the United States until sometime after the year 2057. This seemed to bring about some relief. A census report that Hispanics numbered far more people than was earlier believed had caused discomfort within some minority circles. The nation was accustomed to the black/white divide and its easy-to-understand (but polarizing) sociology, issues and symbolism—from poverty to ebonics to the confederate flag flying at a state capitol. Now, the changing demographics, new immigrants and social diversity challenged a nation on the verge of a nervous breakdown over race-based politics. The challenge went straight to how Americans would think about their country. *Time* magazine noted that the California Hispanic and Asian presence alone had "fueled and complicated the p.c. (politically correct) and multicultural debates that initially arose out of polar conflicts between blacks and whites or men and women."

Now the census was getting caught up in the debate. Larry Lucas, speaking for Director Barraba, tried to assuage fears. He told the nation's mayors that the Hispanic population was 12.1 million and growing at a 2.25 percent annual rate. By 2010, Hispanics would reach 24 million and the black population would number 37 million. Based on that trajectory, Hispanics would take seventy-eight years, or until 2057, to equal the black population, when both would number about 67 million. Not to worry. The Hispanic ascent was a long time off.

The news was well received, even though the Census Bureau admitted it had no reliable count of undocumented immigrants and had a history of undercounting. "Although black and Hispanic leaders are unhappy about it," wrote *Houston Chronicle* reporter Bill Boyarsky, "the politics of poverty has put both groups in competition for their share of dwindling federal dollars."[1] That put new pressure on the upcoming census. It was particularly sensitive because it would serve to reapportion congressional, state legislative districts, and determine where revenue-sharing dollars would go.

By 1980, the census was determining which states and cities would receive more than $50 billion of federal tax revenues. Over a hundred federal programs used census figures, including the Adult Education Act, the Public Health Service Act, the National School Lunch Act, the Economic Opportunity Act, the Manpower Development and Training Act, the National Housing Act, and the Housing and Urban Development Act. When local areas expected more and received less, local officials usually attributed declining revenues to population undercounts. In places like California (cash strapped after the passage of Proposition 13, restricting how much property taxes were allowed to increase), local governments needed to replacement revenues. Cities and states were extremely dependent on an accurate census to qualify for much-needed federal revenues.

A poor response resulted from a 1976 test of census forms conducted in four cities. Only 50 percent of the forms were returned from Camden, New Jersey. In Austin, Texas, INS rounded up scores of illegal immigrants after forms were returned. The Federation for American Immigration Reform (FAIR) and twenty-six members of Congress filed a lawsuit in December,

1. Bill Boyarsky, "Blacks Seen as Largest U.S. Minority Till 2057, Census Bureau Official Says," *Houston Chronicle* (December 6, 1979).

asking for a preliminary injunction to restrain the Census Bureau from proceeding unless they agreed to exclude undocumented immigrants from the count, even though the census forms did not ask about legal status.

On the other side of the issue, local officials wanted high numbers and less undercounting. The Census Bureau estimated that roughly 2.5 percent, or 5.3 million persons were unaccounted for.

Roger Conner, FAIR's director, said that counting undocumented immigrants indicated "if they can get in they can be recognized." A person on a visa would not be counted, but a person overstaying by one day would be. He contended that states with large numbers of undocumented immigrants would get a representation windfall and federal aid. The Justice Department, speaking for the Census Bureau, argued that the Constitution called for counting the total population. All inhabitants had to be counted. If undocumented people were not counted, New York, like many major states, would suffer revenue losses and experience less congressional representation. Mayor Edward Koch said, "any reduction in the formula-based federal grants threatens to plunge the city back into economic crisis."

In fact, contended Esther Estrada of the Mexican American Legal Defense and Education Fund, illegal immigrants contributed to the tax rolls but didn't apply for or collect Social Security, unemployment insurance or other benefits due taxpayers. Not counting them amounted to taxation without representation. Why not count the undocumented immigrants?

Attorney General Benjamin Civiletti, originally opposed by Hispanic groups when he was nominated by President Carter, faced another important confrontation. He was pressured by Latino groups to do something after a federal judge issued a restraining order on immigration officers. The suits alleged that INS officers had improperly detained U.S. citizens and legal resident aliens alike. Immigration agents had broken down doors and searched residents without warrants or probable cause, and local police had acted as immigration agents during neighborhood raids. Civiletti halted the practice three months after INS officials resumed neighborhood raids searching for undocumented immigrants. He pointed out that door-to-door census takers might be mistaken for INS information-gatherers. Even after Civiletti's order came down, other suits were pressed in an attempt to halt future neighborhood sweeps.

Finally, INS officers were directed to change strategies in view of that year's census. The locus shifted to work sites and places where low-income workers congregated, rather than residences. Civiletti's response was an improvement over his earlier stance. With the focus back on employment

sites, Census Bureau director Vincent Barraba appealed to Hispanic organizations and the National Council of Bishops to urge undocumented immigrants to participate in the census count, emphasizing that the information
would remain confidential.

The Census Bureau was up against the wall. Ten years earlier, the White
House had pressured the agency to withdraw its planned 1970 questionnaire (even after the original one had already gone to the printer). They had
worked in a question identifying the "Spanish-origin" population. By 1980,
the "Hispanic" origin category was entered and was presumed to apply to
only 5 percent of the population.

Columnist Georgie Anne Geyer was concerned about differentiating
people by ethnicity. She thought that "citizen" was soon going to mean
nothing. INS, she said, was dealing sentimentally with the identification of
citizens and illegal immigrants. But her criticism was silent on the need to
protect human, civil, and procedural rights, regardless of status. And that
was the real issue. U.S. citizens had suffered the consequences reserved for
illegal immigrants. U.S. Hispanics were confused with the undocumented.
A hostile climate, frustration and confusion prevailed and, in large part,
explains why the Carter administration failed to get the consensus needed
for an amnesty and a guest-worker program.

The census came to represent reapportionment and local financing, as
much as it did enumeration. It served many other purposes, as well, not
the least of which was measuring living standards. Yet, the system begun
in 1790 was not serving 1980 very well. One census official went so far as
to say in court testimony that a scientific sampling would provide more
accurate information than the old form of enumerating every household.
Undercounts had always existed. Even George Washington had complained
that thousands of heads were missed in 1790. But errors had not been so
well documented before. Large cities, with population losses, were unwill-
ing to accept undercounts and financial losses without a fight. After the
census was completed and the analysis begun, some cities charged that the
census had undercounted them.

The census had become so important that the Hispanic Congressional
Caucus, with five members (plus 146 honorary representatives with at
least a 5 percent Hispanic constituency) recognized the importance of the
5 percent swing vote. Congress members, even those with relatively small
numbers of Hispanics in their districts, were beginning to take those constituents into consideration. This enlightenment was helped, in part, by
improved enumeration.

The point was driven home by William A. Medina, Assistant Secretary of the U.S. Department of Housing and Urban Development: "We have enormous potential in twelve states alone," he said, where Hispanics range "from 4 percent of the population to a total of 36 percent of the population. We could influence the votes in those states. As a swing vote, we could deliver to a national candidate, such as a president of the United States, 179 electoral votes. It takes 240 to win; 179 of them are potentially votes that could be delivered by a Hispanic constituency if it could be organized." Census data pointed to precisely where this effort to organize might begin.

Retrenchment and opportunity were like bookends when it came to many Hispanic issues. Those who wanted to help insisted that the federal government and its programs should offer a helping hand instead of relying on strong private initiatives. The arguments seemed persuasive since the economy in general wasn't performing well and had gone through many peaks and valleys during the previous three decades. It was in a valley during much of Carter's term.

President Jimmy Carter made reducing unemployment a priority, putting him in conflict with Federal Reserve chairman Arthur Burns. G. William Miller replaced Burns at the Fed in January, 1978, and introduced an expansionary monetary policy. Yet, even under Burns, the monetary supply had grown 8.2 percent annually during three quarters between 1976 through 1978. Unemployment declined 2 percent, but inflation increased to double-digits in late 1978. Inflation became the main economic problem, and Carter changed strategies by reducing the M1B money supply from September 1978 to February 1979. The money supply grew by only 4.7 percent during that period, and a slowdown, along with rising prices, drove the economy into outright decline.

The strategy to stimulate the economy changed again from February through September 1979. The money supply was increased to an 11 percent annual rate. The recession ended. Investors speculated against the dollar on foreign exchange markets, and dollars fled into gold, silver, and other commodities. Paul Volcker replaced Miller at the Fed on Miller's appointment as Treasury secretary. Volcker held the M1B money supply constant from October 1979 to April 1980. The economy, with tight money, declined and joblessness rose to 7.8 percent by summer. The money supply was again increased—this time by 16 percent between April and November 1980. In a panicky attempt to stimulate the flagging economy during an election year, the money supply experienced the most rapid rise of any six-month period in the two previous decades. The recession was halted. But it came too late to help Carter in his reelection campaign. The economy's ups and downs arranged public opinion against him.

In January, 1979, a *Newsweek* cover story reported the "compelling fact about Chicanos is that there are a lot of them." In fact, 7.2 million, representing a 60 percent increase in eight years. They are a "nation within a nation." Adding surreal imagery to the prevailing stereotype, they called California, Arizona, New Mexico, Colorado, and Texas part of the "Tamale Belt."[2]

The nation was getting its information about Hispanics packaged as part fact and part image. For the most part, the portrayal suggested a pain in the neck. This stood in sharp contrast to the notion accepted during the two preceding decades of a metaphorical "Awakening Giant." Most Hispanic leaders had always thought they represented a social and economic titan that would flex its muscles one day.

By the end of the 70s, that giant was awake, alert, and formidable, so much so that the rest of the nation was taking notice. Hispanics expected accelerated social progress and perhaps less resistance and a more welcoming arena in the drive to acquire a better standard of living and improved representation.

The Hispanic context was often confused with other concerns, especially as the nation turned obsessively materialistic and individualistic. Political ideas were personalized. An out-of-focus magnifying glass was often used to understand this intrusive Hispanic population. Clear understanding was in short supply. And emotions were easily triggered when racial or minority group terms were applied to make the term "Hispanic" a euphemism for social deficiency or economic insolvency. Meanwhile, 75 percent of Hispanics were in the ranks of the lower-, middle-, and upper-middle class. Four out of five Hispanics lived in cities. And only 8.5 percent of Mexican American, so often typified as farm workers, actually were.

Hispanics were increasingly ubiquitous: one in four Texans was of Mexican descent, and one in five Californians. Los Angeles was the second largest Mexican metropolitan area in the world and would have a Latino majority in twenty years. California would have a Latino-dominated "majority of minorities" about the same time. The entire Hispanic-American population, with three-fifths of it Mexican American, would surge past African Americans to become the largest U.S. minority population early in the next century. And almost half of that population was under eighteen years of

2. "Chicanos on the Move," *Newsweek* (January 1, 1979), pp. 22-25.

age, with a median age of 21.3 years compared to 29.5 years for the total U.S. population. Hispanics were forever young, the rest of the population older. Therefore, Hispanic outlooks and concerns contrasted and differed from those of the rest of the nation.

Yet, the imagery often portrayed this population as predominantly needy. Advocacy for the poor fed that notion and, in reality, the Mexican American median-family income was $11,421, as compared to $16,284 for non-Hispanic families. But this income generalization failed to take into account the disparate economic conditions among the different groups, classes and segments of the Hispanic population. Consequently, Mexican Americans, Puerto Ricans, Cubans and others were still largely perceived as one large undifferentiated mass.

The demographic picture at decade's end proffered images of Denver public housing children at play; mustachioed men at an L.A. wedding party alongside dark-haired women in white lace veils and long gowns; black Hispanics in a tenement stoop; deeply wrinkled South Texas farm workers standing alongside long, dry furrows; low-riders standing beside their decorated machines; the ever-present shots of Border Patrolmen on the lookout in the Arizona desert; and Chicano mural art with Benito Juarez look-alikes and Aztec symbols. This was the imagery of what America was becoming—new symbols, new people, new foods, new scares, new problems. This was the Awakening Giant at decade's end—a time designated in a popular poster as the "Decade of the Chicano."

A study, sponsored by California Lt. Governor Mervin Dymally, concluded that the Census Bureau had undercounted the state's minority population by more than 2 million. Consequently, Dymally pursued a coalition approach to politics. He told delegates to the 1978 Mexican American Political Association convention that "If the present trends continue, the emerging ethnic groups will constitute more than half the population of California by 1990, and we will become the country's first Third World state."

Third World state? Clearly, the Lt. Governor meant that the state's population would become more diverse—predominantly Mexican American and African American. For prosperous California, wary of the nation's economic instability, becoming a Third World anything was a scary proposition. In fact, that was one of the great fears—that the nation's economic instability would make them a third-world state.

Nor did the term "minority" necessarily produce comfort, either. Hispanic identity, in fact, alternated back and forth over whether they were that—or not. It was simply not a matter of disturbing concern but became so when others imposed notions about color upon them. Hispanics were, simply, of all racial groups.

Popular political rhetoric, now stringing together "black-white-and-brown," had a discordant ring to it and had no particular appeal to Hispanics, either. They never defined themselves as a "racial" group in the first place. "Race" as genotype or phenotype had little to do with cultural identity, which was a better description.

The term "minority," likewise, did not in itself have relevance. The designation had legal implications but it wasn't a social identity, as was presumed by many blacks and whites who dominated the debate with race-based ideas. Some politicians tried to capitalize on the prevailing notions about race, ethnicity, and minority status by running all the categories together. They mainly imposed a "disadvantaged" template, implying poverty, statistical inequality, and the functional equivalent of "socially handicapped."

Most Hispanics were, in the usual sense, a "minority" group (as a legal definition for an underrepresented group sometimes denied equality and competitive status). But the "minority" yardstick, when used to account for social standing and social status—with thinly disguised racial overtones—was offensive to many Hispanics. Hispanics had national-origin, religious and cultural supports for identity. Efforts to create racial politics with Hispanic participation were doomed to fail. Common cause on issues with other groups was another matter, but not racial politics.

The basic facts were clear: America was failing to assimilate information, knowledge, and imagery about what was occurring. Consequently, many Americans didn't catch on to the meaning behind the changing nature of American society. Popular perspectives incited fear instead of allaying it. Comparing how one group was more privileged, or worthy, or needy than another created a deep-seated angst in social discourse. That perspective would have to change, but no one seemed to know how to do it.

"At some point, the dominant cultural group will have to understand the nuances of difference[s] among the minorities," insisted Luisa Ezquerro, a community leader from San Francisco's Mission District. "To the Anglo, we may all look alike, and they may think we all vote alike, but it doesn't work that way."

By 1980, the Anglo population in Los Angeles County stopped peaking and began descending into the valley of a numerical minority. Twenty years before, they made up 71 percent of the population. The plunge coincided with the emergence of a struggling class of people insufficiently educated or trained to find steady work. As central city schools became predominantly non-white and Hispanic, education meanwhile became the only viable vehicle for self-sufficiency. At the same time, the middle class was in full flight to the suburbs where much of the real estate and economic expansion occurred. *Los Angeles Times* writer Robert Scheer concluded "It is also widely believed, at least among those who are paid to grasp such matters, that middle America has had it with the problems of the blacks, Hispanics and the poor—[after] having done so much for them."

In the general public, defensive attitudes gained acceptance and became increasingly entrenched, reflecting a frustration with special programs to advance the economic opportunity of the nation's poor. The nation's helping institutions, dependent on federal appropriations, were unstable, going from one funding round to the next to see if they would continue their work. About the same time, the traditional middle class was going through a cultural catharsis. It had itself adopted many attributes of lower-class existence and had become a lesser role model to aspire to, except for income.

Incivility became endemic in all economic classes and strata. The rebels without a cause of the Fifties became the archetypes of the Seventies. At the same time, more people consciously feared material deprivation, personal crime and random violence.

On the whole, the value of life and living was increasingly quantified and tallied. People's worth equated with how much they earned. Home and homestead became a real estate investment. Neighborhood became a settlement of mini-warehouses for goods, consumer gadgets, and time-saving appliances needed to maximize the hours breadwinners' spent at work earning enough money to pay for them.

The idea of "family" received lip service, but more people were foregoing the experience with close-knit nuclear and extended families. The value of women was largely assessed in terms of newfound roles in the workplace. Children behaving like brats were universally tolerated and indirectly encouraged.

A slow decline in the quality of teaching, retention of teachers, and scholastic achievement became pronounced. The nation showed little aptitude to re-dignify neighborhood institutions. Teachers seemed to hide cynically behind labor contracts and, in some districts, routinely went on strike or threatened to do so. Teaching was no longer a calling, it was a job. The middle class remained relatively passive in the face of deteriorating schools and retreated to the suburbs.

American society was becoming increasingly professionalized and specialized. The average citizen felt entitled to few important opinions without the backing of popular statistics and support from a Ph.D., psychologist/counselor, physician, or lawyer. Baby boomers were becoming older, conservative, and cautious. Many citizens believed that defense spending was a better investment (with the hope that war products would never be used) than spending on people (as a national human resource).

The social and political ascent of Hispanic groups coincided with this profound transformation in U.S. society. The desperately needed direction, with a unifying outlook, was not yet forthcoming, however. Instead, the same politicians with the same notions made heavy-handed appeals to the greedier side of human nature. The signs were everywhere. Idealism, going into the 1979 elections, was pretty much out the window.

Mexican American political leaders seemed to intuit the changes but were as yet unable to articulate and direct their concerns outside their core group. They were feeling marginal and turning insular. "We are tired of being taken for granted and treated like aliens in our own land," said one participant at the MAPA conference addressed by Lt. Governor Dymally. "We haven't burned down buildings, we haven't been on television getting our heads bashed, and so we haven't called attention to our needs. And a lot of politicians have always assumed they have us in their back pocket. But we're in a new era, and the Anglo leadership can no longer operate in the context of the Sixties and the black civil rights movement. The next decade is the era of the Chicano."

Frustration and impatience was running high. Eduardo Sandoval, a former San Francisco community organizer and lawyer observed, "We have reached a point where our drive toward full economic and political participation is irreversible."

The drive for greater democracy was no longer based on any particular ideology, as had been the case in the off-shoot politics of the 1960s and 1970s. Evidence of the change was seen, for instance, in Abe Tapia's campaign for Democratic lieutenant governor. He was endorsed by anti-abortion activists. Or, the coalitions that formed to support Al Garza, a conservative San Jose, California candidate who ran against the incumbent mayor Janet Gray Hayes. Garza, with the endorsement of the Building Trades Union and the police and fire unions, ran a pro-growth campaign. In the face of increasing federal deficits, extremely tight state budgets, banal or irrelevant public debate, and a professional middle class unable to mentor a working class, "conservative" became the term to describe the trusted values of the past.

No Hispanic candidate was on the California statewide ticket of either major party, even though the midterm elections in 1978 weighed heavily on the state's Mexican American and other Hispanic groups. Governor Jerry Brown, for one, ran a strong Latino campaign that yielded him a landslide reelection victory. Brown knew that California's Mexican American population was a new constituency to cultivate, inclusive of—but not limited to—farm workers. "Brown," said George Pla, deputy director of the state Economic and Business Development Department, "is the first national political figure to recognize the growing economic and political power of the Latino community."

Even here, complications arose. Brown won nearly 79 percent of the Hispanic vote, but it did not equal the 85 percent he had received from all registered Democrats. Were Hispanics turning fickle?

A clue was to be found in understanding that the population wasn't a mass group. Probably the maximum Hispanic voter response was 80 percent, given the population's diversity. There was no 100 percent agreement quotient. To expect more was ludicrous. Furthermore, other political races had to contribute momentum to stimulate a strong turnout by giving voters an incentive to show up to vote for—not one, but—a combination of candidates. They knew—rhetoric aside—that one person could not make things happen. In the gubernatorial election, except for the move by Assemblyman Joseph Montoya to the state Senate, no new Democratic strength was evident. Brown's campaign did not help the incumbents running for office by drawing voters to the polls. From 1972 to the 1978 election, the number of Democratic Latino state legislators remained six. In fact, there was a question about whose coattails pulled whom. Did local candidates draw voters to the polls? Or, did Brown pull voters for the local candidates?

In New Mexico, Hispanics won 30 percent of the state legislature, representing 40 percent of the state's population. Hispanics expected to hold several leadership positions, including House Speaker. They maintained a majority coalition with liberals. They had held power in that fashion since 1970. Bruce King and running mate Lieutenant Governor Roberto Mondragón won against Joe Skeen with a two to one margin. The victory was attributed to strong Democratic registrations, longstanding relationships all the way to the precinct level—and no sudden, panic enlightenment.

If the nation's 20 million Hispanics had been represented proportionately, six Hispanic Senators and forty Representatives would be serving in Congress. Hundreds of state legislators and thousands of local officials would hold office. Instead, going into the 1980 presidential election, not one Hispanic served in the Senate and only five voting Congressmen were in the House of Representatives (a non-voting delegate represented 2.7 million Puerto Ricans). Not many elected officials served even in state and local bodies. And the direction was not altogether promising. For Hispanics, all bets were off concerning representation after a Supreme Court decision on the Voting Rights Act.

The Supreme Court overruled U.S. District Court Judge Virgil Pittman's order establishing districts in Mobile, Alabama's municipal elections. Since 1911, three commissioners elected to at-large districts had governed the city. All the commissioners had been white, despite a 35 percent black population. In a 1976 class action suit, Pittman declared the system unconstitutional and ordered a mayor-council system with ward representatives—after the city's voters had twice previously rejected similar plans. A U.S. Supreme Court majority ruled that the Voting Rights Act protected the right to vote but did not guarantee that African Americans would get elected to office. The Court held that the Fourteenth Amendment required a finding of "intentional discrimination" in voting rights challenges, and there was none in this case. Plaintiffs had to show that the discrimination was intentional. Unequal results were not in themselves proof of discrimination.

Justice Stewart Potter, writing for the majority, said, "Equal protection [of the law] does not require proportional representation." Justice John Paul Stevens, concurred with the majority and wrote that even if Mobile's majority whites supported the plan to keep black's out, "I don't believe [the] otherwise legitimate political choices can be invalidated simply because an irrational or invidious purpose played some part in the decision-making process."

Justice Thurgood Marshall, on the other hand, disagreed: it took only "the smallest of inferential leaps" to conclude that the Mobile system was designed to exclude blacks. Clearly the Court was retreating from this type of race-based challenge to local districting. The decision weighed heavily on Hispanic challengers who aspired to increase representation by challenging elections in districts that historically produced unequal results. Los Angeles was one of the places of dismay. The city and county didn't have so much as a single Mexican American city councilman or county supervisor. All other justifications for lack of representation were so much academic blather. People who dealt in such matters knew districts were gerrymandered. After the 1970 census, incumbent councilman Art Snyder went into a newly created district that was two-thirds Spanish-surnamed, of whom only 40 percent were registered voters. In reaction to the unfairness of the system, a grassroots recall effort was started, backed by Congressman Edward Roybal, Assemblymen Art Torres and Richard Alatorre. The attempt was ultimately defeated. Said David López-Lee, a University of Southern California professor who had collected signatures for Snyder's recall, "When Democrats cut up elective offices, they slice up the Hispanics. . . ."

In 1982, Congress stepped in and revised Section 2 of the Voting Rights Act to require challengers to demonstrate "unequal effects" on potential minority power, not the onerous "discriminatory intent."[3] The hearts of groups seeking minority representation started beating again.

Texas' role in the primaries increased in the 1970s after overtaking Pennsylvania as the third largest state. Northern and eastern populations moving to Texas added to its suburban growth and formed a political mixture of old-line Democrats, new reformists, emerging Voting Rights Act legislators, local politicians, renegades from the Democratic ranks, and a new crop of moderate Republicans. The 1980 voting pattern had its roots in the 1972 and 1976 Texas elections.

In 1972, Richard Nixon appealed to Texas' Mexican Americans and was helped by the widely accepted perception of George McGovern as an "ultra-liberal." Nixon received 25 percent of Texas' Mexican American vote, leading Republicans to perceive a conservative aspect to Mexican American values.

In fact, Mexican American and Hispanic outlooks were given little currency until 1978, when Republican Senator John Tower faced the most difficult reelection campaign of his senate career. He won with less than one-half of one percent of the vote. In that same year, Bill Clements was elected as the first Texas GOP governor since Reconstruction. In both elections, Texas' Mexican Americans cast about 30 percent of their votes, and clearly the winning edge, for the GOP candidates. In Texas, at least, the precedent was set for splitting off the critical 30 percent from the Hispanic voting bloc.

The historical ties between Mexican Americans and the Democratic party broke from the strain over the party's perceived departure from values sustaining family ties, patriotism, personal ethnic awareness, reliance on trust as a vehicle for loyalty to persons and institutions, a work ethic, personal

3. Hugh Davis Graham, "Voting Rights and the American Regulatory State," *Controversies in Minority Voting: The Voting Rights Act in Perspective* (Washington: D.C.: The Brookings Institution, 1992), p. 187.

initiative, and fiscal conservatism. *Newsweek* reported that Hispanics are "a people who are basically conservative, hardworking, religious and family-oriented." In the Tower election, Mexican Americans were acting in their own best interest and in proportions roughly equal to that interest.

A united Democratic Party, organized labor, and a White House supporting Robert Krueger had Tower under attack. But Tower broke with tradition and began courting the Mexican American vote. The advertising agency of Ed Yardang and Associates of San Antonio was selected for the media job. Agency president Lionel Sosa took over control of the Hispanic portion of the Tower campaign, and the rest of the agency took responsibility for other aspects of the account.

Research indicated that Tower's Washington association carried a positive connotation, contrary to the national reaction against Washington ties. Consequently, television messages were designed to show Tower as a strong national legislator committed to defense, education, and equal opportunity. In the follow-through, a media campaign was designed to "humanize" Tower by showing his sensitivity to the needs of Texas' Mexican Americans. A folk ballad was invented for radio.

The identification tagline took. "*El está con nosotros* / He's with us" was constantly reinforced in print and in the electronic media. The campaign boldly appealed to Mexican Americans and addressed them as Texans and as part of a single electorate. The campaign emphasized, without apology, what all Texans could understand—the state's languages, values, and choices. Spanish was not reserved for the Spanish-language radio stations but, instead, ran on all radio stations. Written Spanish was put up on billboards. Election pragmatism (getting the most votes) carried the day.

Preceding the 1978 fall gubernatorial race, Bill Clements persuaded Sosa to produce the campaign's Hispanic political advertising. Similar types of materials as produced for the Tower campaign were used for Clements, who spent twice as much as Tower on the Mexican American vote. The strategy was to sell Clements' conservative philosophy instead of the candidate since he had no clear identification with Mexican Americans. The media messages emphasized family, neighborhood, work ethic and equal opportunity. Radio commercials featured Benjamin Fernández, the Republican presidential hopeful, and entertainer Trini López.

Clements won by 17,000 votes. "No Republican running for governor," said Sosa, "had ever gotten over 5 percent of the Hispanic vote. We got 36 percent, and that put him [Clements] over the edge." Clements reportedly recommended Yardang & Associates to the Reagan Republicans when they looked for an advertising agency. Not surprisingly, the pitch developed for Reagan was that he would provide good jobs, a chance for a good family life, and a future for children.

"We are extremely proud. We are very independent. We do not like to be told what to do. We like to have our own *movidas*, our own little enterprises. We don't want government sticking its nose in everything we do. We respect authority, but the less of it around, the better we like it. We do not like to owe anything to anybody. We do not like handouts," said Los Angeles businessman Fernando Oaxaca, chairman of the Republican National Hispanic Assembly. The Assembly, as the first Latino auxiliary within a major political party, aspired to have a hundred thousand members in 1976, but settled by 1980 for a realistic three thousand in fifteen states.

"We are willing to build our own place within society. The name of the game is making it, and free enterprise is where it's at," said Benjamin Fernández. The Democratic windfall following Watergate—because of unemployment and inflation—was wearing off. Disenchantment with Carter was growing. Oaxaca reasoned, "Latinos are not [as] loyal to a party or a cause as they are to an individual. That is why we are optimistic about our prospects in 1980. . . ."

Republican Hispanic strength and influence was virtually a point of pride even among some Democrats. "Maybe now we can establish a two-party system within our community," said one Democratic higher up. "Our people can fight on two fronts to improve ourselves. This way, regardless of which party is in power, we will always have someone voicing our concerns. For when it comes down to it, we are not fighting to better ourselves as Democrats or Republicans, but as Latinos." One other way to draw attention was by running a candidate.

Out of about 150 candidates who sought the presidency—under various party affiliations—only sixteen sustained national campaigns. Benjamin Fernández, Republican, was one of them. In late November, 1978, he was the second Republican to announce his candidacy. Three months later, he was already making the rounds with three other party hopefuls—former Treasury Secretary John Connally (Texas), Senator Lowell P. Weicker (Connecticut), and Rep. John H. Anderson (Illinois). Fernández planned to raise money in at least twenty states to qualify for federal matching funds. Meanwhile, he would keep his campaign afloat on loans until then.

By summer Fernández was participating in the Republican Presidential forums. Often referred to as "cattle shows," these forums were state party fund-raising events preceding the primaries. Diplomat and former CIA director George Bush, Rep. Phillip M. Crane (Illinois), Senator Robert Dole (Kansas), and perennial candidate Harold E. Stassen, former Minnesota governor, joined the list of candidates.

Ronald Reagan entered the race by the time of the Indiana forum. There, Ben Fernández told the delegates—who gave him a warm hand—"We need an up-front President who scoops up big business and says, "'Thank you for making profits, thank you for making jobs.'" The delegates cheered and whistled. Fernández gave the same basic speech wherever he went. "I'm an American running for President of the United States," he said.

But problems began overtaking Fernández' campaign. Daniel James, his campaign manager, resigned long before the first primary. Yet, Fernández continued. He campaigned through the winter snows of New Hampshire to the tropics of Puerto Rico to his home state, California. Ben Fernández ran side-by-side with the front-runners. In speech after speech, he told his story. He was born in 1925 inside a boxcar parked in a railroad yard in Kansas City. His parents were poor Mexican immigrants. He worked his way through college, earning an economics degree in two years, then an MBA in one. In 1960, he formed a management consulting firm and became a moderately wealthy man. When asked why he became a Republican, Fernández said someone once told him that the Republican Party was the party of the rich. "And I said, 'Sign me up. I've had enough of poverty.'"

When media referred to him as the Hispanic candidate, "I stopped it immediately. I am an American candidate. I never heard about Irish American candidate Reagan, or English American candidate Ford. So don't give me any of this Hispanic American candidate Fernández." The reason was simple: "Our folk have the right to serve this country just as well as anyone else." The same applied to the campaign, "We are going to find the most qualified folk, men and women, and bring them into my administration, at every level, not just as token appointments."

The nation's most serious problem at the time was inflation. "It affects people who can afford it the least," he said, "the poor and senior citizens." He proposed to eliminate waste and to veto every major deficit-creating bill that landed on the president's desk. "The less government interferes in our lives, the better."

"We need a tough energy program, beginning with conservation," the development of alternative energy sources, switching to coal, shale oil, solar energy, gasohol and even recycling garbage. "But, ultimately," he said, "the bottom line is in Mexico. We need a President in this country who can deal with Mexico on a fair and equitable basis."

The United States' future, he said, "lies in the countries of the Western Hemisphere. We are tied geographically, economically and culturally, yet this country has not done its homework." He proposed technical assistance to free countries and offered to normalize relations with Cuba after its political prisoners were released. "We will help Castro's Cuba get back into the free-enterprise orbit," he said.

"As I see it, the shock of my running has been mind-boggling." He remembered campaigning in the Texas Rio Grande Valley, "In the evening, the stories would get back: `Que presumido! Que se cree? No sabe su lugar.' (How arrogant. Who does he think he is? Doesn't know his place.) That's the kind of mentality I found in the market, but it didn't surprise me. I just kept plugging away, giving my speeches in English and Spanish."

The three "front-runners," according, to him, had already offered him the vice presidential position on their ticket. He qualified in fifteen Republican state primaries and Puerto Rico. Kansas and Kentucky gave him one percent, the highest proportion of votes that he got in the campaign. He had complained to the Federal Election Commission in Puerto Rico that his poll watchers had been denied the opportunity to vote, ballot boxes had been stuffed, and many voters had been told that he had dropped out of the race. This was the campaign's low point, even if he finished fourth.

Fernández had even drawn a longer and louder ovation than Ronald Reagan when both men spoke before the Southern Republican Leadership Conference. He conceded defeat soon after casting a ballot for himself in the California Republican primary (he called it a symbolic gesture but an emotionally satisfying one) and said he hoped his personal contacts would serve as the basis for another campaign later. The presidential race had put him $147,000 in debt. He later participated with other Republicans in a series of fundraising events.

In July, 1980, at the opening session of the Republican National Convention, which nominated Ronald Reagan as the party candidate, Benjamin Fernández was the fourth speaker at the podium. Although reportedly willing to accept the vice presidential nod, it was not offered.

9

Changing Attitudes—And Theories

On his first day in office Ronald Reagan ordered a federal hiring freeze. He abolished the Council on Wage and Price Stability and suspended 199 regulations issued by federal agencies after the election and before the inauguration. He named Vice President George Bush to head a commission on regulatory relief, and two-term Congressman David Stockman was appointed director of the Office of Management and Budget. Stockman was already working, a month before the inauguration, on cost-benefit analyses and proposals for a series of budget cuts to fulfill Reagan's campaign pledges.

The Reagan administration was determined to establish its vision of America. It was one with less government. That meant eliminating or minimizing the social welfare programs that had accumulated during the previous fifty years. Suddenly, Hispanic leaders, along with many other Americans, had to defend the programs they had assumed were fixtures.

The Reagan Revolution sought national prosperity by reducing the federal budget, lowering taxes, deregulating business and industry, and getting the government off the people's backs. The prescription was dubbed "Reagonomics."

The administration believed that progress was measured by productivity and income gains that resulted from personal initiative. They tried to weed out the belief that most people needed the federal government for their personal economic well-being. Hispanic advocates were not in agreement in most instances but had a weak voice in the matter. Rubén Bonilla, president of the League of United Latin American Citizens (LULAC), thought that Reagan's influence would pass in due time.

While that didn't quite happen, the other side of Bonilla's scenario did occur. During the decade, two Hispanic governors were elected. Scores of local Hispanic officials emerged, and Henry Cisneros was considered as a potential vice presidential running-mate.

Management and Budget director David Stockman, armed with determination and supply-side ideology, set out to reduce income taxes, encourage investment, practice tight money control, and to balance the budget through reduced government spending. The rules of the game had changed for Hispanic Americans. They had previously persevered and sacrificed to get Washington to address their specific complaints. Now the political strategy was turned upside down and inside out. To the new administration, Hispanics were just another of the federal government's many clients. The drive to get the national government to embrace the Hispanic Americans' economic interests was losing out fast. The ramifications of the budget cutting ran wide and deep. The new administration ushered in an attitude wholly different from that of the preceding ten presidencies. Whether truth was on their side or not, the administration was about to embark on changing America's social policy down to its roots.

Three weeks before the inauguration, Stockman and his staff had already assembled dozens of policy analyses on program reductions and studied national economic forecasts. A computer simulation modeling the nation's economic behavior suggested that the three-year tax reduction and increased defense spending would produce tax deficits ranging from $82 billion in 1982 to $116 billion in 1984. The levels were without peacetime precedent and, if word had gotten out, the estimates would have caused a financial panic. Instead, Stockman proceeded to reprogram the computer and used his knowledge about the dismal projections to instruct Reagan-administration policy insiders to go beyond the vague and painless campaign theme of ending "waste, fraud, and mismanagement" in federal spending as a remedy for balancing the budget. They needed to cut deep into the budget. Stockman hoped they would cut the welfare state right out of the federal budget altogether, or at least render it inconsequential.

Reagan proposed in a February, 1981, economic message to cut more than $41 billion from the projected Carter budget and reduce or end funding for eighty-three federal programs. A *Washington Post*-ABC News poll showed that the President enjoyed better than two-to-one support for his proposals. But cutting the $700 billion federal budget would not be easy. Forty-eight percent of the budget was destined for entitlements, 25 percent for defense, and 10 percent to interest payments on the national debt. The remaining 17 percent included the traditional functions of government, among them the FBI, national parks, county agents and the Foreign Service. Nine percent of that amount provided grants to state and local governments, aid to handicapped children, and highway building. Most of the cuts would have to come from the 17 percent. The bloodletting began at a dizzying pace. The House passed the original budget bill on May 7 with few concessions by a vote of 253 to 176.

In July, the President was back on national television pleading for popular support of a supply-side tax cut, which passed Congress on July 29. But the measure "was a pale and confused version of the [Congressman Jack] Kemp's nostrum adorned with a clutch of special provisions which had little to do with any economic theory except greed," according to journalist Lou Cannon. The measure benefited the oil industry, gave tax relief to savings and loan associations and all corporations, reduced the "marriage penalty" on all two-income families, and accelerated and simplified business depreciation schedules. The proposed 10 percent across-the-board tax cut was reduced to 5 percent on the realization that it would reduce federal revenues too much. Taxpayers would, however, get new 10 percent reductions in July of 1982 and July of 1983.

The original budget cuts were not sufficient. They were soon followed by another round of budget cuts encapsulated in a bill called "Gramm-Latta II." The legislative coalition was a lot shakier now, and more individual concessions were made. But the Reagan approach for the next three years was in place. Budget cuts were used to make up for the staggering deficits.

Stockman was soon back at the White House breaking the bad news. Projections showed that the deficit would rise to $81 billion in 1983 and $112 billion by 1986. He tried explaining that higher real gross national product (GNP) and employment growth would not increase the treasury's revenues. The remedy called for still more budget cuts that even Stockman said were "draconian."

"What Reagan had accomplished," said journalist Lou Cannon, "was not budget balancing or business stimulation but a shift of priorities within the budget." In fact, the military increases nearly offset the Stockman cuts in social programs. Public service jobs under the Comprehensive Employment Training Act were eliminated, as were college education benefits under Social Security. Concentrated Employment Training Act and the Community Services Administration were also scheduled for "zeroing out," Stockman's phrase for closing down a program. Child nutrition programs and unemployment insurance for workers losing their jobs to foreign competition were reduced. Unemployment compensation was lowered from thirty-nine weeks to twenty-six weeks of benefits at a time when joblessness was increasing. Medicare patients were required to pay more of their health care costs; welfare benefits under Aid to Families of Dependent Children were reduced. The food stamp program lost $1.7 billion, and more than one million recipients were eliminated from the program. Even taking a meat cleaver to the federal budget, however, did virtually nothing to reduce the government-spending rate.

Reduced military spending was, of course, one source of savings, but Reagan ruled that out. Entitlement programs were the other major sources of rising government spending. People qualified for these programs when they met certain criteria—government's so-called "check-writing" function. Checks were written for the elderly covered by Social Security, pensions for veterans, hospital and doctor reimbursements under Medicare, welfare checks for dependent children, etc. Social Security, that Reagan was pledged to protect, was by far the largest entitlement. Other entitlements, resulting from Lyndon Johnson's Great Society programs, had quadrupled from $70 billion to $295 billion from 1970 to 1981.

The Fed's tight money policy and continued government borrowing to finance the growing deficit kept interest rates high and business expansion low. Consumer interest rates hovered at nearly 20 percent for most of 1981 before moving downward in December under the impact of a recession that sent unemployment to 9 percent, a full percent and a half higher than the unemployment rate that had led Reagan to label the previous year's economy Carter's "depression."

When Reagan took office, the nation's governors urged a change in state funding away from narrow categorical grants in favor of broad block grants. State governments were pressured by local governments to make up for financial cut-backs after the loss of general revenue sharing. The Reagan administration had cut programs to states by about 25 percent and sought to consolidate eighty-eight categorical programs, but only had congressional approval for fifty-seven. Over four-hundred categorical programs, hobbled by reduced funding, remained on the books.

Reagan proposed in his first state of the union address a new kind of New Federalism. He had made campaign promises as early as 1976 to turn over key federal programs to the states, and to provide the tax sources to pay for them. By early 1982, Reagan promised that Washington would take over responsibility for the states' Medicaid costs, and the states would accept financial responsibility for Aid to Families of Dependent Children and food stamps. Second, the federal government would transfer forty-three social programs to the states—including clinics for black-lung disease, mass transit, and foster care. Lastly, the federal government would establish a temporary trust fund to pay for the programs.

According to New York Senator Daniel Patrick Moynihan, the President's proposed $30.2 billion for the trust fund in fiscal year 1984 (the first year of the new New Federalism) would cost $39 billion, after adjusting for inflation in the two years before the states took over. And the actual cost would come to $43.4 billion. The states would have to raise taxes by a total of $13.2 billion, or cut the programs by one-third. "While the numbers speak for themselves," said Moynihan, "the New Federalism is hardly a bargain for the taxpayer." His state alone would have to raise $1.4 billion dollars or reduce social programs by that amount. The five southwestern states alone would have to come up with close to $2.2 billion, or a little over 16 percent of the total.

The fact remained, wherever anyone stood on the issues, the method of financing America was changing fundamentally. It was the Reagan Revolution. Senator Moynihan was one of the few legislators to give a meaning to the paralyzing deficits. By slashing taxes and doubling military spending, the Reagan administration planned from the beginning to create a fiscal crisis. The Reagan administration had a minimal interest in balancing the budget, said Moynihan. The new administration came into office "with a real interest in dismantling a fair amount of the social legislation of the preceding 50 years." The strategy was to induce a deficit and use that as the grounds for the dismantling.[1]

The $200 billion deficit that resulted by 1984—the year that Reagan had projected a balanced budget—would take fifteen years to work through. A turnaround could not happen before 1999, if then. The nation risked the danger that a future administration would tire of a tight belt and wipe out the debt by inflating the currency. Contrary to what Reaganites believed, the economy had not failed because of the political system, said Moynihan. The problem was that the public-finance crisis was a deliberate plot. "If we can get a truly conservative administration into office by the 1990's," reasoned Moynihan, "we can probably restore stability by the year 2000."

Supply-side theory was bad economics, and even worse politics. Instead of

1. Daniel Patrick Moynihan, "Reagan's Inflate-the-Deficit Game," *The New York Times* (July 21, 1985).

a benevolent government caring for its people and their welfare, the government became the needy one in a wild and reckless way. The nation went roughly $950 billion into debt during the first five Reagan budgets. In eight years, the most "conservative" administration in more than a half-century came close to exceeding its income by $1.5 trillion and made a mockery of public finance.

The Reagan administration believed its Economic Recovery Program would encourage people to increase savings once they were assured that inflation would not consume the interest their capital earned. Lower taxes would transfer the interest from savings straight into people's pockets. The administration was sure that unemployment would lessen, a recession would be averted, and prosperity would reign.

During the Reagan Revolution's first year, Congress cooperated with the administration by cutting programs originally designed as recession life-savers: food stamps, welfare, Medicaid, education grants, job training, and food programs for women, children and infants. The recession of 1981-1982 put 9.5 million workers into waiting lines for unemployment compensation checks. High joblessness continued through the winter of 1982, but inflation came down and so did high interest rates. The recession was followed by five good years, without serious Congressional efforts to reinstate the former welfare state programs that had been choked out of the budget and replaced by high defense spending.[2]

The economic stabilizers, previously constructed one program at a time to support wage earners during economic downturns, were disappearing. For some financially marginal Hispanics, the program setbacks were devastating. "Of the some 100 calls we get each day," said Rebecca Bustamante, aide to New Mexico Lt. Governor Roberto Mondragón, "about eighty percent are from people who have problems and, now with all the cutbacks in human need funding, it's hard just to sit here and tell someone's *abuelito* [grandfather] who really needs to stay on a hot meal program or a housing program that they don't qualify for help. . . ."

The Reagan Revolution touched a raw nerve at the local level. While Democrats tried to retain the programs that had built up over the years, a national attitude was reassessing the helping-programs' value. The administration wanted to place more responsibility for the needy at the state and

2. "The Keys to the White House: The Inside Story of Campaign '88," *Newsweek* (November 21, 1988).

local level. Colorado state senator Polly Baca Barragán criticized the assumption that local jurisdictions could absorb the costs: "The current suggestions that the private sector or local government can fill the gap . . . just does not bear out historically. Had the private sector or local governments accepted this responsibility initially, there never would have been the pressure exerted on the federal government to fill this void [in the first place]."

In that vein, businessman Fernando Oaxaca, who had served in the Office of Management and Budget during the Ford administration, charged that the federal government had been a patron, sponsoring the operatives of a Hispanic social service industry. It was this way, according to Oaxaca, "That upper one or two percent of our community which has, over the last fifteen years or so, participated in and learned to depend on federal largess or programmatic activity for their livelihood or community clout." They were the ones out there "screaming the loudest of all, as the sacred cows of [the] federal dollar flow appear to be drying up." They were the "non-elected 'political' leaders," he said, "who hold their positions through [their] domination of annual meetings of their organizations." Oaxaca observed that by stripping away the programs, many community leaders were losing their support base.

If the social service leaders lost their funding, whom would the constituency turn to? Would they turn increasingly Republican? Would they seek local-level representation?

The Hispanic reaction to the Reagan Revolution was registered in the midterm elections of 1982. The number and quality of political leaders in state legislatures, city halls, and county courthouses became the key to reasonable representation. Adjustments occurred against a background of negotiations, tradeoffs, wrangling, self-promotion, organizational assertions and electioneering. In New Mexico, Toney Anaya, after a spirited primary election, won the gubernatorial race in 1982.

Clara Padilla Jones, a Mexican American, was elected New Mexico's secretary of state. Federico Peña was elected mayor of Denver (only one-fifth of the city population was Hispanic). Henry Cisneros was elected mayor of San Antonio, and Maurice Ferré was elected mayor of Miami. A Black-Puerto Rican coalition in New York contributed significantly to Lt. Governor Mario Cuomo's upset victory over Mayor Ed Koch for the Democratic gubernatorial nomination. Tom Bradley remained mayor of Los Angeles after he got strong support from a coalition that included Mexican Americans. To "Hispanic leaders," said *U.S. News & World Report,* "party affiliation is not as important as a candidate's stance on the economic and civil rights issues."[3]

By mid-1983, the United States had 105 Hispanic state legislators (thirty-one in upper houses and seventy-four in lower houses). Cuban Americans and other Hispanics in Florida reached parity in that state's legislature, while Arizona and New Mexico had almost reached parity. In spite of the impressive gains, Texas, New York, and especially California, were still far behind in representational equity.

After the mid-term elections of 1982, Congressional representation increased from six to eleven—all in the House of Representatives. Nine representatives were elected officials; two were non-voting delegates (Puerto Rico and Virgin Islands). The number was an improvement but still far short of the number that would have to sit in the House to represent Hispanics in approximation to their numbers in the general population.

By August of the following year, a major national voter registration campaign was inspired by the successes of the Southwest Voter Registration Education Project and the Midwest Voter Registration Education Project. SVREP, founded in 1974 by William C. Velásquez, was a Mexican American voting-rights movement in the Southwest that encouraged civic participation by educating Latino community leaders and organizations about how the democratic process works by conducting voter registration campaigns. The Midwest Voter Registration Education Project, founded in 1982, (later becoming the United States Hispanic Leadership Institute) focused on non-partisan voter registration, information, and leadership training.

Voter registration drives helped the election victories of Governor Mark White in Texas and Mayor Harold Washington in Chicago. Two hundred Hispanic leaders met in San Antonio to figure out how to register one million Hispanics before 1984 to increase the Latino electorate to 4.4 million by the next presidential election. Among others present were the Hispanic mayors Maurice Ferré (Miami), Raúl Martínez (Hialeah), Henry Cisneros (San Antonio), and Federico Peña (Denver). Also attending were Assemblyman Richard Alatorre (California), Lou Morett of the Democratic National Committee, LULAC past president Tony Bonilla, Senator Edward Kennedy, and Vice President George Bush. About 300 local campaigns were planned for twenty-eight states. The total projected cost would come to $2.4 million, or $2.40 per registration. Other similar campaigns were estimated to cost as much as $20 per registrant. The campaign would target approximately 40

---

3. "High Hopes of Black, Hispanic Voters," *U.S. News & World Report* (October 11, 1982).

percent of eligible Hispanic voters who were not registered. Sixty percent of eligible Hispanic voters were already registered, compared to 67 percent of all other voters.

President Reagan decided to run for a second term as the voter registration campaigns were getting underway. A *Washington Post/*ABC poll for July 1983 showed a 52 percent approval rating for Reagan. He was close to his highest point and up from a low of 42 percent in January. While Reagan enjoyed the notoriety as an enormously popular president, his approval ratings were in fact lower than those of his predecessors. For example, after the first year, Reagan's popularity decreased to 49 percent. By the end of the second year, public approval had sunk to a dismal 37 percent, which paled by comparison to Jimmy Carter's 50 percent at the same time during his presidency. "One theory," speculated Gail Sheehy, about the belief that Reagan was popular throughout his presidency, was that "there existed an enormous subconscious desire in Washington for the president to succeed after a string of failed presidencies. . . ."[4]

The *Washington Post* poll predicted a close presidential race if former Vice President Mondale was the Democratic candidate (49 percent against Reagan's 46 percent), while Ohio Senator John Glenn (50 percent) rated better than Reagan (43 percent) if he were the opponent. Reagan had not run well in 1980 among women and blacks, and had not made any new gains within those groups during his presidency. The Hispanic "swing vote" was crucial strategically because of the population concentrations in five states that alone accounted for 58 percent of the total 270 electoral votes needed to win. Crucial states (and electoral votes) were Texas (29), California (47), Florida (21), New York (36), and Illinois (24).

As the first primary approached, President Reagan was virtually unopposed by any Republican. Perennial candidate Harold Stassen entered the New Hampshire primary, as did political unknown Gary Arnold. Extremist David Kelley also entered the primary. Among the candidates was Benjamin Fernández, who hoped for enough votes to propel a full-fledged candidacy. A spokesman told the press that Fernández would get the New Hampshire Hispanic vote, "since Hispanics vote Republican. The illegals vote Democratic." The intended humor was lost on most. Illegal immigrants are, of course, prohibited by law from voting.

4. Gail Sheehy, "Ronald Reagan," *Character: America's Search for Leadership* (New York: William Morrow and Company, Inc., 1988).

Fernández had two campaign staff members whom he described as "hard core" Democrats: William Amara, California state finance chairman; and Trini Mestre, New Jersey state chairwoman. Fernández said he was going after the whole Hispanic vote: "I invite *all* Hispanics to participate—Democrats, Republicans and Independents," he said. "I could care less about their political affiliation. What I care about is that they support Ben Fernández." The campaign strategy helped the massive Republican voter registration drives that were soon underway. Reagan ran about even with the Democratic front-runners in the polls at the time of Fernández' announcement.

As far as Fernández was concerned, "I don't think either party is worth the powder to blow it to kingdom come." And running as an independent was futile. He crossed partisan lines and interpreted Hispanic interests. "No president, Democrat or Republican," said Fernández, "has ever appointed a Hispanic American to serve in his cabinet. Who will do it? I'll do it," he said. "When will Hispanics be appointed to the Supreme Court? Probably the day I do it. I make the commitment that at the first opening on the Supreme Court I will name a Hispanic, if I am president."

President Reagan, to offset low ratings among black and women voters, began preparing his campaign by making overtures to the Hispanic constituency that had voted for him in 1980. In May, he attended the Cinco de Mayo observance in San Antonio, sharing the podium with Democratic Mayor Henry Cisneros. Reagan's stepped-up speaking schedule included the U.S. Hispanic Chamber of Commerce in Tampa, Florida. He spoke before the GI Forum in El Paso, Texas, just before meeting with Mexican President Miguel de la Madrid in La Paz, Baja California Sur. The President claimed before the Hispanic groups that he had appointed more Hispanics to high positions than his predecessors, although the actual number was in dispute. In fact, Hispanics groups loudly complained that Reagan had attempted to eliminate the traditional White House office of Hispanic community liaison. Henry Zúñiga was eventually named to the position and was later replaced by Catalina Villalpando.

As the President stepped up his campaign, so did Democratic criticisms. Edward Kennedy and Walter Mondale attacked him for leading one of the most anti-Hispanic administrations ever. Reagan, in turn, increased his speaking engagements with Hispanic groups. He defended his policies three times in one week in November of 1983. A full year before the reelection, he announced plans to provide economic assistance to the states bordering

Mexico—heavily populated by Mexican Americans—that had been hit hard by new peso devaluations.

Of the nine presidential candidates, seven were from states with large Hispanic populations. President Reagan, Benjamin Fernández (Republicans) and Democrat Alan Cranston were from California. Also seeking the Democratic nomination were former governor Reubin Askew (Florida), Senator Gary Hart (Colorado), and Senator John Glenn (Ohio). Former Congressman John Anderson (Illinois) ran as an independent. Only Senator Ernest Hollings (South Carolina) and former Vice President Walter Mondale (Minnesota) were from states with small Hispanic populations. The candidates could not dodge the importance of the Hispanic vote any longer. The recognition of this was reflected in their campaign staffing.

Candidate Alan Cranston, Senate Minority Whip, named Sergio Bendixen, a native of Peru, as his national campaign manager. Richard Vásquez coordinated the strategically important Western states for the senator. Cranston's campaign—endorsed by Congressmen Edward Roybal, Esteban Torres, and Matthew Martínez, and labor leader César Chávez—was oriented toward a Mexican American constituency. In contrast, Reubin Askew, former Florida governor, addressed the international concerns of Cuban Americans and took credit for being intimately involved (1971-78) with the emergence of the Hispanic community in Florida. Ohio Senator John Glenn named a large number of Hispanics to his advisory committee, according to Raquel Frankel, coordinator of Hispanic affairs. Beverly Vigil Ellerman, a Mexican American spokeswoman for Senator Gary Hart, said, "We will not have a 'Viva Hart' group isolated from the body of the campaign. We will be sliding people into all organizational phases of the campaign."

South Carolina Senator Ernest Hollings held off emphasizing Hispanic interests until his campaign reached Texas, California, and the other southwestern states. Spokesman Mike Fernández pointed out that Hollings "has in many respects been their champion." Similarly, Bill Calderón, former Vice President Walter Mondale's spokesman, drew attention to Mondale's sponsorship of the Voter Registration Act when he was in the Senate.

Prior to 1984, the national parties had relinquished directing voter registration. Now, they had to compete for a declining proportion of people who voted.

In each successive presidential election since the turn of the century, voters had demographically become better off and better educated. Non-voters were poorer and less well educated. The United States gained the dubious distinction as the only major democratic nation where the less well off were substantially underrepresented in the electorate. As people became better off, the voter base contracted. By 1983, according to a Harvard/Gary Ackerman survey, the United States ranked twenty-third among twenty-four democratic nations in the percentage of voter turnout.

An uncertain business climate in the 1960s had emphasized government as the mechanism to stabilize American commercial interests. By the time of Reagan's election in 1980, the Republican Party pressed an agenda capitalizing on discontent over Carter's economic policies. Reagan transformed the popular discontent into an economic ideology.

Significantly, Reagan had won in 1980 not because more people voted for him, but because more people did not vote. Fifty-two percent of those who went to the polls voted for Reagan, 38 percent for Carter, and most of the balance for Independent John Anderson. However, surveys showed that non-voters leaned in Carter's favor by 51 percent. Reagan's popular vote margin, the finding suggested, was made possible when prospective Carter voters failed to turn out at the polls.

Additionally, in 1980, 39 to 40 percent of the American electorate was unregistered, or more than 60 million out of an eligible voting-age population of 159 million. Clearly, it was necessary to register this group in order to avoid greater political aberrations. Otherwise, a smaller electorate (those who actually showed up at the polls), and a smaller range of interests, would decide national elections. Studies showed consistently that two out of three of those people who were not registered to vote resided in households with below median incomes. When these individuals registered, 80 percent of them voted.

As the 1984 election neared, Colorado state senator Polly Baca Barragán, representing the Democratic National Committee, expressed pride in how Hispanics were included in all major areas now, with broad-based registration as an integral part of the party's strategy. Bill Greener, of the Republican National Committee, was more blunt: "We're not—no party is—in a position to ignore the political involvement of Hispanic Americans." He added, "Hispanic Americans themselves realize that their community can't be taken for granted. Otherwise people like Toney Anaya wouldn't be working so hard to get the Hispanic vote out." He was referring to Hispanic Force '84, the voter registration campaign organized in San Antonio. "Hispanic leaders have said that the Hispanic vote is up for grabs and that is true." Who would get registration cards into Hispanic hands was up for grabs, too.

New Mexico Governor Toney Anaya, chief spokesman for Hispanic Force '84 was trying to build a base for a vice presidential run or positioning for a cabinet appointment. He had campaigned for Harold Washington in Chicago and had made numerous campaign sorties to assist Democrats and Hispanic candidates. He was credited with delicately guiding a budget through the Republican-dominated New Mexico legislature while avoiding a financial crisis arising from the recession. As his popularity increased outside the state, he became conversely unpopular at home. Bumper strips began appearing: "Call home, Toney!" and "Does Toney Annoya?" His education program was defeated in the legislature and budget cuts meant a resounding rejection of Anaya's priorities. He was late to endorse Walter Mondale, and—even with that—Mondale lost the June New Mexico primary to Gary Hart. By the time of the Democratic National Convention the following month, Governor Anaya was out of vice presidential consideration.

San Antonio mayor Henry Cisneros made Mondale's "short list" of vice presidential possibilities, along with New York Congresswoman Geraldine Ferraro, San Francisco Mayor Diane Feinstein, and Massachusetts Governor Michael Dukakis. Mondale was indecisive, and seemed to lack criteria for selecting his running mate. Polls showed that a woman candidate on the ticket had an inconclusive and contradictory impact. Dukakis was the safe, back-up choice.

Henry Cisneros, the other choice, had emerged in politics from under the tutelage of his uncle, civic leader Rubén Munguía. Cisneros, elected to the city council in 1975, six years later was voted San Antonio's mayor. He rejected welfare approaches to social problems and ushered in a new style of local politics by making "high tech" education a priority, connecting with Austin (forming the "silicon gulch"), and attracting business to the depressed west side (Levi Strauss, Sprague Electric, Control Data). He supported the sale of bonds to raise money for drainage, street improvements, protective services, and participated in highly visible mediations between disputing groups.

Cisneros enjoyed AFL-CIO leader Lane Kirkland's support and became Mondale's wild-card alternative. While he didn't have extensive political experience, he could attract a large, new constituency. Mondale was, by now, far behind in the polls. Cisneros was the long shot. Maybe he could shake up normal election patterns. The Democrats didn't have a compelling program to present. Mondale was certainly aware of the substantial voter registration gains in California, Texas, New York, Illinois, and Ohio. To win, the party needed to enlarge the electoral base. But Mondale decided on Geraldine Ferraro.

Cisneros had his hands full at the Convention. The Simpson-Mazzoli bill on immigration reform had passed the Senate and had gone to the House in the spring. Rep. Edward Roybal (D-Calif.) led the opposition, but the measure passed the House by five votes in June. The Democratic National Convention intervened before the bill went to House-Senate conference. The Hispanic delegation, numbering 343 out of the 3,931 convention delegates, threatened to boycott the first ballot unless Mondale and the party took a firmer stand against the bill. Finally, Cisneros stepped in and succeeded in getting Mondale to use his influence among Democrats in Congress to kill the bill.

After Mondale's name was put in nomination for president, Cisneros delivered a seconding speech. Governor Toney Anaya delivered the seconding speech for Geraldine Ferraro when her name was put in nomination as the vice presidential choice.

The Democrats' response to grievances and criticism registered, but President Reagan's incumbency and outreach to Hispanic groups was a counterweight. The election was boiling down to the numbers.

10

The Deciding Factor

I n 1984, Governor Toney Anaya of New Mexico ordered state agencies (including welfare offices) to provide voter-registration services. Many Republicans, Democrats, editorialists and cartoonists characterized the action as a ploy to register poor Hispanics. New Mexico's attorney general believed that the governor's order violated the state constitution. The controversy continued unabated until Anaya rescinded the order. Yet, Anaya's action sparked a movement.

Governor Mario Cuomo of New York issued a similar order. In response, the state Republican Party claimed that the Governor had invaded the legislature's constitutional power over voter registration. That led a state court to issue a restraining order. Later, an appeal court found that Governor Cuomo had acted properly. Even then, state employees were restricted from asking citizens to register, answering questions, or help filling out the forms. State agencies could only make forms available in waiting rooms. However, the court decision wasn't rendered until after the 1984 election.

A similar suit was filed to reverse Governor Richard F. Celeste's executive order in Ohio. There, a judge—noting the disturbing discrepancy between the number of people eligible to vote but not registered—ruled the governor had acted within his powers and duties.

Later, Texas governor Mark White issued a similar executive order. The director of the Texas Employment Commission balked and filed a complaint with the U.S. Department of Labor, asking whether state personnel—partly paid with federal funds—should distribute voter registration forms. A Labor Department official answered that the procedure was improper, and a letter went out instructing all state employment directors to refrain from distributing these forms. The federal agency, however, had no objection to *the placement of registration forms on tables* in office waiting rooms. This way, federal funds only paid for the rented space directly below the table.

The Labor Department objected, however, when personnel asked or answered voter-registration questions. A distinction was made between "passive" and "staff-active" approaches: Passive—Yes. Active—No. But the issue did not end there.

Donald Devine, director of the Office of Personnel Management, implied in a letter to governors Cuomo, Celeste, and White that state personnel were being forced to influence people to register as Democrats. If true, this was a violation of the Intergovernmental Personnel Act (the Hatch Act) that prohibited state employees who administered federal funds from interfering or affecting the results of an election. The letter wanted the governors to turn over all voter-registration materials used in federal programs and suggested that their grants were in jeopardy if they didn't comply. Florida officials, fearing federal reprisals, did not implement a voter registration program authorized by the legislature.

Governor Celeste called the letter "blackmail." Governor Cuomo said Devine was attempting to curtail access to the ballot box. Governor White convened a news conference at a state agency waiting room, passed out voter registration cards, and announced he was beginning a campaign to implement his executive order at all state agencies. The governors pointed out that it was impossible for state employees to engage in partisan activities. Registration in Texas and Ohio was not by party, and the New York program was not "staff active."

Within days after the letter was made public, the Republican U.S. Senate approved a "sense of Congress" resolution encouraging voter registration drives by all levels of government. There was no violation of the Intergovernment Personnel Act, provided state governments conducted the drives on a non-partisan basis. Republican senators specifically tried to deflect criticism that their party discouraged registration. Hearings by an indignant House Subcommittee on Government Operations bluntly concluded that Devine had selectively applied federal legislation and misused it for partisan purposes to "intimidate" the three Democratic governors "from continuing voter registration during the critical two weeks before the books closed for the presidential election."

The defiant governors in New York, Ohio, and Texas ordered "passive" registration but continued their registration programs. In New York, the court injunction was lifted for two weeks in September, and registration information was made available at employment offices. When the New York courts finally approved the executive order in 1985, long after the election, Governor Cuomo implemented the program in nine agencies, with 389 local offices in fifty-six counties: 41,533 forms were completed (over half in employment offices) in the first six months. Eight additional agencies with seventy-seven local offices were added. The Governor reported in 1987 that state agencies had facilitated the registration of up to 150,000 voters.

During August and September, two months before the 1984 election, Ohio registration forms were distributed through state liquor stores, lottery outlets, and unemployment offices: 59,000 forms were completed and returned to the secretary of state. In Texas, the 450 Department of Human Services branch offices were sent a desktop box of voter-registration forms before the 1984 election. A flier was mailed to welfare, Medicaid, and food stamp recipients urging them to register. However, the mailing did not inform them that registration forms were available at local welfare offices.

The drive to register voters that raged between 1980 and 1984 expanded the electorate to unprecedented numbers. The drive proved that large masses of people would register when customary approaches were supplemented with serious outreach to the public.

The recession of 1981-1982 stimulated new potential voter participation. Marginal populations, affected by job loss during the economic downturn, had some of the highest unemployment figures since the Depression. Registration drives mainly targeted them. The mid-term election turn outs increased the electorate for the first time in two decades to 64 million, 10 percent greater than the last mid-term election in 1978. The *Congressional Quarterly* wondered editorially whether the "have-nots" vote would carry over into the presidential election of 1984: "Both parties are making plans for 1984 on the assumption that it is here to stay." Heavy voting was expected among the so-called "marginal groups"—minorities, the poor, women, and the Christian Right. The Democratic Party expected a windfall benefit from 5.4 million unemployed, 12.5 million blue-collar workers of all races, 7.2 million blacks, and 2.5 million unregistered Hispanics. Except for fundamentalist Christians, the Republicans appeared to lack a natural new constituency. The national Republican Party was largely left out but finally joined the competition for new voters as the presidential election drew near.

The prospect that as many as 10 million new voters would go to the polls in 1984 jolted the Republican Party out of complacency. Columnist James Reston wrote that Reagan was in the process of scaring dropouts and other voters into registering. Similarly newspaperman James Kilpatrick commented that Republicans were facing a possible defeat if they did not get on the stick: "A Republican registration drive must concentrate on middle-income whites and Hispanics, conservative women and young people, and non-union families."[1]

Meanwhile, the Democratic National Committee issued press releases announcing registration campaigns that never materialized. The party depleted available funds during the primary campaigns. By the time Walter Mondale was nominated, a 250-page study urged him to focus a large part of the election campaign on the white working class and minorities. Mondale's own field director Mike Ford urged "high risk strategies," and allocating $12 million dollars to register 5 to 6 million new voters. But the DNC and the Mondale campaign decided to distribute only $2 million dollars to state and local parties for getting out voters already registered.

Reagan-Bush campaign officials estimated that, if the race was close, they would need 2 million new Republican voters to offset the Democratic registration gains. In January, 1984, the Republicans announced a campaign drive alternately described as costing from $10 to $25 million dollars. The Republicans were obviously inexperienced at going deep into the population for registrations. Telephone surveys showed that only 10 to 18 percent of unregistered voters supported Reagan. By setting up folding tables in shopping malls in the traditional way, Republicans inadvertently registered Democrats. Pollster Lance Terrance estimated that for every new registered Republican, the Democrats picked-up two. The losses, however, were short-lived.

Republican organizers re-conceptualized voter registration and created political productivity for their population segment. They bought computer data tapes from the Census Bureau, credit bureaus, motor vehicle bureaus, financial magazines, up-scale mail order houses, and public registers. Analysts pinpointed unregistered affluent people by neighborhood from a merged master list. Telephone banks contacted individuals. If the prospect agreed that Reagan was doing a good job, a canvasser was sent around or a registration card was mailed.

By August, 1984, an army of 55,000 volunteers made 2.5 million telephone contacts at a cost of about $5 to $7 dollars per registrant. Although twenty-five states were designated, the registration campaign focussed massive efforts in Texas, California, Florida, and Illinois. The Republican party's Hispanic National Assembly, working under the project name "Viva '84," was enlisted

---

1. Frances Fox Pivens and Richard A. Cloward, *Why Americans Don't Vote* (Pantheon Books, 1988), pp. 185-186.

to offset the Democratic gains made in the southwest and Florida.

The Republican Latino strategy, riding the coattails of an incumbent president running for reelection, made steady gains going into the 1984 election. The Mondale campaign blundered by not initiating a voter-registration drive for new voters on the same scale as the Republicans. "Ironically," noted two leading academics on voter registration, "one party [Republicans] galvanized itself to cancel out an electoral mobilization that the other party [Democrats] never attempted."

Even though voter registration campaigns were going well, "This year is not the real measuring stick of the Hispanic voting potential," confided Julio Barreto, LULAC's legislative aid in Washington. The Southwest Voter Registration Education Project estimated that one million Latinos had been added to the voter rolls since 1982. Drives in California, Florida, the Midwest and Northeast added another one million registrants. The number of new voters was not expected to crest for several more years.

Meanwhile, Joe Rodgers, finance chairman for the Reagan-Bush '84 Committee announced the formation of Leadership '84 to raise funds to distribute among targeted groups. Part of the strategy was to center on conservative Cuban and Mexican American businesspeople and to make forays into the northeastern Puerto Rican population.

Republicans were differentiating among Hispanic groups. "The difference in views between Cubans, Mexican Americans and Puerto Ricans," said Bill Greener, Republican director of communications, "is considerable. We know we enjoy strength among Cubans and some Mexican Americans, but we want to reinforce it. In the Puerto Rican community, particularly in the Northeast . . . . We're not as strong as we'd like to be. We're going where the opportunity is to make inroads." The Republicans had more to gain than to lose. The 1984 goal was to make Hispanic gains, not necessarily to win a majority. Greener estimated they could get 30 percent of the Latino vote and build a base for the future. Democrats, by contrast, "naturally have more to lose than Republicans," said Barreto. The tendency to take Latinos for granted "is leaving us frustrated and angry." *Nuestro* magazine, encapsulated each party's faults: "GOP [past] indifference is matched by the Democratic [present] tendency to take them for granted."[2]

Overall recognition and responsiveness to Hispanic concerns was improving. An index, devised by Congressional Education Associates, showed

2. Patrick Caffery, "Courting the Latino Vote," *Nuestro* (September, 1984), p. 16.

that senators voted the "right" way with Hispanic interests 50 percent of the time. The average score was not significantly higher for senators from states with large Hispanic populations. The House rated 70.6 percent, and the vote was significantly higher among representatives from districts with 20 percent or more Hispanics. Democrats in both chambers scored better than Republicans.

The Simpson-Mazzoli bill, requiring all employers to document the citizenship of their employees, was a case in point. The Republican Senate twice passed the immigration reform bill over almost unanimous Latino pressure group opposition. In the House of Representatives, Speaker Tip O'Neill prevented passage, even though the leadership was unable to constrain 125 Democrats from voting for it.

Republicans captured a substantial percentage of the Hispanic vote in the 1984 presidential election. The exact number was hotly disputed between Republicans and Democrats. Regardless of the estimates—running between 33 percent and 47 percent—President Reagan won with an unprecedented high approval level from Hispanics. A landmark Republican opening was clearly made into Democratic territory.

About 5.4 million new voters—of both parties— participated in the slam-dunk election won by Reagan. When all voters were accounted for, the electorate was expanded by 2.5 percent between 1980 and 1984. Hispanic Americans increased 3.8 percent above the national rate. In spite of the large gain, the actual number turning out at the polls to vote increased by 0.7 percent (1984 over 1980). Hispanic turnouts increased 2.7 percent, significantly above the national norm. In Los Angeles County, 75 percent of new registrants voted (80 percent of the Republicans compared to 69 percent of the Democrats).

The 1984 campaign, in spite of the major gains, only reached the tip of the iceberg. Most registration campaigns began late. Resistance, especially to the new methods, had been considerable. After the election, the Reagan administration retreated altogether from the new-voter registration methods. Ten months after the election, an administration report concluded that personnel were not misused by the states when they were used to encourage voter registration. The announcement, coming as late as it did, suggested that the earlier ploy had been mainly intended to deter the registration of Democrats. In response to these shenanigans, the Senate refused to reconfirm Donald Devine as Office of Personnel Management director, partly due to his letter to the governors discouraging registration of new voters.

Latino state and local activism was running high before the 1984 election. Carlos Lucero challenged Lt. Governor Nancy Dick in the Colorado primary. In Florida, Evilo Estrella and Ricardo Núñez entered the Republican primary to challenge veteran Democratic Congressman Claude Pepper in the general election. In Illinois, Democrat Joe Gómez lost in the spring primary to incumbent Rep. Cardiss Collins; Chicago Hispanic Democrats planned to find a Latino opponent to Mayor Washington in 1987. In New Mexico, Albuquerque city councilman Patrick Baca prepared to run in the following year's mayor's race. The New York state legislature gained three new Latino elected officials; a heated Democratic campaign developed in the Seventh Congressional district between Caroline Savine-Rivas and Rep. Gary Ackerman; Rafael Espara challenged incumbent Rep. Edolophus Towns in the Eleventh district; and in Rochester's Twenty-ninth district, Democrat Keith Pérez ran against Republican Frank Horton. In Texas, San Antonio county official Alberto Bustamante defeated incumbent congressman Abraham Kazan.

The campaigns made a statistical difference. In 1973, the southwestern states (Arizona, California, Colorado, New Mexico, and Texas), plus New York, counted 1,280 Hispanic elected office-holders. By 1985, the number was 2,859, a 123 percent increase in twelve years. No state, except New Mexico, increased less than 100 percent. Even there, New Mexico showed an impressive 60 percent increase. The gains in New Mexico (a small state, with 219 additional elected officials) accounted for almost as many gains as California (a mega-state, with 235). Texas, alone, added 910 elected officials, and made up 58 percent of the total gain in the twelve years.

With all states considered, the U.S. had 3,202 Hispanic elected officials (91 percent in the southwestern states) by 1985. Ten new seats were gained, or 115, in the state legislatures from 1983. Texas and California each had three Mexican American state senators; however, the Texas senate (thirty-one) was smaller than the California senate (forty), thereby giving Mexican-American Texans greater representation. In the lower house, both in proportions and numbers, the Texas legislature (with twenty out of 150) more fairly represented the Hispanic population than the California assembly (four out of eighty).

Seventy percent of the 3,202 Hispanic elected officials were either city and municipal officials (1,041, or 32 percent) or school board members (2,212, 38 percent). Eight Hispanics mayors were elected to mainland cities of more than 30,000 people.

One of those big city mayors was Federico Peña of Denver, Colorado.

Formerly the state legislature's minority leader, in 1981 he was rated one of the state's top ten legislators by the *Denver Post*. When Peña challenged Denver Mayor Bill McNichol, he had to overcome a low 3 percent name recognition rating. To do so, an army of 3,000 volunteers was organized under the campaign slogan "Imagine A Great City." Governors Bruce Babbit, Toney Anaya and Mayor Henry Cisneros campaigned for him. At the last minute, the local Spanish-language radio station endorsed Dale Tooley, Peña's chief opponent. Still, Peña won, but faced a run-off. In the final three days before the run-off, the Southwest Voter Registration Education Project concentrated on the populations most likely to vote for him—Hispanics, women, union members, environmentalists, businessmen, and minorities. Six thousand new voters turned out, and Peña won.

One hundred days into the new city administration, the *Denver Post* praised Peña for proceeding slowly and cautiously. A year later, the newspaper reported that the thirty-seven year-old mayor had a 61 percent voter approval.[3]

Governor Toney Anaya's voter-registration efforts in New Mexico may have been aborted, but the drive became a national movement. Its net effect helped diminish a stereotype that typified Hispanic *individual* ineptitude. A new image arose: a responsible *public* needed the vote as a way out of government dependence. Hispanics started to gain control over the vote, the instrument that defines the relationship between people and government. While Reaganites talked about taking the economic burden off people's backs, they didn't know that for Hispanics this was not an ideological issue. *The concern was over whether they participated in the decision and were in a position to do something about the consequences.* "Reagan almost destroyed the Republican Party's relationship with Mexican Americans and Hispanics," said political scientist Richard Santillán. The distance between polemics and progress increased during the Reagan years. "Reagan had a chance but he blew it."

The idea was sinking in that people could look less to Washington for policy responses. Yet, state and local representation only made sense if elected officials were responsive to them. An attitude of less ideology and more reality was taking hold as the number of Hispanic elected officials increased. For people seeking solutions, The issue was to either register large numbers

3. Maurilio E. Vigil, *Hispanics in American Politics The Search for Political Power* (Lanham, Maryland: University Press of America, 1987), pp. 98-101.

and get them to vote, or become part of the problem by passively letting others do the decision-making for them.

In 1987, New York Governor Mario Cuomo announced his intention to send voter registration forms routinely through state agency mailings, such as motor vehicle registration and tax forms. After the 1984 presidential election, Idaho governor Evans, Vermont's Kunin and Oklahoma's Bellmon issued executive orders to this effect. Washington and Maryland followed, allowing registration through motor vehicle and human services agencies. Similar methods for agency-based registration were introduced in the California, Texas, Illinois, Nevada, New Jersey, Arkansas, Connecticut, Massachusetts, and Pennsylvania legislatures. In May, 1987, Minnesota required non-profit corporations that contracted with the state to participate in voter registration. The legislation specifically required Community Action Program agencies, prohibited by federal law from registering voters, to provide registration services.

An order from Chicago Mayor Harold Washington took effect two weeks before the 1986 mayoral primary. Roughly a thousand registrations per day resulted. In February, 1987, Los Angeles Mayor Tom Bradley formed a City Voter Assistance Program and made voter registration cards available in 350 locations through fifty city departments.

By August, 1987, San Antonio's ten city departments made fifty locations available. In Houston, 9,000 forms were distributed through city health clinics and courts during the first six weeks of summer, 1987. Then the program was extended through the hospital district. Similarly, the city of Austin, Texas, distributed voter registration forms through libraries, utility company offices, and neighborhood recreation centers. New York City mayor Edward Koch, who won reelection in 1985 with strong Puerto Rican and African American support, ordered many of the city agencies, including the Welfare Department to train 800 city employees in twenty-six departments to distribute voter registration forms and assist in their completion. New York senators Daniel Patrick Moynihan and Alfonse D'Amato supported Koch by mailing out post-paid registration forms (with a copy of the U.S. Constitution) to 2 million unregistered New Yorkers. Other registration activities took place in thirty-three Alabama towns, in New Jersey (Trenton, Jersey City, Newark), San Francisco, and Minneapolis.

In Los Angeles, county supervisor Edmund Edelman proposed that county election officials work with departments to develop a voter-registration program. The motion's defeat caused a major precedent-setting suit against the county. Human SERVE, American Civil Liberties Union,

Common Cause, Southwest Voter Registration Education, and the Southern Christian Leadership Conference charged that Los Angeles county was failing to carry out the California Election Code. In July, 1986, a Los Angeles superior court issued a preliminary injunction ordering the county to instruct 26,000 health and welfare workers to begin soliciting voter registrations. In reaction, the three Republican members of the five-member Board of Supervisors voted to appeal the decision, but the three-judge appeals court upheld the lower court order, and the board of supervisors voted to appeal once again.

In Congress, Senators Alan Cranston (D-Calif.) and John Conyers (D-Mich.) drafted legislation to allow same-day voter registration in federal elections, state mail-in registration, and to require federal agencies and federally-assisted agencies (state, local, and voluntary), to provide registration services. Elected officials, public administration groups, and the League of United Latin American Citizens adopted supporting resolutions. In 1987, even the Democratic National Committee's voting task force recognized the obvious: voter turnouts dramatically increased when state and local governments actively promoted voter registration.

Two years after Ronald Reagan's reelection in October, 1986, Congress finally agreed on an immigration reform bill. This landmark event, by making many persons eligible for amnesty would serve to extend the franchise to millions of new voters in future years. However, getting to this juncture had been nothing less than formidable. According to the *U.S. News & World Report*, similar legislation had been deadlocked for five years "by the increasingly powerful Hispanic voting bloc."[4] The Simpson-Rodino bill was the first reform in twenty-one years of the nation's immigration policy. It granted amnesty and permanent resident status to millions of qualifying illegal immigrants. Employers who hired undocumented workers were sanctioned with fines and even prison terms. The Justice Department set up an office to investigate employer discrimination of citizens and legal residents. The legislation's provisions had been so hard to work out that, instead of the normally expected jubilation, "the silence was deafening" reported *Newsweek*. No one—supporters or dissidents—was fully happy with the final result.[5]

Employer sanctions were particularly controversial. Union leaders had

4. "The Disappearing Border," *U.S. News & World Report* (August 19, 1985), p. 31.
5. "Trying to Reform the Border," *Newsweek* (October 27, 1986).

long argued that undocumented immigrants took jobs away from citizens. They wanted strong measures against employers who knowingly hired them. Farmers and businessmen opposed employer penalties. They argued that the jobs lost to undocumented workers were those that Americans wouldn't take. For instance, Southern Californians could meet less than half of the expected labor needs during the decade, despite the heavy influx of Mexican immigrants. Furthermore, the immigrants didn't cost the country anything, they argued.

The brewing issue was whether immigrants—illegal ones in particular—were adding to the nation's poverty roles, the working poor, taking jobs from Americans, and even claiming benefits (welfare assistance, education, health care, and workers compensation), when they were officially uninvited participants in the U.S. economy. Many people believed that all immigrants were essentially taking more than they contributed. The prospect loomed large that society would eventually incorporate them and they would eventually become voters.

Among those countering some popular beliefs was University of Maryland economist Julian Simon, who estimated that illegal immigrants even paid $5 to $10 in taxes for every dollar in government services they took. Heritage Foundation's Stephen Moore estimated that immigrants—legal and illegal—contributed above-average personal energy, intelligence, and ambition to the national balance sheet. "They are an asset," said Moore.

Immigrants from Mexico and Asia formed a "Fourth Wave," a term from an Urban Institute report. The movement was the largest ever to reach American cities, exceeding the impact of the British, Irish and German immigrations of the mid-1800s. The Fourth Wave had transformed most Hispanic communities. Immigrants made up as much as one-third of the total Hispanic population, which was estimated in 1985 at about 18 million and was expected to reach 27 million by the year 2000. The Simpson-Rodino legislation would neither increase nor stem the immigration tide but simply accommodate a mass movement. One of those accommodations was increased poverty.

Supply-side economics cynically posited that the poor needed poverty as an incentive to prompt them to improve their condition and rise up to the middle class. Writer George Gilder claimed that some government welfare programs supported the poor so comfortably that the poor had no incentive to leave government dependence. Economist Robert J. Samuelson constructed a more complex and serious history of poverty in America. The story had good news: according to one poverty specialist, Sheldon Danziger of the University of Wisconsin, the Reagan welfare cuts only raised the poverty rate by less than one percent.

The bad news was that economic growth, in its fifth year since the end of the 1981-1982 recession, would not lift all out of poverty (mainly immigrants and the structurally poor). The economic expansion had been uneven. Parts of the farm belt, the industrial Midwest, and the oil patch were still depressed. "But that caveat," Samuelson continued, "doesn't alter the basic picture of a two-tiered society." The schism between the haves and have-nots was ossifying. "It's hard to read this year's poverty report optimistically," he said. The economic upturn after 1982 "won't turn low skilled workers into engineers or technicians. It won't mend broken families or eradicate crime. Prosperity is not a tonic for every social ill."[6]

Strong economic growth and government payments had progressively reduced poverty in the 1960s. Rising living standards pulled the increasing numbers of the working poor above the poverty level. As government entitlements increased, more people were helped, especially through Social Security checks for the elderly. An explosion of poor unwed mothers in the 1970s led some critics to blame welfare programs for allowing women to survive alone without holding fathers responsible. While the trends were disturbing, the poverty rate declined from 22.4 percent in 1959 to 12.1 percent in 1969. It was 11.7 percent in 1979. But why did it rise to 13.6 percent by 1986? One reason was that national policy retreated from a full-employment goal because of its inflationary influence, and fewer skilled workers were produced. The second reason was that Hispanic poverty increased five times faster than that of the population average.

Hispanics accounted for about a third of the rise in poverty after 1978 and were the natural target of the poverty plague: more immigrants, more young, and more children. "Will the jump of Hispanic poverty simply reflect the normal pattern of poor first-generation immigrants, who will eventually move into the middle class? Or does it signify a permanent expansion of the underclass? We don't know," confessed Samuelson. A number of Hispanic leaders, especially social-welfare advocates who faced severe budget shortages, were quick to join the chorus warning of a developing under-class.

In 1986, the American median family income rose 4.2 percent to $29,458 (after correcting for inflation). The poverty rate was down after

6. Robert J. Samuelson, "Progress and Poverty," *Newsweek* (August 24, 1987), p. 41.

the deep recession of 1981 and 1982, from 15.2 percent in 1983 to 13.6 percent. Still, it was higher than any year since 1967. The statistical picture portrayed a two-tiered society: an affluent and prosperous layer atop a poverty-stricken segment.

The Southwest Voter Registration and Education Project (SVREP)'s Research Institute released a report showing that dramatic numbers of Hispanics descended into poverty during the first half of the 1980s. By 1986, one in four Hispanics was poor. The study revealed that cash-benefit programs had previously helped 13 percent of all poor families in 1979 (the last year of the Carter government). The same programs only helped 8 percent in 1987 (the Reagan government's last year). In 1979, 28 percent of Hispanic children were poor. By 1985, 40 percent were living in poor families—the highest level ever recorded. The median net worth of Anglo households was $39,135, and the Hispanic household was eight times lower, $4,913.

Hispanics were furious. The findings led to a public outcry. Something had to be done about the developing underclass, said Raul Yzaguirre, president of the National Council of La Raza. Republicans were furious—as well—at the Southwest Voter Registration Institute for releasing the report.

They are not any kind of underclass, wrote White House director of public liaison, Linda Chávez, "Their predictions are misleading." After leaving the White House, she pinpointed her objection. Critics had a political agenda and used the "underclass" idea to further it. "The rhetoric of some Hispanic leaders might make you think," she wrote, "that the government must treat low-income Latinos as though they are somehow different from earlier waves of immigrants, that without such federal programs as bilingual education this group will remain stuck on the bottom of the economic ladder." No, she believed, minimal help, if any, was needed.

Behind the debate and wrangling was the very survival of the Hispanic human services industry—built up over twenty years and assisted by advocacy from national organizations, Democratic officials, and federal agencies. Would it survive or get replaced? Linda Chávez represented one way of looking at the numbers.

The median income for Hispanic families in 1984 was $18,833, compared to $26,433 for the general population, she explained. Unemployment among Hispanics was 50 percent higher than for the rest of the population. But advocates made a mistake by lumping everyone together. The picture was less grim when the subgroups making up the Hispanic population were separated—Mexican Americans (60 percent), Puerto Ricans (15 percent),

Cubans (6 percent), and the remaining Central and South Americans and Iberians.

Cubans were only marginally different from the rest of the population. Coming to the U.S. in the 1960s, they were statistically older and less-well educated than the national average, but their children acquired more schooling than native-born, non-Hispanics. While Cubans' education lagged behind the national average, they earned more the longer they lived in the United States, and the income gap became smaller in the second generation.

Puerto Ricans represented the other end of the spectrum. Forty-four percent of families were female-headed; 51 percent of births occurred outside of marriage. Unemployment was double the national rate, and poverty levels were four times greater than the national average.

Mexican American median family income, at $19,184, was somewhere between Cubans ($22,587) and Puerto Ricans ($12,371). Mexican- American female-headed households (19 percent) and births out of wedlock (16 percent) were more like the Cuban pattern than the Puerto Rican pattern. However, Mexican American unemployment (11.9 percent) more closely resembled Puerto Rican unemployment (14.3 percent) than it did Cuban (6.8 percent). In 1985, only in education were Mexican American adults, (with 10.2 years) faring substantially worse than Puerto Ricans (with 11.2 years), and Cubans (with twelve years).

Mexican American differentials were the result of immigration, according to Linda Chávez. From 1881 to 1950, 814,000 Mexicans immigrated to the U.S. In the next twenty-eight years, from 1951 to 1978, 1.26 million Mexican immigrants entered the United States. If illegal immigrants were taken into account, the arriving population might double the official figures. They mainly took low-paying unskilled and semi-skilled urban jobs in the service and construction industries.

Over time, however, earnings disparities narrowed. After about fifteen years, immigrants' earnings surpassed those of U.S.-born Mexican Americans. Immigrants actually leap-frogged over other citizens who had preceded them.

Forty percent of Cuban and Mexican immigrants owned their own homes after nine years of residency and showed clear signs of following earlier immigrant generations: poor in the first generation and middle class in the second. To Linda Chávez, immigrants were highly motivated risk-takers who made profound contributions to national development—all of which went to show that the classic immigration model was unfolding.

But her compelling argument failed to take into account the role played by national economic development: Had not Puerto Ricans (who were U.S. citizens) suffered from being disproportionately concentrated in the industrial northeast, where the economy was anemic compared to that of the Sun Belt? Weren't Southwestern Mexican Americans and Florida Cubans simply luckier than Puerto Ricans by virtue of historical settlement patterns?

Chávez had a case as long as substantial economic development occurred. But what about the large number of second generation Mexican Americans who had become marginal—between poor and middle class, between languages, between educations, and raising the third, and fourth generations? They didn't show signs of middle-class movement. Surely, Chávez realized that 154 years of settlement was enough time to develop a larger middle-class, and time enough to show better results. The indicators of settlement and permanence—businesses, private schools, colleges, hospitals, banks—were not sufficiently evident to leverage better living standards.

Something was very wrong. Mexican Americans and Puerto Ricans were being short-changed if low income and high poverty rates were the price people paid for the rest of the nation's development. Apologists and historical revisionists contributed little to these important public policy issues.

Linda Chávez had found a basic truth and then generalized beyond the data. Her simple answers took the burden off the administration's shoulders, realizing it was hard—very hard—to give anything other than simplistic explanations without inevitably confronting public responsibility for providing aid.[7]

Fernando Oaxaca, the former White House aide to presidents Nixon and Ford, had a similar attitude toward the social service industry. "Where were our compassionate activists who scream about the exploitation and 'slave labor' implications of Mr. Reagan's Mexican guest worker program when tens of thousands of Latinos were shoved into these job-training, frustrating and mindless tasks created by Department of Labor bureaucrats and some of their own 'manpower training experts?'" he wanted to know: "Have any of them gone into a furniture store in East Los Angeles and tried to buy something on credit and given CETA [Concentrated Education Training Act program] as a job reference and been laughed out of the store?" The program "will not be missed, either by the taxpayer or most of those who were being helped."

---

7. Linda Chavez, "Hispanics: Just Another Immigrant Story?" *Fortune* (November 21, 1988), p. 188.

According to his math, Oaxaca figured that at most the federal government provided about $125 per Latino child needing bilingual instruction. Even under the best of circumstances, the funding was inadequate, but more importantly, the funding was intended for research and development, he claimed. "It is only the 'bilingual experts' who converted it into an alleged 'standard' piece of federal aid to Latino education, and, of course, an insurance policy for their jobs." A 25 percent cut in the program would not make any difference one way or another. Nor would the cut in the food stamp program from $11 billion to $9 billion infuriate "the Latino blue collar worker making $250 a week as a machinist's helper. Will he be upset because his nonworking brothers, or those others who have found the food stamp line at the post office may have been cut back a bit? Not likely!"

To Oaxaca, the heart of the matter was the supporting role of government programs that Latino organizations played. "It may come as a shock to our national leadership who purports to be close to `our people in the barrio,'" said Oaxaca, "but we have millions of Latinos who really don't care to give away their very hard earned bucks to Uncle Sam for his unthinking and uncontrolled redistributions!" Budget cuts brought the debate out in the open. There was no debate, however, over the fact that the federal government was withdrawing from social responsibility. The focus moved to the state and local level.

11

The Countryside Paints Itself

T o control excessive spending in the future, Congress passed the 1985 Balanced Budget and Emergency Deficit Reduction Act (better known as "Gramm-Rudman"). The measure would pull a widely feared budget-cutting "trigger" mechanism if Congress and the President could not agree on a balanced budget (that did not exceed deficits of $171 billion in 1986, $144 billion in 1987, $108 billion in 1988, $36 billion in 1990, and a zero deficit in 1991).

Domestic and defense spending would get equal cuts. The measure spared Social Security, interest on the national debt, Aid to Families of Dependent Children, Social Security Supplemental Income, Food Stamps, and child-nutrition programs.

Later, a federal court case overruled automatic cuts: only Congress, the court said, could decide on the budget. Congress was required to come up with budget cuts, if that's what it wanted. Robert Greenfield of the Center for Budget and Policy Priorities believed social programs were the most vulnerable: "Gramm-Rudman without automatic cuts is more dangerous than Gramm-Ruddman with the automatic cuts," he said. "There are programs, including jobs programs, that are not exempt."

Research commissioned by the Villers Foundation, a public policy organization, joined by the Service Employees International Union and the National Council of Senior Citizens, analyzed Gramm-Rudman's possible impact and showed that a wide variety of federal funds to the states would get cut more than $10 billion by 1987. California and New York would lose $1 billion dollars in funding. Texas, Pennsylvania, Illinois, and Ohio would each lose at least $500 million. Economic development and job training programs administered locally would be particularly hard hit.

Raúl Yzaguirre, president of the National Council of La Raza, caught on to the reality: It seemed to him that "Republicans, Democrats, liberals and conservatives have come to a basic agreement that we have a tremendous deficit and something should be done about it." This was no longer a political observation but a financial imperative.

Although its policies had added stupendously to the debt, the Reagan administration had also molded the mindset that fiscal responsibility was called for. That was the obsession going into the next presidential election.

Encouraged by Reagan's 1984 success, the Republican National Committee launched a nine-state bilingual advertising campaign, called Project Adelante! It encouraged Hispanics to vote Republican in the 1986 mid-term elections. The radio, television, print, and direct-mail campaign emphasized that Hispanics, who had previously voted Democratic, were going to switch.

"They had the Hispanic vote so many years," said media consultant John Ramsey, speaking about Democrats, that "they came to expect it. But Republicans knew that to win they needed the Hispanic vote, and showed they cared." The Democrats did not run a similar effort in 1984 or 1986 and were caught asleep at the throttle. "Democrats are looking for a silver lining if they believe that when Ronald Reagan is no longer president, Hispanic voters will go back to them," said RNC's Terry Wade. "It doesn't mean they're guaranteed to us—that's why we're working so hard to stay identified with the things Ronald Reagan represents to these voters."

A *New York Times*/CBS poll taken in November 1986 showed that 27 percent of Hispanics were Republican, or leaned that way, while 58 percent identified with the Democratic party. Surprisingly, only half of the persons polled were registered to vote. More surprisingly, those who favored Reagan and Republicans were much less likely to be registered. Anecdotal information suggested that a shift, albeit a small one, was underway. "There's a strong conservative streak, particularly related to the family, in Hispanic culture," said Armando Triana, director of DePaul University's Center for Research on Hispanics, "which goes along with the values of the Republican Party."

"The Hispanic community tends to be conservative in values," said Salvador Gómez, a campaign aide to Senator Bob Dole. "But of the many things the Republican Party espouses that are important to Hispanics," the most important value, he said, "is that the American dream is still alive. The Republican party represents opportunity, ownership. "He was giving a political spin to a census report showing that Hispanics owned 400,000 businesses by 1986 compared with 100,000 in 1960.

Nonsense, thought Polly Baca Barragán, Colorado legislator and Democratic National Committee vice-chairperson. Republican inroads were mainly into the ranks of wealthy Hispanic businessmen and Cuban Americans responding to Reagan's anti-communist pronouncements. "As for the family issue," she said, "Democrats are far more family-oriented, support more pro-family policies than the Republicans." Furthermore, the Democrats did not run advertising campaigns similar to the Republicans in 1984 and 1986 "because we don't have that kind of money," she said. In fact, Democrats pinned their hopes on a public record that spoke for itself, and not on advertising.

The Hispanic population's Democratic leanings showed that ten out of the eleven representatives in Congress were Democrats, as were 90 percent of all Hispanic elected officials. Despite this, said DNC spokesman Terry Michael, "they're not a special interest group to be picked off by ringing special bells. We think they respond to the same common-interest themes that cut across ethnic and other differences."

That Vice President George Bush was running for the Republican presidential nomination was evident in the last half of the administration's second term. Senator Robert Dole also sought the nomination. Salvador Gómez, Dole's campaign co-chairperson, wanted to capitalize on the inroads that he thought Reagan had made into the Hispanic community, which he characterized as "a major political transition in the Hispanic community."

Dole's plans seemed to advance when *Al Shiraa*, a Lebanese magazine, reported that the United States had engaged in some irregular arms dealings. After the story appeared in U.S. newspapers, Attorney General Edwin Meese conducted an investigation into the matter. He disclosed in November, 1986, that millions of dollars from Iranian arms sales had been secretly channeled to the Nicaraguan Contras in 1985 and 1986 in an apparent violation of the Boland Amendment, legislation that banned all U.S. aid to the Contras.

The Attorney General said that Lt. Col. Oliver North, an aide to national security advisor John Poindexter, acting on his own authority, was responsible. North was fired the next day, and Poindexter resigned. On television, Senator Robert Dole indirectly criticized Reagan, who claimed to have no knowledge about the deal. Days later, Dole called for a special session of Congress during the Christmas recess, but Reagan and most senators opposed the idea.

Republicans preferred Bush 40 percent to 50 percent in September, just before the exposé, and Dole by only 10 percent. Dole barely rated in opinion polls before the "Irangate" scandal, as it was called, at first. But Bush's popularity plummeted after "Iranscam" (as it was then called). While the President possibly did know about the complex operation, Bush explained he was at an Army-Navy football game during a White House meeting when the Iran-Contra plan unfolded.

Dole's popularity increased, and by January, 1987, 30 percent of Republicans preferred him for the presidential nomination. He was making mincemeat of Bush, aided by the press's relentless "wimp" characterization of the Vice President. Later, a House and Senate joint select committee, followed by the President's Special Review Board (the Tower Commission), exonerated Reagan and Bush. The issue died down for a while but resurfaced when North and Poindexter faced criminal charges in federal court.

Out of the investigation limelight, Robert Dole campaigned in Iowa, New Hampshire and other primary states, saying he was running "on a record" and Bush on "a resume," believing that Bush would stumble during the investigations. But Bush prevailed and continued collecting endorsements and campaign contributions.

By fall of 1987, Dole desperately needed the conservative vote, and he made appeals to it, saying, "Central America wouldn't mind a three-day invasion of Nicaragua," about the off-again-on-again tensions there. When he had announced his candidacy in November, Dole had said, "Someone must make the hard choices," implying that austerity was needed to trim the budget. The deficit had to be reduced or future generations would have the responsibility passed on to them to pay it off. Five days after Dole's announcement, a Florida straw poll gave Bush a stunning 57 percent lead (Bush received 1,322 votes and Dole finished fifth, with only fourteen votes).

In the February, 1988, Iowa Caucus, Dole defeated five Republican rivals with 37 percent of the vote. However, Vice President Bush kept ahead of his rivals in the primaries that followed and ultimately gained the Republican nomination. Jack Kemp withdrew from the running early in March, as did Bob Dole in the closing days of the month. Bush was virtually unopposed in the remaining primaries.

Vice President Bush's campaign began taking heart after a Gallup Poll reported on July 2 that Massachusetts Democratic Governor Michael Dukakis, the Democratic nominee, was ahead by only 5 percent. An ABC/*Money* magazine poll showed a similar decrease in Dukakis' lead that had once been as high as 53 percent to 40 percent. But Dukakis' big lead declined, and

Bush's, whose Republican nomination was virtually assured, began ascending.

On July 6, Bush, speaking to the League of United Latin American Citizens (LULAC) meeting in Dallas, said he was making a "solemn pledge" that "If I become president, my cabinet will be composed of the very best men and women—at least one of whom, finally, will be a Hispanic American. It's time, it's time." His promise was "a pledge that I have never made before to anyone, to any group." A reporter asked later whether he was "pandering" to interest groups in the same way he had criticized the Democrats of doing. "I don't think anybody would make that allegation," replied Bush, "after [such] a long time of no Hispanic ever [having been] appointed." Dukakis, in response, said that Bush was a year behind him in promising Hispanics a cabinet post.

The Labor Department reported during the same week as the Republican National Convention in New Orleans that a record 116.7 million Americans held jobs in June. Unemployment was only 5.2 percent. Reagan received the news with delight and held a special press briefing to announce "more solid evidence that the policies of this administration work, that our philosophy works." Reagan predicted that Republicans would enjoy a "banner year" because more voters were employed. The same employment figures also showed that joblessness among Hispanics remained at 9 percent.

Bush was running 7 to 14 percent behind Dukakis in four major polls when the Republican Convention opened. With his nomination a foregone conclusion, Bush tried to build up suspense about his running mate. Dole and Kemp led last-ditch efforts to receive the vice presidential nod, but Indiana Senator Daniel Quayle was selected instead.

In accepting the party's nomination, Bush said the U.S. was going to create 30 million new jobs in the next eight years, and he was not going to raise taxes. "Thing's aren't perfect in this country," he said. "There are people who haven't tasted the fruits of expansion," but he was going to try for a "new harmony, a greater tolerance." The tone showed how Bush was stretching to capture the loyalty of the American people in an attempt to show Republican politics in a new light, in a different way.

Vice President Bush had his grandchildren in tow when President Reagan departed from the airport the following day after a farewell speech. Reagan, unsure which ones were the Bush's, had them pointed out. Thinking he was out of hearing range from reporters, Bush said, "They're the little brown ones," pointing to them. At a news conference later in the day, reporters asked Bush about characterizing his three grandchildren—children of son Jeb and Mexico-born daughter-in-law Columba—as he did. Visibly disturbed, Bush said the grandchildren are "my pride and joy." His voice taking an uncharacteristically sharp edge, he added, "And when I say pride, I mean it." Then, looking at the reporters right in the eye, he said, "P.S. I don't want to see these kids hurt." The message was clear. The Vice President's family was not to be trifled with. They were not reportorial fodder. The press, in response, gave Bush generally high marks for his words and how he handled the news conference.

The campaign was about pragmatism; it was not about ideologies, declared Governor Dukakis in his acceptance speech to the Democratic National Convention. The election was about who could best handle the nation's challenges. The nation, he said, had become fragmented; "community" needed to be reestablished. He knew about the need to restructure a way of life. After all, he was the son of immigrant parents. All of society's sectors—business and labor, educators, community leaders, and "just plain citizens" could be inspired by the notion of community. That's what guided one man he knew, a man named Willie Velásquez, said Dukakis who "can register thousands of his fellow citizens as voters—*puede inscribir decenas de miles de sus conciudadamos para votar*—and Willie Velásquez can bring new energy and new ideas and new people—*brindando así nuevas energías, nuevas ideas, nuevas personas*—into courthouses and city halls and state capitals of the Southwest—*a los gobiernos municipales y estatales del suroeste*—my friends, we are all enriched and ennobled."

The convention cheered him on.

Wanting to end ideological splits, both Dukakis and George Bush inspired a long, last look at the world before the Reagan administration's divisive policies. They encouraged a fiction, that there had been an ideal earlier time before the discord. While both candidates signaled that Hispanic Americans were a major tributary of the new mainstream, each muddied the waters by reverting to nostalgia. And neither had much new to offer. Perhaps the truth and a source of inspiration existed closer to what Willie Velásquez had been saying and doing all along.

When San Antonio's IMAX theater debuted *The Alamo* in 1988, Willie Velásquez was there to picket. To Mexican Americans, the Alamo, more than any other monument, symbolized a long and dangerous disenfranchisement—underdevelopment, social marginality, the loss of land and liberty, and the beginning of the Texas outcast system. Disguised as history, the movie was pure western-style entertainment and hyperbole, mainly depicting Mexicans killing legendary heroes. The picket line in front of the theater on the 152nd anniversary of the Alamo's fall was supported by the state LULAC chapter, Mexican American Democrats, the American GI Forum, Nosotros—a Los Angeles entertainment industry organization—and the Southwest Voter Registration and Education Project. The film's net effect, said William C. Velásquez, "gets Mexican Americans and Anglos again at each other's throats."

Velásquez, universally know as "Willie," was no stranger to protests and demonstrations. He had participated in the Poor People's March in Washington during the 1960s, and helped organize MAYO, the Raza Unida party, and the Mexican American Unity Council. As a student of political science, he knew the role played by third-party movements. The real goal, he believed, was not to maintain an ethnically separate party but to shake the foundations of the established parties' political consciousness. He left Raza Unida and rejoined the Democratic Party. In the course of his political reevaluation, Velásquez put together a questionnaire that he used to find out what people in Mexican-American barrios and neighborhoods thought—their prevailing opinions and attitudes. He wrote down concerns that people had about drainage, sidewalks, streetlights, parks, crime, education and jobs.

Velásquez, who had lectured at Harvard, spoke with ease the polished language of Washington and Mexico City, the Spanish vernacular of San Antonio's west side, and the dialect used along dusty Texas country roads. "Willie Velásquez' highest calling—and his great passion—is persuading the dispossessed to take political power into their own hands," wrote *Newsweek's* Daniel Pederson. "He does this by talking pavement." Velásquez believed the most important elections were local. "We voted for Roosevelt, Truman, and Kennedy," he said, but "It didn't pave the streets." However, "When we got Mexican-American candidates saying, `Vote for me and I'll pave the streets,' goddamit, that's when the revolution started."

Illiteracy and poverty, he knew, did not keep barrio residents from understanding the problems, issues, and the complex barriers created to keep them from participating in politics. Ignorance did not breed stupidity.

Willie Velásquez formed, and for fourteen years headed, the Southwest Voter Registration and Education Project (SVREP). It served as the wellspring of inspiration for local voter-registration campaigns. He was responsible for more long-term democratic empowerment than any other person in the southwestern states since the annexation of the territories into the union. His national impact was considerable and far more significant than the scant attention he attracted. The key to the organization, he knew, was maintaining locally-based voter registration campaigns with local participation. He developed a voter registration model. Members of civic groups, churches, neighborhood associations, labor groups, and volunteers went door-to-door getting neighbors to register.

Assisted by the Mexican-American Legal Defense and Education Fund, SVREP filed suits charging various governmental jurisdictions with Voting Rights Act violations, or denial of the "one man, one vote" principle. They forced cities, counties, school boards and other elected boards to change from at-large districts to single-member districts. Single-member city council districts, alone, doubled the number of minority representatives in fifty-six Texas cities in the first dozen years after 1974. Velásquez and his organization were party to eighty-two lawsuits. They won all eighty-two.

After 1974, SVREP conducted more than 850 voter-registration drives in 204 communities. In ten years, they helped increase the number of registered Hispanic voters by 79 percent, to 1.7 million in the 1984 presidential election. The number of minority elected officials increased 82 percent during the same decade after 1974.

Their impact changed electoral politics in Texas for all time. April, 1988, for example, marked the third consecutive Democratic presidential primary election in which Mexican Americans in Texas turned out at a higher state-wide rate than did non-Hispanics. Hispanics became recognized for what they had been all along: the fastest growing electorate in the United States. They were growing at a 27 percent faster rate than any other group in the nation. Out of 490,000 public offices elected in the country, Hispanic office-holders doubled to 3,202. Half of those elected were from Texas. As a consequence, a more positive idea about Mexican Americans and Hispanics developed. Image began to correspond more closely with reality.

In his voter registration campaigns, Willie Velásquez' message was simple: "'Register and vote, register and vote, register and vote,'" he would exhort everyone within hearing range. I never heard Willie say just 'register,'" recalled Richard Avena, former southwest director of the U.S. Commission on Civil Rights; "It was always 'register and vote.' I never heard him tell anyone to vote for a Democrat or a Republican, either. Just 'register and vote.'" Willie was tireless in his pursuit of democracy. The dusty little towns of the southwest were not excluded. In fact, they were central to turning it all around. "In my work, I visited communities in Texas and New Mexico," continued Avena. "I remember Pecos, Ft. Stockton, Alpine, Roswell. Every time I would meet with a group of activists, I was always told the same thing: 'Willie was here.' You never asked 'Willie Who?'"

Velásquez and his organization challenged the prevailing assumptions about why Hispanics were politically apathetic and non-participating in many elections. Popular rationalizations ranged from low education to identification south of the border. But Velásquez' showed that the condescending explanations did not hold water. Willie was more to the point: "You don't vote if you can't win," he said.

His approach was magnificently simple. The most important elections to him were local. "If you don't register, you don't win." Southwest Voter had engaged in 958 voter registration campaigns by 1987, and more than a million new Mexican American voters were added to the rolls. It was not easy, nor without resistance: "It's cod liver [oil] for those who have it forced down their throats," said Willie. "It's good medicine, but it tastes like hell."

Austin writer Pedro Ruíz Garza observed that "News coverage of his work . . . was sparse and confined to the back pages. Under-reported was the single-minded determination and the unyielding, uncompromising integrity with which Velásquez changed the political landscape of the Southwest."

He did even more. As Ruíz himself noted, Velásquez understood that democracy is only valid if the governed have a voice in their government. He fomented faith, belief, and trust in a system that had excluded Hispanics for over a century. In a sense, Willie Velásquez took the image of democracy and made it real.

Willie, suffering from kidney cancer, was hospitalized at the Santa Rosa Medical Center in San Antonio when Dukakis mentioned him in his acceptance speech at the Democratic Convention. Willie's friend, Richard Avena was in the room at the time. They reminisced for a while, remembering the time Avena took Homer Bigart of the *New York Times* to the office. Avena tried his hand at translating *De Colores*, the popular movement song of that time. "Of colors, of colors, the countryside paints itself." He and Willie's brother George sang the lyrics alluding to a rainbow-colored sky that spills hope over the land and the people and even the farm animals. The resplendent colors define you and your destiny—like a social karma, like one soul in the company of the spirit of the people, like human will arising like Pegasus. The lyrics, that so impacted and moved common people to action, fell flat. The literal English words failed to carry that transcendental meaning. "Of colors, of colors, the countryside paints itself."

"Yes, it does lose something in translation," said Bigart.

Willie died that week in June of 1988. "*Que bonito es el nuevo mundo*" were his last words. How beautiful is the new world.

San Antonio's mayor Henry Cisneros was with Willie Velásquez in his final hour. "He is as close to irreplaceable as anyone I know," said Cisneros, "yet his work must continue."

Willie was the "single most important political actor since César Chávez," said Rodolfo de la Garza, University of Texas director of Mexican American Studies. "And in terms of representational politics, the most important ever."

Texas Republican governor Bill Clements called Velásquez a statesman and "a strong and effective spokesman."

Willie Velásquez—who had met Michael Dukakis at Harvard in 1981 when both were on the Kennedy School of Government faculty. Willie was on a sabbatical—a time to reflect, think, and write. Dukakis, who had been defeated in the previous Massachusetts gubernatorial election, taught while he pondered his political future.

Dukakis later regained the Massachusetts governorship, and now, as the Democratic candidate, had planned to name Willie his campaign's national co-chairman.

At San Antonio's Church of St. Mary for the funeral mass, Dukakis was somber and low key when he rose to speak. More than a thousand family, friends, and leaders were gathered for the service and eulogy. Ushers wore lapel pins—*Su Voto Es Su Voz*/Your Vote Is Your Voice.

Willie, said Dukakis, was a man "who believed in democracy," and he had "changed the world." Willie Velásquez "loved his country . . . all he asked from it was a fair share of the American dream for himself, and for every American, no matter who they are or where they come from or what color their skin."

In the same week that he died, Willie Velásquez was to have been honored at a meeting of the Mexican American Democrats (MAD), preceding the Texas Democratic Convention. "He's one of the few guys that I've met who were totally committed to the public good without expecting anything in return," said Texas Representative Juan Hinojosa (D-McAllen). Texas Democratic party executive director Ed Martin said officials had expected Willie Velásquez' speech introducing the presidential candidate to the Texas Democratic Convention to have been one of the most emotional moments at the convention, as delegates showed Willie their appreciation for his years of work and service. Willie was to have received one of the few public recognitions ever extended to him. SVREP's work, *Newsweek*'s Daniel Pederson had written the year before, was "almost as unheralded as Velásquez himself."[1] Dukakis said that their task was to continue Willie Velásquez' work to "make democracy come alive."

Five weeks after Willie died, the U.S. 9th Circuit Court ruled, in a case filed by Willie Velásquez' organization against the city of Watsonville (charging that California's at-large election system discriminated against Latinos), that the city had to eliminate the system. The decision set the precedent for similar fights to change election procedures in more than 400 California towns. To press the case in court, the SVREP had expanded into California and conducted dozens of costly voter registration campaigns. U.S. Senator Alan Cranston (D-Calif), after promising to help raise $250,000 for the project, raised only $100,000. Cranston formed his own voter-registration drive, called the Campaign for Participation in Democracy (CPD). He drew financial support away from SVREP. By 1988, CPD had a budget of $3.1 million, while the SVREP had a $350,000 deficit. Tensions and strains characterized the relationship between Cranston and the Latinos who had worked with Velásquez in California.

Cranston called the situation a "misunderstanding" and praised Velásquez as "a great man who I greatly admired." The praise did not change the fact that Cranston's voter registration organization served to undermine SVREP's Latino empowerment mission.

"Although I am a native Californian, said *Los Angeles Times* editorial writer Frank del Olmo, "I have always thought Tejanos were a bit tougher politically, probably because the discrimination they faced in Texas was more overt than in laid-back California." He urged pressure on Cranston to make good on his promise of financial support to SVREP. The editorial sounded right but missed the point: The Texans had become a better model of organization and democratic success. Laid-back California was prone to a sunshine disdain for democratic practices where Latinos were concerned.

Only 300,000 votes separated Bush and Dukakis out of 9.2 million cast in California. When California's forty-seven electoral votes had been critically important to Dukakis, voter registrars set up ironing boards—yes, ironing boards—in front of schools, shopping malls, or on busy street corners to

1. Daniel Pederson, "All Those Guys Owe Willie," *Newsweek* (March 16, 1987).

patrol for unregistered voters. Ironing boards had distinct advantages over folding tables. People did not have to stoop while signing up, and each one held four clipboards at a time. The registrars recruited volunteers at the same time.

Senator Alan Cranston's organization was behind many of the voter registration campaigns. In October of 1985 Cranston, anticipating a difficult re-election campaign, had solicited funds for a voter registration drive. The approach may have been inspired by how Ronald Reagan's supporters had made unlimited donations to Republican-sponsored get-out-the-vote drives after their individual contributions reached the legal campaign limit. The Center for Voter Education, proposed by Cranston, targeted the poor, minority groups, and "total participation." "If that has partisan overtones, if both parties do it, so what?" he said.

His son and campaign manager Kim Cranston contacted Marshall Ganz for help in the senate campaign. After analyzing voter registration data, Ganz—a former organizer for César Chávez and the United Farm Workers—came up with 150 "occasional" voters in each of 1,600 precincts. He hired staff and recruited 3,000 volunteers. By election day, the network produced Cranston's 104,800 winning margin over Republican Ed Zschau, out of 8 million votes cast. Charles H. Keating, chairman of American Continental Corp. of Phoenix, donated $39,000 to the senate campaign and $85,000 to the state Democratic party for a last-minute get-out-the-vote drive.

The experience led Cranston in July, 1987, to form the Center for Participation in Democracy (CPD) as a voter-registration vanguard. Headquartered in Los Angeles, CPD hired ninety-five full-time staff members ($1,500 per month for a twelve-hour, six-day-work week). Kim Cranston served as the organization's secretary-treasurer for a time then became president of another voter-education non-profit organization called the Organizing Institute that Marshall Ganz operated. Kim Cranston claimed CPD registered 350,000 new voters and that the Organizing Institute gave leadership training to 200 young people. Ninety-one percent of the Organizing Institute's funds in the last half of 1987 came from the Forum Institute, a Washington, D.C. organization, whose primary fund-raiser was Senator Cranston.

Cranston solicited $400,000 from Charles Keating for CPD and an additional donation of $450,000 for two other voter-registration non-profit corporations. In response, American Continental Corp., a holding company controlled by Keating, donated $400,000 in February, 1988 to

CPD. Keating, or his affiliates, donated a total of $850,000 in 1987 and 1988 to CPD, USA Votes (a project of New Dimension), and the Forum Institute.

Then in April, 1987, Cranston and two other senators met with federal regulators at Keating's behest, regarding huge losses by Lincoln Savings, owned by Keating's company. A week later, Cranston and four other senators talked with federal regulators at the Federal Home Loan Bank Board's San Francisco office. The senators denied having pressured the regulators to change their minds about certain decisions. But board chairman Edwin Gray said they did. According to Gray, the senators asked him to withdraw a regulation limiting certain risky investments by Lincoln. The senators promised that in turn Keating would make less risky home loans.

"Never, in my presence, was anything like that said," declared Cranston in response to Gray's allegations. In addition to the $850,000 donated to the Cranston voter-registration organizations, Keating and his associates gave $500,000—directly and indirectly—to the other four senators implicated in the influence-peddling scandal.

CPD, formed after Cranston intervened on behalf of Lincoln Savings with U.S. regulators, received contributions totaling $305,414 from the Forum Institute by late 1987. In March and April, 1989 Cranston urged two bank board members to rescind a decision that kept Keating from selling Lincoln Savings after the board found that the prospective buyer did not have enough cash for the transaction.

Lincoln Savings and Loan was seized by Federal Home Loan Bank regulators on April 14, 1989, the day after American Continental Corp. sought Chapter Eleven protection from creditors in federal bankruptcy court. The regulators said that Lincoln Savings was operated unsafely and had dissipated the S&L's $5.3 billion in assets. Losses were posted at $2.5 billion. In May, failing to get a reconsideration, Cranston joined Keating in criticizing regulators for putting Lincoln in receivership.

Other sources disclosed that Cranston-affiliated voter-registration drives benefited from donations by other financial industry firms. Drexel Burnham Lambert, Inc. gave $10,000 to the Forum Institute one month after ninety-eight charges of securities fraud were brought in October, 1988 against Michael Milken and Drexel in relation to their junk bond dealings. Cranston said the contribution arrived before the indictments were handed down. Drexel later pleaded guilty to six felony charges and agreed to pay $650 million in fines and Milken was facing felony charges.

If matters were not serious enough, a class-action suit was brought against Keating, by 24,000 bondholders, alleging that American Continental executives and their professional advisors had sold $200 million of American Continental debt securities through Lincoln Savings and Loan branches. The bondholders claimed that they were led to believe that the bonds were federally insured. Their lawsuit said that Keating and his associates had kept the business afloat by making large contributions to numerous politicians who represented his cause before regulators. "It was one massive political action to assist Mr. Keating," said Joseph W. Cotchett attorney for the plaintiffs. "Mr. Keating's contributions worked to buy him a lot of influence."

The plaintiffs also charged that state regulators, appointed by California's Republican Governor George Deukmejian, were unduly influenced by Keating's $75,000 contribution and $80,000 to the Republican party since 1986. Keating's companies were represented by a Los Angeles law firm that included Karl Samuelian, Deukmejian's chief fund-raiser. The first bond issue was granted by former Department of Corporations Commissioner Franklin Tom, an attorney with Samuelian's firm before and after his state service. The second bond issue was granted by Christine Bender, also previously associated with Samuelian's firm.

Not even retired state Supreme Court Justice Cruz Reynoso was spared. He was CPD's chairman. His law firm had represented some of Keating's business enterprises. The firm was named as a plaintiff in the suit.

Cranston wanted the congressional General Accounting Office to investigate the state and federal agencies overseeing the bond issue. He admitted giving the appearance of favorable treatment to Keating, saying that he "did do a pretty stupid thing politically." But that it wasn't improper. He only tried to get "fair play" for a California firm. Nor was soliciting funds for CPD improper. He said that none of the funds in question went to him "personally or politically."

While funds might not have gone to him directly, the non-profit group Public Interest reported that twenty of his thirty-three non-California trips were paid by voter-registration organizations partially funded by Keating. The trip to see Keating in Phoenix in February of 1988 was paid by New Dimension Resources, and it also paid for a dozen other trips that year.

Talk, plane tickets, and bucks were being exchanged at a fast clip. But for what? What was behind it all?

Obviously, the non-profit organizations were set up to register a million new voters and then to follow up with get-out-the-vote drives. The operation was a thinly disguised partisan attempt. "They were hoping," said former Republican state chairman Bob Naylor, "to register overwhelmingly in Democratic areas and hoping to minimize the Republican registration. They had to portray it [the 1988 campaign] as bipartisan in order to qualify as a nonprofit [organization]."

The most important reason for creating CPD was to knock out Southwest Voter Registration and Education Project from making any new progress toward independent Hispanic political empowerment. The Democrats—under non-partisan, non-profit, disguise—were not particularly scared by Mexican-American political progress but feared being unable to control it. Arrogant power backed up by big bucks and manipulative politics was what the shenanigans were mainly all about.

Alan Cranston promoted Marshall Ganz to state and national party leaders as an election genius in the days following his successful 1986 senate reelection campaign. The pitch to them was that no one before had ever launched a successful voter registration drive in California. Willie Velásquez was despondent over this. Southwest Voter Registration and Education Project (SVREP) had been extremely successful in Texas, New Mexico, and Arizona. His organization had planned all along a similar effort in California but didn't have the money.

Cranston, according to Velásquez, had agreed in 1986 to help raise funds to support SVREP's expansion into California. But Cranston, a bit more street smart after his reelection, started CPD with Kim, instead. When Velásquez figured out what Cranston was up to, they worked out an understanding, agreeing that CPD would not cut into SVREP's funding network. But Velásquez learned subsequently that some of SVREP contributors had switched. SVREP slowly ran out of funds and began cutting back on costs: salaries remained frozen as they had been since 1984; Velásquez even allowed SVREP life insurance policies to lapse.

At a January, 1988 meeting, Velásquez questioned Cranston's decision to concentrate on Latino voters. "A little competition is good for everyone," Cranston replied.

Velásquez, dying of cancer, realized just how powerless his organization really was in the confrontation with big political money and he backed off plans to publicly criticize Cranston for failing to live up to the earlier commitment to help SVREP. Velásquez obliquely alluded to the conflict with Cranston in a speech at the National Hispanic Media Conference in Dallas: "There is a battle building over who is going to deliver the Hispanic vote and for what reason," he said. "It is unwise to have [your] political faith in someone else's hands." He died two months later. Andy Hernández succeeded Willie Velásquez.

Dukakis' 1988 presidential campaign, had hoped to attract large majorities of Hispanic votes in Texas and California. That effort now could be channeled through Cranston. But SVREP had already expanded into California by 1988 and was trying to operate a *national* program on $650,000 when they had previously operated in 1984-1985 on a $1 million budget. "We have experienced a large drop in our income since Senator Cranston came in to help," said Hernández. "This is not a turf fight," he said. "It's a question [of] whether or not Hispanic politics . . . is going to rest in its own institutions, in its own leadership or in someone else's intentions." Los Angeles council member Gloria Molina was "absolutely" sure that CPD was hurting SVREP and spoke to Cranston about it. "Hispanics have to be empowered from within, not anointed from above," she said. "I don't have the kind of confidence in that project that I do in SVREP [and] that we will not be brokered later on."

Cranston denied promising to raise $250,000 for SVREP. However, even Rob Stein, a Democratic party fundraiser, admitted that Cranston had privately and publicly encouraged funding for SVREP; however, he did not take any measures within the organizations he controlled to come to its aid.

The Cranston group was up to something, but what was it? Why would they organize CPD with Keating funding, knowing of an outstanding promise to help fund SVREP? Why was CPD needed if it only duplicated SVREP's work? What was the Organizing Institute really up to?

Kim Cranston was very talkative to writer Darryl Figueroa. As far as Kim was concerned SVREP virtually didn't exist. It wasn't there: "I don't know what to make of it [SVREP charges]. I felt there was a real need to focus on training people to become effective community organizers and register voters. I was not aware of any group that existed that was doing that particular thing," he said. He hid behind the mission's altruism. There are 7.5 million people not registered to vote in California. There's still a lot of work to be done," he said.[2]

True. There was a lot of work to do. And CPD seemed to not be doing it. By the first half of 1988, the year of the big push, CPD (with a $3.1 million budget, two hundred staff members, six offices in Los Angeles and

2. Darryl Figueroa, "Southwest Voter Registration Unit Says Cranston Broke Word," *The San Diego Union* (September 4, 1988).

nine other cities) had registered 139,000. Only 28 percent, or 38,920, were Latinos. At the same time, financially crippled SVREP, running a $350,000 deficit, registered 40,000 Latinos.

Then—deeds not words exposed the real agenda. CPD was particularly active in June, 1989, registering voters for the Salinas City Council elections for one of the first tests after the Watsonville decision, ending at-large elections. CPD ran a slate of candidates against their own former Latino allies. The CPD slate included a Latino candidate who had even opposed the suit. SVREP finally stepped in at the last minute with its own campaign and enabled the Latino activists to win. "If the Democratic Party really had sought successful voter registration in the Latino community," wrote columnist Rodolfo Acuña, "it could have financed such non-profit groups as the Southwest Voter Registration and Education Project. But it, like Cranston, apparently fears the emergence of an independent Latino political force."

Moreover, California Hispanics complained that Marshall Ganz' Organizing Institute directly competed with other Latino organizations. It served no new purpose except to disrupt the structure that had been painfully constructed over time and that was only now beginning to show the fruits of its labor.

"What concerns Latinos," said columnist Rodolfo Acuña "is the damage that Cranston's voter-registration activities in California have had—and will continue to have—on their own efforts to build grass-roots Latino political institutions." In less philosophic language, Richard Martinez and Antonio Gonzales of SVREP said that "This is especially embarrassing with the Democrats, since Latinos are 15 percent of all registered [California] Democrats and regularly vote 75 percent for Democrats." So that no one missed the point, they suggested that a very attractive Latino Republican Orange County official would make a good statewide candidate; he could draw crossover Latino Democratic votes to the Republicans.[3] At this point, the situation had gone beyond a mere scandal: Latino pride was at stake.

3. Richard Martinez and Antonio Gonzalez, "Latinos Should 'Take the Power,'" *Los Angeles Times* (August 14, 1989),

12

The Realization

George Bush declared, "My opponent needs an issue and he's willing to scare people to find it." Dukakis had said that Americans should stand up for American companies and jobs. Bush called it "protectionist demagoguery." In the closing months, the campaign focused on the sunshine states. Surveys showed that Dukakis and his running mate Texas Senator Lloyd Bentsen had gained on Bush and Dan Quayle. But the Republican team had made strategic gains in the states with the most Electoral College votes.

Two Democratic strategists were sent to the Sunshine States and Ohio, where Dukakis was running behind but still had a chance. Bush was considered unbeatable in Florida. In the otherwise lackluster race, the only memorable remark of the campaign was made by Lloyd Bentsen while addressing Quayle in debate: "And you're no John Kennedy," said Bentsen in quick response to Quayle's mild comparison of himself to the former president. "I've never seen a campaign," said Republican campaign aide Sheila Tate, "where a presidential nominee runs against my vice-presidential nominee."

A narrow margin separated Bush and Dukakis in the popular vote, but a wide difference separated the two in the Electoral College. Dukakis, in response, scheduled a last-minute trip to San Antonio immediately after the second and final presidential debate in California. He needed Texas' twenty-nine electoral votes. Mayor Henry Cisneros was there to meet him. Dukakis praised Congressman Henry B. Gonzalez. Gonzalez, who, as chairman of the Housing and Community Development subcommittee, had worked on legislation to provide assistance to *colonias*, impoverished homesteads along the U.S.-Mexico border.

In the campaign's final three weeks, Bush, according to the Associated Press, led with 9 percent of the popular vote. Tino Durán, regional director of the National Association of Hispanic Publications, editorialized in *El*

Informador of Fort Worth that "Bush is familiar with Hispanic concerns, and more importantly, he has a long record of selfless, dedicated service to our country and the Hispanic community."[1]

Going into the campaign's final days, Texas, from the Democrats' point of view, was the key to turning the campaign around. They needed a 70 percent Mexican American voter turnout at the polls. "Texas is winnable," said Bill Richardson (D-NM), a Mexican American congressman and seasoned campaigner, who was sent out at the last minute to organize a major last-ditch push. The Democratic Party doubled the Hispanic-media budget to $1 million and refocused on radio ads delivered by Dukakis in fluent Spanish.

The final election results were solidly in Bush's favor. The Bush-Quayle ticket won 53.4 percent of the popular vote to 46 percent for Dukakis-Bentsen. Bush carried forty states and won 426 Electoral College votes. Dukakis won ten states and 112 electoral votes. Bush only needed 270 to win.

George P. Bush was basically unaided by the Hispanic vote during the 1988 election. Seventy-six percent of Texas' Mexican Americans voted for Dukakis, and only 23 percent cast their ballots for Bush. Similarly, in California, 71 percent voted for Dukakis, and 27 percent for Bush.

The 1988 presidential election had a 50.1 percent voter turnout rate. It was the lowest rate in sixty-four years. Measured against the entire voting age population of more than 182 million, Bush was the choice of barely one out of four adult Americans. Only Harry Truman (1948), Richard Nixon (1968), and Ronald Reagan (1980) had been the choice of a smaller share of voters than Bush. However, all three had significant third-party opposition that took away votes. And all three gained members for their party in Congress. Truman retook the House and Senate. But Bush's election had no coattails. The Republicans actually lost seats in 1988 from their minority standing in both houses of Congress.

The low 1988 voter turn out came on the heels of a low 1986 election turnout when only one in three adults cast ballots. The previous election had the lowest turnout since the 1942 wartime midterm election. Not since the 1920s were turnouts as low as they were in 1988. The downturn was nationwide: forty-five states and the District of Columbia had a lower turnout

1. "Hispanic Newspaper Gives Nod to Bush," *San Antonio Express-News* (October 28, 1988).

in 1988 than they had in 1984. Only Massachusetts, New Hampshire, Nebraska, and Nevada showed increases, and Colorado remained the same.

The *Congressional Quarterly* was so taken aback that it dismissed the explanations of the past: "[T]urnout may be low not because of apathy among voters," it wrote, but "rather an apathy of those in power to improve turnout; grass-roots registration drives . . . are not commonplace; and the conventional wisdom that low turnout helps Republicans may no longer hold." The United States remained the only democracy in the world where voter registration was initiated by the individual and never aggressively pursued at the national level. Political parties and labor unions, spurring voter turnouts for years, were in decline.

The communications and information media were not much help. The press branded Democratic candidates as the "seven dwarfs" and characterized Bush's campaign as a struggle to overcome the "wimp factor." The campaign was long and had struck many as calculated to be negative in tone. The complaint registered in a late October *New York Times*/CBS News poll showed nearly two-thirds of those sampled saying they wished they had an alternative to Bush and Dukakis. More than half of the respondents considered the campaigns boring. And nearly half said they thought the campaign was more negative than past campaigns.

Many Democrats believed that Dukakis could have done a better job of activating coalitions that traditionally supported the party. But the evidence proved, to the contrary, that higher turnouts would have benefited Bush. A *New York Times*/CBS News post-election survey among non-voters showed that Bush was preferred by 50 percent to 34 percent. He would have won with a greater majority if non-voters had gone to the polls. Non-voters, the survey found, were more mobile, less affluent, less educated, less partisan, and less interested in the campaign than those who voted.

In the final analysis, it would have taken more than 5 million additional voters casting ballots to equal the 1984 election turnout. More people did not vote mainly because more people did not register to vote. Of those who did, 80 percent went to the polls.

A lot of introspection followed George Bush's election. Hispanic politics had made notable advances in the two previous decades. But somehow progress had a disappointing edge. Small, incremental accomplishments had been too hard won for what was otherwise a birthright—representation. Victories felt too tenuous to instill much confidence in the future. Setbacks were many. Idealistic dreams were dashed along the way. The happy tomorrows of the past ideologies were marred by vengeful reality. Too much attention was given to government answers for group problems, and individual interests received too little.

At decade's end, the national hang-up with "minority," "race," and "ethnicity," was not diminishing. It became, in fact, even more exaggerated and was acquiring a political life of its own. Popular new reactions were setting in as if too much diversity outside the ritual White and Black racial divide was intruding on the nation's nature, its character. Then, the Equal Employment Opportunity Commission (EEOC) was found out to be one of those instruments of unfairness like a wolf dressed like a lamb. In the end, a kind of political innocence was lost.

It began coming to light in late 1983 when Senator Orrin Hatch (R-Utah), chairman of the Senate Labor and Human Resources Committee, held hearings on a delicate and highly charged issue: whether "the EEOC has primarily assisted the black community and [had] done little if anything to serve other minorities." The hearings were widely believed to help court Hispanics for Reagan's reelection campaign the following year.

"This is the first administration, the first senate committee and the first commission to have confronted the issues head on," said EEOC commissioner Tony E. Gallegos. Some Hispanic leaders speculated that the hearings only served to block Democratic candidate Jesse Jackson's call for a "rainbow coalition," comprised of blacks, Hispanics, and other ethnic minorities. Others were dubious about the whole political enterprise: "They [blacks] have always used us in these coalitions," said a Detroit businessman. "Then they grab the jobs and screw us."[2]

EEOC commissioner Gallegos, former commissioner Armando M. Rodríguez, and former Deputy General Counsel Michael N. Martínez prepared a report, called the "Hispanic Charge Study." It complimented EEOC chairman Clarence Thomas and the commission for looking into the sensitive issue. Some Latino leaders pointed out that EEOC had voted to authorize the study but provided no staff or funds for it. The study showed that the agency had a poor record of pursuing Hispanic discrimination complaints and failed to hire Latinos for important policy jobs.

Two years later, Congressman Matthew G. Martínez (D-Calif.) and other members of Congress became angry when they became aware that EEOC was no longer applying "goals and timetables" to remedy employment

2. Tom Díaz, "Are Some More Equal Than Others at the EEOC?" *Nuestro* (January/February, 1984), p. 19.

discrimination. "They denied they were trying to avoid the guidelines until we caught them," said Martínez. As chairman of the House Employment Opportunities Subcommittee, he ordered hearings to call EEOC commissioners on the carpet.

The EEOC had been created to enforce Title Seven of the 1968 Civil Rights Act, prohibiting workplace discrimination based on race, sex, and national origin. The agency was empowered to reinstate employees wrongfully discharged, levy monetary relief for back pay, and provide other corrections in cases of individual discrimination. Setting goals and timetables was a controversial remedy that raised questions about how civil rights should be enforced. President Reagan and many members of his administration characterized this as favoritism toward minority groups—typifying it as "reverse discrimination"—and said it resulted in little progress and even promoted harm. They preferred a case-by-case review to help people hurt by discrimination. But the policy did not address what to do to a company with a history of discrimination.

"This commission has not 'abandoned' the use of hiring goals and timetables in race and sex discrimination cases," Commission chairman Clarence Thomas charged back. Under his discretionary power, general counsel John Butler was responsible and had instructed EEOC's regional attorneys to make preliminary decisions about when to apply the remedy.

The disclosure made the Congressman see red. "Right now, they are violating the law," said Martínez. "Johnny Butler has no right to arbitrarily set policy [instead of the Commission] and give directives to regional offices to stop enforcing the law. And if Clarence Thomas gave him his marching orders, he is violating the law."

The agency favored a "make whole" approach to address specific instances of employment discrimination. The company might be required to give a damaged person a job and monetary compensation. The company, however, was not required to hire other Hispanics to make up for past discrimination. Not using goals and timetables was "sheer nonsense," when discrimination was longstanding and widespread, said Congressman Martínez. "This 'make whole' theory is only effective *after* massive discrimination has been remedied," *not before.*

The problem started after a 1978 reorganization initiated by Chair Eleanor Holmes Norton. Local EEOC offices were established around the country—based on 1970 census information—to mainly serve African American citizens. The same inaccurate and outdated 1970 census data was used in 1982 when Chairman Clarence Thomas carried out another reorganization.

By 1983 EEOC had become a large bureaucracy with five commissioners, fifty local offices, 3,000 employees, and a $160 million budget.

As the agency grew, the total number of Hispanics filing discrimination complaints dropped steadily from 9 percent in 1979 to 5 percent in 1982. At the same time, the total number of charges received by the agency increased by 76.5 percent.

Those few Hispanics who came forward were largely ignored. In 1980 and 1982, 44 percent of Hispanic employment discrimination charges (numbering 4,936 complaints) were dismissed by EEOC on the basis that the complaining party "failed to cooperate" with the Commission and those complaints received little or no investigation. "It seems unlikely to me, that a party alleging employment discrimination would fail to cooperate in the investigation of the charge," said Michael N. Martínez. By comparison, only 6 percent of the charges filed by African Americans were dismissed for the same reason. Hispanic complaints in actuality were either not investigated or investigated too slowly. Hispanics were assigned a low priority (after black and women filings) and soon ended up as "backlog" cases, which were later "dumped" by busy managers under pressure to "get rid of their backlog."

Another reason for the lack of response was due to the commission's low Hispanic employment rate and alleged employment discrimination. Only 10 percent of the agency's 3,000 employees were Hispanics compared to 60 percent of African Americans. Even in cities where Hispanics were the largest numerical minority group, hiring preference was given to other groups. The Dallas chapter of the League of United Latin American Citizens (LULAC) alleged EEOC job discrimination in 1989. In November of that year, LULAC officials uncovered a similar bias and forced early resignations in San Antonio. Former EEOC investigator Ignacio Ballí, who had investigated job discrimination for eighteen years, said he was pressured to take early retirement or face possible dismissal. "They would start picking on your work" and made you "feel like an incompetent," he said about supervisors.

The agency denied the charges.

Sixteen years earlier, the Nixon administration had initiated the Sixteen Point Program in 1972 to improve Hispanic federal employment, mainly in the higher, policy-influencing levels. Now even the Office of Personnel Management (OPM), designed to assist in recruitment problems, began scaling down. Regional Hispanic Program Managers were eliminated. The OPM/Office of Hispanic Employment Programs was downgraded, reduced in staff size, merged with other programs, and eventually abolished.

The government's own hiring practices were questioned. Five months before Bush's election, in June, 1988, Rep. Pat Schroeder (D-Colo.)—who was testing the waters as a possible presidential candidate—held Civil Service Subcommittee hearings. Congressman Martínez testified that "Federal agency heads give external lip service to hiring Hispanics, but internally fail to set the example of [promoting] affirmative action to their subordinates," he said. "Congress is compelled to fix a problem the executive branch can fix on its own, but won't." He referred to a federal "good old boy network."

According to EEOC data from 1982 to 1987, 5,452 Hispanic federal workers had filed discrimination grievances. Litigation (not the grievance process) however showed better responses. The Federal Bureau of Investigation revamped its promotion system after Hispanic agents slapped the agency with a highly publicized discrimination suit, and the Drug Enforcement Administration had *Muñíz et al. v. Edwin Meese*, a class-action suit pending in court. The earlier Hatch hearings in the Senate had shown that EEOC was very reluctant to take a Hispanic case to court. Fewer than 3 percent of the EEOC suits filed were in behalf of Latinos.

EEOC chairman Clarence Thomas, who had started out as a civil rights activist, was said to have been "taken to the woodshed" by U.S. Attorney General Edwin Meese. Thomas emerged from it a hard-line conservative, emphasizing individual over group interests.

Among his first appointees, Bush nominated Evan Kemp Jr., a legal scholar believed willing to take a firmer stand on fair employment laws, to replace Clarence Thomas. In keeping his campaign pledge, President-elect Bush nominated New Mexico Congressman Manuel Lujan Jr. as Secretary of Interior. Hispanics made up only 3.5 percent of the department's 69,000 employees but posted a net increase in all minority hiring soon after Lujan took over. Two-hundred Hispanic employees were hired, eighty into executive positions. Bush's other Hispanic cabinet appointment, Lauro Cavazos, former Texas Tech University president, was re-appointed Secretary of the Education Department. His nomination had been submitted earlier by President Reagan. Cavazos took over the 4,500-employee agency that had five fewer Hispanic employees, totaling 145, than it had the year before. His predecessor, Edward Bennett, named by Bush to head the administration's anti-drug campaign, thought little of Hispanic-focused approaches to shaping policy. "It was terrible," said an education department employee. "We lost a number of people. Before we had 14 [high level] GS-15 employees; now there are only 4 or 5."

Time had virtually stood still since President Nixon, at Vice President Agnew's suggestion (both motivated by political considerations), had proposed the Sixteen Point Program. Bush's two Mexican American appointments to the cabinet elicited no new ethnic pride. Nor were the appointments, although promised in the campaign, expected as a matter of course. Knowledgeable observers realized that an ethnic appointment was not the mark of overcoming anything anymore. It was, instead, a benchmark that the nation itself had matured sufficiently to enroll the necessary people with the necessary qualities to conduct the nation's business.

The president's appointments were not so much a statement about ethnic assertion as a mark that the nation had begun to transcend social fictions by approaching political reality. Each new appointment seemed less like advancement and more like an approach to normalcy. Incredibly, so much time, effort, grief, and cost had gone unnecessarily into maintaining Hispanic invisibility in the past. "It certainly could be window-dressing," said Mario Moreno of the Mexican American Legal Defense and Education Fund. . . but maybe it will [also] marshal in a new era for Hispanics."

Perceptions were beginning to change in 1988. "As recently as three weeks ago," said Harry P. Pachón, director of the National Association of Latino Elected Officials, "the *New York City Tribune* ran its political analysis of the 1988 Hispanic vote under the banner headline: 'Votes of 20 million Hispanics Called a Sleeping Giant.' A sleeping giant. Imagine the image this conveys—a dormant community about to wake up from its afternoon siesta. So much . . . on Latino politics involves this image."

He was right. The imagery was off-putting. And the results were far more important than the attention they got. For example, California elected one-and-a-half times more Hispanic officials than any other minority group in that state, Texas seven times as many. The number of Hispanic elected officials doubled in a decade. The Hispanic electorate grew 25 percent in two years, or ten times the proportion by the general electorate. How the Hispanic vote was becoming important "at the margins" was even more dramatic.

For instance, Republicans didn't need a majority of the Hispanic votes to decide an election. Puerto Ricans tended to vote Democratic at about a 90 percent rate and Mexican Americans at about 75 percent. Cubans voted for Republicans at about an 80 percent rate. Based on the actual vote in 1986, 10.1 percent of the Puerto Rican/Latino vote in New York could cause a 1 percent shift in a statewide election. Only 6 percent of Latino voters in California (the state with the most Electoral College votes) would cause a

1 percent change in that state's election outcome. In a Texas presidential or statewide race, only 3.4 percent of Hispanic voters could cause a 1 percent change.

A small shift by the Hispanic vote in these key states during a close statewide or presidential election would make the difference between winning and losing. This meant that Democrats, in the future, would have to hold Hispanic loyalty, and Republicans only needed small gains to have a big impact. "Based on figures like this," said Pachón, "the myth of the sleeping giant is seen for what it is. Images need to change. Hispanic political power is not simply a potential but instead is an emerging reality. Hispanic political gains are real."

Impressive gains were again made in local and state elections by 1989. Hispanic elected officials, with representation in thirty-seven states, increased nearly 13 percent from 3,360 to 3,783). Four hundred and twenty-three additional Hispanic officials were elected over the previous year. Texas growth continued (1,611 to 1,693), California (466 to 580), and Florida (50 to 62). Inroads were made in Illinois (41), New Jersey (53), and Washington (18). Ninety-three percent of all Hispanic officials were from seven states: Texas (1,693), New Mexico (647), California (580), Arizona (268), Colorado (208), New York (71), and Florida (62). All other states accounted for the remaining 254 Hispanic elected officials in 1989.

More than a third (1,340) of the officials were elected to boards of education, and nearly another third (1,178) to municipal offices (246 mayors—a 7 percent increase—and 932 to city councils). By 1989, no Hispanic had yet been elected to the U.S. Senate since Joseph Montoya was defeated in 1976; eleven elected officials served in the House of Representatives (including the election of Rep. Illeana Ros-Lehtinen, a Republican from Florida who replaced the esteemed Congressman Claude Pepper after his death). Almost 20 percent (744) of all Hispanic elected officials were women. One governor, Bob Martínez, was elected (Florida), four state executives, 128 state legislators (up from fifty-nine in 1970 and eighty-two in 1982); 338 were in county offices, 575 in judicial and law enforcement positions, and 209 in special offices.

The nation consequently became more democratic. Yet, all Hispanic elected officials accounted for only 1 percent of the total national representation. The nation was better represented, but—as the total Hispanic population made up 8 percent—it was patently still underrepresented.

The expanding base of Hispanic officials also meant that local political organizations and networks had reinforced their capacity to promote national election campaigns. The implication was not lost on the national parties. They had their sights set on the serious advances made at the state and local levels and the effect they could have on future national campaigns. The Republicans were seriously behind in the election sweepstakes, but not so far behind they could not catch up.

After the election, Lee Atwater, Bush's campaign manager, headed the Republican Party. The ideological confrontations that had started eight years before, now seemed part of the nation's past. The Republican Party needed well-crafted strategies. Even conservative Georgia Congressman Newt Gingrich recognized that something other than rhetoric was called for. "To truly govern America," he said, "you have to posit a model of how to govern America." That model had to include a better turnout at the polls to give the government a mandate to govern. Rhetorical flourishes and ideological rectitude were not enough. Republican strategies, to become a majority legislative party, had to replace ideology, but not with a turn to the right or to the center—but a return to the core.

Atwater had been behind Bush's winning strategy and media campaign. Bush beat Dukakis in every major part of the country but did best in the Sun Belt (including the South and West). The Republicans had held the White House for sixteen out of the last twenty years, even if Democrats retained a thirty-four year hold on the House of Representatives and had a comfortable fifty-five to forty-five majority in the Senate.

Lee Atwater, the thirty-eight-year old South Carolinian who said, "My whole life has been about developing a Sun Belt political strategy," knew that Republicans had a "sincerity" barrier to overcome. He wanted a new "attitude" of inclusiveness that needed to get through to the local level, if the Republican Party was to break out of minority party status.

The 1990 census was expected to show that the Sun Belt had gained the most population, and the movement away from the north and east had continued. Florida was expected to get three new House seats, Texas four, and California five. New York, Michigan, Illinois, Ohio, and other traditionally Democratic states in the north were expected to lose representation. These were potential Republican gains and Democratic losses. A Republican strategy could solidify its hold where it was already strong and increase strength in the growing states. Republicans looked to expand where the Hispanic population was also increasing.

The 1990 census was critical to the nation's political direction. A special sensitivity surrounded the count after as much as 10 percent of the Hispanic population was widely believed to have been undercounted in 1980. Consequently, many communities lost potential representation and federal revenues. Fifty federal grant programs distributed funds based on census data. Local governments lost out on about $530 in federal money for each person missed. California may have lost $50 million, Texas $30 million, and New York between $29 and $52 million. To prevent this from happening again, the Carnegie Corporation and the National Association of Latino Elected Officials initiated public service announcements. Civic leaders promoted local involvement. A national information hot-line was installed to help minimize another undercount.

Republicans had their eyes on the marginal gains they wanted and the Democrats on the raw numbers they needed. "It's mind-boggling," said the GOP's Hispanic liaison Ernest Olivas. "But as long as we continue to deny the Democratic party the margins it needs, we'll win." Republicans aimed to attract younger, better educated, and more affluent Hispanics. Their studies showed that this large and increasing segment of the population had been left behind previously in the political calculus. The Republican approach played down notions about "coming to America" and played up the significance of being an American: "Hispanics are much more assimilated now," said Olivas. "More Hispanics entered college and incomes were on the rise. The fact remains that if you're looking at a pattern, Hispanics are in it: urbanization, a move into the service industry and a rise into the middle class."

"The party is going to have to get away from the idea that this is a voting bloc that is going to vote on specific issues. We don't need to be that specific. The issues are very broad. There's no Hispanic crime issue. It's just crime."

The coming collision between Republicans and Democrats appeared at the LULAC national convention less than a year after Bush took office. Arrangements were made to have Lee Atwater and Democratic National Committee chairman Ron Brown (a former Jesse Jackson strategist) debate their parties' future. Brown appeared, but Atwater did not. Brown smoothed his tie, walked to the podium, and from his first words, for the better part of an hour, lit into the Republican Party, calling it racist and cynical. From the Willie Horton campaign ads to discouraging California Hispanic voters, to cuts in the federal education budget, Brown took the Republican Party to task. He wasn't worried about the GOP making good on its promise to capture at least 30 percent of the Hispanic vote in California and Texas, after coming dangerously close in the presidential election, with 23 percent and

27 percent. "I don't think it is plausible again," said Brown.

Then, a woman delegate from the Bronx rose and asked if Democrats had developed any particular programs for Hispanic empowerment that would back Hispanic candidates and develop voter turnouts.

"One of the failures of my party," said Ron Brown, "is an unwillingness to stand up and say what we stand for. We've been trying to out-Republican the Republicans." He avoided any more comment on the issue. Yet, without a plan to encourage political leadership development or appealing to the emerging Hispanic middle sector, how did they expect to keep the lead? Corpus Christi lawyer Rubén Bonilla, thought Brown was short on detail and talked too much about civil rights: "With an audience like this you need to talk economics. These people are professionals, with businesses," he said.

Party politics no longer served as the steam engine that pulled the cars that made up the long economic development train. Entrepreneurs increasingly became the new driving force in directing communities on the infrastructure tracks that government projects had provided earlier. Commercial activity accomplished much of what people previously sought from government. Hispanic trends were in sync with the expanding commercialization in America. Small businesses were expanding because of growing consumer demand and created new demand with their expansion.

Yet, a mischaracterization persisted. Generally, Hispanics were portrayed by social stereotypes, as the takers and less so as the producers. Sometimes the old notions originated from Hispanic advocates themselves when they made the case for greater governmental response to the more needy segments.

"The best kept secret in the United States is what has happened to the Hispanic business community in the last decade," said an executive about a U.S. Chamber of Commerce study. Heralding new data and dying to do combat with old ideas, the report concluded that "Quietly, steadily, Hispanic-Americans have been on the move, building businesses, making jobs, creating wealth," he said. "They show every indication of being a stimulus to the economy in the coming decades and a vital resource for growth."

"It's right on," said Raúl Yzaguirre, president of the National Council of La Raza, about the National Chamber Foundation eighteen-month study. "I don't want to belittle the problems of Hispanic-Americans, they're part of the picture. But the study also presents a part of the real picture, one that doesn't get the headlines." Some opinion leaders had to do a dizzying balancing act between the mental images of Hispanic neediness and the new findings of social and economic diversity. In many non-political sectors, in fact, "Hispanic" represented a balancing notion of community, of diversity without strife, a drive for achievement (individual and group), of overcoming adversity, and—one way or another—always striving. Former spokesmen—bureaucrats, lobbyists, and cause-oriented groups—were slowly displaced as surrogate representatives by a Hispanic congressional delegation, state legislators, and local officials. True, there were still social and economic barriers to overcome. Community social service agencies needed considerable support to serve portions of the Hispanic population needing urgent attention. But local elected officials became increasingly accountable for policy and programs and no longer needed to impersonate social workers, nor did bureaucrats have to resemble politicians.

Some advocacy groups still needed to represent people in gerrymandered districts, which received less than adequate public representation. But advocacy, alone, failed to provide what was often needed—to stimulate both representation and self-sufficiency. Sometimes, these so-called "supplemental representatives" did not understand how the economy worked or that a desirable outcome was non-reliance on government or that grants and contracts were as often doled out as patronage and not so much as community aid.

Business and market-watchers, unlike political advocates, were keenly aware of the changing economic forces at work. Meanwhile, the business community did not play up the economic difficulties, the slow starts, the misadventures, the lack of talent and training, and inefficiencies. Instead they looked only to blue skies and projected market improvements.

The U.S. Chamber of Commerce acknowledged that many Americans perceived Hispanics as dependent on welfare and government subsidies—people perplexed by joblessness, failure, and poverty. "That's never been true, but the realization [that] it's not true is just coming out in the marketplace," said Alicia Conill, who headed a New York advertising agency.

By early 1987, a year and a half before Bush's election, many preconceptions and stereotypes had played out. They served little useful purpose anymore. *Advertising Age*, the advertising industry's trade journal, said so bluntly: "Hispanic marketers and media want to erase the stereotype of the impoverished Hispanic from the mind of corporate America." And the headline of a special report boldly proclaimed, "Buying Power Bursts Poverty-Stricken Image." Past imagery needed a makeover to profitably reflect social realities.

The domestic market was bursting at the seams. Only 11.4 percent of Hispanics lived below the poverty line when income and non-cash benefits were accounted for. Hispanic women entering the workforce contributed substantially to the rise in household income. Late 1987 labor figures showed that 49 percent of Hispanic women, compared with 53 percent for the general population, were at work. As incomes grew, Hispanics' use of products and services paralleled the general marketplace.

Commerce drove comprehension and how Hispanics were perceived. The market was consuming 1.5 times more beer, 3.5 times more baby food and used the telephone for more purposes and longer than the rest of the nation. *Newsweek* noted, more importantly, that "as Hispanics begin to influence Anglo tastes, Hispanic-owned firms . . . should acquire an even larger market."[3] Average household weekly grocery expenses increased only three dollars from 1984 to 1987 (from $99 to $102). This meant that the surge in household income was going toward other purchases, including big ticket items, such as financial and professional services, travel, and luxury items. By 1990, Hispanics represented $172 billion in disposable purchasing power.

Earning and purchasing power was so impressive that the U.S. Chamber of Commerce felt moved to point out that East Coast and Midwest established business sectors missed out on "the spectacular growth of Hispanic business" concentrated in California, Texas, and Florida. Hispanic firms had increased sales revenues by 47 percent from 1980 to 1982 (compared with a 16.7 percent increases in the gross national product).

The most surprising finding was the jump in household income: it kept pace with the U.S. average, rising 15.1 percent from 1985 to 1987. (The total U.S. household income increased 15.5 percent to $32,800). By 1989, the average household income increased to $23,000. When all Hispanic households were put together, income rose 27.9 percent in two years from 1985 to 1987, $134.1 billion in after-tax purchasing dollars.

True, Hispanic households started at a lower base than other U.S. households, but after-tax income grew and "at a faster rate than those of whites or blacks," said Robert Hitchens of Univision/Spanish International Network. The market was growing and the income gap was narrowing.

Since the mid-1980s, values had refined and shifted: Hispanics wanted to be regarded as Americans first and Hispanics second, reported Richard G. Arellano, for the National Chamber Foundation study. They were insulted

3. "Learning the Hispanic Hustle," *Newsweek* (May 17, 1982).

when perceived as other than an integral part of the nation. Hispanic entrepreneurs shied away from reliance on government. They reported that government help was more trouble that it was worth (especially red tape in securing Small Business Administration direct loans and loan guarantees), and they claimed that the injudicious use of the "minority" label provoked a backlash.

A national maturity was developing among buyers and sellers, vendors and suppliers, recognized by Dick McCormick, President of U.S. West Communications, when he addressed the Hispanic Business Conference in 1989. "In the case of Hispanics," he said, "I want to build better business partnerships, selling more to Hispanics, buying more from Hispanics, and working more closely with Hispanics to identify our region's problems and opportunities. They are not 'Hispanic problems.' Nor 'Anglo problems.' They are our problems. It's time to talk about them, to listen, and to act. It is not a time for 'business as usual.'"

★ ★ ★ ★ ★

13

The Insiders

The labor market was reverberating between 1980 and 1987. Hispanics at work jumped 43 percent, to 2.3 million. They accounted for 20 percent of the labor-force growth, with workforce participation expected to increase to 22 percent in the 1990s. The nation's economic expansion had become increasingly dependent on Hispanic workers.

At the same time, the Department of Labor estimated that demand for high-skill jobs, requiring higher mathematics and superior language skills would increase by 23 percent in the next decade. Low-skill jobs would increase by only 12 percent. And the need for workers with less than a high school education would decline from 18 percent to 14 percent of all jobs filled in 1987. Labor needs pressured public education to improve and produce better results.

In 1986, Japan's Prime Minister Yasuhiro Nakasone, in an offhand comment, said his country successfully competed with the U.S. because the Japanese were smarter than Americans. "We have become quite an intelligent nation, much more than the United States," he declared to party officials in Tokyo. "In America there are quite a few blacks, Puerto Ricans and Mexicans. On average [the level] is extremely low."

The comment was readily dismissed in Japan as inconsequential. In the U.S., it drew immediate fire from African American and Hispanic Congress members. Telegrams poured into the Japanese embassy. Nakasone put his foot in his mouth again the following day, saying, "there are things it [the United States] has not been able to accomplish in education and other areas because it's a multiracial society. It's easier in Japan because we're a homogeneous race." The clarification only infuriated minority Congress members even more. Civil rights leader Jesse Jackson called the statements an insult. Congressman Robert Matsui pointed out that only days before, Nakasone had dismissed a cabinet minister for making offensive statements about South Koreans. Finally, Prime Minister Nakasone conveyed a hollow apology: "I have always firmly believed that America's greatness derives from the dynamism of her many ethnic communities," he said.

On reflection, former mayor Henry Cisneros thought Nakasone could have made a significant statement had he asserted that the United States was going to have a very difficult time competing at its current rate and was going to have trouble keeping pace. Nakasone might have been correct to say that no nation can maintain an underclass of 15 to 20 million people and expect to compete in the world.

Since 1980, the Hispanic population had grown five times faster than the rest of the population. Fertility among Hispanic women in 1987 was ninety-six births per 1,000 women of child-bearing age, compared to sixty-nine for other white, and eighty-three for African-American women. Hispanics were expected to leap ahead by about 39 percent in the 1990 census to form 8.2 percent of the total population. However, when the census figures later became available, they showed Latinos had grown 53 percent between 1980 and 1990 and, in the decade before 2000, an astounding 57.9 percent

Immigration and natural increases were about equally responsible for the growth. Looking forward to the year 2000, it was expected that 60 percent of the Los Angeles population would be Hispanic. Further, that Hispanics represented a relatively young population—compared to national demographics—accounted for the large number of children in school. Already by the mid-1980s, about a third of all California school children were Hispanics.

President Bush, with education secretary Lauro Cavazos, appeared to address the brewing public-education crisis by convening the nation's governors. The economy needed more and better prepared people. State and local governments needed to prepare people to become job-ready. And they would have to do it without major new assistance from the federal government. The nation's budget was requiring everyone to do more with less.

The federal debt, estimated at $2.61 trillion in 1988, was the reason. It had increased 11 percent from the previous year. Non-federal (state and local government) debt had increased by 5 percent to $755 billion. The total $3.37 trillion public debt represented a $13,708 burden per American.

An opportunity to alleviate the debt burden arose when the cold war ended and worldwide military commitments were reduced. But Bush, continuing the Reaganomics agenda, proposed to reduce capital gains taxes to mainly benefit the upper-income brackets. Senator Daniel Patrick Moynihan challenged this approach. He proposed instead a reduction in Social

Security payroll deductions. That way, low and medium-income workers, whose real earnings had fallen between 9 percent and 15 percent during the Reagan years (1979 to 1987), would benefit directly. Employers would also benefit from having to contribute less of their share of the payroll tax. Bush's tax reduction passed; Moynihan's did not.

President Bush was very popular at the end of his first year in office. This was in part due to the success of a quick military intervention in Panama that resulted in the overthrow and capture of General Manuel Noriega, who was taken to Miami to stand trial on drug trafficking charges. Bush, in mid-January, 1990, had an amazingly high 80 percent approval rating. It was far better than that of any of the preceding three elected presidents—Reagan (49 percent), Carter (55 percent), and Nixon (61 percent).

With a popular president in office, Democrats explored new directions. One little-noticed delegation of Democratic representatives met with Mexico's Agriculture Secretary Carlos Hank Gonzáles concerning trade and the exchange of farm technology. Co-chaired by House majority whip Richard Gephardt (Missouri) and House Agriculture Committee chairman Eligio (Kika) de la Garza (Texas), the delegation, included Ronald Coleman (Texas) Solomón Ortiz (Texas), Alberto Bustamante (Texas), and was accompanied by Ambassador John D. Negroponte.

At the end of the visit, Gephardt said he thought speculation about a North American free trade zone including Mexico was premature. The idea had come up as a measure to offset the expected effects of the European Economic Community. "It took three years of long, hard negotiations with Canada," to establish free trade with them, he said, "and they're the country most like the United States in the world."

Bush kept his popularity high and Democrats off balance with mainly one issue. "I'm the one who will not raise taxes," he had said when he was nominated by the GOP. . . And they'll push, and I'll say, `No.' And they'll push again, and I'll say to them: `Read my lips: no new taxes!'"

Bush had signed a letter the year before pledging no new taxes. Senator Bob Dole refused to sign it. The refusal contributed to his primary loss to Bush in New Hampshire.

Less than two weeks after Bush was sworn in, Secretary of the Treasury Nicholas Brady reportedly considered a commercial-bank and savings-and-loan depositors' fee to cover insurance. Bush's intervention quelled conservative protests in Congress. He explained that it was merely an option that had not even reached his desk. By mid-1989, Federal Reserve Board chairman Alan Greenspan warned that the slowing economy could slip into recession. Unemployment, at only 5.2 percent, could rise.

White House chief of staff John Sununu convinced Bush that talk about recession was unwarranted. The new year brought other warning signs: 79,000 manufacturing jobs were lost in 1989. Production prices had gone up 4.8 percent. Banks dropped their prime lending rates to counter the economic slowdown.

The administration's new budget, based on optimistic assumptions by the Congressional Budget Office and some independent economists, included many cuts previously proposed by Reagan and rejected by Congress. Democrats vowed not to go along with Bush's second budget, while conservatives complained about the budget's priorities. Bush proposed the capital gains measure to shore up conservative strength.

The administration opposed a civil-rights bill intended to further curb job discrimination and characterized it as a "quota bill." Lee Atwater, the administration's major link to conservative Republicans, collapsed while giving a speech in March of 1990 and was diagnosed as having a brain tumor. His health deteriorated quickly. White House chief of staff John Sununu replaced Atwater as chief advisor on what the president needed to do to satisfy conservatives.

In Congress, Democrats worried about the growing deficit. They pressed for action to reduce it. The Republican Party's right wing seemed reassured that the president would not give in on attempts to raise taxes. By March, 1990, House Ways and Means committee chairman Dan Rostenkowski came up with a plan to freeze spending and raise income tax rates. The White House gave mixed signals. Meanwhile, Congress dismissed the president's budget, and passed its own proposal, leading to a White House meeting between the president and congressional leaders. They agreed to negotiate on a bipartisan deficit-reduction package.

Nineteen House Republicans wrote to Bush reminding him to keep his no-new-taxes pledge and pressed for a capital-gains tax-rate cut. Eight GOP Senators wrote asking Bush to reject any budget proposal that included new taxes. Fifty-seven percent of respondents to an NBC News/ *The Wall Street Journal* poll in May said that Bush should stick to his no-new-taxes pledge.

In June, on the threat that the Democrats were about to walk out, Bush admitted needing "tax revenue increases" among other budget measures. Eighty-nine House GOP members signed a letter to Bush saying that tax increases were "unacceptable." and that they were "stunned by your announcement."

Bush's fateful decision to repudiate his solemn pledge led to the belief that the administration lacked a political core. Sununu, who claimed to represent conservatives after Lee Atwater's death, was blamed for a cavalier approach to tax measures. The president was perceived as having broken not only his pledge but also his personal word.

The transformation of the Soviet Union and Eastern Europe obscured the significance of these 1989 national political maneuverings. In June, the Chinese communist regime brutally suppressed a pro-democracy movement at Beijing's Tiananmen Square. Then in December, the U.S. invaded Panama. Domestic concerns, superseded by global events, looked minor by comparison.

During the Bush administration, the Hispanic Caucus of the 100th, 101st, 102nd sessions of Congress (1987-1992) was not yet truly powerful but its members became increasingly influential because of committee assignments, seniority standing and through party roles that its members played. During those years, members included non-voting delegates (Ben Blaz, R-Guam), Ron de Lugo, (D-Virgin Islands) and Jaime B. Fuster (D-Puerto Rico). Antonio Colorado (D) replaced Fuster as Puerto Rico's delegate in 1991. Up to the 100th Congress (at the end of the Reagan administration), Texas, California, New Mexico, and New York provided the elected Hispanic representation. By the 101st and 102nd Congresses (during the Bush years), new Hispanic House members were elected from Arizona and Florida. The expanded representation helped to outline broader issues and more diverse interests than had previously characterized the Hispanic perspective and political character. Older House members—because of their seniority in committees—flexed their legislative muscles and left their mark on national policy.

Albert G. Bustamante (D-Tex.), for example, was one of the Hispanic Caucus' older members who served on the Procurement and Military Nuclear Systems Subcommittee, the Subcommittee on Energy, and the Natural Resources Subcommittee. He supported nuclear test ban amendments and voiced concern for environmental and safety problems in the nation's nuclear production plants. He played an important role in delaying the funding for a Special Isotope Separation project in Idaho. Bustamante at first supported the administration's policy toward Nicaragua, voting in 1986 to authorize aid to the Contras, insurgents opposed to the revolutionary Sandinista government in power. But in the following two years he voted against Contra aid. As a member of the Select Committee on Hunger, he worked to increase nutrition funding and brought national attention to the "colonias," the rural slums along the U.S.-Mexico border. In December, 1990, Bustamante became a member of the House Democratic Steering and Policy Committee, voting for a civil rights bill and a family and medical leave bill over President Bush's veto.

Tony L. Coelho (D-Calif.) had served as Chairman of the Democratic Congressional Campaign Committee prior to the 100th Congress. The committee dramatically increased Political Action Committee contributions. In 1985, Coelho became the first elected Democratic Party Whip (he would resign both this position and his House seat in 1989 after questions arose about his personal finances).

Robert García (D-N,Y) and Jack Kemp, (R-N.Y.) introduced legislation in 1980 to create urban "free enterprise zones," providing businesses with tax incentives for moving into depressed inner-cities areas. Garcia persevered and in 1988 a plan for inner-city development was enacted. In 1984, he had taken a temporary seat on the Foreign Affairs Committee where he focused on Central American issues, including defending previous Inter-American Foundation grants. He signed a letter, along with ten other House Democrats, addressed to Nicaraguan general Daniel Ortega, stating opposition to U.S. funding of the Contra rebels. In the 100th Congress, he chaired the Banking Subcommittee on International Finance, Trade, and Monetary Policy until his resignation from Congress in 1990.

Henry B. González (D-Tex.), already in Congress in 1961, became Chairman of the Subcommittee on Housing and Community Development in 1981. From there he worked on legislation to approve a program to assist families facing home foreclosure. He battled the Reagan administration's proposed public housing program cuts. Then as Chairman of the Banking, Finance, and Urban Affairs Committee, he helped enact many pieces of legislation, including flood insurance reform, major housing initiatives, increased credit access for small businesses, and strengthened laws addressing money laundering and other financial crimes. During his tenure as Chairman of the Banking Committee, González dealt with the collapse of the savings and loan industry (a crisis he had predicted throughout the 1980s) and in 1991 he led a restructuring of the federal deposit insurance system. He was once again in the national spotlight in 1992 (as he had been in the 1970s as Chairman of the House Assassinations Committee investigating the murders of John F. Kennedy and Martin Luther King, Jr.) when he requested an investigation of the Bush administration's involvement in loans to Iraq.

Eligio (Kika) de la Garza (D-Tex.), as Chairman of the Committee on Agriculture from 1981 to 1994, was the first Hispanic since 1917 (when Ladislas Lázaro chaired the Enrolled Bills Committee) to chair a standing committee in the House of Representatives. During his tenure, de la Garza successfully led three omnibus farm bills (1981, 1985, and 1990) to passage, a major overhaul of the agricultural lending system, federal crop insurance reform, an Agriculture Department reorganization, pesticide law reforms, numerous assistance measures, rural economic development, and human nutrition improvement. In 1990 the Food, Agriculture, Conservation and Trade Act re-authorized commodity and nutrition programs, reformed export assistance programs, and established new initiatives to strengthen environmental protection for agricultural lands. De la Garza also strongly supported improved access by the elderly and veterans to health care, better living conditions for low-income and impoverished individuals, and educational opportunities for all.

Manuel Lujan (R-N.M.) served as the only Republican member of the Congressional Hispanic Caucus in the 1970s and most of the 1980s. He had faced a strong challenge from Bill Richardson in 1980, when the district he represented changed from a largely rural one to almost exclusively urban, concentrated in Albuquerque, with aerospace and high-technology industries. Lujan won reelection with a slim margin but he gave up his ranking Republican spot on the House Interior and Insular Affairs Committee in 1985 to become the ranking Republican on the Science and Technology Committee. As one of five congressional members on the President's National Space Commission, Luján helped develop long-term U.S. space policy. Although he usually supported the Reagan administration, he sided with Hispanic leaders and opposed the 1986 legislation revising federal immigration laws that included the levying of sanctions against employers hiring illegal immigrants. In 1989 President George Bush appointed Luján Secretary of the Interior,

Matthew G. Martínez (D-Calif.) was elected to the House in 1982. He opposed the Reagan administrations' Central America policy and in 1983 voted to bar covert U.S. aid to Nicaragua. The following year he voted to bar aid to anti-Sandinista forces in Nicaragua. A loyal Democrat, Martínez supported legislation affecting the welfare of children, young adults, and the elderly. In 1991 he became Chairman of the Human Resources Subcommittee, where he sponsored legislation for drug abuse education and delinquency prevention programs. That same year he sponsored a bill that required literacy and child development training for parents of children in Head Start programs.

Solomon P. Ortíz (D-Tex), elected to the House in 1982, was assigned to the Merchant Marine and Fisheries Committee and the Armed Services Committee. During the Cold War he voted for MX missile funding and opposed a 1983 resolution to ban nuclear weapons testing. He proposed legislation in 1984 that was enacted into law allowing oil and gas leasing on federal lands in Corpus Christi (his district). Ortíz also worked to maintain open South Texas' military installations facing closing during the early 1990s. Ortiz worked on the Voting Rights Act of 1992 to increase voter access to second language election materials.

Bill Richardson (D-N.M.) had unsuccessfully challenged incumbent Congressman Manuel Luján in 1980. Following the creation of northern New Mexico's Third District, Richardson won the 1982 election. During his first term in Congress, Richardson was assigned to a coveted seat on the Energy and Commerce Committee. In the 101st Congress, Richardson supported a plan to promote the use of non-gasoline cars, parts of which were included in the Clean Air Act re-authorization. As a member of the Interior and Insular Affairs Committee, he supported expansion of national parks and the designation of wild and scenic rivers.

Illeana Ros-Lehtinen (R-Florida) was the first Hispanic woman elected to Congress, beginning service in 1989 after a special election. She supported legislation dealing with education and served on the Foreign Affairs and Government Operations Committees, committee assignments of particular importance to her Cuban American constituency. She played a key role in the discussion of the Cuban Democracy Act, which became part of the 1993 defense authorization that specifically prohibited subsidiaries of U.S. corporations from trading with Cuba.

Edward Roybal (D-Calif.), in the 1980s, showed leadership in various important posts: he was named Chairman of the Treasury-Postal Service-General Government Subcommittee and served on the Labor-Health and Human Services-Education and Related Agencies Subcommittee. Both Appropriations Committee panels fit in well with Roybal's legislative goals. He also served on the Select Committee on Aging, becoming Chairman in the 98th Congress. In the 100th Congress, Roybal worked for the expansion of rural mental health-care programs and the establishment of a national mental health education program. He played a key role during the 101st Congress in passing legislation to reverse a 1989 Supreme Court decision allowing age-based discrimination in employee benefits. During that Congress, he continued his work on health-care issues and he was instrumental in renewing legislation to support research leading to the prevention and treatment of Alzheimer's.

In 1991, Ed L. Pastor (D-Ariz.) won Arizona's Second District seat, left vacant after Morris K. Udall's resignation. Pastor was assigned to the Appropriations Committee, where he served on two Subcommittees—Agriculture, Rural Development, Food and Drug Administration and Related Agencies; and Energy and Water Development.

José E. Serrano (D-N.Y.) was elected to in a special election in 1990 to fill the unexpired term when Robert Garcia resigned. In his first term in Congress, he served on the Education and Labor Committee, where he successfully sponsored a bill to encourage school districts and community leaders to create programs to reduce dropout rates in schools. After he was elected to a full term in the 102nd Congress, Serrano was the principal sponsor of the Voting Rights Language Assistance Act, which strengthened and expanded the Voting Rights Act of 1965.

Estaban Torres (D-Calif.), elected to the U.S. House of Representatives in 1982, was appointed to the House Committee on Banking, Finance and Urban Affairs, where he served until the 102nd Congress. He also served on the Committee on Small Business during this time. His efforts led to numerous successful pieces of legislation. In the 102nd Congress, he became Majority Deputy Whip and participated in the House-Senate conference committee on a bill making important changes to federal housing programs. He influenced a disaster-assistance program for low-income people. During the same Congress, Torres became Chairman of the Consumer Affairs and Coinage Subcommittee, where he worked to grant consumers easier access to their credit histories and to help them correct mistakes in their credit reports. He also authored a bill, the Truth-in-Savings Act of 1992, to simplify the disclosure of interest rates and conditions for savings accounts, which was signed into law.

Broad Hispanic interests were beginning to be expressed in the legislative process. The House of Representatives—but not the Senate—was gaining noticeable Hispanic representation. By now, some of the nation's Hispanic character was also expressed in the Executive branch through presidential appointments. The mix of actors from the inside out onto the national stage was getting better. Better, not great, but better. That was the case in two of the three branches of the federal structure. The same was not the case for the Judiciary, however.

After Thurgood Marshall announced his resignation from the Supreme Court in June, 1991, President Bush met with assistant C. Boyden Gray, Attorney General Richard Thornburgh, John Sununu and Vice President

Dan Quayle about a replacement. Bush was eager to fill Marshall's seat with Clarence Thomas in order to please conservatives and avoid an acrimonious situation that would incense liberals, as had happened before when David Souter was nominated the previous year.

Bush had nominated Thomas to the Court of Appeals just two years earlier. He liked Thomas' conservative, black self-help philosophy; it fit in with Bush's beliefs that he should oppose "quotas" yet encourage minority members to become part of mainstream America. Thornburgh too was impressed with Thomas after meeting with him for an hour at the Justice Department on June 28 but warned that Thomas' record with civil rights groups and an unenthusiastic recommendation from the American Bar Association could cause problems getting him confirmed by the Senate. Thomas, just forty-three-years old, had practiced law for only five years in his career, had served on the Court of Appeals for only fifteen months, and his few legal writings were uninspired.

Thurgood Marshall was a legend and a giant in the legal profession, Clarence Thomas a judicial dwarf. The two could not be measured with the same yardstick. Marshall, as a lawyer for the National Association for the Advancement of Colored People, had pioneered civil rights cases that challenged segregation. He had served as a judge and then as Solicitor General before Lyndon Johnson nominated him to the Supreme Court in 1967. Marshall and Thomas seemed only to have in common that both were members of the bar.

Thomas' youth assured that he would serve on the court for a long time and could influence it with the conservative perspective required by Reagan and Bush. Inexperience, in the administration's view was not a deficit when weighed against the need for an orthodox conservative.

Thornburgh and Sununu pushed Bush to consider a Hispanic nominee. Bush had tried earlier, in fact, to put Judge Ricardo Hinojosa, a trial judge from South Texas on the Fifth Circuit Court of Appeals, but he turned down the offer. Clearly, the president wanted to get a Hispanic in line among possible choices for Supreme Court consideration. And he did not want to get boxed in by specific ethnic choices. "American presidents don't like having terms dictated to them. They want to make their own political choices," Chase Untermeyer, a White House personnel advisor, confided later.[1] Thornburgh and Sununu argued that the President would reap better political rewards from a Hispanic choice.

---

1. Interview, Chase Untermeyer, former White House Personnel Director, (October 9, 1993).

Gray, backed by Vice President Quayle, argued forcefully for Thomas. They began background work, despite Thornburgh's objections. Even if part of the White House staff strongly supported Thomas, Bush was persuaded to keep his options open. Gray, furious at Thornburgh for derailing the plan to nominate Thomas that same day, set out to sell civil-rights groups with the administration's best case for Thomas. The main obstacle was the powerful political argument favoring a Hispanic person.

After reviewing the possibilities, Bush's men came up with Emilio M. Garza, a lesser-known judge on the federal Court of Appeals in Texas. Other Republican judges were better known and more experienced but none could be counted on to have a conservative, pro-life ideology, a virtual qualification for consideration as a nominee.

Thornburgh and others advising Bush asked Garza to get on the next plane for Washington. But after the interview, they decided that Garza was too inexperienced. He was the same age as Thomas and had served as a federal district court judge for only two years before his appointment to the appeals court. But Garza had served on that court for only two months before Marshall's announcement to leave the Supreme Court. In private practice, he had represented clients in malpractice and product liability suits that had produced few of the kinds of sparks that distinguish a great jurist.

All of the attention turned back to Thomas—his character, his background and the resistance to his nomination. With his mentor, Missouri senator John Danforth and NAACP's Benjamin Hooks on board, the nomination announcement proceeded. Bush was adamant that Thomas was selected on merit and not on the basis of race. Yet the White House had previously made clear to reporters through a contradictory statement that Bush wanted a black or a minority nominee.

The Mexican American Legal Defense and Education Fund opposed Thomas. "The nominee," said Guadalupe Luna, "does not demonstrate affirmative support for advancing the civil rights and constitutional guarantees of all persons." A twenty-two page report by the organization, said Luna, documented Thomas's "unyielding opposition to affirmative action in employment and school desegregation and a disregard for the constitutional right to privacy." He did not have adequate legal or judicial experience to serve on the high court. His performance as EEOC chairman and as director of the Office of Civil Rights in the Education Department was questionable, according to the report. Latinos were disappointed that Bush did not nominate a Hispanic, and they were disenchanted with the ultimate choice.

Syndicated columnists Jack Germond and Jules Witcover recognized that Bush's decision "misses a political opportunity." They reasoned that a Hispanic American on the court "could have been persuasive," especially in Texas and California, because the traditionally Democratic Hispanic vote had been "trending Republican."[2]

Thomas' nomination stumbled before the Senate Judiciary Committee when Anita Hill, a tenured professor at the University of Oklahoma, alleged sexual harassment by Thomas when she worked for him from 1981 to 1983 at the Department of Education and the Equal Employment Opportunity Commission. Her testimony before the all-male Judiciary Committee turned bitter. Was the nominee the "best qualified" person to fill Thurgood Marshall's shoes, a possible decisive voice on women's rights and abortion rights challenges? The televised hearings portrayed a committee hostile to Hill's testimony. The cross-examination made committee members appear contentious to women's claims of workplace sexual harassment. In the end, the Senate confirmed Clarence Thomas by this century's closest vote for a Supreme Court nominee, fifty-two to forty-eight.

President Bush's popularity slipped as the economy moved into recession and unemployment figures rose. The downturn actually ended sometime in 1991, but it was not matched with a quick or perceptible economic lift. Instead, the recovery floundered near zero. Up until the New Hampshire primary, Bush appeared headed for an easy re-nomination. Patrick Buchanan, a former Nixon aide and newspaper columnist, however, mounted a primary challenge. Arkansas governor Bill Clinton, defining himself as a different kind of Democrat, emerged from the tumultuous Democratic primaries to gain his party's lead. Independent Ross Perot posed a third party challenge, dropped out, then reentered the presidential race again with a write-in campaign.

Perot was the biggest threat to Bush's reelection. He represented neither Right nor Left but the "radical middle," people angry at Washington for the budget deficit and despairing at "gridlock" (viewed as a dysfunction, an inability to pass needed legislation). The tension between the branches of government was perceived as the problem. Analyst Joshua Muravchik reasoned, however, that the complaint was really about "the way the system is intended to work. We were all taught its genius in school, except then it was called the separation of powers."[3]

2. Jack Germond and Jules Witcover, "How Did Thomas Suddenly Get So Experienced?" *Houston Post* (July 3, 1991)
3. Joshua Muravchik, "Why the Democrats Finally Won," *Commentary* (January, 1993),p.21.

As the campaigns took off in earnest, not one Hispanic was an intimate insider as part of the strategy-making for either the Bush, Clinton or Perot campaigns. If there had been, the Bush campaign would have known that a segment of Latino leaders, a full year before the Republican convention, already showed signs of disaffection with the Bush administration. President Bush's dilemma was that Reagonomics didn't work for most Hispanics, who were now primarily concerned about their own job security, where future jobs would come from, unemployment, and they feared a worsening economy.

Considering the amount of support Bush had received from Hispanic voters in the 1988 election, the President had actually not done so badly for his Latino constituents. Bush had appointed two cabinet members of Hispanic backgrounds. Also, Dr. Antonia Novello was named U.S. Surgeon General; Catalina Villalpando, U.S. Treasurer; former Florida Governor Bob Martínez, Office of National Drug Control Policy director; Ana María Farías became Associate Deputy Secretary of Labor; Jaime Ramón, Office of Federal Contract Compliance Programs director; Cari Domínguez, assistant secretary for Employment Standards Administration; Patricia Díaz Dennis, State Department assistant secretary for human rights and humanitarian affairs; and José Villamil undersecretary of economic affairs at the Department of Commerce.

In May of 1992, a Hispanic National Bar Association report showed that Hispanics still only occupied twenty-two of 816 federal judgeships (2.7 percent) and only 644 of 28,475 state level judgeships (2.3 percent). New York had the worst record, with no Hispanic federal judges and less than 1 percent, or twenty-six, state judges. Finally, in late June, 1992, the Senate Judiciary Committee approved attorney Sonia Sotomayor for the New York Southern District.

Numerous other appointments were made throughout government. But the Bush administration did not want to release updates on how Hispanic appointments fared. The "president has included Hispanics at all levels of his Administration," said George Ríos, a New York Republican National Hispanic Assembly founder. More Hispanics were in "policy-making positions than [under] any other president." Perhaps the claim was true but the recognition game had changed. Equal significance, critics claimed, needed to be placed on the policy-making importance of positions and not just the numbers.

For instance, slippage was detected in the handling of education. In September 1990, President Bush signed Executive Order 12729 establishing an advisory commission on education. The president's order came after Education Secretary Lauro Cavazos held a series of task force hearings around the country. But just a few weeks after the president's order was signed, and before an executive director was named, Cavazos resigned. Follow up was slow and no director was named for almost a year.

The executive order lacked teeth, failed to recognize discrimination as a factor inhibiting educational attainment, and failed to recognize that the government lacked consistent and systematic data on the issue. Nor were federal agencies required to cooperate. Furthermore, the seventeen-member commission was only given a year to draft a report and make its recommendations.

After meeting a few times, its recommendations were similar to others that "have been put forth for a decade," said two close observers. It let "the federal government off the hook," they said, by emphasizing the need for change at the local level, instead of focusing on federal policy that they were in a position to affect.[4]

Similarly, Bush supported the National Coalition of Hispanic Health and Human Services Organizations' ambitious efforts to address Hispanic children's health issues. But these, and similar initiatives didn't help the president's image. Many Latinos felt their concerns were shut out of the national agenda. Free trade negotiations with Mexico and Canada—one of the important post-Cold War measures for economic expansion—was a logical area for Hispanics to advise and represent the United States. But no Latino was part of the negotiating team. In fact, Raúl Yzaguirre and other leaders didn't like the direction that the negotiations were taking.

Bush was thought to have broken a promise under the proposed accord to protect workers. One often-cited example predicted that 2,600 union members at a GM plant in Van Nuys, California (about half of them Latinos) would lose their jobs due to plant competition from Mexico. Others objected to Bush's expected veto of legislation pending in Congress to prohibit the permanent replacement of striking workers.

The Bush administration's intention with respect to Hispanic interests, if it had a position, was questioned. Some even suggested that pains were taken to antagonize some elements. For instance, the Foresight Award was at first expected to go to the National Council of la Raza for distinguished service in the 1990 census. Then the honor was rescinded, and Commerce

4. Janice Petrovich and Elizabeth Weiser Ramirez, "Did Executive Order Shortchange Latinos?" *Hispanic Link Weekly Report* (October 5, 1992).

Secretary Robert Mosbacher canceled his appearance at the NCLR convention, sending a substitute instead.

Once again, every step forward seemed to come with two political steps back. Latino leaders felt that the national administration misperceived them, and thought they were only allies when it was necessary or convenient. They were alternately tolerated and rejected. Too many other important events easily overshadowed their concerns and moved their interest out of the picture. They were perceived as representing parochial issues and being out of step with the changing political landscape, part of which was suburban expansion.

Suburban growth exploded during the decade before the 1980s. The population of fourteen states became largely suburban. Six were among the ten most populous (California, Pennsylvania, Ohio, Michigan, Florida, and New Jersey). Five of the nation's ten fastest-growing counties were majority suburban, and nineteen of the twenty-five fastest growing "cities" were suburbs.

Suburban life, though stressful, did not stimulate any back-to-the-city movement, and was, in fact, expected to continue far into the next century. The opposite effect was in full force; cities were emptying in a rush to the outer loops. For instance, 43 percent of Boston residents, 48 percent in Los Angeles, and 60 percent in New York City said they would leave the city if they could.

The suburbanization of America produced a distinct ideology. "The prevailing imperative of suburban life," said William Schneider, "is security—both economic and physical. . . Presidential politics these days is a race between Democratic cities and Republican suburbs."

Suburban expansion meant Republican growth, producing a third of the national vote in 1988. That year, suburbs represented 48 percent of the vote, split 28 percent Republican, 20 percent Democratic. The eight point Republican lead in the suburbs canceled out the Democratic lead in the cities. In 1988, Bush could have carried such states as Ohio, Michigan, Georgia, Louisiana, Maryland, California, and Missouri without a single vote from a large city. The suburban voting pattern suggested a changing view of government.

Suburbanization spawned a heightened preference for private over public in government matters—and the attitude turned highly tax sensitive. Government was seen as an agent equalizing the distribution of tax-supported services. Suburbanites tended to oppose notions about equity that entitled direct benefits to some but not others.

The only politically secure social programs were those that benefited everyone. Social welfare programs—targeting the needy with housing, food, and medical care—were supported when the benefits went to the "truly needy." Entitlement programs, like public works, were understood as categories that everyone belonged to. Taxes, unlike broad spending, were to be applied narrowly so that they didn't hurt everybody. The more affluent were inclined to believe government had too much power; some voters doubted that government had the ability to do good. Government's potential had to be narrowed by term, pay, spending, and taxing limits.

President Bush's dilemma was that Reaganomics didn't work anymore. The economy had only expanded by 1.6 percent from 1989 to 1992, lower than under Reagan (3.0 percent), Carter (3.1 percent), Nixon and Ford (2.2 percent), and Lyndon Johnson (4.6 percent). Bush had promised 30 million new jobs in eight years but was only reaching toward 5 million by 1996. He had promised prosperity, but the nation got a major economic restructuring (due largely to defense cut-backs, a foreign trade expansion economy, and rapid technological and production displacement) that boiled down to a lingering recession.

Democrats sought to shore up traditional pockets of support by appealing to the "forgotten middle class," and proposed to manage better than had the Republicans by putting a president in office of the same party as the congressional majority, consequently breaking the gridlock. Perot could play into the Democratic strategy by taking votes away from Bush in the West. The approach would break into the Republican power centers in the suburbs. Clinton downplayed the traditional Democratic promise, derisively referred to as "a government program for every problem." Instead, he wanted the wealthy to pay a larger share of taxes to finance government, and he appealed to caring as an appropriate response for the plight of others. Most of all, he promised jobs and prosperity.

In April, 1992, both Bill Clinton and George Bush spoke by satellite hook-up to a National Association of Hispanic Journalists meeting in Albuquerque, New Mexico. "The economic news is a little better," said Bush. "I think we'll see a little more optimism." In particular, he emphasized his family-values campaign theme and reminded the 700 watching that he had three Hispanic-American grandchildren.

Later, Clinton pirated Bush's issue. "What I would like to point out," he said, "is [that] the president has an obligation to go beyond loving his own family and loving the idea of family and recognizing what has happened to American families."

Bill Clinton was the presumed Democratic nominee when he appeared at the LULAC national convention in July, 1992. Bush's family values, he claimed, were reflected in a 9 percent decrease in Hispanic family income and an increase from 11 percent to 22 percent of working Hispanics living in poverty. "Where is the day care? Where are the pre-school programs?" Clinton stressed education, LULAC's top priority. And without making specific promises, Clinton said he would appoint Hispanics to key cabinet posts, federal judgeships, and possibly the Supreme Court.

The presidential candidates should consider a Hispanic vice presidential running-mate, said LULAC president, José Vélez. "If anyone in this country can represent us and do justice for Hispanics . . . it would be Henry," added Velez. Cisneros just shook his head.

The Democrats had all of the attention, as George Bush and Ross Perot declined invitations to speak. LULAC, a non-partisan organization, would not endorse any candidate but gave Bush an indirect boost when the 576 delegates endorsed the North American Free Trade Agreement on condition that it include job training and environmental protection provisions.

Some Latino delegates were offended by the lukewarm reception from Clinton's political machine by the time of the Democratic National Convention in New York. Latinos were urged, even ordered in some cases, to hold back on "special interests." The appearance of unity basically succeeded, except when New Mexico's former governor Toney Anaya pushed for more Hispanics to serve in campaign policy positions and on the road with Clinton. "What I see unfolding at this convention is exactly what I see every four years paraded before us in this country. We are told, and we tell ourselves . . . that we are important, and then we walk out of here and nothing ever changes."

José Villareal, Clinton's deputy campaign manager, the top Hispanic on the team, quieted the revolt. He admitted the campaign needed more Hispanics in top jobs but assured the delegates, "It's going to get better." The campaign later named Los Angeles county official Gloria Molina as national campaign co-chair. In August, after the convention, Henry Cisneros was appointed campaign advisor.

Hispanic delegates made up 7.7 percent (330) of the convention. The delegation was greater than the 6.8 percent in 1988 and the 6.4 percent of 1984. California, Texas, and Puerto Rico sent the largest delegations.

Rep. Bill Richardson (D-NM) explained to the Mexican television network Televisa that Bill Clinton came from a state with very few Hispanics and was unaccustomed to dealing with Hispanic issues. Yet, the theme was all too familiar. Hispanic delegates were having to struggle again for recognition by virtually beginning from square one. The history of Hispanic recognition was forgotten. One convention experience did not build up to another. Nor did it matter that former candidate Jimmy Carter's recognition of the Hispanic delegation took him a long way. Anyone knowing that Clinton had not met with Hispanic delegates would have been embarrassed to hear Richardson make it sound as if this were a milestone.

Former New Mexico governor Toney Anaya was dissatisfied with the party's wishy-washy approach and how they deliberately downplayed race and ethnicity. Hispanic involvement was reduced practically to the point of political invisibility, he believed. "We want a major role to play," he said. "We want people in scheduling and policy positions. Let's force them to make the commitments, or else we are going to be here in four years looking in from the outside." Colorado state senator Bob Martínez echoed the sentiment. "I hope that Clinton will not write off the millions of Mexican Americans and Hispanic voters, because they will be the deciding factor."

José Villareal claimed that a lot of people just didn't know about the Hispanic involvement already going into the campaign. Hispanics had managed the campaigns in New Mexico and Nevada and were political directors in Texas and California. Marcella Sandoval was the western states regional director, and María Echeveste was appointed national Latino coordinator. "I actually helped manage the entire campaign," said Villareal, a San Antonio attorney. Jack Otero, a Democratic National Committee vice chair, disagreed with the dissenters and backed up Villareal: "I'm never satisfied, but we have greater presence than we've had with any other presidential candidate."

Texas Railroad commissioner Lena Guerrero was a keynote speaker, as was Texas attorney general Dan Morales and Congressman (Kika) de la Garza (Tex). "I think we have to stop pandering to gender, geography, or ethnicity," Guerrero later confessed. "I think we have to stop looking backward and start looking forward." After all, she had reached the pinnacle of her success. "It doesn't matter if he's black, brown or white at that level," said Roberto Alonzo, a Texas delegate, about Tennessee senator Al Gore's selection to the ticket, "What is most important is that we have access. Hispanics have agreed that the most important thing is to get Bush and Quayle out."

The political landscape had changed from four years before. Local campaigns took on new importance. Redistricting based on the 1990 census heated up competition. The push was on, through court challenges and electioneering, to clear a way for greater Hispanic representation, especially in New York, California, Texas, and Illinois. What did strike a nerve was that Hispanics (8 percent of the national population) were concentrated mainly in states critical to the election.

During the Democratic national Convention, independent Ross Perot withdrew from the presidential race. A *New York Times*/CBS News poll showed Perot's support had eroded the week before the announcement. He placed third (with 25 percent), behind Bush (33 percent) and Clinton (30 percent). Perot had run second the previous month, two points behind Bush and six ahead of Clinton.

The election equation changed with Perot out of the picture. Clinton was gaining in the popularity polls, and now he had a chance to appeal to Perot's loyalists. Similarly, the Hispanic vote was again coming into play, but in a quiet way, as Clinton cautiously avoided any "minority" over-identification. Hispanics were needed to hold the line as part of the Democratic core.

Two weeks after he got the nomination, Clinton campaigned in California. "It's no coincidence that we're going to the heart of Perot country to cultivate support soon after the convention," said Jay Ziegler, Clinton's California press secretary. The core of Perot's support—suburbanites, ideological conservatives and disaffected Democrats—was the traditional California Republican presidential voter. California held one-fifth of the electoral votes but had voted for a Democratic presidential nominee only once since the 1940's.

After Ross Perot abandoned the presidential race, Hispanic voters would have to turn out in large numbers to influence the outcome if the two candidates split the difference. Latinos had hardly supported Perot, although there was some detectable interest in the candidacy. "There will be an all-out war for the Hispanic vote," predicted Juan Andrade, head of the Midwest/Northeast Voter Registration Education Project. His group, founded in Chicago in 1982, provided nonpartisan information on candidates and issues to Latino voters in seventeen states. "It is great for us. It enhances our ability as power brokers," he said.

"The Latino vote will be crucial," agreed Manuel Casanova, chairman of the Republican National Hispanic Assembly. He pointed out that the Latino vote had been decisive in Republican Pete Wilson's gubernatorial election in California and Democrat Ann Richards' in Texas.

One of the connecting points between the campaigns and Hispanic interests was through Henry Cisneros. Before he resigned as a director of the Federal Reserve Bank in Dallas to campaign for the Democratic ticket,

Cisneros had been one of the driving forces behind the National Hispanic Leadership Agenda (NHLA).

NHLA, founded in 1991, served as the premier non-partisan coalition of major Hispanic organizations and leaders to provide public policy advice. Not since the Barbazon Terrace agreement, the first known non-government, non-party national policy meeting in 1969 forming the Hispanic alliance between organizations and leaders, sectors and Hispanic ethnicities, had such group consensus gone public. The NHLA group, headed by Cisneros, drafted recommendations for the two national party platforms and for the Perot campaign to consider. The recommended policies included removing voter registration barriers, curbing INS civil right abuses, addressing education funding inequities, health care as a right, home rental assistance for more Latino families, and minimum wage increases. The proposals went to the two major parties' platform committees. They were in luck as Bill Richardson chaired the Democratic Platform drafting committee, and he was sympathetic to their interests. The committee also had four other Latino members. The Republican platform committee's interim chairman, meanwhile, was Orange County, California supervisor Gaddi Vásquez.

Other indictors showed that Hispanics were primarily concerned with about employment, and the economy. A Los Angeles research focus group polled by the Southwest Voter Research Institute registered concerns about rising crime and education funding cutbacks. The California state lottery's lack of contributions to public education cast suspicion on government. "I thought they were going to give that money to the schools. Where's the money," said forty-five-year-old construction worker Gerónimo Carazco.

Four Los Angeles focus groups were held, plus two in Dallas and two in San Antonio. Homelessness and poverty, health care and health insurance, and the North American Free Trade Agreement's possible negative effects were other issues that concerned Hispanics. The focus groups shared mixed views on abortion, but they held a strong opinion that it was a personal or a religious issue and not a public-policy one decided by government.

A week after the GOP convention, Clinton met with the National Hispanic Leadership Agenda board members in Washington, D.C. He took notes on the five subject areas that were part of the briefing and only objected to one. "On the issue of employer sanctions," he said about the request to repeal sanctions against businesses that hired undocumented workers, "I don't know as much as I need to know." He said if elected he wanted to meet regularly with the group and pledged to review immigration policy. The National Hispanic Leadership Agenda sought but failed to get a similar meeting with Bush. Issues were not, however, driving the campaign. Core support was. And the nation's focus had shifted to the suburbs.

The day before the GOP convention opened, George Bush's son, Jeb, brought an emotional moment to a Republican National Hispanic Assembly breakfast meeting. Three hundred thirteen of the convention's delegates and alternates were Hispanics. The Hispanic Assembly claimed to have 6,000 members in twenty-two states, according to chairman Manolo Casanova. Jeb Bush eulogized Arturo Hevia, who he said was "Perhaps the strongest supporter of my dad." Bush seemed to fight back tears when he asked for a moment of silent prayer for Hevia, the Bush friend and advisor who had recently died. Hevia, highly regarded in the Cuban community, had drawn large numbers into Republican politics. "Arturo led the politicization of Cubanos when they did not want to integrate into the U.S.," said Washington businessman and former White House assistant, Henry Ramirez.

Foreign and domestic policy were increasingly interwoven, added Bush. "The world is interconnected," he said. "The closest allies are in this hemisphere." The recently negotiated North American Free Trade Agreement "is the first tangible result of that" yet Democrats were increasingly critical of the trade deal.

"Where were they when the Canadian free trade agreement was passed?" he said. The agreement with Canada gained relatively easy acceptance. "Is there something wrong with Mexico?" he asked rhetorically, suggesting that criticism was motivated by anti-Mexican sentiment and was not focused on the trade pact itself.

The other campaign issues he said that were shaping up included welfare reform, home ownership as a public housing substitute, education vouchers, and campaign reform. "The cold war is over. We have yet to define what the next era will be," he added. "The future can be filled with optimism and hope going into it *brazo a brazo*."

U.S. Treasurer Catalina V. Villalpando, speaking to the New Jersey delegation, linked former San Antonio mayor Henry Cisneros to womanizing allegations made of Bill Clinton. "Can you imagine two skirt-chasers campaigning together?" she said. The shock waves from the remark reached President Bush. "Nobody is going to be able to control everything that everybody says," he responded. Bush seemed to contradict an earlier statement that he would fire anybody who dealt in private innuendo, including "the issue of marital infidelity." Cisneros had withdrawn three years earlier from public office after acknowledging an extramarital affair. Villalpando's broadside came as a surprise, given that she had served earlier with Cisneros on the bipartisan Hispanic Leadership Agenda policy group.

A GOP statement, the following day, apologized for Villalpando and for a similar statement made by campaign chairman Robert Mosbacher. Clinton's communications director George Stephanopoulous called Bush a "hollow man" for failing to eliminate "sleaze" from his campaign. The president should fire Mosbacher and Villalpando, he said.

Before the Republican convention opened, the Platform Committee clarified its plank on illegal immigration, proposing to support the Border Patrol with the necessary "tools, technologies, and structures." The controversial wording was widely interpreted as a veiled endorsement of ditches and walls, barriers to deter illegal immigration at the U.S.-Mexico border, as Patrick Buchanan had proposed.

Roberto de Posada, GOP director of Hispanic Affairs strongly denied that interpretation. Past administrations had been criticized for various proposals to curb illegal immigration at the border. Pat Buchanan wanted the government to construct a 200-mile fence along the frontier in California and another section in El Paso, Texas. Buchanan's sister and campaign manager Angela Marie "Bay" referred to "structures" in the platform as one of seven planks that Buchanan wanted. "They don't build lighthouses on the border," she said.

Buchanan's America First campaign took flight after the New Hampshire primary. He advocated cutting immigration and foreign aid, reducing armed forces commitments around the world, reviewing treaty commitments, and defending industry with trade barriers. "We got our platform four years early," Bay Buchanan bragged. Press spokesman James W. Cicconi called the Buchanan assertions as "a lot of hooey." He said it was outrageous to interpret "structures" that way.

Yet, a few platform committee members, the Hearst News Service reported, didn't know what "structures" meant in the platform's context; they thought they were voting on guard houses. "If the Republican delegates have the courage of their insensitivity, they ought to change 'structures' to 'fence,'" said Fernando Dovalina, of the *Houston Chronicle*. "They could get smart and eliminate a Democratic weapon that would be pretty potent across the Southwest between now and November."[5] The plank, according

5. Fernando Dovalina, "GOP Plank on Border Fence Insults Once-Courted Hispanics," *Houston Chronicle* (August 16, 1992).

to Roberto de Posada, referred specifically to checkpoints, office space, highway improvements and excluded the controversial barriers. "The president is on the record opposing anything like a ditch or a wall."

The platform language was an embarrassment, and "I think nobody believes them. The way I see it, they are trying to backtrack" on the issue, said Leonel Castillo, former Immigration and Naturalization Service commissioner under Jimmy Carter, who observed the Republican convention from the sidelines.

The controversy arose one week after negotiations were concluded between the U.S., Mexico and Canada for the North American Free Trade Agreement. The "structures" plank alienated some Hispanics and sent out a contradictory message. NAFTA intended to lower trade barriers, while the platform suggested raising human ones.

Near the end, Barbara Bush, speaking to the convention delegates from the rostrum, asked her grandson to make some remarks. "Thank you, Ganny," said 19-year old George P. Bush, Jeb and Columba's son.

"The family is what makes my grandfather tick," he said, before reading from a letter written to the boy by President Bush. "I just wish," said George P. to the delegates, with hundreds of millions of television viewers watching around the world, that "people who see George Bush on TV or read about him in the newspapers could know him as I do." Then, almost as an afterthought, he burst out, with his right arm in the air, "Viva Bush!" he shouted.

Pep squads picked up the call "Viva Bush!" Then the delegates on the floor. "The hall was electrified," said Illinois Bush/Quayle campaign deputy Arabela Rosales, one of the Hispanic delegates. Illinois' stately Governor Jim Edgar pitched his arms into the air "Viva Bush!" he shouted.

"Everybody felt 'this is my family,'" said New Mexico delegate Rita Núñez. "He was one of us in the family," said New Mexico senate candidate Lou Gallegos about the young speaker. "He was one of us extending out."

The next day reporters gathered around de Posada, the twenty-six year old GOP operative. "Do you have a fact sheet? How many Hispanics are there in the country? What proportion?"

"About nine percent," he responded, unflappable, in a business suit and sneakers.

The defining moment did not arrive spontaneously, but it was not altogether engineered either. An ebullient Manolo Casanova, RNHA leader, announced to the Viva Bush! organizers that the theme was picked up after his group produced 15,000 bumper stickers and 10,000 caps. "Viva Bush!" buttons became instantly popular and scarce. They were actively traded among the faithful. "Oh, where can I get one," said a young woman in an evening gown, arriving for a reception at the Four Seasons Hotel.

The message had gone out. The divisive connotations that had variously defined Hispanic (as ethnic, minority, heritage group, other, them) went into a "suspense" category, much like that used in accounting, until new terms could be found to denote "inside the mainstream" and "part of the whole." The defining moment was what all the yelling was about —a presumption of inclusion, heralded by the president's 19-year old grandson.

Across town, a small Democratic crowd gathered at the Holiday Inn for drinks and a fundraising raffle to benefit Yolanda Navarro Flores' campaign for the state legislature. Many of the politicos were in a hurry to rush off to a Democratic "Bush and Baloney" gathering.

"I think they put him up to it," said Sylvia Medina, a young campaign worker, about George P's speech.

"We did showcase on the podium," said de Posada "because we had something to showcase with. That's what they [Democrats] were ashamed of doing." Republican Hispanic delegates actually formed a larger proportion of the convention than at the Democratic Convention. Two Hispanic Republicans were top platform committee leaders and six others served there. "These people are more in the mainstream" than Democrats, he said. "The Democrats were nowhere near on this radar screen," adding that Hispanic GOP'ers "were not appointed to minority positions, but to positions [that] went to the most qualified." Sheepishly coy, he added, "They say Bush has Hispanic professionals; Clinton has professional Hispanics."

De Posada knew that he was on the cusp of valuable political knowledge. Hispanic voters did not vote consistently as a Democratic bloc. Republican Illinois Governor James Edgar, for instance, had received 40 percent of the Hispanic vote. They no longer "pull the big lever." Straight party ticket voting was going by the boards. Hispanic voting represented the "evolution of the electorate," he said.

The party lines were drawn just seventy-five days before the election. The president was behind in the polls. The GOP strategy had intended to hammer away at Bill Clinton but the advertising campaign was in disarray. Pressure was building to change the campaign advertising. Roger Ailes, responsible for the negative Willy Horton campaign against Michael Dukakis in the previous election, was brought in to advise. Meanwhile, Leonel Sosa—who had successfully led Republican Hispanic campaigns in the past—still remained unclear about the campaign's direction at the end of August when it entered its final, decisive stage.

14

The Supermajority

Three weeks after Clinton's election, Henry Cisneros and Gloria Molina, top advisors to the president-elect, met with seventy-five Latino leaders to discuss the transition. Molina had already announced plans to continue as a Los Angeles County supervisor and said that she would not seek a position with the new administration. The group sought to forge a new kind of relationship. "We don't just want numbers [meaning, appointed positions], but the ability to have a say," said Tony Morales, American GI Forum executive director. Others felt that once installed in office, administration members would forget their promises. "There is some skepticism because we heard the same pitch from Carter sixteen years ago," said Morales. The meeting, said Southwest Voter Registration Project head Andy Hernández, served "notice that we will very closely monitor progress."

Clinton named Cisneros to head the Department of Housing and Urban Development. Federico Peña became secretary of the Department of Transportation. Bruce Babbitt, former Arizona governor and environmentalist, was named secretary of interior over Bill Richardson, who was considered. Clinton selected Zöe Baird for attorney general, even after she had told a transition aide that she had hired an illegal-immigrant couple to help manage her household. Later disclosures showed that she had failed to pay the employer portion of Social Security taxes. After she withdrew her candidacy Janet Reno was eventually confirmed as attorney general.

Enlightened self-interest made Bill Clinton attentive to Hispanics. He won the 1992 election with only 43 percent of the popular vote. It was a lower victory margin than that of every member of Congress. This dilemma encouraged Congress members to go their own way on voting when they chose to. Clinton had few passionate supporters and the advantage of having few permanent Washington enemies. Clinton governed through "floating coalitions," according to presidential advisor David Gergen.

Voter Research and Surveys reported that Clinton won 62 percent of the nationwide Hispanic vote. In California, he won 65 percent while a combined 35 percent went to Bush/Perot. The proportions by which he won in other large states with a big Hispanic electorate were: Texas, 58 percent to 42 percent ; New York, 59 percent to 41 percent ; and Illinois, 60 percent to 40 percent. He lost Florida 31 percent to 69 percent .

Clinton won by the smallest percentage of the popular vote since the 1912 election. Ironically, his 5.6 percent victory *margin* (the difference between him and the next closest vote-getter) was also the largest of any Democratic winner since Lyndon B. Johnson in 1964. Clinton carried two-thirds of the states (thirty-two and the District of Columbia), but only topped 50 percent of the vote in the District of Columbia and his home state, Arkansas.

Congressional district voting was the key to Clinton's victory. He won 256 out of the nation's 435 congressional districts. He won ninety-eight of them by a majority. Those voters became his core support. Clinton got a "supermajority" (at least 60 percent of the vote) in forty-nine of the districts. Forty-two of the forty-nine super-majority districts were "majority-minority" (that is, predominately black, Hispanic, Asian—or a combination of these populations). Minority districts became Clinton's "backbone of support" and the key to his victory. The other seven supermajority districts were white, but "certifiably liberal," located in New York, Massachusetts and California, said *Congressional Quarterly* analyst Rhodes Cook. Most of Clinton's supermajority districts were urban.

Clinton's other core forty-nine districts (that he won with between 50 percent and 60 percent) were in Appalachia, the Mississippi Delta, and the Hispanic Southwest. Clinton won two types of districts with less than a majority—those with voters that he steered back to the Democratic fold (after they voted for Republicans in the 1980s) and districts that represented a breakthrough into the Republican rural heartland and the suburbs. Having only exploded onto the national scene eighteen months earlier, his unstable constituency expanded, shifted and contracted dramatically during the first year. By his sixth month in office, Clinton's support fell back to "true-blue" Democrats composed of blacks, Hispanics, Jews, liberals, low-income voters and the elderly.

Clinton turned to his core support during the first crucial test —the budget. Core supporters provided the votes in the House, allowing Clinton to win the budget vote there. In the Senate, the measure only squeaked by after Vice President Al Gore broke a tie.

In the final analysis, 98 percent of Clinton's support came from districts where he had won a majority, 85 percent where he had a plurality, and only 60 percent where he had failed to carry the district. That left him with a two-vote winning margin since Republicans were unanimously opposed. The 218 votes roughly defined the Democratic core, Clinton's ruling majority.

Columnist David Broder, after studying the voting pattern, noted that the Congressional black and Hispanic caucuses in the House favored his program. But Clinton still faced "a delicate and risky political maneuver" in forming majorities beyond his core support. "Governing will never be easier for him until he gets a stronger mandate from the voters."[1]

Nine new members elected to Congress increased Hispanic representation to nineteen (including delegates from the U.S. Virgin Islands and Puerto Rico, both with limited voting privileges). The seventeen-member *voting* contingent included eleven Mexican Americans, three Cuban Americans and three Puerto Ricans. Hispanics composed about 9 percent of the population but made up 4.4 percent of the House membership. "We have a long way to go, but it's a start," said Rita Elizondo, the Congressional Hispanic Caucus Institute's executive director.

In fact it was not a start at all. The start occurred 170 years earlier when Rep. Joseph Hernández went to Congress to represent the Florida territory. Prior to 1992, a total of twenty-three Hispanics had served in Congress, two in the Senate and twenty-one in the House. Dennis Chávez (1935-62), followed by Joseph Montoya (1964-77) were elected to the Senate from New Mexico; they served for forty years (a two-year gap between the end of Chávez' term and Montoya's election). No Hispanic had sat in the Senate in the following fifteen years.

In the House of Representatives, Romauldo Pacheco (R-Calif.) went to Congress in 1877. During fifty-one of the next seventy-four years (1878-1952), a Hispanic served in the House, but never more than one representative at a time (from either California, New Mexico, or Louisiana). Texas, for instance, had no representation until Henry González was elected in 1960. The tide turned that year, and the number of representatives increased slowly over the next thirty-two years.

Sixty of the 435 congressional districts in the 1992 election had Latino

---

1. David Broder, "Slim Election Margin Hobbles Clinton," *Houston Chronicle* (August 23, 1993). Broder mistakenly suggested that Texas congressman Henry Bonilla, a Hispanic Caucus member, voted for the bill. He did not.

populations greater than 100,000; twenty of them had Latino majorities. Two Hispanic Congressmen (Bill Richardson of New Mexico and Robert Menéndez of New Jersey) represented districts without a majority Latino constituency. Six non-Hispanic Congress members represented districts with between 46 percent and 70 percent Hispanic populations.

Three Hispanic House members served for the first time on the House Appropriations Committee—Esteban E. Torres (D-Calif.), Ed Pastor (D-Ariz.), and José E. Serrano (D-N.Y.). Members with seniority began taking influential positions in the committee structure. In the House leadership, Bill Richardson was one of four chief deputy whips elected by the Democratic Caucus. This happened as the Hispanic Caucus diversified its focus (especially with the delegation's strong urban character) and became increasingly important to the President's governing coalition. When congressman José Serrano from the Bronx, N.Y. replaced south Texas Rep. Solomón Ortiz as Hispanic Caucus chairman, speculation arose that the leadership change gave the group "too much of a liberal bent."

"There will be some issues that divide us," said former chairman Ortiz, "but there are more issues like education, housing and jobs that unite us than divide us."[2]

After sixty days in office, Clinton's presidential appointments troubled the National Hispanic Leadership Agenda group. Signs indicated that Hispanics were getting overlooked—again. It didn't make political sense, since the administration needed Hispanics to maintain a governing coalition in Congress. Yet, Hispanic interest groups were willing to attribute much of the oversight to normal transitional disarray. They were still largely swayed by Clinton's pledge to advance diversity through his political appointments. The administration would "look like America," Clinton had announced. "And that to me," said Nydia M. Velázquez (D-N.Y.), who had just been elected to the House, "means hope that [Hispanics] will no longer be an invisible group in this country." But doubts arose among National Hispanic Leadership Agenda members, as appointments—which had been expected to move right through—ran into snags. Leaders cautioned patience; it was still early in the selection process, NHLA members were told.

By May, NHLA issued a "report card," giving Clinton a "C-." His performance was barely passing. High-level appointments lagged seriously

2. Inés Pinto Alcéa, "Hispanics Gain Members, Power," *Congressional Quarterly* (January 2, 1993).

behind. Only fifteen Hispanic appointments were announced during the first hundred days. Less than five of the total number were upper level enough to require Senate confirmation. HUD Secretary Henry Cisneros and Transportation Secretary Federico Peña alone produced a third of the jobs for their departments. White House officials shot back that NHLA had compared Hispanics with the total available positions instead of the appointments filled so far. Otherwise Hispanics would make up 9 percent of Clinton's appointments, roughly equal to the Hispanic population. The administration had made fifteen appointments out of 186 from a total of 324 available slots.

Still, the administration had named only one Hispanic among thirty-one top White House positions. It was a bothersome thorn in NHLA's side, as White House personnel sifted through applicants, with few if any Hispanics doing the sifting. Then in August White House appointee Regina Montoya resigned as assistant to the President for intergovernmental affairs when her husband was named U.S. Attorney in Dallas. The following month, Clinton quickly named Joe Velásquez as White House political affairs deputy director.

The situation was not better by October, and in fact, had grown worse from NHLA's point of view. Clinton was given a "D" for making only fourteen new nominations. The total had declined by one since May (five others awaited confirmation). Hispanics made up only 5.4 percent of the high-level appointments to date. Clinton, said Republican political consultant Roberto de Posada, "does not care and his campaign and political advisors think the Hispanic vote is something he doesn't have to worry about."

"The future, unfortunately, does not look promising," said Frank Newton, NHLA executive director. The complaint was symptomatic of the problem. In 1992, a Merit Systems Protection Board study disclosed that Hispanics made up 8.9 percent of the national workforce but 5.6 percent of all federal workers. They were the only major ethnic group underrepresented in the federal workforce, with only 2 percent of senior management jobs, compared to 92 percent for whites and 5 percent for blacks.

At the end of Clinton's first year in office, only one out of forty-eight nominations by the new administration to the federal bench was a Hispanic. Eighteen top positions were unfilled in the Commerce Department, more than thirty places in the Defense Department, as well as some top spots in the Department of Justice. After surveying similar openings at the Agriculture, Veterans Affairs, Environmental Protection Agency, State, Interior, and "every other department of the government," commentator

Raoul Lowery Contreras asserted that Clinton's people "can't find any Mexican Americans to fill appointive jobs." Yet, he noted, an experienced Latina prosecutor in San Diego was passed over for U.S. Attorney in favor of a Yale alumnus, an old Clinton college chum (who had never worked as a prosecutor). Thousands of Hispanic lawyers, teachers, professors, doctors, civil servants, law enforcement officials and business executives were also getting passed over. "They, more than anyone," said Contreras, "should be resentful that Clinton can't find them. They remain invisible. They, and I, remain unhappy."[3]

The low number of appointments—especially in the judiciary (district and circuit court judges in particular)—meant that only a small potential pool would gain the experience for the higher judicial ranks and that fewer judges would become available for Supreme Court nominations when they were sought. The 3,800-member Hispanic National Bar Association, in response, compiled a Supreme Court candidate list to avoid a last-minute scramble if a vacancy occurred. The group interviewed candidates, and finalized recommendations in March of 1993.

Coincidentally, Justice Byron White announced his resignation at the end of the current session. Press accounts reporting possible replacements, which included José Cabranes (chief judge of a U.S. District Court in Connecticut), Antonia Hernández (president of the Mexican American Legal Defense Fund (MALDEF)), Vilma Martínez (former MALDEF president), Cruz Reynoso (former California Supreme Court justice), and Dan Morales (Texas Attorney General) among others on the long list. Hispanic leaders were buoyed by Clinton's statement that the next justice "should be familiar with the problems of real people." But they were passed over in favor of Ruth Bader Ginzberg, whose reputation was founded on gender issues.

On June 3, Clinton met with two-dozen members of the National Hispanic Leadership Agenda to discuss a variety of topics, including appointments, education equity, and health reform. His nominee to head the Civil Rights Office, Lani Guinier, was in trouble. After the meeting, Clinton met the White House press corps to announce he was withdrawing the nomination. By December he still had not found a candidate for the Civil Rights office after John Payton withdrew his name from consideration. More than a year after the election, almost all of the federal civil rights offices remained

3. Raoul Lowry Contréras, "Hispanics Invisible in Clinton's Administration," *National Minority Politics* (February, 1994), p. 26.

vacant or were headed by Bush appointees. Clinton was considering non-legal remedies to open up economic opportunities. He was said to favor government anti-poverty approaches that targeted need and not race.

At a Congressional Hispanic Caucus dinner, Clinton spoke about his anticipated national health plan. His presence reinforced the perception that the president was increasingly dependent on Hispanic leaders as part of the legislative coalition needed to pass major bills. He had already successfully guided legislation through Congress that allowed parents to take leaves of absence from jobs during certain family emergencies, and he signed a "motor voter" bill, that encouraged expanded voter registration when applying for a driver's license. He was responsible for a barely-noticed, earned-income tax credit that raised millions of working poor above the poverty level.

Early in the administration's first year, rumors circulated that Housing and Urban Development secretary Henry Cisneros would leave his position to run for the U.S. Senate from Texas. Governor Ann Richards had appointed Bob Krueger to the post when Lloyd Bentsen resigned to become Treasury Secretary. Kay Bailey Hutchison, the Republican state treasurer, defeated Krueger in a special run-off election. (José Angel Gutiérrez ran as a Democrat in the same race). Hutchison was considered vulnerable for the 1994 general race after a Travis county grand jury indicted her for allegedly using the state treasurer's office for personal political fundraising and destroying public records. (The charges were later dropped.)

Cisneros, however, was moving full-speed ahead on another kind of campaign. In April he met with Margarita Robles to inspect her 300 square foot apartment in El Paso's *Segundo Barrio*. He rode a van from the airport and stopped to meet with County Judge Alicia Chacón, Congressman Ron Coleman, and members of EPISO (the Industrial Areas Foundation's local affiliate). Community organizer Ernesto Cortés Jr., a MacArthur Foundation fellow, was also present. He and Cisneros had a friendly reunion then left to inspect the apartment. Later, Cisneros told reporters that he would move funds to help families like the Robles. "There's no running water in the apartment units, the building doesn't meet code . . . It's hard to believe that in this country people are living like that in the '90s." Then he added, "I'm meeting with the President tomorrow morning and I intend to tell him what I've seen here today."

It seemed like another shallow resolve by a seasoned politician-bureaucrat. He had seen similar conditions in San Antonio and the Rio Grande Valley. President Clinton, too, had seen conditions like it in Arkansas. But in the six months after the El Paso tour, Cisneros spent a night at the Ida B. Well housing project in Chicago. He checked into a Queens, New York shelter for the homeless, where he shooed away city officials who went to greet him. He flew to Vidor, Texas where he seized control of the all-white county housing authority after the Ku Klux Klan had driven away the last two remaining African-American public-housing residents. Cisneros, after only nine months in the Cabinet, got the homeless back on the national agenda. He warned Democrats that the party was drifting to the right, criticized the Democratic Leadership Council, and used his office to attack racism. He referred to some party members, who considered minority problems unworthy of a major public policy focus, as "New Democrats."

Nevertheless, Cisneros was able to hold on to politically-advantageous business backing. Even the usually crabby *Texas Observer* called Cisneros "the best of the Clinton Cabinet."[4] Many insiders considered him the logical Democratic candidate for the U.S. Senate seat held by Kay Bailey Hutchison. But in mid-October, 1993 Cisneros announced that he would not run. Later that month he rebuffed requests from White House aides that he approach housing discrimination patterns as an economic issue. Instead, he identified the elimination of racial discrimination as one of HUD's priorities. On his first anniversary after taking office, President Clinton signed an executive order creating a new Cabinet-level working group, headed by Cisneros, to review all federal housing programs and to remove discriminatory practices preventing minorities, the disabled and families with children from access to financial assistance. The urban agenda was back on the block.

Similarly, Federico Peña, the other Hispanic in the cabinet, played a key role, with Labor Secretary Robert Reich, in the agreement reached between American Airlines and its striking attendants. The action helped ameliorate relations between the administration and organized labor after the fractious split over the North American Free Trade Agreement. Clinton had appointed Peña as Transportation secretary over William M. Daley, son of Chicago's legendary mayor Richard J. Daley, whose brother was the current mayor. Daley later led Clinton's drive to pass the North American Free Trade Agreement.

Clinton took office just as a new demographic picture came into focus from the 1990 census. Hispanics' spectacular population growth, begun in the

4. "Henry Come Home," *The Texas Observer* (November 12, 1993).

1970s, continued into the 1990s. The increases, however, encouraged some unrealistic expectations about Latino electoral power.

By 1993, 5,174 Hispanics held office in thirty-four states. They comprised just slightly more than 1 percent of all United States elected officials. Ninety-three percent came from six states—Texas (2,030), California (797), Illinois (797), New Mexico (661), Arizona (350), and Colorado (204). New York (93), New Jersey (44) and Florida (68) added another 205 officials to the total. The nine states accounted for 86 percent of the Hispanic population.

Acknowledging that "few would argue that it is anything but desirable to try to give minorities more power in House elections," *Congressional Quarterly* writer Phil Duncan complained that the elections of Nydia M. Velásquez (New York), Luís V. Gutiérrez (Illinois), and Lucille Roybal-Allard (California) attracted few voters. NALEO official Harry Pachón also had low voter turn-outs in mind when he said that population growth created "unrealistic expectations about Latino electoral power among some observers."

Sixty-six percent of the population was over eighteen years of age, and old enough to vote. However, only 19 percent of all Hispanics were in the fifty-five and over age category that casts the most ballots in elections (contrasted with 30 percent for the general population. Twenty percent was between eighteen and twenty-four, the age category that least participates in elections (compared to 14 percent for the general population. Therefore, Hispanic demographic youthfulness made them less likely to participate or to have a stronger impact on elections.

Linda Chávez offered another point of view. She believed that Hispanic immigrants inflated the population because of increasing numbers and helped increase greater representation, even when many of them were not eligible to vote in the districts where they lived.[5]

In 1992, four in ten adult Hispanics were not U.S. citizens. Non-citizenship prevented a greater impact at the polls throughout the 1990s. Six million were ineligible to vote (40 percent compared to 11 percent white and 8 percent black non-citizens). This alone distinguished Hispanics from other voting groups. On the other hand, over three million legalization applicants were expected to increase the voter pool by 1993. The trend was expected to continue at least until 1996.

---

5. Linda Chávez, *Out of the Barrio: Toward a New Politics of Hispanic Assimilation* (New York: Basic Books, 1991).

Even before that new wave of voters materialized, Hispanic elected officials had already increased by 41.3 percent from 1984 to 1993. The average official represented a district with a 56 percent Hispanic population. Single-member districts (mostly made possible because of Voting Rights Act guidelines and court challenges) changed government when Hispanics were present in sizable numbers.

Between 1981 and 1990, the increasing political representation coincided with a Latino population explosion and the greatest immigration in U.S. history. Along with high birth rates, the Latino population increased by 53 percent in one decade. Consequently, a 1993 census report—showing that many Hispanics lagged behind in income, education, and other indicators—fueled a debate over whether immigration or discrimination factors were responsible.

The report tended to affirm what many Hispanic policy leaders had been saying all along—greater public assistance was needed because the population was falling behind. The census seemed to prove that. Many had contended that Hispanics were often left out when it came to government help. Assistance was needed to catch up and lift people out of education, income, housing and other social welfare deficits. The Reagan administration's budget cutbacks in the 1980s had driven many Hispanics into the "underclass," some alleged. Recent findings showed that almost one-third of Hispanics had no health insurance (compared to 20 percent of blacks and 13 percent of whites); and 28.7 percent were below the new $14,350 poverty level. National Council of La Raza president Raúl Yzaguirre said that educational reform and other public programs were needed. "We haven't raised our voices enough. We haven't had the data. We haven't had the policy decision-makers."

Linda Chávez frontally attacked that line of thinking. She argued that immigrants had been responsible for the increased numbers of the economic and socially disadvantaged. But all "Hispanics" had been lumped together into one designation. When Mexican Americans, Puerto Ricans, Cubans, Central and South Americans, the groups making up "Hispanics," were differentiated between newcomers and first, second, and third generations, the groups seemed to statistically improve their life situations the longer they were in the country. They took on the characteristics of previously assimilated immigrant populations.

This optimistic scenario went against the interest of advocates, who championed government intervention and assistance, Chávez argued. They lumped all "Hispanics" together and had an ulterior motive in doing so. This was the "civil rights approach," intended to alleviate problems with government programs and extending entitlements to Hispanics, who they had designated, by definition, as a disadvantaged minority group. Advocacy groups self-servingly broadcast an untrue image of what "disadvantaged" meant. In fact, solutions that advocates proposed actually backfired and tended to create government dependence. Welfare approaches to problems encouraged female-headed households inside a vicious poverty cycle, she claimed.

The clash turned into virtual combat over how to conceptualize the "Hispanic" population. The fight contrasted perspectives into two camps, each side trying to persuade the public to accept a way of thinking. The duel was also over what government should do. The "social-welfare statists" lumped data together and tended to urge government interventions. Financial support would make people more equal and less poor. The "government minimalists" split data and encouraged less or no social-welfare assistance, alleging that the measures discouraged personal initiative.

The encounter took on urgency, as new census figures projected that Hispanics would become the nation's largest minority by 2010. Census reports did not distinguish between immigrants (about 40 percent of the Hispanic population) and non-immigrants. In fact, newcomers from Mexico, El Salvador and Guatemala were among the least educated and least affluent in contrast to college-educated immigrants from other parts of the world. Latin American immigrants depressed the figures for native Hispanics. Many studies failed also to differentiate immigrant from non-immigrant. In fact, most of the generational studies focused on Mexican Americans, to the exclusion of other Hispanic groups. The concern was not mere intellectual hair-splitting. But was it really true that each generation was better off than the one before?

Urban Institute demographer Jeffrey Passel found that second-generation incomes tended to improve; yet the third-generation Hispanic "isn't making gains above that." Perhaps education explained the pattern. Michigan State University sociologist Ruben Rumbaut came up with intriguing mixed results. He found that recent studies showed that some second- and third-generation Hispanic children did less well in school than Hispanic children who came to the U.S. as immigrants. The studies suggested that when generational differences were taken into account, some improvement occurred but the gains peaked in the third generation.

By the early 1990s an interesting demographic dualism appeared. The

Census Bureau had reported that from 1978 to 1990 the Hispanic poor increased from 2.61 to 6.01 million (21.6 percent to 28.1 percent of all Hispanics). The Increasing numbers were widely used as proof that the Reagan/Bush years had been detrimental to Hispanics. On the other hand Hispanic unemployment dropped 7.3 percent (from 15.3 percent to 8.0 percent) from 1982 to 1989.

Twenty-seven percent of Hispanic households below the poverty line had at least one full-time worker. That contrasted with 21.8 percent for white and 11.8 percent for African American families. A 1991 study by the National Council of La Raza—compiled from data provided by the census, academic groups, and think tanks—showed that many Hispanic families in the poverty ranks were part of the "working poor"—those with year-round workers, sixteen and older, who earned less than $12,195 in 1990.

"There have been stereotypes that lump us in that category of victim—people constantly looking for more welfare," said Cecilia García, spokeswoman for the Congressional Hispanic Caucus. "This could finally give recognition to the struggle that so many Latino families undergo. We do work. We do whatever we can to feed our families." However, the analysis did not segment (data splitting) to show how many were the immigrant working poor and whether the native population was prospering.

Another mixed finding resulted. This one tilted a little toward the splitters. The *San Francisco Chronicle* found that thirty-year-old Hispanic males with a college degree earned 13 percent less than similarly educated Anglo males, and similar immigrants earned only about half that of an Anglo. A thirty-year-old female Hispanic citizen earned 12 percent less than a similar Anglo female; and immigrant Hispanic females earned about 24 percent less than their Anglo counterparts. A study of 700,000 census records also found that, contrary to the bleak assumption that Hispanics dropped out of school en masse, actually 70 percent of Hispanic citizens over twenty-five had a high school diploma. That compared better than the 30 percent of immigrants who did so.[6]

Another study suggested that immigrants might assimilate too well. Ruben Rumbaut reported to the Association for the Advancement of Science that foreign-born children averaged better in school than their U.S.-born counterparts. The records of 5,000 children in Miami and San Diego showed that the longer a foreign-born child resided in this country the

6. Ramon G. McLeod, "Latino Men Having a Harder Time in Recession," *San Francisco Chronicle* (August 23, 1993).

chances increased that he would become like the U.S.-born, and his performance would decline. "There does seem to be this extraordinary draw of American culture," responded University of California, Irvine, sociologist Judith Treas, "not always with good consequences."

The "lumpers" and "splitters" distinctions went to the "Hispanic" core. "There are those who learned that depicting us in the bleakest possible terms was a way to get policy made," said David Hayes Bautista, of UCLA's Center for Latino Health. "But that has created the false impression that Latinos are this dysfunctional minority, mired in poverty and living off welfare. Yes, there are problems," he said. "But it is true that we need to look at the entire picture. There are many people making it and succeeding." A 1993 census report showed that Hispanic incomes increased with schooling, business startup and acceleration for entrepreneurs, and when consumer purchasing power rose.

Perhaps public perception had been all wrong, driven by the mainstream media's obsession with portraying America's Hispanics as an impoverished group, said William O'Hare, director of policy studies at the Population Reference Bureau. "The truth is more complex. A "significant share" of the Hispanic community had moved into affluence since the 1970s. Affluent Hispanic households increased 234 percent from 1972 to 1988.

Largely perceived as concentrated in ethnic communities, it seemed to follow that immigrants overpopulated old, stagnant settlements, mainly in inner cities. In part that was true, but deviation from the old pattern accelerated. Some immigrants never went to the inner city.

Some newcomers fit in closely with the native Hispanic population. University of Texas professor Rodolfo de la Garza described Hispanics as likely to be U.S.-born (instead of foreign born), affluent, and well educated. One report about a family in affluent, suburban Marin County, California frankly confessed—"The Perels don't look 'Hispanic'" or "the stereotype of a Latino immigrant."[7] The old stereotypes weren't as useful as in the past. The population was too robust, variable, diverse, and mobile for the old, tired discrediting mental pictures that had been so popular in the past. However perceived, Hispanics packed a big demographic wallop and accounted for 40 percent of U.S. population growth.

Instead of a bland monolingual, monolithic orientation, as most commentators presupposed, another pattern was taking shape. The trend was

7. William H. Frey and William P. O'Hare, "¡Vivan los Suburbios!" *American Demographics* (April 1993).

toward acquiring Spanish language skills, and not away from it. Seventy percent of Hispanics spoke Spanish at home in 1990, 30 percent did not. That was a 57 percent increase from 1988. Three-quarters of the people surveyed in one study said Spanish was more important to them now than it had been five years earlier.

Clearly, the population was integrationist because 30 percent to 40 percent of the group intermarried. That would lead to a new generation that would form a new cultural synthesis. For others, religion (70 percent Roman Catholic), history, identity, and attitudes tended to pull them into a shared cultural core. Spanish-language television cemented mutuality between people of distinct national roots.

Forty-one percent of Hispanics identified with Democrats, and 24 percent said they identified with Republicans. Regionally, Hispanics in the South were less likely to be Democrats; those in the West and Midwest were less likely to be Republicans, but more likely to register as Independents. A study of political identity suggested that Hispanic America resembled "white America" in class and local political cultures, and that the Republican Party stood to benefit the most as Hispanics became more affluent.

Movement—from south to north and from traditional Latino population centers in all directions—was striking. The migration acquired the dimensions of a diaspora.[8] Minnesota's Hispanic population, for instance, jumped 68 percent (from 32,000 in 1980 to 54,000 in 1990). Similar increases occurred in the upper Midwest. "They come for three reasons—" said Roy Garza, Minnesota Spanish Speaking executive director in St. Paul, "job, jobs, jobs."

Rhode Island, Nevada, Massachusetts, New Hampshire and Virginia doubled their Hispanic populations in the 1980s. Edwin Meléndez, head of the Gaston Institute, a Boston-based Latino think-tank, said that Puerto Ricans left New York for Massachusetts, New Jersey and Connecticut in search of better economic prospects. Declining schools, drugs and crime drove them away. Cuban Americans in Florida pressed into the suburbs while Central and South Americans moved into the urban areas around Miami near production and construction jobs.

The movements were too new for analysts to ascertain their long-term political impact. Garden City, Kansas, an older settlement, for instance, experienced a 105 percent Hispanic increase in the 1980s; people were lured

8. Christian R. González, "Migration Creating New Latino Enclaves," *Hispanic Link Weekly Report* (December 6, 1993).

by the opening of a meat-packing plant. Dennis Mesa became the town's first Hispanic two-term mayor. In distant Idaho, Iowa, and Oregon, a Hispanic presence became evident.

Hispanics also burst into the suburbs. About 43 percent lived in suburban communities in 1990, compared to 40 percent in 1980. These suburbanites increased from 5.1 million to 8.7 million, or 23 percent of total suburban growth. They tended to be better educated and more affluent by 32 percent than their central city peers. Seventy-seven percent of the Hispanic suburban population lived in thirty-eight metropolitan areas. Fourteen of those suburbs were in California, eight in Texas, five in Florida, three in New Jersey, and one each in Arizona, Colorado, Illinois, Massachusetts, Nevada, New York, Pennsylvania, and Washington, D.C.

As communities diversified and solidified, Hispanic affluence became more pronounced and self-evident. It appeared in advertising and target marketing, the ethic of educational attainment, inter-marriage, and mobility. "Affluent Hispanics are redefining Latino roles in America," wrote researchers William H. Frey and William P. O'Hare. In political terms, it would add to, and moderate, the emerging suburban ideology. Government had a role to play in helping those without recourse. It should do so fairly and on the basis of income (not race) as long as the rules were fair and well-regulated for non-discrimination. Beyond that, government was obligated to stand aside once the helping hand had done its part by concentrating on its traditional police and defense roles and to organize development in the common interest.

The immigrant scare of the 1990s was a fearful reaction provoked by structural economic problems, unresolved illegal immigration issues, mass appeals to public antipathy, and confusing racial/ethnic attitudes (especially prevalent after riots in Los Angeles following the Rodney King verdict). The ingredients led to the unique American nativist rhetoric founded on insecurities, prejudice and misinformation. Some people thought they were victimized and were less well off because of immigrants. Many Americans were convinced that foreigners were exploiting immigration laws and social benefits.

Yet, in spite of the perceptions, immigration had actually declined during the twentieth century. Rates were far below historic-high levels (when compared to the nation's base population). Most people had grown up during this unusual period and believed that the United States was traditionally less ethnically diverse that it had actually been previously.

Mainly, the public reacted to changes in the law that scrapped the quota system in 1965. This was believed to have caused greater immigration. The 1986 Simpson-Rodino Bill (the Immigration Reform and Control Act) drove legal immigration to a post-Depression high (3.1 per 1,000 U.S. residents from 1981 to 1990). The rates were still below those of every decade after 1830 until 1930 and ran about the same as the long-term immigration rate since American independence. In fact, the percentage of foreign-born in the population declined from 8.8 percent in 1940 to 6.8 percent in 1993. But even if the rates declined, the numbers were still high.

Nearly 40 percent of the total immigrants since 1987 lived in southern California, New York City, south Florida, Texas and Chicago. They often filled the vacuums left by native urban populations that had escaped into the suburbs in the diaspora from city to suburb to edge city. The irony was that immigrants shored up the numbers in some places. New York City, for instance, after losing over one million inhabitants, became the only major city east of the Mississippi to gain population between 1980 and 1990.

The increases helped local tax revenues. Immigrants reclaimed inner-city neighborhoods after decades of decline. They did not displace native workers but mainly went into jobs that did not exist before they came. One study estimated that even when the immigrant labor force doubled, wages for young blacks fell by only 4 percent or less, and those of other minorities were unaffected, casting doubt that immigrants significantly lowered wages.

Southern Californians, however, felt that illegal immigrants exacerbated racial tensions and took away jobs from minorities. Pat Buchanan's pronouncements during his presidential campaign emboldened nativists who felt the country was losing ground to illegal immigrants.

Behind the emotions was a startling economic restructuring. Fully 27 percent of all jobs lost between June 1990 and December 1992 were in the five-county Los Angeles area. Los Angeles was responsible for 540,000 of the 2 million jobs lost nationally. Massive defense cut-backs and the slowing of the construction industry following the savings-and-loan crisis, corporate downsizing, and a state budget crisis forcing tight public service budgets. California, by itself, accounted for 38 percent of the whole national job loss. California, New York and Connecticut were responsible for three-quarters of the employment loss. As the problem was not national in scope, every American was not similarly affected. For that reason, nativism did not hit fever pitch in all places.

But it did happen in gateway areas, where immigrants traditionally settled. Nearly 40 percent of all immigrants since 1987 settled in Southern

California, with large cohorts in New York City, south Florida, Texas and Chicago. Otherwise sensible people perceived that immigrants—especially illegal ones—depleted the public treasury, placed excessive demands on public schools, increased welfare programs, demanded health care aid, and contributed to rising crime rates.

Nowhere else was the correlation made more shrill than in California. Tensions mounted right before the 1992 election. In April, a riot broke out in south-central Los Angeles after a suburban jury (where the case was taken after a change of venue) found all but one of four Los Angeles police officers not guilty in the brutal beating of Rodney King. Street pedestrians and motorists were beaten, stores were looted, and arsonists torched buildings. George Bush's perceived inattention to the nation's economy did not spark the incident but did not help, either.

The INS was called in (after the National Guard) to seek out undocumented immigrants, some of whom were reportedly involved in looting. INS officers rounded up Mexican undocumented immigrants and deported them across the border. Tensions rose as marauders were pitted against good citizens. The undeserving underprivileged were seen running with loot from stores while the city burned. Incredulous Latino storeowners couldn't understand why people they serviced had opportunistically looted them.

Up against a fiscal wall, some cash-strapped local officials couldn't see immigrants as part of the solution to their problems, even if immigrant parents contributed more than the $5,000 needed per schoolchild through taxes. Or that children had filled schools not only in Los Angeles but also in New York, Chicago, and Miami. The school systems, said writer Peter Salins, were dying before the immigrants came and breathed new life into them. "[T]he immigrants rescued the schools, not only from bankruptcy, but also irrelevance."

In California, many thought that immigrants couldn't help rescue anything. They were the problem. A study sponsored by the Los Angeles County Board of Supervisors claimed that immigrants (including illegals and their children), cost the county about $808 million during fiscal year 1991-1992. They exhausted about 68 percent of the county's health care services. Immigrant children were responsible for about 23 percent of the total education system's budget. The thrust of the public complaint was against illegal immigrants. Many thought that legal immigration was also out of control.

When Rebecca Clark and Jeffrey Passel of the Urban Institute investigated, they found that the Los Angeles Internal Services Department's costs were overstated by $80 million. Local officials, with tight budgets and deficit spending, exaggerated the case. Instead, long-term immigrants made significant contributions to the areas where they lived. But the federal government —not the state —benefited the most from the revenues gained. Local officials were pointing their fingers at the wrong people. However, the scare was about fear —not about reality.

The California Assembly introduced twenty pieces of legislation to restrict access by illegal immigrants to health care, public assistance, workers compensation, employment assistance, driver's licenses, and education. Most of the measures failed, but some remained viable. "The key to controlling the illegal immigration problem is to stop subsidizing them," said Los Angeles-area Republican assemblyman Dick Mountjoy. Border walls would not deter illegal crossings, he said, "because we've made it too beneficial for them to come here." Novato, California resident Bette Hammond, leader of the 450-member Stop The Out-of-Control Problems of Immigration Today (STOPIT), blamed petty and major crimes, homelessness, jail overcrowding, and the education system's downfall on illegal immigration. "There's parts of Los Angeles you walk through you wouldn't even know you are in America," she said.

The attitude in California was infectious, and some other parts of the country found the vector contagious. Sixty-one percent of respondents to a *New York Times*/CBS News Poll said they favored a decrease in immigration, compared to 42 percent in 1972 and 33 percent in 1965. Most Americans misperceived and believed that illegal immigrants made up the bulk of all immigrants.

According to the INS, 8.9 million legal immigrants came to the U.S. in the past decade, along with three million illegal immigrants. However, speculations ran as high as 10 million legal and 4 to 5 million illegal immigrants. "Economics, not xenophobia," said writer Tony Freemantle, "tends to trigger anti-immigration sentiment, although fear and distrust of new ethnicities cannot be dismissed."

University of Maryland economist Julian Simon reasoned that immigrants had no negative economic consequences but were, instead, a national asset. He calculated that immigrant families cost $1,400 in welfare and schooling benefits, compared with the average native household receiving $2,300. But University of California economist George Borjas reasoned that since the 1950s, immigrants had fallen into a class more likely to seek public assistance. By 1980, 8.8 percent of all immigrants to the U.S., he found, received some sort of welfare, compared to 7.9 percent of native households.

The greatest outcry, however, was in reaction to a study by Donald Huddle, economics professor at Rice University. He estimated that all immigrants —legal and illegal, refugees, and asylum seekers —cost the country much more than the taxes they paid. He estimated that 11.8 million legal immigrants settled in the U.S. from 1970 to 1992. Projecting forward, Huddle forecast a cost to taxpayers of $668 billion from 1993 to 2002.

Urban Institute researcher Jeff Passel evaluated Huddle's projections and found an error. "He assumes that after their first year, immigrants would not pay taxes at all," said Passel. "This is a gross exaggeration of numbers," said NCLR policy analyst Cecilia Muñoz. Early the following year, another Urban Institute report by Passel and Rebecca Clark (sponsored by the Tomás Rivera Center) contrasted sharply with Huddle's study. It found that U.S. immigrants contributed $70.3 billion in taxes in 1992 and used $41.6 billion in government services. The study also found that California immigrants contributed $30.7 billion in taxes and used $18.7 billion in government services. Passel and Clark included tax contributions left out by Huddle such as gas, social security, FICA and insurance taxes.

Undaunted, Huddles conducted a study for Texas similar to the one in California. Again Passel pointed out how the study, paid for by the Carrying Capacity Network, was flawed.

Clinton proposed to control illegal entry with reforms and new expenditures. Those measures were not enough for Wyoming Senator Alan Simpson (R), who also wanted to reduce legal immigration. "I think we went too far," he said about the law he had originally sponsored. He proposed new fees for border-crossings, revision of the asylum laws, and that citizens carry tamper-proof identity cards.

Interestingly, Simpson's proposed measures were actually less restrictive than those offered by other legislators.

15

Convergence

Congress felt pressured by loud outcries to stop encouraging immigration. In 1993, a congressional measure would have sent $300 million to states disproportionately impacted by immigrants and would have prevented legal immigrants with less than five years of residency from receiving benefits. House Ways and Means Committee chairman Dan Rostenkowski wanted to add to the bill that new immigrants would have to wait five years before becoming eligible for welfare payments, unemployment compensation, and other benefits. The government could save $331 million with the delay. Representative José Serrano (D-N.Y.), Congressional Hispanic Caucus chairman, complained that the floor debate was misleading and "antithetical to everything this country stands for." Congress, he said, was "pitting the unemployed against the poor, disabled, blind and elderly immigrants." Under current legislation, immigrants were eligible to apply for government benefits after three years.

Freshman California Congressman Xavier Becerra was instrumental in exposing a bipartisan plot to impose the five-year exclusion. That led senior Hispanic Caucus members to work out a deal with Rostenkowski. After a bargain was struck, the coalition supporting the reconciliation bill threatened to fall apart. Rostenkowski wavered on his commitment to the Hispanic Caucus and threatened to change his mind. Other House members threatened to oppose extending unemployment benefits, also part of the bill, if he didn't support expending the qualifying period from three to five years. Representative Rick Santorum (R-Penn.) complained that employed citizens were being asked to pay for the benefits of non-citizens. Serrano called similar arguments "disgraceful. Impoverished legal immigrants were getting scapegoated." Then, at a closed-door Democratic session to count votes, Becerra openly thanked the Democratic leaders "for backing the objections to the unfair provisions. . . ."

"Why don't you shut the fuck up," barked Rostenkowski. A heated, expletive-filled exchange followed. In the end, Rostenkowski called the deal off.

"Xavier really messed up," said one representative. "If this hadn't happened, we'd be declaring victory." More than a hundred Democrats joined a solid Republican bloc to include the two extra years in the legislative package.

The administration cautiously stayed out of the rising clamor to take action against immigrants. California Governor Pete Wilson, however, moved aggressively, and signed four state bills designed to restrict their mobility. The laws required proof of citizenship or legal residency to apply for a driver's license, denied undocumented persons job training or placement assistance, overturned local sanctuary laws preventing local police from working with the Border Patrol, and stiffened health care fraud penalties. Wilson vetoed a bill to allow non-profit organizations to offer naturalization courses and to establish immigration outreach and applications centers.

Eighty-one percent of California Latinos opposed California Governor Pete Wilson's other proposals to restrict immigrant children the right to schooling, according to an August, 1993 survey sponsored by the National Association of Latino Elected Officials Educational Fund, KVEA-TV and the newspaper *La Opinion*. Seventy percent believed that the debate over illegal immigration fostered greater discrimination against Latinos, and 29 percent felt threatened by the anti-immigrant sentiment that swept the state. El Paso writer Joe Olvera observed that Wilson "is trying to fight the Mexican-American War of 1846 all over again."[1]

Meanwhile, the federal government formed another kind of plan. By December 1993, the U.S. Border Patrol planned to erect a ten-foot steel fence on the border along El Paso, part of Arizona and in southern California. In all three border locations, the solid-steel walls were made of military surplus mats used to make aircraft landing pads, welded together into sections by military units that provided the labor. In El Paso, the new protection added to miles of chain-link fence along the Rio Grande.

Border Patrol agent Silvestre Reyes had a few hundred of his subordinates take positions along a twenty-mile stretch in mid-September, as part of Operation Blockade. The agents effectively stopped illegal immigrants who had boldly defied most previous barriers, and the number of illegal

---

1. Joe Olvera, "California's Gov. Wilson Wants to Start Another War with Mexico," *The Houston Post* (August 20, 1993).

crossings were driven down to negligible numbers. After the operation, apprehensions declined from about 700 to 200 per day. Mexican diplomats called the action an "unfriendly act." Reyes' superiors recognized the operation's negative political fall out, but found it effective.

El Paso county residents noticed that crime decreased after the measure took effect. Many others supported the measure as a way to reduce recent tax hikes for non-reimbursed social services stemming from immigration. (A later evaluation found that the approach had little effect on illegal "long distance crossings," nor decreased human rights violations and other alleged Border Patrol abuses, and was inconclusive about whether Mexicans were even responsible for the crimes—mainly against property—that were reduced.)

Officials at Dallas' Parkland Memorial Hospital, in another example, were concerned that their facility was not being reimbursed for most of the Hispanic infants delivered there to undocumented parents. Then, on publication of the report, chief executive officer Dr. Ron Anderson informed journalist Richard Estrada that Parkland had actually said they believed the majority to be documented. However, since Parkland and other hospitals in Texas were prohibited from asking the patient his legal status, there was no way to really know. Other social-service providers in the region also reported surges of new demand for services from impoverished, undocumented Mexican immigrants.[2] Again, the presumption was that Hispanic attributes suggested first an illegitimate status and, secondly, a public burden.

President Clinton responded to complaints by recommending immigration policy measures that curbed human trafficking by crime syndicates that facilitated illegal entry. Meanwhile Congress received more than seventy bills seeking to restrict legal and illegal immigrants. In December of 1993, Clinton named former Texas Congresswoman Barbara Jordan to head a nine-member U.S. Commission on Immigration Reform to assess the impact of recent immigration policy changes. A new thrust was in the offing.

Finally, after Doris Meissner was appointed as INS commissioner, a new policy was announced by trial balloon. The administration wanted to defuse tensions over illegal immigrants by enfranchising the estimated 10 million residents who had lived in the U.S. without benefit of citizenship. The proposal recognized that the federal government had not previously

2. Richard Estrada, "El Pasoans Might've Been Canaries in Immigration Coal Mine," *Houston Chronicle* (November 28, 1993).

encouraged naturalization. "I am very concerned about the anti-immigrant feelings we see in various parts of the country and in Congress," said Meissner. "We have never been very aggressive in encouraging resident aliens to naturalize."

The policy was inspired after the 1986 amnesty law encouraged 3 million immigrants to gain legal status. Lawful residents could apply for citizenship after maintaining U.S. residence for five years or longer, demonstrating an ability to read and write English, and possessing knowledge of U.S. history and government. The proposed policy offered the administration a bonus—a new bloc of potential Democratic voters once citizenship was obtained.

The policy measure had promise, but the antagonistic public mood simmered and did not quell easily, while local public funds grew scarcer. Latino groups became alarmed at the mounting anti-immigrant sentiment. In mid-January of 1994, the American Friends Service Committee organized a meeting in Tucson concerning the Miranda incident.

In June, 1992, Darío Miranda was shot in the back twice by INS agent Michael Elmer in Nogales, Arizona. Elmer, thirty, was on a drug stake out at sunset when Miranda, twenty-six, ran toward him, then changed directions. Heading back toward the border, he took the bullets in the back. A Tucson federal jury acquitted Elmer, who admitted hiding the body after a fellow Border Patrolman reported the incident. When faced with charges arising from having violated Miranda's civil rights, a Phoenix federal jury acquitted Elmer in February of 1994.

Activists believed that the jury was influenced by the prevailing anti-immigrant hysteria. Early in 1994, Attorney General Janet Reno, responding to the outcry from human rights groups on both sides of the border, announced she would look into the civil rights implication of the case. Later, she announced a major new initiative, costing about $540.5 million and modeled after El Paso's "Operation Blockade." The proposal would place new INS agents, install five miles of border lighting and use new equipment. The current number of judges and investigators who handled asylum cases would double to address the backlog. And up to 20,000 criminal immigrants were scheduled for deportation (when they were released from prison or jail). The policy would make it easier to get a job by decreasing the number of documents needed for employment, would increase enforcement against employers regularly hiring illegal immigrants, and it promoted naturalization through community-based outreach. Commissioner Meissner referred to "a full reinventing of the INS" with the advent of a computer network that would share data with the FBI, the U.S. Customs Service and U.S. consulates worldwide. Immigrant advocacy groups were generally favorable.

Clinton's first major presidential test was the budget. The second benchmark, also in the first year, was the North American Free Trade Agreement. The building blocks, leading up to NAFTA began when President Carlos Salinas de Gotari signed six agreements with President Bush, one to open trade and investment opportunities. Later in the year, Salinas became convinced that Mexico's foreign policy would have to rely more on United States investments and less on those from Europe and Asia. By December of 1990, Salinas, already two years into his six-year term, proposed a free-trade agreement. Former U.S. ambassador Abelardo L. Valdéz had advanced a similar idea twelve years earlier. President Reagan had broached a comparable notion. Mexico was in a good position now to promote free trade as the United States' third largest trading partner. In May of 1991, Congress had granted President Bush "fast track" negotiating authority to assure the measure would get to a Yes-No vote when it arrived for approval.

Canada was involved from the beginning to safeguard its own free-trade pact with the U.S. A North America free trade zone, with 360 million people and a combined $6 trillion dollar economic output could serve as a global counterweight to the European Common Market and the East Asian block led by Japan. Salinas needed free trade's foreign capital and technology to permanently stabilize Mexico's economy. In turn, the United States wanted lower production costs, access to the Mexican market, investment opportunities, and energy.

To help out, the Hispanic Alliance for Free Trade, headed by Elaine Coronado, was formed to promote "fast track" passage. The group was intended to serve as a liaison between the Hispanic community and NAFTA negotiators. Raúl Yzaguirre, National Council of La Raza president, also gathered Latino support for fast-track authorization. Latino leaders were certain that the Bush White House needed their participation in the negotiations and political support for the legislation to pass. Free trade was for them a way to open doors inside new power centers and an attractive non-partisan issue.

But the secret negotiations miffed Hispanic leaders, who were kept out of the "loop." The Bush administration did not court Hispanics for ideas to the same extent that the Mexican government did. The two approaches were clearly different.

By May 27, 1992, the Mexican government had already spent $25 million since 1989 for consultations and to promote NAFTA in the U.S. The Center for Policy Integrity, a Washington watchdog group, released information showing that the Mexican government paid substantial amounts to Latino leaders for technical assistance. They included former New Mexico governor Toney Anaya; Eduardo Hidalgo, Carter's Secretary of the Navy; Abelardo Valdéz, an assistant administrator for Latin America and the Caribbean at the U.S. Agency for International Development during the Carter administration; Jerry Apodaca; Sosa and Associates; Campos Communications; and Moya, Villanueva and Associates.

The report may have underestimated the real costs due to the Justice Department's lax disclosure requirements. *The Wall Street Journal* estimated that Mexico might have spent more than twice the reported amount, Latinos receiving under 10 percent of the amount spent.[3]

By July of 1992, President Bush and Salinas met for the tenth time following a major breakthrough earlier in the month. Trade officials, meeting in Mexico City, tried to conclude the negotiations before the August Republican National Convention to give Bush the NAFTA issue in the campaign, observers noted.

In Congress, Democratic House Majority Leader Richard A. Gephardt criticized the pact as deficient in environmental, worker rights and labor-related provisions. Bush's 1988 pledge to serve as the "environmental president" was thrown in his face. Under the pact, Mexico gained greater access to some U.S. markets and had fifteen years to eliminate some of its own subsidies. Some observers speculated that an August deadline had been set so that Congress would have ninety days to ratify the agreement before the election. "We have said time and time again there is no deadline," trade representative Carla Hills insisted.

On August 12, Salinas vigorously defended NAFTA in a televised speech. Mexicans feared losing industries to American and Canadian capital just as U.S. organized labor feared losing jobs to Mexicans. On the tenth day of final negotiations, President Bush appeared at the White House rose garden to announce a "new era" in North American trade. NAFTA, he said, is "part of my long-term economic growth plan."

The pact was "chock-full of firsts," said Hills. For instance, Mexico would open its market to U.S. cars, light trucks and motor vehicle parts. Agricul-

---

3. Patricia Guadalupe, "Study Identifies Top NAFTA Lobbyists," *Hispanic Link Weekly Report* (June 7, 1993).

ture would have full-market access after fifteen years. Textile quotas would be eliminated for the first time in an international trade agreement. NAFTA created free trade in services and opened Mexico's $6 billion telecommunications and $3.5 billion insurance markets to its northern neighbors.

Special briefings were prepared in Houston for Hispanic Republicans at the Republican National Convention. In October, one month before the election, Bush—accompanied by Salinas and Canadian Prime Minister Brian Mulrooney—witnessed the signing in San Antonio of NAFTA's final draft.

Clinton's position on NAFTA was unclear. He had enunciated in mid-August that "foreign policy and domestic policy were now two sides of the same coin." House majority leader Richard Gephardt considered NAFTA a bad coin toss and said "Without changes, Congress could not responsibly approve the NAFTA agreement." If Clinton decided to reject the agreement, the campaign needed to take a strong position against it. But if he were in favor, the campaign needed something else besides a "me-too" position.

Clinton's campaign staff went to work around labor and environmental group objections. Strategists sent Henry Cisneros—Salinas' friend and former Harvard classmate—to tell the Mexican president about Clinton's qualified approval. On a campaign swing to Democrats Abroad, a branch of the party in Mexico City, Cisneros broadly gave the impression that Clinton's mind was made up and the decision was favorable. Then he met with Salinas at Los Pinos, the president's residence. Clinton's position would emphasize the need for greater consideration of environmental and labor factors.

Twenty-four hours later, on October 4, Clinton made his position public. He did not oppose NAFTA but objected to parts of it and defined a difference between Bush and himself.

Speculation arose in Mexico over what would happen if Clinton were elected. Was the entire pact subject to re-negotiation because of the objections? From the Mexican government's point of view, the treaty was already signed and sealed after the negotiators signed off. "Fast track" assured Congress' speedy consideration.

Cisneros' meeting had triggered other high level contacts. Mexican representatives met at least twice in deep background with members of Clinton's team until word eventually leaked out. The Mexicans seemed receptive to adding provisions to the treaty, even if the government had maintained several times that NAFTA was an agreement with a government and not with a candidate.

Sandy Berger and Barry Carter, Clinton's campaign assistants on international policy, met with Salinas' representatives: Herman Von Bertrab, commercial officer at the Mexican embassy, ambassador Gustavo Petriocioli, and Herminio Blanco, chief of the Mexican negotiating team. Mayté Junco, assigned by the Clinton campaign to Hispanic affairs, confirmed that the meetings took place. Representative Bill Richardson similarly acknowledged that such meetings took place as did Raúl Benítez, international affairs expert at Mexico City's Iberoamerican University.

"There's no official arrangement, neither with Bush's team nor with Clinton's," said Van Bertrab. The Mexican government didn't want to get entangled in the campaign. There had been "25,000 meetings with 25,000 persons," he said, with Republicans and Democrats alike, but no "official" contacts with the campaigns.

Bertrab obfuscated the issue. He referred to "official", not "unofficial" ones as had evidently taken place. "Unofficial" channels, during a political campaign, were highly suspect and questionable practices. Mexican officials were vulnerable and could have been charged with interfering in an election. The controversy could have been devastating for Clinton and the Mexican government. But Bertrab handled the matter delicately and left it blurry enough so that it could be affirmed, if that was useful, or denied, if necessary.

Salinas said in a speech to party officials that his policies would remain unchanged if Bush were defeated. "Independently of who governs in Washington," said Salinas, "we will continue working with this same strategy." Two weeks later, Clinton won the election. The following day, at eight in the morning, Clinton telephoned Salinas to assure him that the free trade agreement would get his support.

"Well, you know that mutual friends have led him [Clinton] to understand the process of change in Mexico," said Salinas the same day. The "mutual friends" alluded to were Henry Cisneros and Texas governor Ann Richards. Keeping his eye on the prize, Salinas dispatched Ambassador Gustavo Petriccioli to Little Rock with a formal congratulatory letter, lauding Clinton for campaigning vigorously, particularly among women and Hispanics. Salinas was the first head of state to meet with Clinton after the election. Clinton restated his intention to review NAFTA on labor and environmental concerns. After Mickey Kantor was confirmed as the U.S. trade representative, the new administration began negotiating the "parallel agreements."

In 1991 many Latino leaders, feeling left out of NAFTA deliberations, reversed the exclusion by organizing dozens of conferences, debates, town-hall meetings and briefings through the summer of 1992. A consensus resulted. Research and computer modeling showed that NAFTA would create a small job gain but that Latinos would get few benefits and would possibly suffer greater losses than other groups. Opinion polls suggested that Latinos supported the NAFTA concept but feared job loss. They would support an agreement that included workers' interests, border and environmental development.

In March of 1993, the Southwest Council of La Raza, the Mexican American Legal Defense and Education Fund, and the Southwest Voter Registration and Education Project convened a national summit. Leaders ironed out an opinion, predating the conclusion of the "parallel agreements." Armed with "conditional support" from 65 percent to 67 percent of California and Texas Latinos, nine recommendations were made for job training, labor and environmental standards, border infrastructure, economic and small business development, inclusion of immigration and Caribbean Basin issues, and the formation of a North American Development Bank. The NAD Bank idea originated from House Congressional Resolution 121, sponsored by Los Angeles congressman Esteban Torres, to make $1 billion in low-interest, long-term loans for development and retraining. That winter's Hispanic recommendations became a mainstream national agenda by late spring and summer when negotiations on the "parallel agreements" were concluded. In late August 1993, Clinton recruited William Daley to guide the legislation through Congress. Meanwhile, Texas billionaire Ross Perot opposed the measure. Daley was chosen because of his labor connections and as a concession after he lost out to former Denver mayor Federico Peña in the competition for the Department of Transportation cabinet post.

Ross Perot's opposition to NAFTA was a major obstacle. To counter him, Trade Representative Mickey Kantor attacked Perot's claim that job loss would be extensive. "There's a lot of misinformation floating around," said Kantor.

If NAFTA failed, Bush's strategy to include other Latin American nations and the Caribbean Basin in a free trade zone would also fail. Chile had already indicated willingness to sign on, and Colombia and Argentina were close behind. A hemispheric free trade zone would dwarf any similar trade bloc in Europe and Asia.

Texas governor Ann Richards's strong pitch for NAFTA at the National Governor's Conference in Tulsa encouraged a perception that Mexico's stability was in imminent danger if NAFTA failed. The Texas hyperbole heated up when Ross Perot, as a routine part of his anti-NAFTA argument, referred to the "giant sucking sound" of jobs that would drain out of the U.S. on their way to Mexico.[4]

A break in the side agreements occurred in mid-August. The U.S. demanded that environmental and labor violations should be punished with trade sanctions. Canada was opposed but finally agreed to a compromise. Mexico would raise wages, and Salinas proposed to link the minimum wage to productivity gains. The side agreements created labor and environmental commissions, each with a minister and a secretariat to enforce the provisions.

House Majority Leader Richard Gephardt announced his reservations about the pact but left the door open if changes were made. House majority whip David Bonior (D-Michigan) defected outright from the President's ranks. NAFTA could not pass without a majority of Republicans approving it. And Clinton, ironically, became more reliant on Republicans than on Democrats for support.

Deputy whips Bill Richardson (D-N.M.) and Robert Matsui (D-Calif.) assumed the leadership roles for NAFTA in the House. Matsui complained that Clinton's staffers were getting in the way of passage, especially irksome in light of Bonior's defection and Speaker Tom Foley's passive commitment.

Inside the White House, a policy struggle was taking place over whether national health care (and keeping organized labor's favor) was a higher priority than NAFTA. Bonior sent a letter to Clinton, co-signed by a hundred House Democrats, saying that the NAFTA debate would detract from building a health care reform coalition.

Clinton's candle was lit from both ends. Labor charged that the administration encouraged job flight to Mexico. Employers felt that pro-labor bills (higher business taxes and anticipated higher health care costs) added new financial burdens on them. AFL-CIO president Lane Kirkland simply dismissed NAFTA as a "poison pill left over from the previous administration."

NAFTA was in bad shape by Labor Day, 1993. House Majority Leader Richard Gephardt told colleagues he would oppose it. Gephardt's defection influenced ten to fifteen others on the NAFTA vote. Bill Richardson admitted that Gephardt could carry votes with him "even if he doesn't try."

House Republicans were not doing much better than the divided Democrats. Minority Whip Newt Gingrich (R-Georgia) admitted that an increasing number of Republicans opposed NAFTA. He doubted that

4. "Overdrawn: Unwarranted Alarms Ill-Serve Whip Says," *Houston Chronicle* (August 29, 1993)

the Republicans alone had the votes to pass the treaty without more solid Democratic support.

Office of Management and Budget Director Leon Panetta didn't help either. He, in fact, infuriated the Salinas administration when he declared NAFTA dead. The Mexicans thought they were being made to walk the plank. Mickey Kantor interpreted Panetta to mean that the pact would have a hard time in Congress without supplemental agreements like the ones being negotiated—in Washingtonese, "it's dead for now." Panetta was misquoted, said Kantor. Then two days later, at the National Press Club, Kantor said that NAFTA's defeat could signal instability in Mexico. The statement was received in Mexico as intending to destabilize the pact.[5]

In a strategic move, Clinton appointed former Oklahoma Congressman James R. Jones in August to replace Ambassador John D. Negroponte. In an opening statement preceding Jones' confirmation hearing, Senator Jesse Helms (D-N.C.), called the Mexican government the most corrupt in the world. The story was published by the Mexico City daily *La Jornada*, soon followed by other Mexican newspapers.[6] Some Mexican representatives (called deputies) condemned Jones as an interventionist. One of them demanded that the government refuse to accept Jones as ambassador. Columnists for the conservative *Excelsior* agreed. And in an interview with the newsmagazine *Proceso*, Jones denied the United States had ever pursued interventionist policies.[7]

As Clinton's team took positions in Mexico City, the administration tried to define a strategy. The economic argument for NAFTA was persuasive, but the free trade idea had no emotional appeal. And opposition was fed up with a recession that lingered and a recovery that didn't seem to take.

Salinas was concerned that Capital Hill assigned no real urgency to the measure. He was so chafed that he spoke about the "great interest" of Pacific Rim nations and Europe "in intensifying their relationship with Mexico."

Representative Robert Matsui admitted they were about seventy-five votes short of approval in the House. By mid-October, Representative Chris Cox (R-Calif.) estimated that pro-NAFTA votes were about thirty short in the House. Clinton was perceived as procrastinating while Ross Perot and his forces undertook a series of revival-style appearances characterized as

5. David Haskel, "Kantor Seeks Support For NAFTA," Mexico City, *The News* (May 5, 1993).

6. "Getting to Know You," Mexico City, *El Financiero* (August 23-29, 1993).

7 Anita Snow, "Mexico is Doubtful of New U.S. Ennoy," *Houston Chronicle* (October 8, 1993).

"Rant-O-Rama." Pro-NAFTA forces were running while Perot's organization, United We Stand, set the agenda by defining the issue as a net job-loss
proposition. Working people readily responded to the perceived threat.

The argument for NAFTA was helped slightly by a GAO report that
acknowledged government had the means and the responsibility to assist
workers displaced by trade and concluded that the agreement would deliver
an unexpected economic boost in 1994.

The case was coming down to how NAFTA would offset a perceived un-
comfortable relationship with Mexico. "I'm getting a little weary of hearing
people criticize Mexico as not perfect," said Clinton. "Do you think that
anybody else in the world that we trade with is perfect?"

Clinton had a month to get the support he needed before the House
voted on November 17. Administration initiatives were trumped at every
turn by anti-NAFTA forces. Perot was especially effective on talk radio programs that promoted his point of view. To stop the slippage, administration
spokesmen affirmed that they would consider opting out of the agreement
after three years if job losses occurred.

Lawmakers, contrary to fast-track intentions, proposed twenty-four
amendments. Furthermore, Mexico, opposed to any new amendments, said
so. San Antonio's congressman Henry B. González was one of those opposed to NAFTA. The influential representative's position surprised many
local business leaders because their city stood to benefit substantially from
the pact. González, chairman of the House Committee on Banking, Finance and Urban Affairs, said he was concerned that NAFTA would allow
banks to set up operations in Mexico to evade U.S. banking regulations.

Immigration policy became indirectly linked to NAFTA. In the month
before the critical NAFTA vote, while the U.S. mounted a major campaign
to halt illegal border crossings, Clinton claimed that NAFTA, with U.S.
investments improving conditions there, "will dramatically reduce illegal
immigration pressures from Mexico," in a matter of a few years. With three
weeks remaining, Treasury Secretary Lloyd Bentsen announced support of
the North American Development Bank. Representative Estaban Torres, a
former NAFTA critic who had done a complete turn around, introduced
the bank legislation. He and four other Hispanic House members had
negotiated the NADBank agreement with the administration. Bentsen's
announcement triggered formal NAFTA endorsements from the Southwest
Voter Research Institute, MALDEF, and the National Council of La Raza.

Fourteen undecided members of Congress, including four Hispanics,
agreed to support NAFTA, Torres asserted now that the financing mechanism

was in place. But some players in the scenario missed their cues. As the administration tried to round up every possible vote and made wholesale deals during the critical four days before the House voted, an anonymous source admitted that the administration had believed that NADBank support would bring as many as eight votes. But following Bentsen's announcement, Torres only affirmed his own. "When you make a deal," said the source, "you have to sit people down and say, 'If I do this, will you all go with us? If you don't, we're not going to do it.' In this case, that was not done. There was an assumption that one man brought eight votes."

Later, after the administration endorsed NADBank, other representatives with large Hispanic constituencies followed: Nancy Pelosi, Xavier Becerra, Lucille Roybal-Allard, Ed Pastor, Karen English, and others. A five-city poll showed substantial pro-NAFTA support. The Latino Consensus intensified its national pro-NAFTA grassroots campaign.

The administration was desperate for votes. Their distress showed in a hastily arranged trip of undecided House members to meet with President Salinas. The group, guided by Representative Bill Richardson and Jim Kolbe (R-Ariz), flew into Mexico City on October 22 by private government plane. William Daley accompanied the group. Ambassador James Jones met them. Arriving in the afternoon without press notification, the ten undecided members met with President Salinas at Los Pinos.

Time was running out. Speculation abounded that Clinton had missed the opportunity to get an upper hand by not embracing NAFTA early. He had treated it like leftover business from the Bush administration. He had over-reached by focusing more on health care. The only meeting with Salinas had not been a particularly warm parley, nor had he arranged for a joint signing ceremony when the side agreements were reached. Many speculated that the Mexican president was being snubbed. Others thought that Clinton's team was simply inexperienced and didn't understand high level negotiations.

Then the other shoe fell. Jean Chrétien, Canada's Liberal party prime minister candidate, was elected on October 25 by a large majority three weeks before the House vote. He defeated the Conservative Party candidate Kay Campbell, who had taken over the party leadership from Brian Mulrooney before the parallel agreements were negotiated. Chrétien's campaign called for NAFTA's revision.

The Clinton administration's hunt for new votes was at a standstill. Tensions increased. The administration intensified its rhetoric and warned of dire consequences if NAFTA failed. United States officials admitted the fight for NAFTA was going down to the last minute but insisted that the strategy was on track. NAFTA critics said they had a solid advantage to defeat the measure, with ten votes to spare. The administration insisted that support was leaning in their favor.

Just one week before the House vote, Vice President Gore, in a nationally televised debate with Ross Perot definitively knocked out NAFTA's opposition. Gore won by a *"Nocaut,"* read the banner headline in Monterrey's major newspaper, *El Norte.* In one overnight survey, NAFTA support jumped twenty-three points—to 57 percent —while opposition remained unchanged. Clinton was buoyed by the debate. "I honestly believe we're going to win it now, and that's not just political puff," he said.

In the closing days before the vote, each movement, report, and change of mind counted. Perot lobbied Capitol Hill the day before the vote, while Democratic congressional leaders tried to distance themselves from him.

Tom Donahue, AFL-CIO Secretary, presented petitions to Gephardt and Bonior from 1.8 million workers seeking a negative vote on NAFTA. Opponents claimed they had acquired four more House votes. The White House applied all the pressure it could, and the pool of potential votes dwindled.

The NAFTA debate challenged the Democratic coalition that had brought Clinton into office. It was also a test to determine whether Clinton was really a New Democrat, favoring trade expansion, while the old Democrats often sought protection. Like those on the pro-NAFTA side, Senator Bill Bradley (D-N.J.), argued that Democrats could protect their constituents' core interests by providing domestic "security" programs (including health care, job training, crime prevention, college loans) that prepared workers for international competition. Restricting free trade was a doomed ploy.

Clinton worked feverishly to save his presidency from a humiliating defeat. Hard lobbying and trade-offs led to accusations that Clinton was buying votes. For instance, Mickey Kantor offered twenty-two concessions to the Florida fruit and vegetable industry; more than $33 million were involved. Concessions were also made on peanut butter and wheat. Clinton was constantly on the telephone to undecided representatives.

On November 17, the House NAFTA debate began. It continued the entire day. The same arguments for and against were made all over again. Members moved in and out of the chamber wearing for and against NAFTA buttons on their lapels.

No surprises came from the debate except for the intensity and vehemence of the positions. Those opposed often alluded to anti-democratic practices in Mexico. Some representatives argued that "free" trade was only possible between democratic countries. House Agriculture Chairman Kika de la Garza had heard enough. In an indignant and stirring defense of the measure, he lashed out at members for judging the rest of the world with an American yardstick. Mexico might not be democratic enough, but that was no reason to claim that the Mexican president was a dictator.

"This vote is about the dignity of work, it is over human rights, it is over democracy," said David Bonior toward the end of the debate.

"We the Republicans," said House Minority Leader Robert H. Michael, "don't sacrifice the rights of tomorrow for the fears of today."

As the House prepared to vote, opponents realized they would lose. President Clinton invited selected national leaders to the White House to watch the vote on television. Benjamin Chavis, NAACP president, who like three-fourths of the Congressional Black Caucus fought against it, was invited. Raúl Yzaguirre, NCLA president, who had fought vigorously for it, was not.

The House approved NAFTA on a 234 to 200 vote. The coalition forged to support it was made up of 132 Republicans and 102 Democrats. Presidential scholars could not remember when a Democratic president had needed so many Republican votes for a key piece of legislation. Of the seventeen voting Hispanic representatives, nine voted Yes, eight voted No. All of the votes in favor came from border states—Texas (4), California (4) and New Mexico (1). The votes opposed to NAFTA came from New York (2), Florida (2) and one each from Illinois, California, and New Jersey, and Texas. The count showed the regional nature of the interests involved, except for the votes of Matthew Martínez of California and Henry González of Texas.

NAFTA provided a defining moment for the congressional Hispanic delegation. "America's fastest growing ethnic group," said *The Wall Street Journal*, "has shown in this debate that it doesn't want to be a slave to one political party or interest . . . The Nafta debate has produced a refreshing diversity among Hispanics that suggests an important new opening to the politics of growth and opportunity."[8]

A regional North American internationalism was emerging—not because anyone had thought it through but because "foreign" and "domestic" had converged. It was also an acceptance of the United States' own changing

8. "Hispanics and Nafta," *The Wall Street Journal* (November 16, 1993).

nature. "Nafta has provided a useful sorting out," concluded *The Wall Street Journal.* Different from before, however, Hispanic Americans were playing a role in the unfolding to make it a more democratic scene. After two decades of struggle they had a heightened decision-making stake in the outcome of the nation's and the hemisphere's future.

On November 23, the third day after the U.S. Senate passed NAFTA, the Mexican Senate approved the treaty. Canada's Prime Minister Jean Chrétien announced, after talking with Clinton by telephone, that his government was dropping opposition to NAFTA after the United States offered to help establish codes to prohibit unfair trade and "dumping," that floods the market with products.

Six weeks after the measure passed, some of the tension was still in the air and an internal political brawl among Hispanic representatives broke out in the open. Bill Richardson complained that the two Republican Hispanic Caucus members, Lincoln Díaz-Balart and Illeana Ros-Lehtinen, had failed to support NAFTA. "My frustrations were compounded," he said "by an unwillingness of many . . . in the Cuban American community to consider arguments for NAFTA outside the narrow and stormy Mexican-Cuban bilateral relationship." This was in reference to Mexico having maintained relations with Cuba throughout the long history of a U.S. economic boycott of the island nation. "I was alarmed," he said, "at some unfortunate Mexico bashing."

"Why?" the two Republicans wanted to know of Richardson, especially since two hundred House members did not support it, "has Richardson chosen to show his displeasure only with Cuban Americans?" Finally, the issue was on the table. The protagonists were policy-makers in a democracy, not members of a church choir echoing each other's voices.

"The trio's darts will no doubt be replaced by smiles the next time a camera catches them together," said *Hispanic Link's* satirical, often outspoken, columnist Kay Bárbaro, "Such is life on Capitol Hill."

★ ★ ★ ★ ★

16

The Rise of Hispanic Political Power

P resident Clinton governed with an ebb and flow of support and opposition that made his presidency quite different from his immediate predecessors. Republicans had widely supported his North American Free Trade proposal. But acrimony doomed a national health-care plan prepared by a task force that first lady Hillary Rodham Clinton headed. The proposal was vehemently opposed even before the plan was announced.

In 1994, President Clinton and the Democratic Party were dealt a serious setback in the mid-term congressional elections when a Republican majority took control of the House and Senate. The new "conservative" majority wanted to redefine the social contract between the federal government and the people. In May 1995, the House approved cuts aimed at balancing the budget by 2002 and provided $9.1 billion less than the previous year. The new budget reduced or eliminated many education and social programs. Hispanic members voted along party lines: three Republicans for and fourteen Democrats against. "We recognize the need to reduce spending," said Rep. "Kika" de la Garza (D-Tex.), "but this is going too far." The Hispanic congressional delegation had nineteen members (including two non-voting delegates).

In June 1995, the Supreme Court struck down the establishment of congressional districts where race was a dominant factor in forming the community of interest. Justice Clarence Thomas, the only justice of color, voted with the majority in the five to four decision. The Supreme Court seemed to have put a cap on the previous political expansion, which had led to explosive Hispanic political growth during the preceding decade. The 1975 revision of the Voting Rights Act of 1965 was the cornerstone legislation that had stimulated voter-registration campaigns and court-sanctioned single-member district elections—where candidates run for several small districts instead of one candidate running "at-large"—and formed a more competitive system. In the last decade alone, from 1984 to 1994, the number of Hispanic elected officials increased 74 percent, from 3,128 to 5,459. At a Capitol Hill news conference, Hispanic Congressional Caucus chairman Ed Pastor (D-Ariz.) said, "They've taken away our economic opportunities, educational opportunities and now our political opportunities."

At the same time, the rest of America was undergoing an urban/suburban mutation. Increasingly, Hispanics in Congress represented urban areas, with large ethnic and lower-than-average income constituencies. They were often pegged as liberal districts. The new majority was often suburban, with large white middle-income constituencies, who identified themselves as conservatives. They sometimes launched assaults on the very measures that were responsible for the Hispanic electoral successes. In a sense, the Republican majority returned to a way of thinking reminiscent of President Richard Nixon's New Federalism policy.

Two decades earlier, Hispanic leaders had been prompted into action because state and municipal representatives were unresponsive to community needs. Nixon's policies—through employment training and social services—aimed to put more responsibility in state and municipal government hands. When that happened, local political leaders had to make most of the hard choices about who got what. Also, how could cities maintain current levels of service with fewer funds? "The role of local government will be made almost impossible," complained Angel Ortiz, the only Latina on the seventeen-member Philadelphia city council. Mary Rose Wilcox, the only Hispanic on the five-member Maricopa (Phoenix) County board of supervisors saw the trend as leading local decision-makers "trying to out-conservative Washington, so they want to cut back even more." Tight budgets forced all legislators and representatives to choose, prioritize and target who would benefit. But, different from the Nixon years, a semblance of Hispanic elected representation sat at the table where the hard choices were made.

More than 96 percent of all Hispanic elected officials served at the local level, mainly as school board members and on city councils. The next highest category was in county government, followed by those in the state legislatures. The arrangement had begun to resemble, albeit still not equitably, the way the United States government is arranged.

Yet, the building blocks to democratic representation did not begin with elected officials but with the community organizations that had sought recognition from bureaucrats when elected representatives didn't or wouldn't serve their interest. Then as Hispanic elected officials gained visibility and, more importantly, seniority inside government chambers, a clearer reflection of the people began to emerge. Local grassroots organizations had served as the essential building blocks, like a protein for the new democracy.

Ever since the 1930s, when groups like the League of United Latin American Citizens were founded, political action has been the way to counteract discrimination and to advocate economic betterment. Government was seen as the way to set the example and through it to create initiatives on how society ought to make opportunity accessible to everyone. Yet, the hardest part of the case to present was denial of opportunity because of discrimination. Those practices were often regional, capricious, arbitrary, variable and sometimes confined to portions of the population and not to all. And that form of prejudice was beginning all over again at the end of President Clinton's first term. Hispanics witnessed how California Governor Pete Wilson's appeal to the electorate's less admirable side gave pent-up social disdain a new voice.

In 1995, Wilson, announcing his candidacy for the Republican presidential nomination at the Statue of Liberty, said that immigrants who arrived at Ellis Island had come to America "the right way." He implied that the others—whose ancestors arrived in slave ships or had become Americans because of land acquisition or who were more concerned about fleeing war, revolution, economic wreckage and ruin—didn't merit the same licit claim on the country as the European immigrants from the turn of the century.

Wilson was following the old Republican nostrum—moving to the right to get the nomination then to the middle to win the election. His anti-immigrant positions were part of that hard right positioning. He championed restricting access to health, education and other public services when people lacked proof of citizenship (mainly women and children), as contained in Proposition 187, passed by California voters in 1994. (He didn't point out that proportionately, Canadians in California were the worse foreign-visa offenders, a common form of illegal entry.) Wilson fanned the enraged belief that some people were getting a free ride, not the least of which was "affirmative action." Twenty-two states had already stepped in to keep American culture from dissipating further by passing English-only legislation aimed mainly, but not exclusively, at the Spanish-speaking.

Pat Buchanan trumpeted an "America First" theme in his quest for the Republican nomination and also played on divisive sentiments. His audiences exhibited the kind of animosity that had turned its discriminatory anger against German Americans right before the twentieth century. Buchanan blamed NAFTA for unemployment and he proposed isolationist economic measures.

But these campaigns sputtered. Some of the issues that would have inflamed more demagogic fervor had trouble taking flight because many people at the local level resisted or were more amused than converted by them. What these demagogues were saying didn't square with everyone's experience. The average citizen around the country didn't see himself as a victim of immigration. In fact, many saw benefits. And, although they were proportionately few, Hispanic elected officials acted like a firewall who protected the target public and the average citizen from the further corruption of issues. By 1994, American voters had elected 5,459 Hispanic officials to office. Whether elected to school boards or Congress, Hispanic elected officials served in thirty-five states, representing roughly 5,459 coalitions within, between and across groups. While all regions were not similarly impacted by immigration, all people could be affected by the demagoguery. The resistance succeeded because Hispanic leaders around the country had already formed local-level, cross-group coalitions. At first, these had been self-serving collaborations to win elections. Now, they were part of an infrastructure of understanding between groups. That was one reason why the venom did not spread everywhere.

The lack of democracy explains why the phenomenon took form in California. The state accounted for nearly 30 percent of the Latino population in the United States (the proportion growing to 32 percent during the decade). The state had the largest Hispanic population in the U.S. but it elected 14 percent, 796, of all Hispanic officials. California was woefully underrepresented. Even Illinois with eighty-five, had more representation than California in proportion to the state population. Consequently, all Americans paid the price by way of rhetorical deception when presidential candidate Wilson exploited public concerns, raised false fears and baited immigrants. He put the average American of Hispanic descent on the defensive and it seemed for a while that the public was turning on immigrants. In California, Wilson didn't have democracy as a counterweight to moderate his frenzy. There was good reason why the same didn't happen in other parts of the country.

Texas, for instance—with nearly 40 percent fewer Latino voters than California and the second largest Hispanic population—had 2,215 Latino officials, over 40 percent of the national total. When George W. Bush, the former president's son, won the gubernatorial race in 1994, his first act was to name Antonio O. Garza Jr. secretary of state. Bush declared before taking office that he didn't think Texas needed anything like a Proposition 187, the California measure intended to deny health care, social services, and education to undocumented immigrants. Bush spoke out unequivocally against then-Republican Pat Buchanan's "isolationism," he supported NAFTA and warned, "I will speak out strongly at the [GOP] convention and any chance I get if the Republican Party chooses to bash Mexico."

Hispanic interests were now the focus and not deferred. The public interest was now us—all of us. No matter that reactionaries were reverting to the methods of bygone times, there was no turning back. This was now, with its own issues, a new phase of American life. National politics had matured in spite of the divisive rhetoric.

At the dawn of the millennium, many Americans were beginning to think about Latinos in terms of the present and future. Reflected in the arts and music fusion and other cultural forms, Latino expression sought "crossover" and to harmonize. Writer Ilan Stavans referred to that phenomenon as the "Hispanization of the United States, and the Anglocization of Hispanics."[1] To quadrate like that was very important to American identity because it began liberating the society from race-based ideation and contrived, trivial, diversity fluff.

The blending was evident everywhere. Partisanship, for example, was much more mixed than stereotypes had people believe. Researcher John García found that many Mexicans and Puerto Ricans were Democrats and Cubans more often were Republicans but crossover was taking place on a wholesale basis. A majority of Cubans were Republicans but others were Democrats or leaning that way. A substantial level of Mexicans and Puerto Ricans reported lower than expected Democratic partisanship and a substantial number said they were former Democrats. These people, often typified as coming from liberal districts, considered themselves conservative to moderate.[2] The self-identifiers didn't matter much in the grocery store line, but they did to campaign strategists, who watched the numbers and psyched out the public as the 2000 election approached. The Hispanic vote was not going to be taken for granted because of this crossover potential. It could tip the balance in several crucial states.

An important apprehension going into the 2000 election was whether Hispanic voters, once mobilized, would show up at the polls. Six million Hispanic voters were expected to vote in the national election. (The final count indicated that 7 million actually did). In general, fewer voters overall

1. Ilan Stavans, *The Hispanic Condition: Reflections on Culture & Identity* (New York: Harper-Collins Publishers, 1995), p. 9.
2. John A. García, "Latino National Survey, 1989-1990: Explorations into the Political World of Mexican, Puerto Rican, and Cuban Communities," *ICPSR Bulletin*, September 1997).

tended to vote each election year. In California, for example, two-thirds of all voters went to the polls in 1972. By 1996, the proportion was 52 percent. Meanwhile, California's Latino voters expanded rapidly in the 1990s, growing from 1.35 million to 2.35 million in ten years. They were 87 percent of the total growth of registered voters. The impetus was a reaction to the anti-Latino campaigns and initiatives of the 1990s. The question, then, was whether Hispanic voters would continue accelerated voting after 1998—the year Proposition 227, restricting bilingual education, was on the ballot. This was one sure-fire issue relevant to them. The inflammatory rhetoric had led Latino leaders to urge bloc-voter participation and that galvanized new Latino voters.

Going into the 2000 presidential campaign, strategists had needlessly questioned whether the new voters would turn out to vote when no anti-Latino issue was on the ballot. In the 1996 primary election, California Latinos had formed 9 percent of all state voters. By 2000, they were already turning out in large numbers and made up 13.4 percent of the presidential primary voters. Elsewhere, Latinos were now one in four of the electorate in at least six states (California, Florida, Illinois, New York, Pennsylvania, and Texas). These states alone were responsible for 184 electoral votes of the 270 needed to win. Moreover, the Hispanic vote was growing fast in all of the states. The Tomás Rivera Policy Institute, for example, forecast that New York alone would increase from 7.5 percent in 1996 to 13 percent in 2000.

The stage was set for a spirited campaign over competing ideas about government's role in domestic life. However, it mainly boiled down to a plebiscite on President Clinton's presidency. Vice President Al Gore, the Democratic Party's nominee, as if to distance himself from the controversies surrounding the president, took amazingly little credit for his contributions to the Clinton administration. He and running mate Senator Joe Lieberman (Conn.) ran on having helped make the prosperous economy possible, yet all the while uneasy about the association to the incumbent president.

Meanwhile, George W. Bush came out of the Republican convention saying, "The night is passing and we are ready for the day to come." The unprecedented national prosperity was due to people's efforts, Bush and running-mate Richard Cheney (former Defense secretary under President George P. Bush) claimed, and not because of government. How important and how necessary was government to unleash the economy, in a sense, went to the heart of the matter. Yet the candidates were not taking their case to the public. Instead, Clinton's character was as much the unspoken issue, as was policy. And the media evaluated the candidates more by style and strategy than by content.

The Clinton presidency had been marred by scandals— money dealings ("Travelgate" and then the Whitewater affair investigated by special prosecutor Kenneth Starr), White House advisor Vince Foster's suicide, fundraising methods (accused of letting out the Lincoln bedroom to big money contributors), and the President's untoward personal behavior (Gennifer Flowers, Paula Jones and Monica Lewinsky). In 1997, the President had faced impeachment—and was later acquitted by the Senate—because he lied about his relationship with Lewinsky. As a result, a Clinton fatigue had set in with part of the public.

Yet, President Clinton's policy accomplishments were formidable. He presided over the best economy in U.S. history. In 1997, Clinton negotiated a balanced budget with the Republican majority. A budget surplus was a serious prospect for the first time in thirty years. Republicans claimed that the surplus justified a tax cut. The administration reasoned that the baby-boom generation would soon cause a burgeoning retirement age population. Replacements for tax-paying workers were shrinking. Productivity from lower-skilled workers cast doubts that they could support the retirees. The White House wanted the surplus to help preserve Social Security.

Clinton had redefined Democratic politics into a New Democrats agenda—support of free trade, universal health insurance, welfare reform and affirmative action—that cut across partisan liberal-conservative views. According to writer Joe Klein, Clinton had also managed the nation's transition from the Industrial Age into the Information Age. The president had referred to his strategy in the 1998 state of the union address. Lower interest rates, he said, would stimulate growth, investments in education and skills development would prepare people for the new economy and markets, and with the revenue surplus "save Social Security first."

Clinton succeeded where Ronald Reagan's ideological presidency had failed. The Reagan administration had tried to end the welfare state. Clinton, by reforming welfare, created a balance between personal and social responsibility. Then he focused on the concerns of the middle class.

Expanding earned-income tax credits was Clinton's New Democrats hallmark. They especially benefited the lowest-wage earners—the cafeteria workers, janitors, and hospital orderlies, who worked below poverty wages. Fifteen million families (earning less than $27,000 a year) gained $21 billion in just over five years. By using the government's taxing mechanisms, Clinton expanded the ranks of the middle class and through welfare reform shrank the number of poor people. The welfare monster was tamed by limiting how long people were allowed on the welfare rolls. The policy required recipients to take steps to become skilled in jobs for the new economy. This, along with earned-income tax credits, was the right combination in an expanding economy.

By 2000, the United States was in its tenth year of economic growth. Unemployment was down to 4.1 percent. The wage dollar stretched further because "core inflation" (excluding food and energy) was just 2.4 percent, even though it had recently edged up to 3.5 percent. Corporate profits rose 33 percent since 1996. The Dow Jones average hovered around 10,700 at the time of the first presidential debate. At the end of the second, it was at 10,400.

Two months before the election, unemployment dropped to 3.9 percent, matching the thirty-year low reached in April. Campaign issues focused on health care, education, and the economy. The Gore campaign had hard numbers to show the job begun was unfinished. More than 15.5 percent, of the U.S. population lacked health insurance. Among Hispanics the rate was 33.4 percent because of the higher proportion of immigrants and children and the loss of health coverage when people moved from welfare to entry-level jobs. Texas had the second highest uninsured rate in the nation, although it had declined slightly under governor George W. Bush.

Latino poverty rates declined during Clinton's eight years in office. "This is good news for the nation," said National Council of La Raza president Raúl Yzaguirre, "not just for Latinos, because our country's economic progress is linked to the well-being of Latino workers." The political adage that a rising tide raises all boats seemed to be in play. Median Hispanic family income rose for four consecutive years. An additional $1,779 was added to the average household between 1998 and 1999. During the campaign, George Bush emphasized lowering taxes from the expected budget surpluses. Gore trumpeted how the tax credit idea could be applied to other specific needs. This became the basic distinction between the candidates. Republicans wanted to return tax money to people to do with as they pleased (if they had any money coming). Democrats wanted to provide incentives for specific categories of people. Sloganeers compared the cliché approaches as "read my lips" vs. "a program for every problem."

Still, the campaign was reaching out to a changing national population. The future was not as easy to predict as before. Technological change was rapidly transforming the economy. It was reminiscent of the 1896 campaign when a candidate made direct appeals to the new American immigrants. And that was why William McKinley won. He understood that the United States would not remain predominantly English, Scottish and Irish—but increasingly Italian, German and Russian. Bush's political strategist Karl Rove understood the 1896 election. He had, after all, written a dissertation on it. More importantly, the candidates were giving the Hispanic vote increasing attention. And for good reason. It had grown to 7 percent of the overall U.S. electorate and was concentrated in states critical to the election's outcome.

By the spring of 1999, the Hispanic population was about 32 million, or about 12 percent of the nation's total. It had increased by a third since 1990. By the time the new president completed his first term in 2005, Hispanics were expected to be the largest minority group, and by mid-century to comprise 25 percent of the nation's population.

California, Texas and Florida especially experienced huge Hispanic population increases. The growth trend in these states was especially relevant to the election because no candidate had won the presidency since the 1960s without winning two of these three states.

George W. Bush had received 29 percent of the Texas Latino vote when he first ran for governor in 1994. By the time of his 1998 reelection bid, he received 48 percent. Texas, was virtually assured to Bush for the 2000 election.

By fall, Gore campaigned in New York with first lady Hillary Rodham Clinton (running for the U.S. Senate). In Albany, he tried saying "*acompáñanos*," "join us," before a Latino audience but he botched the Spanish. But they didn't mind. Assemblyman Roberto Ramírez (D-Bronx) estimated the state's Latinos had voted for Gore by eight-to-one. Gore's yodel was a touching gesture but he got big applause for pledging to aid the poor and the uninsured.

A month before the election, eleven Puerto Rico residents filed suit in the First Circuit Court of Appeals demanding the right to vote. "We run the same risks and you can vote. Why not us? We are U.S. citizens like you," said Gregorio Igartúa, a litigant and the group's lawyer. Two and a half million Puerto Rico voters have no Electoral College status because the island is a territory. That creates an anomaly. A Puerto Rican moving to the continental U.S. can vote in a presidential election, but a U.S. citizen moving to Puerto Rico cannot. "Puerto Rico could make the difference in the 2000 elections," said Governor Pedro Rosselló, if it had the right to vote.

By Labor Day, 2000, polls showed that Bush had begun to lag—one poll showing by 10 percent—after holding dead-even following the convention "bounce." Polls had generally tracked the race as even by the time of the first presidential debate on October 3. Gore started to pull ahead but fell back. Texas was foregone to Bush. California was assumed for Gore. Florida, where Jeb Bush, the candidate's brother was governor, was a surprising toss-up. A major contest was being waged in Pennsylvania.

Two weekends before the balloting, Gore campaigned in Michigan. He called Bush the special interests candidate and said Bush's policies would take the country back into deficit spending. "We tried that," said Gore. "Been there, done that, still paying the bills." Joe Lieberman said Bush was not qualified for the White House: "Maybe sometime, but not now."

A week before the balloting, Reuters estimated that Gore was leading Bush 222 electoral votes to 216. One hundred were a toss-up. Bush campaigned hard in California. He was clearly a long shot there but he had 310 county and local headquarters make 1.5 million phone calls during the final month. Bush told the Republicans gathering in Anaheim by satellite from Austin in the week before the election, "While my opponent has been busy counting the votes of California, I've been working hard to earn them."[3]

A *Los Angeles Times* poll reported that Gore had a razor-thin lead in Michigan and Bush had one in Florida and Pennsylvania. The election was too close to call. As many as eighteen states were up for grabs. Every vote would count in almost every part of the country. Latinos were the balance of power in 68 percent of the electoral votes coming from major states. Hour-by-hour, each state became increasingly important.

Bush was gaining slightly on Gore in the national popular vote, according to the Sunday newspapers, especially in Michigan, Illinois, New Jersey and Pennsylvania. Republicans historically had to score big there to win nation-wide. A CNN/Gallup poll showed Bush supported by 49 percent of likely voters and Gore by 42 percent. Ralph Nader (Green Party candidate) pulled 3 percent and Pat Buchanan (Reform Party) only 1 percent.

Vast millions were spent in the feverish quest for Hispanic votes. Bush and Gore made themselves available for interviews by Univision and Telemundo. They appeared on the popular variety show "*Sabado Gigante*," took questions from call-in listeners over Radio Unica, and courted Spanish-language newspapers. Both campaigns had Spanish-language press operations. The

3. Clay Robison and R.G. Ratcliffe, "Bush is Confident About California," *Houston Chronicle* (October 30,2000).

Democratic National Committee and the Republican National Committee coordinated direct mail and voter-contact programs targeting Hispanic voters. However, only Florida, with its large Cuban American concentrations, was considered in play of the states with the largest Latino populations.

A Public Policy Institute survey showed that Bush had gained 2 percent among all California voters, but among Latino voters he had lost 3 percent in the same period. The reason for this wasn't so much Bush as the Republican Party. Many voters, Latinos in particular, were wary of the restrictive policies that the state Republican party and its former governor Pete Wilson had championed.

Targeting Florida, New Mexico, Nevada, Pennsylvania, Georgia and Washington, the Republican National Committee had launched a $2 million Spanish-language media campaign in the last two weeks of the campaign to counteract the negative image. The Bush campaign spent about $4 million altogether on Spanish-language media. Republican strategists observed that Latino support could also provide a turning point in the smaller battleground states, the ones where very small numbers mattered a lot. The *Los Angeles Times* in the final week called the campaign the closest presidential fight in four decades and that both parties were spending record amounts to encourage voter turnouts. Grassroots ferocity was at a level unseen in a generation.

The Cuban population's focus galvanized right before the 2000 election. On Thanksgiving Day, 1999, of the previous year a child, Elián González, was found floating off the Florida coast. He was one of three survivors from a capsized boat. Fleeing Cuba, Elián's mother and ten others had drowned. The boy was placed in his great uncle Lázaro González's home. A seven-month custody battle ensued that culminated—to the shock and dismay of many—in an INS commando raid that seized the boy from the home and the neighbors supporting Lázaro González. Elián's father gained custody in June and returned the boy to Cuba. How the INS nabbed Elián turned the Cuban community's misgivings into bitterness toward the Clinton administration, referred to as "*voto castigo*," the revenge vote, that was awaiting Gore in Florida for supporting the administration's actions.

In the administration's closing days, after Congress approved a preferential permanent trade partnership with China, an opportunity arose to crack the trade embargo with Cuba, originally imposed in the 1960s. Clinton said he would sign legislation that would allow some minor trade and limited travel to Cuba. A month before the election, House and Senate Republican negotiators had agreed on a plan, as part of an $80 billion agriculture bill. U.S. farmers would be allowed to sell grain and rice to Cuba, Libya, Sudan, and North Korea—although U.S. banks were not allowed to finance the transactions with Cuba. Still, Democrats attacked the agreement for not going further.

The Havana regime's newspaper *Granma* editorialized that the legislation actually toughened the embargo because it restricted U.S. banks from financing food sales to the island. Cuba would have to pay cash or obtain financing from a third country. The newspaper said Cuba "will not buy a single cent of food or medicine" through the legislation and accused "the extreme U.S. right and the terrorist Cuban-American mafia" for the legislation's restrictions. Yet, the legislation demonstrated that embargo supporters no longer had a strangle hold on the agenda, even though the legislation also stripped the president of power to expand travel to Cuba. Florida Republican representatives Lincoln Díaz-Belart and Ileana Ros-Lehtinen were generally credited with the final compromise.

Other factors impinged on the election. The suburbanization of America was now a prevalent factor. A national attitude favoring more limited government was ascending. Urban issues were receding. The closest and most controversial election in a hundred years was coming down to the concern about how the nation was going to handle prosperity made possible by a president half of the nation disliked.

The election's results were inconclusive. But the importance of the Hispanic vote was firmly established. Who won was not final for forty-two days. While the results were deadlocked. Each candidate fell short of the 271 electoral votes needed to win. The controversy centered on Florida's twenty-five electoral votes. In fact, some of the confusion in the dawn hours following election night arose because the weight of Florida's Hispanic balloting was overlooked in the prognostications.

Gore won the majority popular vote and 255 electoral votes from twenty-one states (including the District of Columbia) and Bush 248 electoral votes from twenty-nine states.[4] Nationally, more than 7 million Hispanic voters

4. The figures cited come from Hispanic Trends, Inc. The *Los Angeles Times* polling reported 61 percent for Gore and 38 percent for Bush among Hispanics nationally. In California, Gore was reported to have received 75 percent of the Latino ballots and Bush 23 percent. The William C. Velásquez Institute exit polls reported Gore getting 65 percent of the Texas and 77 percent of the California Hispanic vote, while Bush got 33 percent of the Texas and 23 percent of the California votes.

went to the polls.[5] Sixty-four percent of them voted fot Gore. George W. Bush received 34 percent of the Hispanic vote. The results of the national Hispanic voting were proportionately much on par with previous national elections.

In New York, for example, Hispanics gave Gore and Hillary Clinton about 80 percent of their votes, contributing to Clinton's 12 percent win over her Republican opponent. New Mexico's Hispanic voters gave the Democratic ticket a two-to-one margin. In New Jersey, 58 percent to 35 percent. In the Midwest, 66 percent to 34 percent, and in Colorado, 68 percent to 25 percent. But the big story was in the three major Hispanic states—Texas, California, and Florida. Texas Hispanics, with 10 percent of the statewide vote, gave Bush 43 percent and Gore 54 percent of their votes. California went overwhelmingly for Gore at 64 percent to 32 percent. Commentators speculated that California was now solidly a Democratic state and that Republicans would have a tough time statewide for another decade. Nationally, of all Hispanic voters, more than 50 percent were foreign-born, forming a new dynamic for future national elections. The confusing situation in Florida, however, by going back and forth held the nation in suspense. First Bush was declared the winner, then Gore, then Bush again, then the election was inconclusive and remained so for forty-two days.

Had the Cuban-American *voto castigo*, the revenge vote over the Elián González incident, cost Gore the election? George Bush won Florida with about 50,000 more Cuban-American votes than Republican Bob Dole received in his 1996 presidential bid. This indicated a higher than expected turnout for Bush. Voter News Service (VNS), an exit-polling firm for the news media, caused confusion by first projecting Bush the winner, then back-tracking. After the disputed recounts and recriminations in the days following the election, one of the fatal errors found was that VNS had interviewed a small 2 percent of Cuban-American voters while the Cuban vote represented 8 percent of the Florida electorate. The actual Florida Cuban vote was 78 percent for Bush and 20 percent for Gore. And here is why it is important to differentiate between Hispanic groups. Cubans in Florida voted Republican by four-to-one. Other Hispanics in the state voted two-to-one

5. VNS final exit poll, Hispanic Trends, November 20, 2000. This source is known for accuracy in national polling, however it made some miscalculation in Florida that added to the confusion and controversy over the election results. VNS did not report on the Hispanic vote for states where the sample was less than 5 percent of the statewide sample (such as Illinois, 4 percent).

for Gore. Not enough Cuban-American voters were in the VNS sample to measure their effect. Consequently, VNS revised its projected Bush victory in the early morning following election night with about a 6 percent lead for Gore in Florida.

VNS's projection was based on previous state elections.[6] But the method failed in Florida. The so-called "key precinct" method did not work because Republican Cubans were missing from the exit polls in proportion to their voting strength, and the mistake added to the erroneous vote totals from the northern part of the state, leading the news networks to declare Florida going to Gore. At the time, the actual vote returns showed Bush ahead by 2 percent to 4 percent.

At two a.m. EST, with 98 percent of the vote counted, Bush was still 2 percent ahead of Gore. It seemed unlikely that Gore could pull ahead, but he did because of African-American Democratic precincts in South Florida that went nearly 100 percent for Gore. The networks made another wrong call about the winner when they underestimated these voters, who set a turnout record.

Bush's statewide lead was 1,700 on the day after the election, then it fell to a thousand, then it was officially certified nineteen days later at 537. Lawsuits in Florida and before the U.S. Supreme Court eventually upheld the official, certified results. Realistically, it was impossible to determine the actual vote count from the number of contested ballots.[7] Not since 1886 was an election so controversial. And not since 1960 had a candidate won the presidency without two of the three key states—Texas, California, and Florida—where Hispanic voters are critical to any close races.

Even before the inauguration, the new administration aimed on a new understanding about relations with Mexico. President Vicente Fox's conservative party, the *Partido Acción Nacional* had ended the *Partido Revolucionario Institucional*'s seventy-one year rule. As governors and now as presidents

---

6. When the exit polls showed a 5 percent lead, and the computer analysis of key-precinct balloting did not disagree with the trend from previous elections, the analysis was assumed to be accurate and the data was supplied to the news networks.

7. Long after the official results, two independent probes of Florida's election disputed the conclusion that Bush won. A survey for the *Washington Post* showed that Gore won nearly a three-to-one majority among 56,000 Florida voters, which were discounted because they contained more than one punched hole. A survey by the *Palm Beach Post* found that Gore won a majority of 682 among the discounted "dimpled" ballots in Palm Beach county. In each case, if the examined votes would have counted, Gore would have won a narrow victory in Florida. Martin Kettle, *The Guardian* (January 29, 2001).

Bush and Fox had met and conferred to the point of personal friendship. A new immigration policy seemed imminent. Even the notion of a hemispheric free trade market—extending to the Caribbean, Central America and South America—was back on the block.

Seven months into the new administration, a new political strategy was already in play. The new president had to improve on the 34 percent to 35 percent of the Hispanic vote he had captured in November. A simple calculation showed that Bush would lose the 2004 presidential race by 3 million votes if Hispanics and other groups voted in the same proportions as they had in 2000. He made key appointments and called for ending in three years the naval bombing tests at Vieques, Puerto Rico (before the time he would seek reelection). A White House task force headed by Secretary of State Colin Powell and Attorney General John Ashcroft proposed, as a "work in progress," granting legal status to 3 million undocumented Mexican immigrants in the U.S. *The New Republic* said the announcement signaled that anti-immigrant politics were over. "And it probably took a Republican to strike the blow."

President Bush appointed Mel Martínez, the elected Chief Executive of Orange County, Florida, as Secretary of the Housing and Urban Development. Martínez was a close ally of Florida Governor Jeb Bush and co-chairman of the state Bush presidential campaign. He was also a former board member of the strongest Cuban exile lobby, the Cuban American National Foundation that expected Bush to toughen or at least maintain the trade embargo against Cuba. Martinez had paid for Elian González' trip to Disney World the year before during the bitter custody battle between Miami relatives and the boy's father in Cuba. Martínez was himself a child refugee who had left Cuba at age 15 in 1962.

Commentator Linda Chavez was nominated as Secretary of Labor but she withdrew following news reports about an illegal Guatemalan immigrant who had lived at her home. Bush later nominated Richard Carmona of Tucson as the first Hispanic U.S. Surgeon General. Gaddi Vásquez, the former Orange County (California) Supervisor was named Peace Corps director under a cloud of criticism. The Republican activist was criticized for lacking any notable foreign-relations experience. Trouble also awaited another Bush nominee, as well.

A year and a half into the administration, Senate Judiciary Committee chairman Patrick Leahy (D-Vt.) was miffed by assertions concerning Miguel Estrada's nomination to the U.S. Court of Appeals. Nomination hearings seemed to have been delayed over whether Estrada met the qualifications and had the temperament for the job. An immigrant from Honduras who worked his way up through Harvard Law School, Estrada had argued fifteen cases before the U.S. Supreme Court. Those opposing his nomination compared his conservative views to those of Supreme Court Justice Antonin Scalia. Estrada's former supervisor at the Solicitor General's office said, "I think Estrada lacks the judgment and he is too much of an ideologue to be an appeals court judge." Estrada was a partner in the law firm that had represented Bush before the Supreme Court during the post-election legal fight with Al Gore. But to make matters worse, Estrada's proponents said ethnicity was the reason why the hearing was delayed (as a deflecting ruse, while partisanship was the culprit). Senator Leahy shot back: "It is Democrats who have long championed diversity in the federal courts."[8]

From another angle, Los Angeles-based commentator Rodolfo F. Acuña, wrote that Hispanic advocates make "a tremendous error in pushing Latinos for appointed positions just based on the nebulous identity of being Latinos." He said that Estrada did not "identify with the struggles or aspirations of most U.S. Latinos, he never experienced discrimination or unequal educational experiences. He opposed affirmative action and sided with large corporate interests." Acuña added that Latinos "cannot afford to have people in high office who do not know our community, who are not part of it, yet who can be considered *representatives* for Latinos by virtue of having a Spanish surname."[9]

He had a point. A Spanish surname was not entitlement but an opportunity to identify and build upon the contributions of others. That was one lesson coming from the past. The other was that the Hispanic political tradition that emerged challenged ideas, strategies and practices that excluded people from civic, social, educational and political participation. The Brown Mafia episode had made it clear that a deliberate political strategy to discourage participation is fraudulently unethical. The Hispanic view of society is inclusive, not exclusive or compartmentalized. Furthermore, government policy, like Nixon's New Federalism, is a shell game when it virtually assured that Hispanic communities would not benefit from economic development programs because they lacked local elected representatives. Ever since those experiences, Latino political efforts have been about gaining representation at all levels of government.

8. Press release, "Comments of U.S. Senator Patrick Leahy, Chairman, Senate Judiciary Committee, On Assertions Made About The Nomination of Miguel Estrada," (April 10, 2002)
9. Rodolfo F. Acuña, "Not Representative of Latinos," *The Miami Herald* (April 26, 2002).

Yet to know this virtually silent history has been until now the domain of a few persons who were there, who participated, or had concatenated the details. Now, instead of passing into lore, the story of the Hispanic political legacy in an object lesson in practical democracy—how it is gained and what it takes to maintain it. The values underlying the legacy are those to pass on the next generation. And it is not acquired by surname alone.

Now, nearly thirty years following the reactions to the Nixon administration that sparked the movement, the focus turned back to whether appointed public policy officials can represent the Latino community and not be of it. The short answer is yes, if they embrace the Latino experience and the values resulting from the thirty-year experience.

The patrimony is lost if the focus becomes solely that of ethnic diversity, which has been trivialized and called "status diversity" in some places. It has been also called "non-functional representation," referring to symbolic value of little or no substance or applicability. Cynics hide behind reductionism like that.

Instead, the past thirty-years have taught us that representative government is both intellectual (ensconced in dry books and debates) and a physical engagement (by pounding the sidewalk). Its open-admissions policy encourages people to join organizations to represent their interests and help elect responsive officials. "Register and vote. Register and vote," Willie Velásquez exhorted everyone within hearing range. Not just register. But also participate when it counts. That is how inequities are reversed and the course of events corrected. Redress is hard-won but it speaks eloquently about the armies of ordinary people who contributed portions of their lives, without the promise of gain—except as the founding fathers said, "to create a more perfect union."

The rise of Hispanic political power is a unique chapter in the history of American democratic practice. It shows how a complex course correction in this country's political agenda was made, beginning in 1972, resulting from chicanery originating from the White House. The 1975 amendments to the Civil Rights act served to enfranchise many of our fellow citizens who were otherwise unaccounted for. To make the legislation happen and to make it real, we see a remarkable collusion between many—Edward Roybal and Barbara Jordan in the House of Representatives, Fernando de Baca in the White House, and later Willie Velásquez— to make the idea come alive. In the end, the idea that government representation and economic participation are inexorably linked emerges as a guiding political value. The late Congressman Henry B. González brilliantly extolled that philosophy. "I believe in the

Constitution," he said, "—and in groceries, too."

Because the Latino political tradition was hard won, its inheritors and those aspiring to lead need to know it exceptionally well, especially in relation to what happened next.

In December, 2000, President Bush had named Alberto Gonzáles to serve as White House Counsel. "I understand how important it is to have a person who I can trust and whose judgment I trust. . ." Bush said at the press conference announcing the appointment. As Texas governor, Bush had named Gonzáles as his general counsel in 1995. Two years later, he appointed Gonzáles as Secretary of State, where he served as Texas' chief election official and conducted the state's relations with Mexico. In 1999, Gonzáles was appointed to the state Supreme Court and ran unopposed for the seat the following year (an elected position in Texas). Gonzáles was a Bush administration insider and was often mentioned as a possible future U.S. Supreme Court nominee.

In making the rounds as a speaker, Gonzáles liked telling audiences about working in the West Wing and about the time Bush asked him if he wanted to see the White House residence. They went upstairs and were looking out into a garden when a rather naïve question came to Gonzáles' mind and he asked before he could really think about how the it might sound: "And what's it like being President of the United States?" he said.

A thoughtful George W. Bush half-smiled and said, "It's a really big deal."

Gonzales knew about real big deals. He was born in San Antonio but grew up in Houston. After attending the Air Force Academy, he completed college at Rice University and earned a Harvard Law School degree. Now, as White House Counsel he could influence all major policy involving the president, all legislation signed and vetoed, and he could influence who would get appointed to federal courts and to the U.S. Supreme Court when vacancies occurred.

One source speculated that four vacancies might arise during Bush's four years.[10] In Texas, Gonzáles, as a state supreme court judge, had made business-minded conservatives comfortable by siding with the majority to overturn a lower-court ruling allowing class action suits against the Ford Motor Co. Social conservatives were bothered that he sided with the court majority allowing some minors to have abortions without notifying their parents.

10. "The Supremes," *Texas Monthly* (June, 2001).

As White House Legal Counsel, Gonzáles was usually out of public sight except when there was serious trouble. His authority comes directly from the president to deal with sensitive situations. "Nothing Justice Gonzales has done has fully prepared him for his new job," said Nixon White House Legal Counsel John Dean. Surprises awaited him, he said.[11]

Certainly nothing had prepared most of the public for the morning of September 11. Gonzáles was in Virginia Beach, Virginia to give a speech. A short time later, he was on his way back to Washington under military escort, following the terrorist attacks, beginning at about 8:45, that crashed American Airlines Flight 11 into the World Trade Center's North tower in New York City. Eighteen minutes later United Airlines Flight 175 slammed into the South tower. At about 9:40, American Flight 77 crashed into the Pentagon. At about 9:58, the South tower collapsed, followed by the North tower at 10:28. Less than a half-hour after the third crash, United Flight 93 crashed near Shanksville, Pennsylvania. Six hours after the New York crashes, debris was still falling from the remains of the World Trade Center. Firefighters could get no closer than two blocks of the burning disaster site. Altogether 266 people perished in the four planes. Nearly, three thousand were known dead on the ground.

The campaign to root out the al-Qaida terrorist organization led to the overthrow of the Taliban in Afghanistan that harbored it and its leaders. Nearly a thousand individuals were apprehended, held, detained, or jailed during the emergency in the United States. In November, two months after the attacks on the U.S., Gonzáles was before the news media explaining the procedures for bringing certain people under military justice. Some captured al-Qaida and Taliban war prisoners were taken and imprisoned at the U.S. Marines military base in Guantanamo, Cuba. "This is an extraordinary action, generally. [But] It is not extraordinary in a time of war. There is a long line of precedent for this type of action during these times of war," he said.

Attempts were made on the lives of congressional leaders by placing anthrax bacterium in letters sent via the United States Postal Service. Postal workers and civilians sustained five deaths. Public alarm over the national security breach by the nineteen suicide terrorists who commandeered the airplanes set off public apprehension about foreign nationals living in the country and the relative ease to obtain and breach visas. How was border security so routinely violated? Public opinion slammed shut talks about opening the

11. John Dean, "Being White House Counsel: What Al Gonzalez, Bush's Pick, Will Face in Washington," *Find Law's Legal Commentary* (December 22, 2000).

borders or liberalized immigrant policy. One terrorist alert followed another. All goods and human movement by land, sea and air came under watchful, suspicious eyes. On American Airlines Flight 63 from Paris to Miami on December 23, 2001, Richard Reid was stopped when he sought to light a fuse to ignite an improvised explosive in his shoe. Another incident involved the arrest and capture of Abdullah al Muhajir, a U.S. citizen "enemy combatant." Muhajir, aka José Padilla, 31, was a former Chicago street gang member and convict who converted to Islam in 1993. The State Department said Muhajir had trained in Pakistan and Afghanistan with al-Qaida and posed a threat to several cities. Under surveillance in Pakistan, Muhajir was alleged to have plans at the time of his arrest by the FBI to build a radioactive explosive devise, or "dirty bomb," a weapon of mass destruction. Muhajir was turned over to the military by civilian authorities on May 8, 2002.

Terrorist attempts against the people and government of the United States seemed light years removed from the simple lives of destitute people seeking to eke out a living by entering the U.S. to work. Their movements along the U.S.-Mexico border, albeit illegal, were vigorously interdicted. National security became a consideration in the maddening issue intertwining civil rights, immigration, free trade, community development and homeland security.

The U.S.-Mexico border's increased surveillance and patrols led many illegal entrants to cross from more dangerous places than they had before. Fifty-three related deaths were recorded in the Arizona desert in one-year ending in 2002. Nine months after September 11, Mexican Foreign Minister Jorge G. Castañeda called for resumption of talks to "regularize" the status of approximately 3 million Mexicans living in the United States illegally.

Clearly the mood was unfavorable for resumption of those talks with Mexico. This caused Congressman Gene Green (D-Tex.), not of Hispanic background but who represented a Hispanic-majority district in Houston, to pledge he would work toward a national anti-terrorism policy that "strikes a balance" between constitutional rights and the protection of Hispanic immigrants. "We need to make sure that we know that the war on terrorism has nothing to do with someone who is a hard-working immigrant coming into this country only to support their family," he said. In fact, among the missing at the World Trade Center were firefighters, foreign visitors, bond brokers, and some of those hard-working illegal immigrants. How many undocumented workers were casualties will forever remain unknown. They were often referred to as the "invisible dead." They were the ones who cleaned the offices, swept the floors, scrubbed the toilets. They delivered sandwiches and pizzas. They were mainly the maintenance and food service workers—mostly from Mexico, Honduras, Ecuador, Peru, Colombia, the Dominican Republic and other Latin American countries. They were often anonymous in daily life. And among the dead, they cannot be identified because there were few body parts left or no one had listed them as missing. Some faraway families may not have even known their loved ones were working in or around the financial complex. And employers may not have listed them on the roster.[12] Or when a person turned up missing, sometimes families were unable to obtain death certificates from uncooperative employers. In some cases, people just vanished.[13] We would not even know about the vanished were it not for the work of Asociación Tepeyac, an advocacy group in New York City, and others like them. In the past, it had been difficult enough for Hispanic advocacy groups to gain recognition to represent the living. Now, they are doing it for those who weren't there.

12. "WTC Dead Still a Police Case," *Associated Press* (March 8, 2002).
13. Ernesto Portillo, "Terrorist Attacks Also Left Invisible Dead," *Arizona Daily Star* (October 20, 2001).

Epilogue

At the dawn of the 1980s, columnist David Broder in *Changing of the Guard* wrote that we would witness "a new generation of young leaders sharply different from their predecessors coming to power."[1] Yet, that didn't happen. Instead, the oldest President in our history took office. The World War II generation's tenure was extended through Ronald Reagan's election and beyond. Instead of a new progressive generation taking the leadership helm, a new conservative generation took over. The changing of the guard in another way did begin within the Hispanic political movements that foreshadowed what would transpire later in other segments of American society. Its hallmark was civic improvement through the application of government in key places. That was an important driving force in the rise of Hispanic elected leaders. And this direction was already evident in the closing days of the 1970s.

David Broder, pulled together in 1979 (with Louis Núñez's help, a staff official of the U.S. Civil Right Commission), a round-table group to talk about what was significant about Hispanics and the emerging leadership. Among the participants were Henry Cisneros, Vilma Martínez, Alfredo Durán, Robert García, Joseph Aragón, and a number of others, who touched on many of the topics and trends we have encountered in previous chapters. However, from that long ago perspective, looking into the future, three themes stood out.

Broder had found the commitment to "community" to be an "innovative" idea. He quoted Herman Gallegos with capsulizeing it as "a better life for the many and not just the good life for the few." It was a commitment that still holds but may become less strong. As political aspirants leapfrog

1. David S. Broder, *Changing of the Guard: Power and Leadership in America* (New York: Penguin Books, 1981)

to political careers, more and more leaders—often claiming merit accruing from education achievement rather than from life experience—less often come up the community activism ranks. In the past, commitments were made to people with faces and not just to the idea of people. These new leaders run the risk of disconnecting from their constituents when their sponsors with money contributions can make holding office easier than having to press the flesh so much. There is also a risk that, like the rest of the United States, a political class can arise, skilled in moving numbers, making constituents into markets, and deterring the cleansing effect of occasional turnover. That can happen also as constituents become increasingly ethnically and socioeconomically mixed and as more "crossover" and "fusion" leaders arise.

What will remain the same, however, is what Broder attributed back before the 1980s to Albert Bustamante, who said that Hispanic leaders were much more willing than others "to mix private and public resources, entrepreneurial initiatives and social motives, in a single blend." Up to that time, the World War II generation had parsed political ideas into Good and Bad, Right and Wrong, Right and Left, Conservative and Liberal. It was a natural adaptation to the Cold War but had spawned prejudicial ideological attitudes. Now, however, Hispanic leaders' work to mix the relationship into a national development recipe had two main ingredients—government participation and private initiative. Ultimately, the guiding principle is the Bustamante axiom: "social motive, single blend."

Finally, immigration was seen even before 1980 as a blow-back, the unintended consequence of other misadventures and policy errors. Back then, Joseph Aragón said it could potentially cause a "tremendous amount of damage domestically and internationally" and it could become "a divisive issue" among Hispanics. It was both, but it eventually solidified, rather than atavized, Latinos.

Latin American immigration to the United States has many underlying reasons. However, in almost all cases the lack of local opportunity in the home country makes the prospect of a job across the border in the north worth the risk. Rather than seeing this as someone else's problem, a more secure future requires us to make it our own. And the gateway is thorough Mexico. Pulitzer Prize-winning correspondent Andrés Oppenheimer, said: "No single country in the post-Cold War era affects the U.S. national interest in more ways than Mexico. This may sound [like] an overstatement in light of the traditional U.S. foreign policy focus on the former Soviet Union and Europe, but it is becoming increasingly evident in the late nineties as

Americans center their attention on day-to-day problems that directly affect their lives."[2]

Future leaders will need to revisit the North American Free Trade Agreement and determine why it is a stunning macroeconomic trade success and a microeconomic failure. Why does it fail to follow the pattern of the European Union that "harmonized" poorer countries to become partners in that economic powerhouse? We only invite someone else's problems to our side of the border when hard won measures like NAFTA are not real solutions for both sides. In fairness, NAFTA was not part of immigration policy but it was intended to stabilize and not destabilize the ability of low-skill workers to make a living. Some immigration between the North American countries is to be expected, and some is even beneficial, but not as gross displacements that deplete productive workers from whole regions, break up families, and produce disjointed growth. That day-to-day reality needs re-focus.

It is tempting to try to distinguish the emerging Hispanic leaders—that will increasingly come from all regions of the country and from town, urban and suburban areas—and imply some racial content. But that does not make sense anymore. Hispanic leadership expansion occurred at a time when American society needed an exit from the divisive and obsessive concern with race, ethnicity and identity. Meanwhile, world citizens and the "global spirit" were more in tune with the direction the rest of the world is taking. It falls on the United States to reconcile its past and to find an international identity.

What does matter is what makes Hispanic leaders tick and the contributions they make as individuals. As a group, they increasingly bring to public affairs a national life experience that had been previously absent. That is how national decision-making perspective is gained. It is how we tune up our system and provide increasing security to our citizens. The nation is stronger when it balances a perspective of itself as a nation and as people of the earth.

Following the September 11 terrorist attacks, normalcy did not return quickly to the United States. In the self-questioning aftermath, the nation pondered its role in the world and "why do they hate us?" and even reflected on whether we were in a "war of civilizations," where Islamic culture perceived itself in a kind of *jihad*, a commitment against American culture. The better perspectives came from analysts who combined Middle Eastern

2. Andres Oppenheimer, Bordering on Chaos: Mexico's Roller-Coaster Journey Toward Prosperity (Boston: Little, Brown and Company, 1996, 1998), p. xi.

history, demographics, economic and cultural perspectives in the context of globalization. What many Americans had not pondered before was that the negative consequences in faraway places could have a proportionate reaction in their own neighborhood. What ought to be the nation's future course? What national definition would we take? What was our national purpose now that the country resembled world citizens more and more?

Meanwhile, as the introspection continued, homeland defenses went up.

References

Chapter 1: THE BROWN MAFIA

Jack Anderson, "Official Powers Used to Get Votes," *The Washington Post* (May 8, 1974).

Jack Anderson, "Minority Groups Badgered for Votes," *The Washington Post* (May 11, 1974).

Hearings of the Subcommittee of the Committee on Appropriations, House of Representatives Ninety-third Congress), *Treasury, Postal Service, and General Government Appropriations for Fiscal year 1975*, Part 3, Executive Office of the President (Washington, D.C.: U.S. Government Printing Office, 1974).

Hearings of the Subcommittee on Minority Small Business Enterprise and Franchising of the Permanent Select Committee on Small Business, House of Representatives (Ninety-third Congress, First Session, *Government Minority Enterprise Programs,* Volume I (Washington, D.C.: Government Printing Office, October 3 and 4, 1973).

Hearings of the Select Committee on Presidential Campaign Activities of the United States Senate, Ninety-Third Congress, First Session, Presidential Campaign Activities of 1972, Senate Resolution 60, , November 7, 8, 13, 14, and 15, 1973, Book 13 (Washington, D.C.: U.S. Government Printing Office, 1973), p. 5232-5285 and Exhibit 262-2. The U.S. Senate Select Committee on Presidential Campaign Activities is best known as the "Watergate Committee" or as the "Ervin Committee." The original hearing transcript was used extensively in its original typewritten photocopy form, then as a printed document from the U.S. Government Printing Office, then in the version published by Dell. All versions were used, as there were some slight differences (corrections, inclusions of exhibits, and condensations) that make each publication slightly different.

Malcolm R. Lovell, Jr., "Progress Report: The Quest for Equality," *Manpower*, IV (September, 1972), p. 2.

Mark R. Levy and Michael S. Kramer, *The Ethnic Factor* (New York: Simon and Schuster, 1972).

Jeb Stuart Magruder, *An American Life: One Man's Road to Watergate* (New York: Atheneum, 1974).

Jerry Rankin and José de la Isla, "Mexican-Americans and the New Federalism: What Role for the Bureaucracy?" *The Bureaucrat*, Vol. 2, No. 2 (Summer 1973).

The Senate Watergate Report: The Final Report of the Senate Select Committee on

Presidential Campaign Activities (the Ervin Committee), Volume One. (A Dell Book, 1974), pp. 322-338.

Duncan Spencer, "Malek's Management System," *Washington Star-News* (February 22, 1974).

Sub-Committee of the Committee on Government Operations, "Activities of the Cabinet Committee on Opportunities for Spanish-Speaking People," Ninety-Third Congress, First Session, July 23 and September 12, 1973 (Washington, D.C.: U.S. Government Printing Office).

CHAPTER 2: THE PRICE OF INFLUENCE

Agenda, newsletter of the National Council of La Raza, December, 1973.

Jack Anderson, "Charming the Spanish Americans," *The Washington Post* (December 30, 1973).

"Banuelos Plant Chief Refuses Search," *Houston Chronicle* (May 7, 1972).

Barry Browne, "Treasurer Hails Race Goals," *San Antonio Light* (March 19, 1972)

"Californian Named New Treasurer," *The Washington Post* (September 21, 1971).

Ken W. Clawson, "U.S. Nominee's Firm Raided," *The Washington Post* (October 6, 1971).

"CREEP and La Raza," *The Texas Observer* (December 14, 1973)

Gaylon Finklea, "Treasurer Pro Nixon," *San Antonio Light* (October 18, 1972).

"Food Firm Raid Nets 53," *The Denver Post* (December 9, 1972).

"Food Firm Ruled Unfair by NLRB," *San Francisco Chronicle* (November 22, 1972).

Dick Gazi, Sanchez Praises President," *The Arizona Republic* (October 22, 1972).

Robert Gruenberg, "Skeptics Eye Chicano Appointments," *San Francisco Sunday Examiner & Chronicle* (October 3, 1971).

Hearings before the Select Committee on Presidential Campaign Activities of the United States Senate, Ninety-Third Congress, First Session, *Watergate and Related Activities, Phase III: Campaign Financing.* Washington, D.C., November 7, 8, 13, 14, and 15, 1973. Book 13. The liaison between the Spanish-speaking Task Force and the National Hispanic Finance Committee for the Re-Election of the President was documented in the weekly reports from William Marumoto to Charles Colson and Fred Malek on the following dates: April 3, April 21, April 28, May 5, May 19, May 26, June 9, June 16, August 18, September 1, October 6, 1972. These exhibits were part of William Marumoto's testimony on November 7, 1973. Mr. Fernandez testified before the Committee on November 8, 1973).

"The Indictment of Senator Gurney," *The Washington Post* (July 14, 1974).

George Lane, "Picket Threats to Keep Hispano Officials From Celebration," *The Denver Post* (April 7, 1972).

"La Raza Unida Founder Calls McGovern a `Damn Liar'," *El Sol* (Houston, Texas), December 27, 1972.

"Magazine Links Tip to Banuelos Raid," *New York Times* (October 11, 1971).

Gayle McNutt, "Mrs. Banuelos urges Latins to Vote for Nixon," *Houston Chronicle* (August 29, 1972).

Memorandum to Rob Davidson and Stan Anderson from Mo Marumoto. Published in *Agenda*, newsletter of the National Council of La Raza, December, 1973.

Memoranda and Reports released by Senator Lowell P. Weicker, Jr. (R-Conn.), *The Washington Post* (April 14, 1974).

"Mexican-American Rallies Planned for Nixon Drive," *The Arizona Republic* (October 21, 1972).

"Mexican-Americans Say `Viva Nixon,'" *The Arizona Republic* (October 22, 1972).

"Mrs. Banuelos Sees Politics Behind Raid," *New York Times* (October 7, 1971).

"New Raid on Treasurer's Former Firm," *San Francisco Chronicle* (December 9, 1972).

Bruce Oudes (ed.), *From: The President, Richard Nixon's Secret Files* (New York: Harper & Row, Publishers, 1989) [Memorandum To: H.R. Haldeman, From: Charles Colson, December 20, 1971, p. 351.

"PASO Plans `Poor People's Dinner' To Protest Nixon Fund Event Here," *Houston Chronicle* (August 29, 1972).

Press Release from the Committee to Re-elect the President, July 27, 1972. Armando Rodriguez, "A Chicano Looks at Bureaucracy," *The Bureaucrat* (Summer, 1973).

RASSA Lobbyist (Official Publication of Raza Association of Spanish Surnamed Americans), July/August, 1973.

"Reveals Agreement to Protect Gurney," United Press International (July 11, 1974).

Steven V. Roberts, "Chicano Leaders Upset Over Raid," *New York Times* (October 8, 1971).

Select Committee on Presidential Activities, Vol. 49, Hearings held Wednesday, November 7, 1973. (An early unpublished transcription).

The Senate Watergate Report: The Final Report of the Senate Select Committee on Presidential Campaign Activities (the Ervin Committee), Volume One, a Dell Book, 1974.

"Treasurer Firm Hit By Strike," *The Denver Post* (March 9, 1972).

"Tells of Offer," *El Sol* (Houston, Texas), December 21, 1973.

U.S. Senate, Select Committee on Presidential Activities, *Hearings, Watergate and Related Activities*, Phase III, Campaign Financing, 93rd Congress, 1st Session (November 7, 8, 13, 14, and 15, 1973), Book 13.

U.S. Senate, Committee on Finance, *Hearing Nomination of Romana Acosta Banuelos To Be Treasurer of the United States*, 92nd Congress, 1st Session (November 29, 1971).

"U.S. Treasurer's Firm Found Guilty," *The Denver Post* (November 22, 1972).

CHAPTER 3: THE TRANSITIONAL PRESIDENCY

"A Spanish Accent Is Very 'In' These Days On Madison Avenue," *Wall Street Journal* (January 24, 1975).

Authorization Bill for the Cabinet Committee on Opportunity for Spanish-Speaking People, September 25, 1973, Ninety-third Congress, First Session, House of Representatives, Report No. 93-528.

Grace Bassett, "Congress Stalls on Wetbacks," *San Francisco Chronicle* (November 17, 1974).

"Bay Area Man Gets U.S. Post," *San Francisco Chronicle* (September 19, 1976).

Fred Buckles, "Montoya Says 'Too Conservative,'" *Santa Fe New Mexican* (August 15, 1974).

Susanne Burks, "Institute Examines Chicano Higher Education Problems," *Arizona Journal* (July 26, 1975).

Marquis Childs, "Democrats' Shell Showing Cracks," *The Washington Post* (November 21, 1972).

Ben Cole, "Equal Opportunity in U.S. Called Aid to Ties With Latin America," *Arizona Republic* (August 15, 1975).

"Ex-Ford Campaign Aide Gets Interior Dept. Job," *Los Angeles Times* (July 22, 1976).

Frank del Olmo, "1974: The Year Latins Rediscovered Politics," *Los Angeles Times* (December 26, 1974).

Frank del Olmo, "Amnesty for Illegal Aliens Urged by Latin Leaders," *Los Angeles Times* (May 23, 1975).

Frank del Olmo, "Chicano Activists Ask Ford to Seek Saxbe's Resignation," *Los Angeles Times* (November 18, 1974).

Frank del Olmo, "Chicanos Criticize Saxbe on Alien Deportation Proposal," *Los Angeles Times* (November 8, 1974).

Frank del Olmo, "Ford's Top Chicano Aide Raps Saxbe," *Los Angeles Times* (November 17, 1974).

Elizabeth Drew, "Conversation With A Senator," *The New Yorker* (May 19, 1973).

"Faults Found in Revenue Sharing" *San Francisco Chronicle* (December 11, 1974).

"Ford Hears Requests From Spanish Speakers," *El Paso Times* (October 18, 1974).

"Ford 'Racist' INS Leader Targets of GI Forum Chief's Fiery Speech," *El Paso Times* (June 2, 1975).

"Gov.-Elect Apodaca Hopes Innuendo Forgotten By '78," *Santa Fe New Mexican* (November 10, 1974).

"HBG Nixes Veep Post," *San Antonio Express* (August 25, 1974).

Phil Kimball, "Hispanic Group Deals With Researching Data," *El Paso Times* (October 20, 1974).

Tom Kuhn, "Panel Planned To Study of Farm Labor," *Arizona Republic*

(October 22, 1974).

Sarah McClendon, "White House, State Department Probe Alien Influx," *El Paso Times* (August 28, 1975).

James McCrory, "Harlan Cites Bracero Plan Practicality, *San Antonio Express* (October 24, 1974).

"Minority Candidates Score Election Gains," *Los Angeles Times* (November 7, 1974).

"Montoya, Lujan Pleased," *Santa Fe New Mexican* (September 5, 1974).

Evan Moore, "Muniz Mysery: Downfall from Destiny," *Houston Chronicle* (July 10, 1994).

Richard P. Nathan, *The Plot That Failed: Nixon and the Administrative Presidency* (New York: John Wiley & Sons, Inc., 1975).

"Mr. Nixon on the Economy," *The Washington Post* (July 27, 1974).

Kevin Phillips, *The Emerging Republican Majority* (Garden City, N.Y.: Doubleday, 1969).

Jerry Rankin and José de la Isla, *Political Responsiveness*, unpublished monograph, 1974.

Subcommittee of the Committee on Government Operations, "Activities of the Cabinet Committee on Opportunities for Spanish-Speaking People," Ninety-third Congress, First Session, July 23 and September 12, 1973 (Washington, D.C.: U.S. Printing Office).

James L. Sundquist and David W. Davis, *Making Federalism Work* (Washington: Brookings, 1969).

Phil Niklaus, "Aide Supports Job Approach," *Albuquerque Journal* (March 22, 1975).

"Panel On Illegal Aliens Formed," *Los Angeles Times* (January 7, 1975).

"Pardon John Dean, Too, Says Gonzalez," *San Antonio Express* (September 10, 1974).

"President Reiterates Alien Bill Support," *San Antonio Express* (November 19, 1974).

James Reston, "Mexico's One Hundred Million," *Denver Post* (August 31, 1975).

"The Rising Flood of Illegal Aliens," *San Francisco Chronicle* (August 17, 1975).

"Saxbe Wants One Million Aliens Ousted," *San Antonio Express* (October 31, 1974).

Ann Schmidt, "Gallegos CSA Role Criticized In Probe," *Denver Post* (January 27, 1976).

Ann Schmidt, "Hispanic Aide Notes Irony," *Denver Post* (September 6, 1975).

Ann Schmidt, "Hispano Lobbyist Asks House To Strengthen Anti-Alien Bill," *Denver Post* (March 14, 1975).

Aziz Shihab, "U.S. Cracks Down On Wetbacks," *San Antonio Express* (October 6, 1974).

Michael Stachell, "It's Not Illegal To Hire An Alien—But Immigration Officers Were Embarrassed To Find Four of Them in Their H.Q.," *San Antonio*

Express (December 8, 1974).

Social Indicators of Equality for Minorities and Women, U.S. Commission on Civil Rights (August, 1978).

"Texas Chicanos Voted GOP; New La Raza Unida Got 6 percent," *The Washington Post* (November 13, 1972). *Washington Post* (November 13, 1972).

"Texas Politicians: System Is Strong," *San Antonio Express* (August 9, 1974).

John Toohey, "Sam Martinez Believes CSA Still Has A Mission," *Denver Post* (April, 1976).

"U.S. Latins Lose Ground On Income," *Washington Post*

Maurilio E. Vigil, "Jerry Apodaca and the 1974 Gubernatorial Election in New Mexico: An Analysis," *Aztlan*, Volume 9, 1978, pp. 133-149.

C.W. Webb, letter to editor, *Albuquerque Journal* (March 12, 1975).

Benjamin Wells, "Illegal Aliens Causing Unemployment in U.S.," *Denver Post* (December 27, 1974).

Jim Wood, "Ford Hails Hispanic Heritage," *San Antonio Express* (September 5, 1974).

Edwin M. Yoder, Jr., "Power and Purse Strings," *Book World/The Washington Post* (September 17, 1972). A review of Michael D. Reagan's *The New Federalism*.

CHAPTER 4: POLITICS AND RELEVANCE

"Americans In Mexican Jails," *San Francisco Chronicle* editorial (September 8, 1976).

"Arizona: Illegal Aliens Stripped, Stabbed, Burned," *El Paso Times* (August 22, 1976).

Judith Anderson, "A Champion For Chicanos," *San Francisco Chronicle* (August 12, 1976).

"Bilingual Vote Required in 30 States," *San Francisco Chronicle* (April 22, 1976).

Bill Boyarsky, "Black-Latin Coalition Wins House Voting Rights Fight," *Los Angeles Times* (June 4, 1975).

Bill Boyarsky, "Support Rises For Latin Rights Move," *Los Angeles Times* (March 26, 1975).

"Castro and Governor of Texas To Join Border-Issue Lobby Group," *Arizona Republic* (March 17, 1976).

Rosie Castro, "Texas Voting Rights," *San Antonio Express* (May 26, 1975).

"C. de Baca Appointed HSSD Chief," *Albuquerque Journal* (January 13, 1976).

"C. de Baca Explains Decision," *Albuquerque Journal* (January 19, 1976).

"C. de Baca Urges Act Enforcement," *Albuquerque Journal* (September 4, 1975).

Ben Cole, "Equal Opportunity In U.S. Called Aid To Ties With Latin America," *Arizona Republic* (August 15, 1975).

Rudolph O. de la Garza, "The Politics of Mexican-Americans," *The Chicanos: As We See Ourselves*, Arnulfo D. Trejo, ed. (Tucson, Arizona: The University of Arizona Press, 1979).

Frank del Olmo, "L.A. Spanish Daily Marks 50th Year in Circulation," *Los Angeles Times* (September 27, 1976).

Kemper Diehl, "GOP Needs a Stronger Spanish Accent," *San Antonio Express* (February 9, 1975).

Kemper Diehl, "GOP Pushes Party's Future Among Mexican-Americans," *San Antonio Express* (February 2, 1975).

"Discrimination Of Another Sort Laid To Agency," *Arizona Republic* (November 26, 1975).

"Echeverria Levels Blast At U.S. Alien Treatment," *San Antonio Express* (September 2, 1976).

"Ford Appoints Phoenix Attorney Special Aide on Hispanic Affairs," *Arizona Republic* (July 30, 1976).

"Ford OKs Charges In Immigration Quota," *San Francisco Chronicle* (October 22, 1976).

"Gains for the Spanish-surnamed," *Los Angeles Times* (December 30, 1974).

Margaret Gentry, "Concern For Voting Rights of Minorities Grows As Law Nears Expiration," *El Paso Times* (April 13, 1975).

"GOP Women Urge Priority for Hispanics," *San Antonio Express* (April 21, 1975).

"Henderson, NM Group Ready To Voice Woes," *El Paso Times* (November 9, 1975).

Phil Kimball, "EP to Host Border Meet," *El Paso Times* (November 25, 1975).

"Language Rule's Effect on Counties In California," *San Francisco Chronicle* (April 22, 1976).

"Latin Minority Predicted To Be Largest," *El Paso Times* (October 21, 1975).

"Latinos Political Success Hailed," *Santa Fe New Mexican* (December 26, 1974).

"Law Will Slash Ranks Of Hispanic Immigrants," *San Antonio Express* (October 22, 1976).

Daryl Lembke, "Ethnic Barriers Fall in Southwest Elections," *Los Angeles Times* (November 17, 1974).

Sara Martinez, "Mexican-Americans Told To Live Up To Potential," *San Antonio Express* (September 9, 1976).

"Mexican Chief in Texas," *San Francisco Chronicle* (September 8, 1976).

"Mexican Envoy Will Be Guest At Convention," *Arizona Republic* (May 4, 1976).

"Mexican President Wins Bout With Protester," *San Antonio Express* (September 8, 1976).

"Mexican-Americans and Blacks Fear Voting Act Rift," *Arizona Republic* (December 26, 1974).

"Mexico: Protest Pending," *El Paso Times* (August 25, 1976).

"Mexico Chief Seeks Truce With Business," *San Antonio Express* (October 23,

1975).

"Mexico Shows Interest," *El Paso Times* (June 16, 1976).

"Mexico To Propose Law For Foreign Prisoner Exchange," *Los Angeles Times* (September 6, 1976).

Bill Mintz, "Cantu Convicted—Now Wanted In Mexico," *San Antonio Express* (September 10, 1976).

James McCrory, "GOP Called Loser," *San Antonio Express* (December 18, 1974).

Wilson McKinney, "Lopez Portillo Backs Trade Fair," *San Antonio Express* (April 5, 1978).

David McLemore, "Echeverria To Be Picketed," *San Antonio Express* (September 5, 1976).

Harold K. Milks, "Mexico's President-elect Will Face Hassles On Peso," *Arizona Republic* (September 22, 1976).

"New, Broader Voting Rights Bill Speeded to Ford," *San Francisco Chronicle* (July 29, 1975).

Fernando V. Padilla and Carlos B. Ramirez, "Patterns of Chicano Representation In California, Colorado and Nuevo Mexico," *Aztlan* (Spring and Fall, 1974).

"President-Elect of Mexico To Meet With Ford," *San Francisco Chronicle* (September 24, 1976).

Joe Quintana, "Chairman of GI Forum Says Hispanics Suppressed," *El Paso Times* (October 21, 1975).

Julie Smith, "S.F. Anger Over Alien Job Order," *San Francisco Chronicle* (September 4, 1976)

Robert E. Storey, "It's Not Really A New Idea. It Has Been Kicked Around The Cloakrooms of the House and Senate For a Number of Years," *Santa Fe New Mexican* (December 1, 1974).

"Texas: Kreuger Frowns on 'Cactus' Suggestion," *El Paso Times* (August 17, 1976).

"Two Border Talks Set For Mexico This Week," *El Paso Times* (December 2, 1975).

"U.S. Envoy Remark Enrages Mexico," *Denver Post* (March 23, 1976).

"U.S. Fails to Plan For Hispanic-Americans, Agency Says," *Arizona Republic* (April 8, 1976).

"U.S.-Mexico Relations Hit Bottom," *El Paso Times* (September 7, 1976).

Ramon Villalobos, "Mexican President-Elect Plans Meeting With Gerald Ford In U.S.," *El Paso Times* (June 20, 1976).

Ramon Villalobos, "Portillo Reassuring During Ford Meeting," *El Paso Times* (October 10, 1976).

"Vote Law Waived For N.M." *Albuquerque Journal* (August 6, 1976).

Donald K. White, "Mexican Peso's New Role," *San Francisco Chronicle* (September 2, 1976).

George Williams, "Alien Hiring Case Reopened," *San Francisco Chronicle* (October 19, 1976).

CHAPTER 5: SYMBOLISM JUST WASN'T ENOUGH

Joseph Albright, "The Rising Power of Spanish-Americans," *San Francisco* (December 22, 1975).

Alan Baily, "Gonzales To Oversee Viva Carter," San Antonio Express (July 4, 1976).

"Alicia Chacon Disappointed at Demo Meet," *El Paso Times* (October 15, 1975).

"Area Demo To Attend Committee Meeting," *El Paso Times* (October 13, 1975).

"Bernal Praises Carter's Stand," *San Antonio Express* (July 3, 1976).

"Briscoe Fights Grant," *San Antonio Express* (September 5, 1976).

"Carter Pledges Battle Against Discrimination," *El Paso Times* (July 2, 1976).

"Carter To View Jobs For Minority," *San Antonio Express* (June 3, 1976).

Jim Dawson, "Reporter: Montoya In Trouble in '76," *Albuquerque Journal* (September 4, 1975)

Jerry Deal, "Grand Jury Indicts Four," *San Antonio Express* (September 30, 1976).

Jerry Deal, "Gutierrez Denies Grant Charges," *San Antonio Express* (August 25, 1976).

Jerry Deal, "H.B.G: Grant Buys Votes," *San Antonio Express* (August 22, 1976).

Kempter Diehl, "State Crystal Probe Threatens Big Grant," *San Antonio Express* (September 5, 1976).

Kemper Diehl, "Mystery Letter May Be Zavala Grant Key," *San Antonio Express* (September 22, 1976).

"Demos To Meet On Role," *San Antonio Express* (November 18, 1976).

"Drive to Begin For Registration," *San Antonio Express* (August 22, 1976).

William Endicott, "State's Affirmative Action Efforts Stirring Backlash," *Los Angeles Times* (January 22, 1976).

Richard Erickson, "Mexican-American Demo Seats Urged," *San Antonio Express* (June 14, 1976).

"Governor Asks Carter to Dump Sen. Gutierrez, *Arizona Republic* (August 22,1976).

Michael Harris, "An Old Reagan Foe Returning to Capital, *San Francisco Chronicle* (April, 1976).

"Hispanic Unit To Strive For Voter Signup," *Denver Post* (November 3, 1975).

"Hispanics Aiming For Power Base in GOP," *Albuquerque Journal* (August 25, 1976)

"Kissinger Will Attend Mexican's Installation," *Arizona Republic* (November 12, 1976).

"Latin Democrats," *San Francisco Chronicle* (December 16, 1975).

"Latino Caucus By Democrats," *San Francisco Chronicle* (November 2, 1975).

"La Raza Nominee Presents Views," *Denver Post* (September 26, 1976).

James McCrory, "Bernal Defends M-AD," *San Antonio Express* (May 20,

1976).

James McCrory, "Briscoe: Grant Would Mean A Cuba-In-Texas," *San Antonio Express* (September 19, 1976).

James McCrory, "Gutierrez: Probes Are Political," *San Antonio Express* (November 25, 1976).

Dick Merkel, "Court Okays Review of Grant To Zavala," *San Antonio Express* (October 29, 1976).

Dick Merkel, "Zavala's 'Little Cuba' Now Political Football," *San Antonio Express* (October 28, 1976).

"Mexican-American Demos Will Fight For '76 Delegates," *San Antonio Express* (January 11, 1976).

"Mexico Invites 11 Arizonans To Inauguration," *Arizona Republic* (November 4, 1976).

"Montoya Criticizes Press Role," *Albuquerque Journal* (August 15, 1976).

"Nation's Long-Time Illegal Immigrants," *Los Angeles Times* (July 2, 1976).

Charles Overby, "Carter Warned Not To Take Votes Of Latinos For Granted," *El Paso Times* (July 15, 1976).

Charles Overby, "Mexican-Americans' Votes Being Sought," *El Paso Times* (November 7, 1975).

Steve Peters, "El Paso's Chacon Nominated to DNC," *El Paso Times* (June 19, 1976).

Fernando Pinon, *Myth and Realities: Dynamics of Ethnic Politics* (New York: Vantage Press, 1978).

Emma E. Pullen, "Democrats Urged to Make Use of Latins," *Los Angeles Times* (November 1, 1975).

Joe Quintana, "Chairman Of GI Forum Says Hispanics Suppressed," *El Paso Times* (January 30, 1976).

Kenneth Reich, "Carter Backs 'Legitimate Status' for "S.A. Democrats Start Viva Carter Campaign," *San Antonio Express* (July 3, 1976).

"Sen. Gutierrez' Fortunes," *Arizona Republic*, editorial (August 22, 1976).

Lloyd Shearer, "Intelligence Report," *Parade* (July 2, 1978).

Sharon Sherman, "Full Latino Census Vital, Valdez Says," *Denver Post* (November 2, 1975).

Sharon Sherman, "Valdez Scores At Latino Conference," *Denver Post* (November 2, 1975).

Larry Stammer, "Presidency Attracts Brown, Aide Says," *Los Angeles Times* (August 23, 1975).

"Three Coloradans Selected For Latino Panel," *Denver Post* (November 3, 1975).

Paul R. Wieck, "Montoya Calls on Hispanos To Use Votes," *Albuquerque Journal* (November 2, 1975).

Paul R. Wieck, "Montoya May Introduce Gun Legislation," *Albuquerque Journal* (October 6, 1975).

Chapter 6: TURING POLITICS INTO GOVERNMENT

Robert V. Beier, "Schmitt Defeats Sen. Montoya," *Albuquerque Journal* (November 3, 1976).

Bill Boyarsky, "Carter Tells L.A. Chicanos, Blacks he Backs Drive To Get Out Minority Vote," *Los Angeles Times* (August 24, 1976).

"Carter OKs New Border Agency," *San Francisco Chronicle* (July 3, 1978).

Mike Cortes, "Has President Carter Come Through on Capital Hill for Hispanics?" *Agenda* (March/April, 1980), pp. 4-9.

"Crowd Chants 'Viva Carter' In McAllen," *El Paso Times* (October 31, 1976).

Frank del Olmo, "Bell Will Warn Police," *Los Angeles Times*, " (June 22, 1978).

Frank del Olmo, "Dole Meets With Chicanos In L.A.," *Los Angeles Times* (September 25, 1976).

Frank del Olmo, "Latins Charge Insensitivity by Carter Aides," *Los Angeles Times* (February 18, 1977).

Frank del Olmo, "Latins Form Unit To Support Ford," *Los Angeles Times* (October 15, 1976).

Thomas D. Elias, "Zero Population: A Time Bomb," *Sacramento Bee* (December 8, 1978).

"Farm Union Endorses Carter," *San Francisco Chronicle* (September 6, 1976).

"Farm Bureau Is Unhappy With Carter," *San Francisco Chronicle* (September 8, 1976).

Mervin D. Field, "Majority Swings To No on 14," *San Francisco Chronicle* (October 15, 1976).

Michael Harris, "A Big Push To Register California Voters," *San Francisco Chronicle* (October 4, 1976).

David Harris, "Illegal Mexican Immigration Is Part of What Has Been Called the Most Serious Problem Facing the Country: The U.S.-Mexico Border," *San Francisco Chronicle* (March 4, 1980).

Andrew Hernandez, *The Latino Vote in the 1976 Presidential Election: A Political Research Report*, (San Antonio, Texas: Southwest Voter Registration Education Project, 1977).

"Huge Increase in Latin Population is Forecast," *Oakland Tribune* (July 27, 1980).

Karen Kramer, "Hispanic Appointees in the Carter Administration," *Agenda* (November/December 1979).

Abe Mellinkoff column, *San Francisco Chronicle* (October 22, 1976).

Harold K. Milks, "Leaders Throughout Latin America Uncertain About Carter," *Arizona Republic* (November 10, 1976).

"Minorities Chalk Up Legislative Gains," *San Antonio Express* (November 4, 1976).

"Minority Demos To Reassess Roles," *El Paso Times* (November 18, 1976).

Philip Nobile, "Closing Loopholes in American Immigration Laws," *San Francisco Chronicle* (March 4, 1980).

Neal R. Pierce, "Refugee Influx A Real Sore Spot For Big City Mayors," *Oakland Tribune* (February 8, 1980).

Jackson Rannells, "Carter Finally Meets State Labor Leaders," *San Francisco*

Chronicle (October 8, 1976).

Doug Shuit and Frank del Olmo, "Mondale Courts Middle-Class Voter in L.A.," *Los Angeles Times* (October 19, 1976).

"Talks Planned On Peso Impact," *Arizona Republic* (November 27, 1976).

"Why the Tide of Illegal Aliens Keeps Rising: Interview with Leonel J. Castillo, Commissioner, Immigration and Naturalization Service," *U.S. News & World Report* (February 20, 1978).

Narda Zacchino,"Farm Workers Cheer Chavez—Even in Defeat," *Los Angeles Times* (November 4, 1976).

Chapter 7: THINGS COULD BE BETTER, YES

"1980 NCLR Affiliates Convention to be in Albuquerque," *El Noticiero*, National Council of La Raza (First Quarter, 1980).

"Alien Pupil Ban Upheld," *San Antonio Express* (September 12, 1976)

Eric Bazil, "Plan To Rescue Bilingual Education," *Oakland Tribune* (February 6, 1980).

"Bilingual Programs Fall Short, Court Told," *The Houston Post* (December 6, 1979).

"Bilingual Teachers Scarce, Consultant Says," *The Houston Post* (December 12, 1979).

"Bilingualism And the Melting Pot," *Washington Post* (September 27, 1979).

"Entry of Alien Children Into Texas Public Schools Delayed," *San Francisco Chronicle* (August 13, 1980).

"Envoy Nurtures Mexico-US Ties," *The Sacramento Bee* (November 28, 1980)

Lawrence Feinberg, "College Entrance Exam Results Show Blacks Are Averaging Far Below Whites," *San Francisco Chronicle* (December 10, 1979).

"Gas Importers Express Surprise With Export Limits Set by Mexico," *The Wall Street Journal* (November 21, 1980)

"HEW Clarifies Bilingual Ruling," *Denver Post* (April 19, 1976).

"Hispanic Nominated," *Oakland Tribune* (March 7, 1980).

"Mexican Immigration and the United States Labor Market," *Agenda* (March/April, 1979).

"Minorities Remain Scarce Among College Students," *Oakland Tribune* (February 15, 1980).

Alan Murray, "Issues of Census Undercount May Go On Until 1990," (October 8, 1980).

"Regional Report: The INS vs The Census," *Nuestro* (March, 1980).

Robert Reinhold, "Should Census Count the Illegal Alien," *The New York Times* (February 7, 1980).

"Rising Criticism of Census' Ethnic Focus," *San Francisco Chronicle* (May 15, 1978).

Tomas Saucedo, "Historical and Legislative Perspectives on Bilingual Education and the Lau Regulations," *Agenda* (March/April, 1981), pp. 10-14.

Mark Seibel, "Mexico Has Reservations About Nava Choice,"

George Skelton, "Brown Raps Carter on Oil Talks," *Los Angeles Times* (February 7, 1979).

Kit Smith, "How Presidents Play Politics with Fed," *The Sunday Star-Bulletin & Advertiser* (March 1, 1981).

William K. Stevens,"U.S. and Mexico Governors Find Value in First Meeting," *The New York Times* (June 29, 1980).

Chapter 8: A FORMIDABLE GIANT

"About Those Other Presidential Hopefuls—" *U.S. News & World Report* (March 24, 1980).

Alex Armendariz, "Reagan/Bush Si, Carter No," *Nuestro* (November, 1980).

Ellen J. Bartlett, "Cynicism is Up: America Has a Big Problem With a Real Downer Attitude," *Houston Chronicle* (August 15, 1989).

David Broder, "Fears In the Black Community," *San Francisco Chronicle* (December 3, 1980).

"Campaign Director Quits," *New York Times* (August 31, 1979).

Lou Cannon, *Reagan* (New York: Putnam, 1982).

Adam Clymer, "G.O.P. Women Cheer Connally At Parley," *New York Times* (September 29, 1979).

"Conservative Group Urges Civil Rights Policy Reversal," *Los Angeles Times* (November 13, 1980).

Frank del Olmo, "Also-Ran to Vote, Concede," *Los Angeles Times* (June 3, 1980).

Frank del Olmo, "Politicos Point to Latino Vote as Proof-But of What?" *Los Angeles Times* (November 13, 1980).

Ann Devroy, "Democratic Voting Blocs Went Against Tradition," *Oakland Tribune/Today* (November 5, 1980).

Tony Dominguez, "Jimmy Carter: A Worthy Record," *Nuestro* (November, 1980).

Douglas Dowie, "Why Carter Must Win In California Vote," *East Bay Today* (September 10, 1980).

"Ethnic Political Advertising Comes of Age In Texas," *The Hispanic World's Fair Forum: Minority Marketing in '80s* (November, 1980).

Facts on File, World News Digest With Index (February 22, 1980), p. 130.

José Garcia, "King's Kingmakers," *Nuestro* (March, 1979).

Jack W. Germond and Jules Witcover, *Blue Smoke and Mirrors: How Reagan Won and Why Carter Lost the Election of 1980* (New York: The Viking Press, 1981).

Ray Gonzalez, "California's 'Virgin Territory,'" *Nuestro* (March 1979).

Georgie Anne Geyer, "Citizenship May Become Irrelevant," *Oakland Tribune* (February 26, 1980).

Louis Harris, "Reagan, Carter Running Even," *East Bay Today* (September 10, 1980).

"I Am Presidential Timber," *Nuestro* (March, 1980).

Jonathan Kirsch, "Chicano Power: There is One Inevitable Fact. By 1990, California Will Become America's First Third World State," *New West* (September 11, 1978).

Douglas E. Kneeland, "Republican 'Presidential Forums' Get Big Turnouts, But Candidates Grumble," *New York Times* (August 5, 1979).

The Latino Vote in the 1980 Presidential Election: A Political Research Report (San Antonio, Texas: Southwestern Voter Registration Education Project, 1981).

Frank Lynn, "Bronx Leader Acts To Close Breach In Democratic Party," *The New York Times* (February 19, 1979).

Julio Moran, "The GOP Wants Us," *Nuestro* (August, 1980), p. 26.

Joe Nolan, "Reagan and 5 Former Opponents Preach Party Unity, Raise Funds," *Houston Chronicle* (June 28, 1980).

Eleanor Randolph, "Reagan Attempts to Reassure Blacks," *Los Angeles Times* (November 24, 1980).

"Reagan and Former Rivals Pooling Fund-Raising Lists," *The New York Times* (June 10, 1980).

Elisa Sanchez, "John Anderson: The Alternative," *Nuestro* (November, 1980).

Robert Scheer, "Urban Plans: Much Talk, Little Action," *Los Angeles Times* (June 23, 1978).

"Selling the Dream," *Forbes* (November 10, 1980).

"Teddy and Jimmy in Texas," *Newsweek* (September 15, 1980).

CHAPTER 9: CHANGING ATTITUDES—AND THEORIES

Lou Cannon, *Reagan* (New York: Putnum, 1982).

Ronnie Dugger, *On Reagan: The Man & His Presidency* (New York: McGraw-Hill Book Company, 1883).

Rowland Evans & Robert Novak, *The Reagan Revolution* (New York: E.P. Dutton,1981).

William Greider, "The Education of David Stockman," *The Atlantic Monthly* (December, 1981).

Haynes Johnson, "An American Revolution," in Paul Duke (ed.), *Beyond Reagan: The Politics of Upheaval* (New York: Warner Books, 1986).

Robert Lekachman, *Visions and Nightmares: America After Reagan* (New York: MacMillan Publishing Company, 1987).

Robert Lekachman, "The Economy," in Alan Gartner, et al. *What Reagan Is Doing to Us* (New York: Harper & Row Publishers, 1982).

David Stockman, *The Triumph of Politics: The Inside Story of the Reagan Revolution* (New York: Avon Books, 1986).

CHAPTER 10: THE DECIDING FACTOR

Carlos Acudelo, "Wooing the Hispanics," *World Press Review* (November, 1983). [Originally in *El Tiempo* of Bogota, Columbia].

Polly Baca Barragan, "Democrats: Reagan Budget Cuts Devastating for

Latinos," *Nuestro* (October, 1981), p 26.

Ellen J. Bartlett, "Cynicism Is Up: America Has A Big Problem With a Real Downer Attitude," *Houston Chronicle* (August 15, 1989).

Sidney Blumenthal, "Reagan The Unassailable: How Come His Gaffs Never Seem to Hurt Him?," *The New Republic* (September 12, 1983).

Beth Bogart, "Political Power Gives Market Vote of Confidence," *AdvertisingAge* (February 9, 1987).

Linda Chavez, "The Next underclass? The Truth About Hispanic Poverty, *The New Republic* (August 3, 1987).

Tom Diaz, "Congress Rates On Black and Hispanic Issues," *Nuestro* (September, 1984), p. 41.

Stephen Goode, "Cathi Villalpondo: Special Assistant to the President," *Nuestro* (January/February, 1985).

"High Hopes of Black, Hispanic Voters," *U.S. News & World Report* (October 11, 1982), p. 46.

Larry Hufford, "Chicano Challenged America to Live Its Ideals," *National Catholic Reporter* (July 15, 1988).

"In Search of Hispanic Voters," *Nuestro* (August, 1983).

"The Keys to the White House: The Inside Story of Campaign '88," *Newsweek* (November 21, 1988).

Morton Kondracke, "White House Watch—Q:Is He Running? A: Why Not?" *The New Republic* (September 12, 1983).

Guernsey LePelley,"Lightly:Voice A Choice," *The Christian Science Monitor* (February 13, 1984).

Julio Moran, "Esteban Torres: Our Hot Line to The President," *Nuestro* (March,1980).

Fernando Oaxaca, "Republican: Reagan Puts Nation on Prudent Path," *Nuestro* (October, 1981).

Richard Parker, "The Hispanic Strategy," *Hispanic* (May, 1989).

"Politicians You Didn't Vote For," *Nuestro* (November, 1981), p.19.

"The Political Parties Respond," *Nuestro* (September, 1983), p. 19.

"Presidential Election 1984," *Nuestro* (September, 1983).

Gail Sheehy, "Ronald Reagan," *Character: America's Search for Leadership* (New York: William Morrow and Company, Inc., 1988).

David Stockman, *The Triumph of Politics: The Inside Story of the Reagan Revolution* (New York: Avon Books, 1986).

CHAPTER 11: THE COUNTRYSIDE PAINTS ITSELF

"Activist Willie Velasquez Dies at 44 of Kidney Cancer," *Houston Post* (June 6, 1988).

Rodolfo Acuna, "Don't Count Cranston Among Latinos Friends," *Los Angeles Herald Examiner*

Richard Avena, "One Last Vote for Willie Velasquez," *Los Angeles Times* (June 18, 1988).

Charles R. Babcock, "Cranston Aided S&L, Solicited Funds," *The Washington Post* (July 19, 1989).

Beth Barrett, "Cranston Aided Project's Supporter," *Daily News* (Los Angeles), (July 18, 1989).

"Cranston Used Non-Partisan Group to Raise Partisan Cash," *Register-Pajaronian* (Watsonville, California), (August 7, 1989).

Ilana DeBare, "Cranston, Duke Caught in Fallout of S&L Failure," *The Sacramento Bee* (July 23, 1989).

Frank del Olmo, "Opening for Latino Voting Marred by Dispute Between Cranston,Velasquez's Heirs," *Los Angeles Times* (August 7, 1988).

"Drexel Gift To Cranston Group Reported," *Los Angeles Herald Examiner* (July 24, 1989).

"Dukakis Starts Spanish Media Blitz," *San Antonio Express-News* (October 28, 1989).

Jane Ely, "Noted Political Leader Velasquez Dies at 44," *Houston Chronicle* (June 16, 1988).

Facts on File: World News Digest With Index (April 17, July 15, July 22 and August 19, 1988).

James S. Granelli, "Solicited Donations From Firm Chief, Cranston Says," *Los Angeles Times* (July 18, 1989);

"Group Cranston Aided Funded Son's Institute," *The Sacramento Bee* (July 26, 1989).

Robert H. Gunnison and Jerry Roberts, "Cranston's Trips on Behalf of Favorite Causes," *San Francisco Chronicle* (July 19, 1989).

Stanley G. Hilton, *Bob Dole: American Political Phoenix* (Chicago: Contemporary Books, 1988).

Larry Hufford, "Chicano Challenged America To Live Its Ideals," *National Catholic Reporter* (July 15, 1988).

David Lautor, "Dukakis Eulogizes Latino Political Leader Velasquez," *Los Angeles Times* (June 19, 1988).

"Looking for Mr. Right," *Newsweek* (November 21, 1988), p. 36.

Mary McGrory, "Dukakis' Ironing-Board Power," *The Washington Post* (June 5, 1988).

"North Predicts Mexico's Fall If Communists Take Nicaragua," *San Antonio Express-News* (October 15, 1989).

Leslie Phillips, "Role of Tax-Exempts Debated," *USA Today* (January 22, 1990)

Joe Scott, "Causes the Conservative and `Sen. Liberal' Shared," *Los Angeles Herald Examiner* (July 21, 1989).

Amy Simmons, "Getting Past the Doorstep, *Hispanic* (November, 1989).

Martin Smith, "Looking Beyond Cranston," *Sacramento Bee* (January 12, 1989).

"Turnout Hits 64-Year Low in Presidential Race," *Congressional Quarterly* (January 21, 1989).

Chapter 12: THE REALIZATION

"Another Zero Sum Game," *Nuestro* (April, 1986).

Beth Bogart, "Political Power Gives Market Vote of Confidence," *Advertising Age* (February 9, 1987).

Gloria Borger, "The Retooling of the Right," *U.S. News & World Report* (August 22, 1988).

Barbara Caplan, "Linking Cultural Characteristics to Political Opinion," *Ignored Voices: Public Opinion Polls and the Latino Community*, in Rodolfo E. de la Garza, ed. (Austin: University of Texas Press, 1987).

"Close-Up: WIC Report—Officials May Have Misled Public," *USA Today* (January 24, 1990).

Rhodes Cook, "Political Notes: Atwater Takes the Reins at Republican Party," *Congressional Quarterly* (January 21, 1989).

Democratic Party and the Hispanic Voter," *Hispanic* (September, 1989), p. 54.

"Dukakis Comeback Could Be Difficult," *San Antonio Express-News* (October 15, 1989).

"Dukakis To Visit S.A.," *San Antonio Express-News* (October 11, 1989).

"First Latina in Congress," *National Report*, NALEO Newsletter (Third Quarter, 1989).

Ed Fitch, "Buying Power Bursts Poverty-Stricken Image," *Advertising Age* (February 9, 1987).

Jack Germond and Jules Witcover, *Mad As Hell Revolt at the Ballot Box, 1992* (New York: Warner Books, 1993).

"Goals & Timetables—A Civil Rights Remedy?" *Nuestro* (May, 1986).

"Hispanic Elected Officials Numbers Jump by 12.6 Percent," Press Release, National Association of Latino Elected and Appointed Officials (September 4, 1989).

"Hispanics on The Rise," *Newsweek* (October 6, 1986).

"Hispanic Votes Up for Grabs," *National Journal* (September 9, 1989), p. 2212.

Gene Koretz, "How the Hispanic Population Boom Will Hit the Work Force," *Business Week* (February 20, 1989), p. 21.

Julia Lieblich, "If You Want A Big, New Market. . . ." *Fortune* (November 21, 1988).

Mark Linsalata, "EEOC Accused of Racial Bias," *San Antonio Light* (November 25, 1989).

Dick McCormick, "The Importance of Hispanics to Our Nation," Speech delivered at the Hispanic Business Conference, Phoenix, Arizona, February 16, 1989.

Walter S. McManus, "Labor Market Costs of Language Disparity: An Interpretation of Hispanic Earnings Differences, *The American Economics Review*, Vol. 75, No. 4 (September, 1985).

Robert Mena, "Business World," *The News* (Mexico City) (January 19, 1990).

"More People Than Power," *The Economist* (September 17, 1988).

Julian Morrison, "The Quiet Success of Hispanic Businesses," *Nation's Business* (July, 1984).

"NALEO's 1990 Census Fullcount Project," National Report. NALEO *Naturalization Quarterly*, vol. 4, issue 3 (Third Quarter, 1989).

NALEO Press Release (September 7, 1989).

NALEO Newsletter (Third Quarter, 1989).

Harry P. Pachon, "Politics and Public Policy: The Hispanic Community," Speech delivered before the 1988 Black and Puerto Rican Legislative Caucus, Albany, New York, February 14, 1988.

Richard Parker, "The Hispanic Strategy," *Hispanic* (May, 1989).

"Turnout Hits 64-Year Low in Presidential Race," *Congressional Quarterly* (January 21, 1989), p.137-138.

Richard Parker, "Ron Brown: The "HBG Says No to Dukakis Invitation," *San Antonio Express-News* (October 15, 1989).

"USA Snapshots, *USA Today* (January 17, 1990).

"U.S. Congressmen Talk With Gonzales," *The News* (Mexico City) (January 19, 1990).

Murray Weidenbaum, *Rendezvous With Reality* (New York: Basic Books, 1988).

Chapter 13: THE INSIDERS

Rodolfo F. Acuna, "Latinos Big-Time Losers in Bush Administration," *Houston Chronicle* (August 19, 1991).

Kay Barbaro, "Sin Pelos en la Lengua," *Hispanic Link Weekly Report* (July 6, August 3, October 5,1992).

Henry Cisneros, "Dinamismo Estadunidense y La Cultura del Nuevo Mundo," *El Nacional Textual* (Enero, 1990).

José de la Isla, "Ganny, Gampy, & George P.—the Crystalizing of Hispanic Politics," Hispanic Link News Service *Los Angeles Times* Syndicate, (August 18, 1992).

José de la Isla, "GOP Platform: The Border Controversy That Won't Go Away," Hispanic Link News Service dispatch (August 17, 1992).

José de la Isla, "Jeb Bush Addresses Hispanic GOP Group—Tribute to Arturo Hevia," Hispanic Link News Service dispatch (August 17, 1992).

José de la Isla, "'Tortilla Curtain' Lowered" Hispanic Link News Service dispatch (August 17, 1992).

"Done Deal," *U.S. News & World Report* (August 31, 1993), p. 30.

James Evans, "With Justice For All," *Vista* (November 8, 1992).

"Family Values Touted at Hispanic Meeting," *Houston Chronicle* (April 25, 1992).

John J. Fialka, "Loner Gonzalez Toils to Expose White House Role In Aiding Iraq in Years Leading Up to Gulf War," *The Wall Street Journal* (July 31, 1992).

Douglas Frantz, "Rep. Gonzalez calls Plea Deal in Iraq Loan Case a

'Whitewash,'" *Los Angeles Times* (September 4, 1993).

Christopher Georges and Clara Bingham, "Who's Who Inside the Clinton and Bush Campaigns," *The Washington Monthly* (July/August 1992).

Jack W. Germond and Jules Witcover, *Mad As Hell: Revolt at the Ballot Box, 1992* (New York: Warner Books, Inc., 1993).

Ken Herman and Mary Lenz, "Transcript Tells All on Guerrero," *The Houston Post* (September 17, 1992).

Steven A. Holmes, "Perot Breaks with Agency That Produced Reagan Ads," *The New York Times* (July 14, 1992).

Jan Jarboe, "The Eternal Challenger," *Texas Monthly* (October, 1992).

Mary Lenz, "Guerrero Didn't Graduate from College," *The Houston Post* (September 12, 1992).

Neil A. Lewis, "Former Bank Official Says Bush Supported Iraq Loans," *The New York Times* (September 4, 1993).

Sandra Martinez, "Perot Exit Changes Hispanic Voter Equation," *Hispanic Link Weekly Report* (July 27, 1993).

Sandra Marquez, "Latinos at Democratic Convention Focus on Unity," *Hispanic Link Weekly Report* (July 20, 1992).

Lisa Paikowski and John O'Connor, "GOP Sets Strategy," *AdWeek* (August 24, 1992).

Janice Petrovich and Elizabeth Weiser Ramirez, "Did Executive Order Shortchange Latinos?" *Hispanic Link Weekly Report* (October 5, 1992).

Press Release, Southwest Voter Research Institute (August 28, 1992).

"Racial Slur Stirs Up Storm, *Newsweek* (October 6, 1986).

"RNHA of New York State Holds Rally to Endorse President Bush," *The American Hispanic* (April-May, 1992).

William Schneider, "The Suburban Century Begins," *The Atlantic Monthly* (July 1992), p. 34.

Tom Shale, "Mrs. Bush Warming Up the TV Home," *The Washington Post* (August 20, 1992).

Kelley Shannon, "Clinton Vows Appointments for Hispanics," *The Houston Post* (July 2, 1992).

Kelley Shannon, "Hispanic Group Opposes Thomas' Court Nomination," *The Houston Post* (August 15, 1991).

Kelley Shannon, "LULAC Opens U.S. Conclave," *Houston Chronicle* (July 1, 1992).

Norman B. Ture, "To Cut and To Please," *National Review* (August 31, 1992).

Tom Wicker, "Tax-Cut Plan Turns Tables On Bush," *The News* (Mexico, D.F., January 19, 1990).

John E. Yang, "Clinton Mines for Perot Votes In Calif.," *Chicago Sun Times* (July 27, 1992).

Chapter 14: THE SUPERMAJORITY

"Anti-Immigrant Sentiment Rises," *Houston Chronicle* (July 4, 1993).

Kay Bárbaro, "Sin Pelos En la Lengua," *Hispanic Link Weekly Report* (October 25, 1993 and January 3, 1994).

Debra Beachy, "Study Estimates Immigrants Cost Texas $4.68 Billion in 1992," *Houston Chronicle* (March 3, 1994).

Sidney Blumenthal, "The Making of the Machine," *The New Yorker* (November 29, 1993).

Patricia Braus, "What Does Hispanic Mean?" *American Demographics* (June 1993).

David Broder, "Striking High, Low Points in Clinton's First Year, *Houston Chronicle* (January 16, 1994).

Stephen S. Cohen, "Where the Jobs Were," *The Washington Post* (March 14, 1993).

Rhodes Cook, "Clinton Struggles to Meld a Governing Coalition," *Congressional Quarterly* (August 7, 1993).

Phil Duncan, "Minority Districts Fail to Enhance Turnout," *Congressional Quarterly* (March 27, 1993).

Tony Freemantle, "Land of Milk, Honey Turning To Curds and Whey," *Houston Chronicle* (July 4, 1993).

Christian R. González, "Rice Economist's Numbers Rile Activists," *Hispanic Link Weekly Report* (November 15, 1993).

Christian R. González, "Study: Immigrants Paid $70 Billion in Taxes in 1992," *Hispanic Link Weekly Report* (February 28, 1994).

Patricia Guadalupe, "Clinton Gets `C-' for Appointments," *Hispanic Link Weekly Report* (May 24, 1993).

Patricia Guadalupe, "Study Finds Immigrants Less of a Burden than Previous Findings," *Hispanic Link Weekly Report* (September 13, 1993).

Patricia Guadalupe, "Study Finds Latinos Only 5.6 percent of Federal Workforce," *Hispanic Link Weekly Report* (December 20, 1993).

Jonathan J. Higuera and Carolina Pica, "Clinton Receives Court Candidates, *Hispanic Link Weekly Report* (March 29, 1993).

"La Raza Study May Lay Lazy Latino Stereotype to Rest," *Houston Chronicle* (July 20, 1993.

"Latinos Threatened by Tone of Anti-Immigrant Debate," *Hispanic Link Weekly Report* (September 13, 1993).

Frank Cota-Robles Newton, "Presidential Appointments and Disappointments," *Hispanic Link Weekly Report* (October 18, 1993).

Harry P. Pachón and Juan Carlos Alegre, "An Overview of Hispanic Elected Officials in 1993," *National Roster of Hispanic Elected Officials.*

Robert Pear, "U.S. Sets Policy On Naturalization," *New York Times* (November 26, 1993).

Felix Pérez, "Meeting Held to Secure Input With Clinton," *Hispanic Link Weekly Report* (November 23, 1992).

"The Rise of Hispanic Affluence," *American Demographics* (August 1990).

Peter D. Salins, "Take a Ticket," *The New Republic* (December 27, 1993), p. 14).

Rad Sallee, "Making Sense of Hispanic Census," *Houston Chronicle* (August 24, 1993).

Joe Schwartz, "Low-Wage Workers Growing Rapidly," *American Demographics* (July 14, 1992).

"Study: Immigrants Top U.S. Students," *Houston Chronicle* (February 23, 1994).

Margaret L. Udansky, "Report on Status of Hispanics Likely to Stir Debate Over Causes," *Houston Post* (August 23, 1993).

Chapter 15: CONVERGENCE

"A Greenspan le preocupa un rechazo al Tratado," *El Heraldo* (Houston, June 3, 1993).

Rodolfo F. Acuna, "Latinos Big-Time Losers in Bush Administration," *Houston Chronicle* (August 19, 1991).

José Armas, "Media Masks Hispanics' Considerable Role in NAFTA Passage," *Hispanic Link Weekly Report* (December 6, 1993).

"Audiencia Sobre TLC, Televisada a EE.UU. Para Solo Dos Senadores," *Unomásuno* (Mexico, D.F., October 22, 1993).

James Bornemeier, "Researchers Praise New Border Policy But Say It Is Not All-Purpose Solution," *Houston Chronicle* (July 28, 1994).

Keith Bradsher, "NAFTA Controls on Environment Are Far Stronger Than On Labor," *Houston Chronicle* (September 19, 1993).

"Bush Hails Progress of 3-Nation Free-Trade Talks," *The Houston Post* (July 15, 1992).

"Canada Hopes to Solve NAFTA Kinks," *Houston Chronicle* (November 22, 1993).

Jim Cason and David Brooks, "Cambios en la Implementación de TLC Para Captar Votos A Favor," *La Jornada* (Mexico D.F., October 28, 1993).

Andrew Cawthorne, "Clinton's Victory Ushers In New Era Of Mexico-U.S. Relations, *The News* (Mexico, D.F., November 4, 1992).

William E. Clayton, Jr., "Dem Whip Won't Quit For Fighting NAFTA," *Houston Chronicle* (August 30, 1993).

"Clinton Da Marcha A Su Plan de Elevar Impuestos," *Novedades* (October 23, 1993).

"El Comercio Crece 10 percent entre Mexico-EEUU en Primer Trimestre," *El Mexica* (Houston, June 3, 1993).

"Custionan Democracia en México," *El Norte* (November 18, 1993).

William E. Clayton Jr., "Bush, Salinas Sign 6 Accords Covering Trade, Environment," *Houston Chronicle* (October, 1989).

William Cormier, "Trade Negotiators Yield To Mexico on Subsidies," *Chicago Sun-Times* (July 27, 1992).

"De Retirarse Canada, Seguirán México y EU," *El Sol de San Luís* (Potosí, October 29, 1993.

Augusta Dwyer, "Salinas Comes Out Swinging on NAFTA," *El Financiero*

International (Mexico, D.F., October 11-17, 1993).

Thomas B. Edsall, "The Tradeoffs of NAFTA for Democrats," *The Washington Post National Weekly Edition*," (November 1-7, 1993).

Dolia Estévez and Rebeca Lizárraga, "NAFTA Gets Green Light," *El Financiero International* (December 14, 1992).

Martha Frase-Blunt, "On the Fast Track to Free Trade," *Hispanic* (August, 1991).

Dan Freedman, "Reno Unveils Plans to Tighten Up Border," *Houston Chronicle* (February 4, 1994).

Michael K. Frisby and James M. Perry, "Clinton's NAFTA Dealing Shows Gambler's Instincts," *The Wall Street Journal* (November 18, 1993).

Johaben Garcia Garces, "Antes de llegar al Congreso el TLC Sufre Severos Embates," *Punto* (Mexico, D.F., May 10, 1993).

Tim Golden, "Salinas Changes His Tune on NAFTA," *Houston Chronicle* (September 15, 1993).

Antonio González, "For a Prosperous and Equitable North America," *Latino Consensus on NAFTA*, N.D.

John Gravois, "Gephardt, Others Ask President to Renegotiate Free Trade," *The Houston Post* (September 10, 1992).

Patricia Guadalupe, "An Elusive 'Consensus' on NAFTA," *Hispanic Link Weekly Report* (March 29, 1993).

Patricia Guadalupe, "Clinton Agrees to NADBANK; Torres On Board," *Hispanic Link Weekly Report* (November 1, 1993).

Patricia Guadalupe, "Hispanic Caucus Loses Fight on Immigration Benefits," *Hispanic Link Weekly Report* (October 28, 1993).

Patricia Guadalupe, "Hispanic Congressional Members Split 9-8 Pro-NAFTA," *Hispanic Link Weekly Report* (November 22, 1993).

Evangelina Hernandez, "Funcionarios Mexicanos Hablaron con el Equipo de William Clinton," *La Jornada* (Mexico, D.F., November 3, 1992).

David Hess, "Gephardt Reportedly Will Oppose NAFTA," *Houston Chronicle*, September 11, 1993).

Cragg Hines, "Clinton Buoyed by NAFTA Debate Fallout," *Houston Chronicle* (November 11, 1993).

Jim Hoagland, "The Baker-Clinton Policy," *The Washington Post* (August 17, 1992).

Ernest F. Hollings, "Reform Mexico First," *Foreign Policy* (Winter 1993-94).

"Hopes for NAFTA," *Reuter News Service* (September 27, 1993).

Laurence Iliff, "Mexico Breaks With Political Tradition," *Houston Chronicle* (September 29, 1993).

Interview with David Robinson and Susana Gousker, Democratic Americans Abroad/Mexico, Mexico, D.F., November 3, 1992.

Rosalind Jackler, "Key Democrat Says Health Care More Important Than NAFTA," *The Houston Post* (July 28, 1993).

Cynthia Joyce, "Mexico's Taste for U.S. Good Touted by Clinton," *The News* (Mexico, D.F., October 21, 1993).

Kathy Kiely, "INS, Reno Move to Retake Control of Mexican Border," *Houston Post* (February 4, 1994).

Latino Summit on NAFTA, Latino Consensus Position on NAFTA, March 12-13, 1993, Washington, D.C.

"Legisladores de EU Llegan a Mexico Para Hablar Con CSG," *Novedades* (Octubre 23, 1993).

Carmelo Lodise, " San Antonio: A Hotbed of NAFTA Support," *The News* (Mexico, D.F., October 21, 1993).

Greg McDonald and Bill Mintz, "Bipartisan Backers Make NAFTA Pitch," *Houston Chronicle* (November 3, 1993).

"Mexico Ha Comprometido Mas que Otros en Favor de la Apertura: Clinton," *La Jornada* (Mexico, D.F., October 21, 1993).

"Mexico May Join Economic Group, *The Wall Street Journal* (August 20, 1992).

Bill Mintz, "Lawyer Daley to Lead Charge for Trade Pact," *Houston Chronicle* (August 20, 1993).

Bill Mintz, "NAFTA Supporters Say They're Turning the Tide of Opposition," *Houston Chronicle* (October 9, 1993).

Bill Mintz, "Plan Would Double Border Fees to Offset Losses from NAFTA," *Houston Chronicle* (October 8, 1993).

Bill Mintz, "You Scratch My NAFTA, I'll Scratch..." *Houston Chronicle* (November 13, 1993).

"Most House Democrats Oppose NAFTA, Majority Whip Says," Reuters News Service (August 30, 1993).

"NAFTA Fate Threatens Econ, Relations With US," *Guadalajara Reporter* (Mexico, May 15-21, 1993).

Robert Novak, "NAFTA, Health Care Test the President's Control," *The Houston Post* (September 7, 1993).

"Organized Labor Sings Clinton's Praises Despite Sharp Disagreement on NAFTA," *The Houston Post* (September 7, 1993).

President Plans Major Address As Part of Administration's Push for NAFTA, *Houston Post* (September 6, 1993)

"Quayle Prognostica la probación de TLC," *El Heraldo* (Houston, June 3, 1993).

James Risen, "U.S., Mexico, Canada Near Trade Pact OK," *Chicago Sun-Times* (July 26, 1992).

"Salinas Calls Ratifying NAFTA Once-in-Generation Opportunity," Reuters News Service (August 29, 1993).

Fidel Samaniego, "Repercusiones a Nivel Mundial, Si EU Rechaza al Tratado," *El Universal* (Mexico, D.F., October 24, 1993).

Sergio Sarmiento, "Breaking Protocol During A Presidential Tour," *The News* (Mexico, D.F., October 22, 1992).

Jennifer Smith, "Cisneros Says Clinton's Position On NAFTA Will Be A Clear One," *The News* (Mexico, D.F., October 3, 1992).

"Speculation Already Begins On Clinton's Future Cabinet," *The News* (Mexico,

D.F., November 5, 1992.

Starr Spencer, "Salinas Optimistic About Clinton, Trade," *The News* (Mexico, D.F., November 5, 1992).

"Statement of Ambassador Mickey Kantor, United State Trade Representative— NAFTA and the Perot-Choate Book," The White House, September 2, 1993.

Mark Stevenson, "Service Surcharges Being Considered To Fund Environment Clean-Up," *The News* (Mexico, D.F., October 21, 1993).

Television interview of President Carlos Salinas de Gortari by Jacobo Zabludosky, *Televisa* (Mexico, D.F., November 4, 1992).

Wilbert Torre, "Mayor Energía Dureza Contra El Bloqueo, Exigen," *El Unversal* (Mexico D.F., October 24, 1993).

"What if NAFTA Loses?" *Business Week* (November 22, 1993).

Antonio Vazquez, "Daño al Comercio Mundial Si Fracasa el TLC: Kolbe," *Unomásuno* (Mexico, D.F. October 24, 1993).

"Would Kill Pact, Salinas Insists," *The Washington Post* (October 8, 1993).

CHAPTEr 16: THE RISE OF HISPANIC POLITICAL POWER

Henry J. Aaron, *Politics and the Professors: The Great Society in Perspective* (Washington, D.C.: The Brookings Institution, 1978), p. 17.

Luís Arteaga, "To Vote or Not to Vote," The California Latino Vote 2000, Latino Issues Forum (www.lif.org/Vote_2000.2.html).

"Clinton Reflects on Learning Curve of Being President," Associated Press (October 9, 2000).

"WTC Dead Still a Police Case," *Associated Press* (March 8, 2002).

Anthony Boadle, "Hispanic Leader Criticizes Bush Over Appointments, *Reuters* (January 19, 2001).

David S. Broder, "Voters' Views Sharply Divided," *Washington Post* (November 8, 2000).

"Terror Attack Hits U.S.," CNN.com (September 11, 2001) www.cnn.com/ 2001/US/09/11/worldtrade.crash/

Kim Cobb, "Americans Uninspired by Election," *Houston Chronicle* (October 29, 2000).

Matt Coker, "Gaddi Damn It," *OC Weekly* (November 16-22, 2001).

José de la Isla, "The Election from Austin and Taquería Chapala," *Hispanic Link Weekly Report* (November 13, 2000).

John Dean, "Being White House Counsel: What Al Gonzalez, Bush's Pick, Will Face In Washington," *Find Law's Legal Commentary* (December 22, 2000).

Zachary R. Dowdy, "Gore, Clinton Court Latinos," *Newsday* (March 11,2000).

Editors, "Border Crossing," *The New Republic Online* (June 25, 2002).

"Foot Soldiers Fight to Boost Turnout," latimes.com (October 30,2000).

Juan González, *Harvest of Empire: A History of Latinos in America* (New York: Viking, 2000).

"Gore Campaigns in Michigan, Bush Makes California Speech by Satellite," CNN.Com (October 30, 2000).

Edward Hegstrom, "Mexican Official: US Policy Leading to Deaths on Border," *Houston Chronicle* (June 27, 2002).

Judy Keen, "Republican Party on a Crusade to Win Over Hispanic Americans," *USA Today* (August 7, 2001).

Joe Klein, "A Reporter At Large: Eight Years, Bill Clinton and the Politics of Persistence," *The New Yorker* (October 16 & 23, 2000).

Joe Klein, "Eight Years: Bill Clinton and the Politics of Persistence," *The New Yorker* (October 16 & 23, 2000).

Kevin O'Leary, "Gaddi Vasquez, 46," *OC Metro: Business Lifestyle Magazine* (N.D.)

Cynthia L. Orosco, "California Latinos Like Gore Even More, See Government as Friend," *Hispanic Link Weekly Report* (October 30, 2000).

"Positive Economic Indicators for Hispanics Reveal Opportunity to Focus on the Nation's Working Poor," News Release, National Council of La Raza (September 26, 2000).

Ana Radelat, "Senate Passes Embargo Bill," *The Miami Herald* (October 19, 2000).

Patrick Reddy, "Analysis: How the Networks Blew the Florida Call—Twice," Hispanic Trends.com, December 7, 2000.

Press Release, "Comments of U.S. Senator Patrick Leahy, Chairman, Senate Judiciary Committee, On Assertions Made About The Nomination of Miguel Estrada," (April 10, 2002).

Ernesto Portillo, "Terrorist Attacks Also Left Invisible Dead," *Arizona Daily Star* (October 20, 2001).

Clay Robinson and R.G. Ratcliffe, "Bush is Confident About California," *Houston Chronicle* (October 30, 2000).

Anita Snow, "Havana Protests Proposed Embargo," Associated Press (October 18, 2000).

Gary Solis, "Even a 'Bad Man' Has Rights," *Washington Post* (June 25, 2002).

Ilan Stavans, *The Hispanic Condition: Reflections on Culture & Identity* (New York: HarperCollins Publishers, 1995).

Jared Taylor, "The Myth of Diversity," *American Renaissance* (July-August 1997).

"The Supremes," *Texas Monthly* (June 2001).

U.S. Census Bureau, Current Population Survey, March 1999, PGP-2.

Index

H

Haldeman, H.R. 28, 29, 37, 38, 297
Hammond, Bette 251
Harold Washington 155, 160, 170
Hart, Gary 158, 160
Harvard 159, 184, 187, 259, 284, 286
Harvard Law School 284, 286
Hayes, Janet Gray 140
health-care 217, 269
health insurance 229, 243, 276
Hearst News Service 231
Heller, Walter 53
Helms, Jesse 263
HemisFair 81, 82
Henderson, Don 79
Heritage Foundation 172
Herman Von Bertrab 260
Hernández, Alfred J. 39
Hernández, Andy 193, 234
Hernández, Antonia 239
Hernández, Rick 102
Hevia, Arturo 230, 312
Hicks, Floyd V. 97
Hidalgo, Eduardo (Edward) 108, 258
Hill, Anita 221
Hill, John 96, 100
Hills, Carla 258
Hinojosa, Juan 187
Hinojosa, Ricardo 219
Hispanic Advisory Committee 102, 107
Hispanic Alliance for Free Trade 257
Hispanic Business Conference 209, 311
Hispanic Committee for President Ford 103
Hispanic Congressional Caucus 134, 270
Hispanic elected officials 70, 168, 169, 180, 202, 203, 243, 270, 272
Hispanic Force '84 159, 160
Hispanic Link 223, 247, 258, 268, 312-319
Hispanic National Assembly 89, 165
Hispanic National Bar Association 222, 239

Hispanic population 19, 20, 27, 45, 58, 68, 73, 76, 77, 107, 131, 132, 136, 137, 158, 167, 168, 172, 174, 180, 203, 204, 207, 211, 237, 238, 242-244, 246, 247, 272, 277
Hispanic Trends 18, 280, 281, 319
Hispanos 17, 18, 68, 86, 107, 304
Hitchens, Robert 208
Hollings, Ernest 158
Holman, Benjamin F. 77
Holmes, Peter 77
Honduras 108, 283, 289
Hooks, Benjamin 220
Horton, Frank 168
Horton, Willie 205
House Appropriations Committee 130, 237
House Committee on Banking, Finance and Urban Affairs 218, 264
House Operations Committee 52
House Subcommittee on Government Operations 163
Housing and Community Development 195, 215
Housing and Urban Development Act 132
Houston Chronicle 42, 132, 231, 236, 255, 262, 263, 278, 296, 297, 299, 307-310, 312-319
Huddle, Donald 252
Hufstedler, Shirley 129
Human SERVE 170
Hutchinson, Ray 98
Hutchison, Kay Bailey 240, 241

I

Idaho 76, 130, 170, 214, 248
Igartúa, Gregorio 277
illegal immigrants 51, 60, 61, 63, 64, 65, 66, 93, 95, 101, 103, 109-115, 117, 120, 122, 123, 132-134, 171, 172, 175, 216, 231, 248, 249-251, 254-256, 264,

Y

Z

About the Author

José de la Isla is a writer and former public policy analyst. A University of Houston graduate, he has a master's degree in anthropology from the University of Oregon and a Master of Public Policy degree from the University of California, Berkeley. He has served on the faculties at both Oregon and Berkeley.

De la Isla reported from the Republican National Convention in 1992, covered the NAFTA debate from Mexico City in 1993 and the Mexican presidential election in 1994. His reports and comments have been heard on "World Radio Morning News" on Houston's KPFT-FM and on National Public Radio. In 1994, he received the National Hispanic Literary Award.

His frequent articles have been syndicated by the *Los Angeles Times* for op-ed and editorial pages in newspapers around the country.

About the Book

This book was typeset in Adobe Garamond, a typeface based on the types of the sixteenth-century printer, publisher, and type designer Claude Garamond (1499-1561), whose sixteenth-century types were modeled on those of Venetian printers from the end of the previous century. The Garamond typeface and its variations have been a standard among book designers and printers for four centuries; nearly every manufacturer of type or typesetting equipment has produced at least one version of Garamond in the past eighty years. Adobe designer Robert Slimbach went to the Plantin-Moretus museum in Antwerp, Belgium, to study the original Garamond typefaces. These served as the basis for the design of the Adobe Garamond romans; the italics are based on types by Robert Granjon, a contemporary of Garamond's. This elegant, versatile design, the first Adobe Originals typeface, was released in 1989.

Book design and composition by JTC Imagineering, Santa Maria, CA.

Printed in the United States by Patterson Printing Company.